THE TRANSFORMATIVE CITY

The Transformative City
Charlotte's Takeoffs and Landings

WILBUR C. RICH

The University of Georgia Press | Athens

© 2020 by the University of Georgia Press
Athens, Georgia 30602
www.ugapress.org
All rights reserved
Designed by Melissa Bugbee Buchanan
Set in Minion Pro

Most University of Georgia Press titles are
available from popular e-book vendors.

Printed digitally

Library of Congress Cataloging-in-Publication Data

Names: Rich, Wilbur C., author.
Title: The transformative city : Charlotte's takeoffs and landings / Wilbur C. Rich.
Description: Athens : The University of Georgia Press, [2020] |
Includes bibliographical references and index.
Identifiers: LCCN 2019044401 | ISBN 9780820356754 (hardback) |
ISBN 9780820356761 (paperback) | ISBN 9780820356747 (ebook)
Subjects: LCSH: Charlotte-Douglas International Airport—History. |
Economic development—North Carolina—Charlotte—History. | City
planning—North Carolina—Charlotte—History. | Charlotte (N.C.)—
History. | Charlotte (N.C.)—Economic conditions.
Classification: LCC F264.C4 R53 2020 | DDC 975.6/76—dc23
LC record available at https://lccn.loc.gov/2019044401

To all the young people who call me Gramps—

Kailani, Nikolai, and Mikhial Reynolds

Miah, Symphony, Liliana, and Benjamin McDonnell

CONTENTS

Preface	ix
Acknowledgments	xiii
INTRODUCTION | Charlotte as a City of Change	1
CHAPTER 1 | Textile Charlotte Learns to Fly	19
CHAPTER 2 | Postwar Years and the New Airport	47
CHAPTER 3 | Charlotte in an Era of Deregulation	71
CHAPTER 4 | Organizing the City's Greatest Asset	97
CHAPTER 5 | The Pro-Growth Coalition and the Hired Help	123
CHAPTER 6 | Meshing City Politics and the New Economy	152
CHAPTER 7 | City Council Oversight Style	182
CHAPTER 8 | The Plot That Failed	204
Conclusions	228
Notes	245
Index	271

PREFACE

THIS BOOK REFLECTS MY FASCINATION with urban economic development, city airports, and airlines. When I was growing up in Montgomery, Alabama, the local airport was named Dannelly Field. The army used it as a training field during World War II, and the city took it over in 1946. Montgomery has had a storied airport history with Maxwell and Gunter Fields. Today Dannelly Field is called Montgomery Regional Airport. To fly anyplace, one usually has to first fly to Atlanta Hartsfield Airport, the regional hub. Hartsfield, now Hartsfield Jackson International Airport, connects the southeastern United States to the world. The airport also helped make Atlanta one of the nation's largest and leading cities. This book examines how the city of Charlotte also used its airport to grow and develop.

In researching this book, I discovered several early historical parallels between Charlotte and Montgomery. Cotton proved critical to both cities; Alabama grew it, and North Carolina turned it into textiles. Montgomery and Charlotte also shared a racial tradition. Yet one grew while the other stagnated and lost population. Montgomery features fewer tall downtown buildings than Charlotte, and it has no corporate headquarters or professional sport franchises.

Why did Charlotte grow faster than Montgomery? Why did the banking industry select Charlotte? Who led the city, when, and how? Was its leadership just a matter of politics? Just as Charlotte mayor Benjamin Douglas (1934–1941) led the fight for Charlotte Municipal Airport, Montgomery mayor William A. Gunter (1919–1940) advocated for aviation before Douglas and stood behind the creation of Montgomery Municipal Airport (1929). After the war, the two cities diverged, and Gunter's successors did not grow the airport.

It can be argued that a larger airport and more dynamic leadership could have changed Montgomery's history. Enticing airlines, at least regional ones, to the city could have made Alabama's capital an airline hub. With a more diverse economy and a supportive pro-growth coalition, Montgomery could have grown into a larger city with a better-developed economy. Montgomery also lacked the likes of Daniel A. Thompkins, Bonnie Cone (president of Charlotte College, now the University of North Carolina at Charlotte), Ben Douglas,

Harry Golden, Harvey Gantt, Edward Crutchfield, Hugh McColl, and John and Tom Belk. None of these leaders were born in Charlotte, but they were all key to its development. However, I only mention Montgomery to explain my personal interest in the city's economic development. This book is not a comparative analysis of Charlotte and Montgomery.

This book offers a case study of the rise of Charlotte's pro-growth coalition and its promotion of the Charlotte-owned airport, a critical part of the city's infrastructure. The building of Charlotte during the twentieth century underwent several generational changes in leadership. The point I am making in this book is that a pro-growth coalition matters in terms of the city's ambience: its race relations, business decisions, and uses of state and federal government grants-in-aid. Sunbelt cities like Atlanta, Charlotte, and Miami, with their international airports, have a transportation advantage that overwhelms global competition from other southern cities. Why? The short answer to this question seems intuitive, but the long answer lies at the intersection of built infrastructure policies, civic boosterism, and the changing nature of American cities. Simply put, Charlotte leaders invested in the future and took advantage of its opportunities.

In 2015, Charlotte was the second leading national center for banking. The city's pro-growth coalition supported building and expanding its airport, and leaders recognized that the city had to play on a universal stage. Hosting the 2012 Democratic National Convention gave Charlotte worldwide name recognition and proclaimed its aspirations to be a global city. Reporters from around the world came to the city to hear Pres. Barack Obama speak. The convention also "injected $91 million in new spending into the local economy, for a total economic impact of nearly $164 million."[1] Charlotte's two major professional sports franchises, the Carolina Panthers and Charlotte Hornets, brought the city additional national visibility. With help from real estate developer Johnny Harris, the city won even more national notice from hosting the 1994 NCAA Final Four Basketball Tournament. Harris also started the annual Wells Fargo Championship Golf Tournament at Quail Hollow Club. Sports talk radio, teams, and events build residents' pride in their city.

This book discusses a variety of subjects—aircraft and airport development, city political history, Charlotte's changing airport management and business community, the Uptown/airport linkage, and the vagaries of citizen participation. I am sure that some important actors in the airport's history remain unidentified and their contributions overlooked. Some events overlapped each other while others happened parallel to each other. The point is that Charlotte did not isolate itself from national trends. It embraced social and economic change, and it grew as a "transformative city."

Charlotte is becoming a global city because of its linkages with the new financial class that dominates the world economy. The city is increasingly one of bean counters (e.g., financial and credit analysts, accountants, auditors, and loan advisors) and members of an Internet-monitoring class (e.g., informational security analysts and computer network architects) working from their Uptown offices (downtown). Charlotte is also a Democratic Party oasis in a state dominated by the Republican Party. At the time of this writing the city had elected two African American mayors. Moreover, it elected a female mayor before cities like Detroit and New York City. Charlotte grew without being the home of the state's flagship university (University of North Carolina at Chapel Hill) and without the presence of a major law or medical school. Native Charlotteans are proud that their city is the nation's second-largest banking center and that the airport serves Metrolina, which includes two states.

Finally, this book grew out of an unanswered mystery. In light of the city's praiseworthy investments and energy directed to its airport, why would the state of North Carolina try to take over Charlotte Douglas International Airport? After all, the airport is one of the city's major engines of growth, and it had a sterling reputation for being well managed. Did a growing partisan base split the time-honored pro-growth coalition? Did the attempted takeover portend a fundamental change in the relationship between the state and the city? I tried to answer some of these questions in a paper presented at the Southeastern Conference of Public Administration (2014). It was clear that I needed to provide more historical information concerning the airport and the city's economic development. Accordingly, this work devotes two chapters to the airport's history and Charlotte's related political/economic development. The book also examines the role of the federal government in airport development, banking, and race relations reforms. This review of Charlotte politics, airport, and economics covers events through 2015. Though many aspects of the city and local banking decisions have changed in the last four years, the basic conclusions of the book remain the same.

ACKNOWLEDGMENTS

I WOULD LIKE TO THANK colleagues Janet Bednarek, Marion Orr, Walter Turner, Thomas W. Hanchett, and Donna Patterson for reading earlier draft chapters and helping me improve the overall manuscript. In addition, I extend appreciation to interviewees Jerry Orr, LaWana Mayfield, Ron Carlee, Brent Cagle, Sue Myrick, Harvey Gantt, Richard Vinroot, H. Edward Knox, Sue Friday, Bob Hagemann, Bob Morgan, David Goldfield, Bill McCoy, Michael Gallis, Mary Newsom, William Graves, Hugh McColl, Ely Portillo, Rick Rothacker, Pam Syfert, Scott Syfert, Chuck McShane, Jim Morrill, Ann William, Jim Williams, and Betty Kuester for providing their time and insights into the city history in general and economic development in particular.

Of course, some actors and participants did not return my call or did not want to be interviewed. This was especially true for a few former elected officials; it was as if they had signed a nondisclosure agreement. Longtime airport director Thomas J. "Jerry" Orr graciously invited me into his home, but he met me by saying, "I am not going to tell you any secrets." Academics may never know secrets and rumors about the airport and its economic development.

In this book I had to rely on key actors' public statements in the newspapers. Obviously, I could not have written this work without the great assistance of librarians at the University of North Carolina at Charlotte's Special Collections and Archives Room. I am indebted to them for help with the papers of former mayors. Furthermore, I want to thank one of the manuscript reviewers for alerting me to the Goldmine collection at the university library. The staff of the Dolphin D. Overton Aviation Library provided me with information and photographs concerning the development of aircraft and flying in Charlotte. The staff at Charlotte Mecklenburg Public Library Uptown branch's Robinson-Spangler Carolina Room was also extremely accommodating, helping me find material and suggesting places to look for information. This was especially true for Tom Cole, who helped me locate old newspapers and other references.

My thanks to Wellesley College for its generous funding of faculty research and travel. I would also like to thank audience members at conferences, as well as several colleagues who offered their corrections, suggestions, and criticisms.

I learned a lot from those who wanted to spend more time on one issue or another. Of course, my daughters Rachel and Alexandra have always let me talk endlessly about my latest writing project. They have also been great critics and supporters of my work. Again, my appreciation to all who have read the early drafts of this book. All the omissions, errors, comments, and conclusions are mine.

Finally, I would like to thank my editor James Patrick Allen and his assistant Katherine Grace La Mantia for their encouragement and support. I also would like to thank my copy editors Misha Lazzara, Rachel Reynolds, and the final publisher copy editor Elizabeth Crowder. They made the book more readable.

THE TRANSFORMATIVE CITY

INTRODUCTION

Charlotte as a City of Change

THERE IS A GREAT LINE in the movie *The Leopard* (1963) in which one of the characters says, "If we want things to stay as they are, things will have to change." This axiom could apply to all American cities. Stagnation and maintaining the status quo are not viable options—cities must change to survive and grow. In the past century, Charlotte, North Carolina, triumphed over its past as a sleepy textile center and became second only to New York City as a wide-awake banking complex. The reinvention of Charlotte began after World War II and was consolidated with its selection as a hub for airlines and with the growth of its major banks, First Union—Wachovia National Bank (now Wells Fargo)—and North Carolina National Bank (NCNB; now Bank of America).

A critical element in this fundamental transformation was an early recognition of the need for a sustainable piece of infrastructure, a city-owned airport. The takeoffs and landings at the airport accelerated the demographic and economic changes necessary for making Charlotte a major postindustrial city. Simply put, having such an airport allowed the nascent banking industry to recruit the talent it needed.

Charlotte built and sustained the airport at a relatively low cost. The growth of the airport—indeed, air travel in general—is in part the result of federal largesse. As author Daniel Bubb states, "Government funding enabled the airline industry to thrive. Without Uncle Sam's financial assistance, the airline industry was too expensive for private financiers to sustain, and would have faced imminent collapse."[1] Urban planning scholars Alan Altshuler and David Luberoff observe, "The hallmark of successful mega-project finance is that projects should appear costless, or nearly so, to the great majority of voters. The easiest way to achieve this is to rely on funding from higher levels of government."[2] Airports *had* to expand and maintain runways and maintenance facilities. To attract airlines, airports also had to continuously redecorate and upgrade their terminals. In doing so, Charlotte's airport competed with other cities' airports for passengers, airport jobs, and nonstop flights.

The nation has invested a large amount of resources in the funding of airport infrastructures. This federal government investment has generated a fascinating history of airline industry competition as well as of local airport politics. Airline and airport politics refer to local, state, and federal government actions taken to provide essential services to the flying public. Incentives had existed from the advent of commercial flight, but cities had to act decisively.

Some city leaders had the acumen to foresee the economic potential of this mode of transportation. Postindustrial southern cities such as Charlotte and Atlanta selected their airports as one of their main forces of economic development. In deciding to use the airport as the engine to take the city from its textile past to its current destiny as a financial center, Charlotte's pro-growth coalition (i.e., business leaders and politicians) exhibited great foresight. Making this change represented a long-term commitment that required the pro-growth coalition's constant attention and support.[3] Yet urban academics have overlooked the relationship between airlines and airport politics within the overall development of cities.[4] This omission is especially true for so-called New South cities like Charlotte.

Transportation infrastructure is critical to a modern city's economic development. Transportation helps explain why some cities have been stymied and others have become globalized. Charlotte's pro-growth coalition understood this relationship and acted on it without too much disruption by day-to-day politics of the city. Developing an international airport in the American hinterland is difficult; indeed, several cities have gotten mired in city and regional politics when attempting to develop or upgrade their airports.

The 1994 replacement of Denver's old Stapleton Airport with the nation's largest airport, Denver International Airport (DIA), offers several lessons in this regard. The airport's director offered six reasons for building the new facility: (1) a visionary mayor, (2) strong federal government support, (3) sufficient undeveloped land, (4) an entrepreneurial spirit, (5) a poor economy, and (6) the airlines' inability to derail the project. A cynical biweekly newspaper publisher offered three additional reasons: (1) the city's major newspapers were favorably biased toward the airport, (2) elected officials did not provide proper oversight of federal funds, and (3) an effective public-interest opposition group did not exist. A local aviation consultant attributed the building of DIA to greed. DIA, in other words, was built for businesspeople, landowners, and developers. In their study sharing these various views of the DIA, Paul Stephen Dempsey, Andrew R. Goetz, and Joseph S. Szyliowicz conclude that the effective pro-growth coalition, willing politicians, and favorable external circumstances (i.e., postairline deregulation pressures, congested airports, and federal support) facilitated the replacement of Stapleton.[5]

The task of building an airport in a large coastal city is not without its perils. Historian Nicholas Dagen Bloom's history of John F. Kennedy International Airport (JFK), *The Metropolitan Airport* (2015), tells a fascinating story of infrastructure evolution. Despite being a part of the Port Authority of New York and New Jersey, the airport was not insulated from local politics and mafia corruption. Mistakes are evident in its terminal designs and its methods of transporting passengers to the facilities. Although JFK is hemmed in by its Queens neighbors, it has still overcome its structural and locational limitations to serve "a region of approximately 18 million people."[6]

CHARLOTTE'S COMPARATIVE ANALYSIS

This book traces the economic transformation of Charlotte led by several generations of pro-growth coalitions—a mix of political and business leaders. Initially, the city airport was regarded as a requisite infrastructure for a growing city, one that would transport and connect passengers and cargo. The economic significance of the airport has changed over time. In most cases, airports can define what a city is and what it can become. The location and politics of a city intersect with the role of airport in the local economy.[7] For example, Denver and Charlotte are hub cities with somewhat similar situations but quite different histories. Charlotte Douglas International Airport and Denver International Airport evolved differently and yielded different lessons for those involved. The major lesson for Charlotte is that air transport changed the ethos of the city.

This book addresses the following key questions: What was the role of the pro-growth coalition in the making of Charlotte, the "transformative city"? What political events shaped the city's economic development? Who were the men and women who played a critical role in the expansion of the airport? How has the pro-growth coalition worked? How was Charlotte's airport, a critical element in its transformation, funded, planned, designed, built, and debated? What have been the roles of the various consultants in the planning and financial development and strategy for the airport facilities? Airline companies, this study shows, are neither disinterested tenants at the airport nor bystanders in city politics. They have been constantly involved in airport operations. Indeed, the airline industry influenced what was built at the facility and what happened between airport management and city government. Accordingly, the industry is not just a tenant but is a legitimate stakeholder in the politics of city airports.

SEEKING AEROMOBILITY IN THE NEW ECONOMY

The ordinary passenger is rarely concerned with the politics of airlines and airports. For most Americans, air travel is simply the fastest and most efficient way to travel and exercise their "aeromobility." Members of the public want to go places, visit, and do business. Aeromobility begins at a permanent starting and ending point, the airport.

Alone, building a modern airport with a first-class infrastructure cannot make a city transformative. This conversion requires an open-minded and ambitious leadership, a talented workforce, and a solid economic foundation. The Charlotte pro-growth coalition understood this obligation. Because of its talent needs, the banking industry had to be in the forefront of the transformation. Former Bank of America head Hugh McColl put it succinctly:

> We needed to attract brainpower. The Bank [North Carolina National Bank (NCNB)] was early in employing Affirmative Action in hiring and we put them on the promotion ladders. It was not perfect, but we were beginning the march. I wanted to change the city to attract people. People travel a lot; they go to San Francisco, Chicago and Hong Kong. We had to build a city that attracted people to live downtown. Downtown [Uptown] is just 4 square miles. They never have to leave the areas for arts and sports. We needed a performing arts center and pro sports arenas. We attracted lawyers and CPA firms. Other businesses like Duke Energy shared in the growth of the central city. Duke Energy was growing. Electrical engineers came to the city to work. UNCC was growing.[8]

In order to be "transformative," a city must abandon its old ways and adopt a stylish and compelling modern profile. Achieving a consensus about overall city economic aspirations is the first step in such transformation. The second step is to titivate the downtown area's built environment. This requires refurbishing landmark buildings, upgrading the skyline, and improving street appearances. The "dress-up imperative" facilitates a city's presentability. A swanky airport, nonstop flights, a ready workforce, and a growing and glowing skyline make the sale easier than a shabby downtown and airport.

Historian Paul Barrett asserts, "Cities viewed airports as adjuncts of the CBD [Central Business District], and this fact diverted attention to highway building and other panaceas that did not entail substantive land use planning."[9] Few people understand this concept better than civic boosters. This might explain why McColl served as chair of the Charlotte Uptown Development Corporation (CUDC) from 1978 to 1981. In 1986 he served as chair on an interim basis. Other business elites also understood this critical transformation, its talent assortment challenges, and their consequences for the city.

The third step in developing a transformative city is building a modern transportation system consistent and current with changing economic activities. Air travel is essential to this goal. Accordingly, the central question for Charlotte was whether the pro-growth coalition would keep its focus on the changing needs of the airport infrastructure so as to prepare the city to meet the challenges for a postindustrial economy.

The answer to this question is more complex than it seems. Keeping the focus on an infrastructure can consume leaders' attention and may lead to neglect of other public policy challenges. Solving social problems is more commendable than arranging and upgrading an airport's concrete, steel, and glass. The task for the pro-growth coalition was to achieve a balance between devotion to the built environment and concern for social conditions.

As will be argued in this book, Charlotte Douglas International Airport was a product of Charlotte's history and economic transformation. And the elaboration of its economic transformation has had a spillover effect on other aspects of the city's politics. When Charlotte began to grow, its leaders recognized the need for an efficient and attractive airport. Having a lackluster airport was inconsistent with the transformative aspirations of the city leaders and the ever-demanding airline industry.

Charlotte's economic history provided another competitive advantage. Having never been a serious heavy metal–oriented production center (notwithstanding the presence of the small Ford assembly plant from 1924 to 1929 and the Charlotte Army Missile Plant from 1956 to 1965), Charlotte had little reason to mourn its loss. As the nation's economic foundation shifted from its manufacturing centers, the city had the space and climate to attract parts of the mushrooming new economy. Sociologist Daniel Bell saw the rise of the postindustrial society as early as the 1970s.[10] The nation was gearing up for a knowledge-based economy that required new and fewer workers and a high capital-intensive base. Banking was critical to that new economy. In the past, state laws had restrained bankers' interstate and international transactions. However, these laws were changing as the world moved toward a global transactional platform.

Charlotte business leaders realized that in order to participate in that new environment, the city needed to expand the airport infrastructure. They recognized the place of air travel in a postindustrial economy, and they urged their elected officials to keep the local airport current in terms of runways, terminals, and airline tenants. Hugh McColl of NCNB (now Bank of America), once said, "No one is going to move to your city without good air connections and hangars for their own planes."[11]

To remain current, an airport has to expand to meet the needs of the airlines and population it serves. This condition is significant because the United States has the highest number of local airports in the world and serves over 800 million passengers a year. Airport expansion requires multimillion-dollar construction loans that take years to repay. The city's general obligation bonds were used for this purpose. For decades, states and the federal government have also poured billions into building and expanding airports.

CHARLOTTE CHANGED

The transformation of Charlotte, a fast-growing southeastern Sunbelt city, is both a cultural and demographic story. When Pres. George Washington visited this burgeoning settlement in 1791, he found forty houses, a courthouse, and a gaol (i.e., jail). In his diary, Washington declared, "Charlotte is a trifling place."[12] How did this "trifling place" become a textile center of the southeastern United States and the principal trading center of what journalist Samuel Lubell called the "booming Piedmont Carolina"?[13] In 1951, Lubell went so far as to assert, "Probably no other city is so dramatic a product of social and economic revolution that is currently remaking the South."[14]

After World War II small unincorporated neighborhoods or suburbs surrounded Charlotte. Charlotte's land area subsequently grew by a series of city-initiated and voluntary annexations. In 2000 political scientist Timothy Mead stated, "[Since] 1970 85 annexations have resulted in the city's land areas increasing by 170 square miles and its population by 207,088."[15] In 1976, a special issue of *U.S. News and World Report* compared four cities in their quest for growth. It pointed out that Charlotte had "annexed contiguous urbanized areas without vote by those inside or outside," adding, "Since 1960 the city had added 42 square miles that way."[16] The magazine also attributed Charlotte's expansion to liberal annexation laws that "keep it from being hemmed in."[17]

The population growth started before World War II. From 1930 to 1950, Charlotte's population grew from 82,675 to 134,042. Some of that growth can be attributed to Mecklenburg County's "unique political geography." Geographer Russell M. Smith observes, "In 1984, the municipalities of Mecklenburg County developed and agreed on spheres of influence around their existing city limits that divide up the county for future land use planning and service delivery. These spheres of influence became de facto annexation boundaries, that neighboring cities cannot cross. This eliminated the competition for annexable land and allowed Mecklenburg County municipalities to annex when desired and not due to fear of losing territory to a surrounding city."[18]

Overall growth in the county redounded to Charlotte's economic image. In Mecklenburg County "retail sales rose by 405 percent between 1970 and 1987 compared with 328 percent nationally. The number of foreign companies operated in Charlotte increased from 60 in 1970 to 225 in 1989."[19] Charlotte leaders then began to call Charlotte Douglas Airport's catchment area Metrolina. The area represents ten North Carolina counties—Anson, Cabarrus, Cleveland, Gaston,

Table 1. City of Charlotte Population Changes by Race and Ethnicity

Decade	Total Population	% White	% Black	% Latino	% Asian	% Other
2010	731,424	45.1	35.0	13.1	5.0	10.1
2000	540,828	59.0	32.1	7.1	3.4	7.4
1990	395,934	65.6	31.8	1.4	1.8	0.4 (+0.4 Native Amer.)
1980	315,474	67.4	31.0	1.1	0.3	0.3 (+0.5 Native Amer.)
1970	241,420	69.4	30.3	0.6–1.1	0.1	0.4 (+0.2 Native Amer.)
1960	201,564	72.0	27.9	n/a (part of white race)	<0.0003	<0.001 (+0.1 Native Amer.)
1950	134,042	72.0	28.0	n/a	<0.0002	>0.0001
1940	100,899	68.9	31.1	n/a	<0.0003	n/a
1930	82,675	69.5	30.4	n/a	<0.0003	n/a
1920	46,338	68.4	31.6	n/a	<0.00009	n/a
1910	34,014	65.4	34.6	n/a	<0.00009	n/a
1900	18,091	60.5	39.5	n/a	<0.0002	n/a

Source: U.S. Census, table 34, North Carolina—Race and Hispanic Origin for Selected Large Cities and Other Places: Earliest Census to 1990. University of North Carolina at Charlotte's Special Collections and Archives, Charlotte, N.C.
Statistically, Asians and other races made up 0 percent of the population from 1900 to 1960. Native Americans were statistically 0 percent of Charlotte's population from 1900 to 1950.

Iredell, Lincoln, Mecklenburg, Rowan, Stanly, and Union. Metrolina also includes Lancaster and York Counties in South Carolina. In 1985, the Charlotte Chamber of Commerce asserted in a research report, "Metrolina's population is currently growing at a faster rate than the nation as a whole."[20] Today the metro area of Charlotte (seven counties) is home to 1.2 million people. Geographers William Graves and Heather A. Smith observe, "Charlotte's evolution into what scholars view as an incipient world city is remarkable given its regional disadvantages. The city's unexceptional location (far from ports, navigable rivers, or mountain gateways), the cultural baggage of its impoverished southern heritage, its economic history as a low-wage industrial center, and its politically peripheral position in state politics make it an unlikely site for a globally ascendant center."[21]

For the purposes of this book, it is important to point out that over 10 million people live within 150 miles of the airport. Charlotte's population is becoming increasingly diverse, and residents of the Metrolina area identify with the city of Charlotte proper. Table 1 shows how the transformative city has changed with each decade.

In the 2010 Census, the population of Charlotte proper grew by 35.2 percent to 731,424. The city proper population is greater than that of Atlanta (420,003), Miami (399,452), and Nashville (626,681). Whites represent 45.1 percent of Charlotte's residents, meaning that the city remains predominately white. Blacks represent 35 percent of the population, and the growing Latino population accounts for 13.1 percent of Charlotteans. Of the city residents, 19.1 percent speak a language other than English. The city has changed significantly since the 1950s, when whites represented 72 percent of the population and 99 percent of residents were native born.

The browning of Charlotte—that is, its burgeoning minority population—is creating a visible difference in the city. Equally important is the growing number of retirees and foreign immigrants. At first glance, the Immigration and Nationality Act of 1965 seems unrelated to Charlotte's transformative goals. A closer look reveals that the section 101 H-1B visa law allowed the banking industry to recruit workers (bean counters and data analysts) from as far away as Bangalore, India. The second Yankee invasion of Charlotte came in the form of relatively affluent retirees who brought with them the conservative ideology of their former hometowns. The integration of this type of conservatism and southern ways proved an interesting transition. Political scientist Kim Q. Hill believes that the newcomers have added to the nascent competitive party system evolving in the South. He asserts, "Migration to the South from other regions brought many new voters with Republican loyalties. And the enfranchisement of the southern blacks made state politics more divisive. All these changes have made the politics of the South more complicated and less susceptible to one party control."[22] A growing partisan divide makes the engineering of consensus more difficult. As this work will show, developing and nurturing a consensus is critical to the building and expansion of an airport.

WHY WERE CITY-OWNED AIRPORTS CREATED?

Simply put, city-owned airports were created to provide transportation magnets for businesses and for the air-traveling public needing to get in and out of the city. Put more simply, city-owned airports function as more than landing and boarding platforms, terminals, runways, traffic towers, hangars, and maintenance facilities. Indeed, they have evolved into a community within a community. Airports and their host cities are undeniably linked in that they grow alongside each other. As the city's economy changes, so does the type of airport it needs.

Airlines have become the linchpin of the manufacturing economy and more recently the financial economy. Passengerwise, cities can be divided into three basic types of landings: feeder, hub, and obligatory. Feeder-landing airports are located in small and midsize cities, and they are serviced mostly by commuter airlines. Hubs are airline-designed centers for maintenance and the collection and redistribution of passengers. Obligatory landings are cities where major national and international airlines must have gates. Examples include Atlanta, New York City, Boston, Los Angeles, Washington, D.C., San Francisco, Dallas, and Chicago. More people and commerce mean more scheduled flights, representing a city moving up landing scale. Yet as writer David Esler observes, an airport needs to be marketed to its host city:

> With modern city governments being pulled in so many directions by ever-escalating—and often conflicting—demands for services from residents and businesses, with declining tax bases, unemployment issues, crime, educational needs and all the other problems that fill our nightly news reports, how can they be convinced of the importance of retaining a cash-neutral or cash-draining municipal airport when developers are telling them how much money they can rake in by replacing it with condos and strip malls? How do you persuade a community that it needs its airport as a fully functional, unencumbered public asset?[23]

City leaders found ways to promote and maintain the growth of the Charlotte Airport. A unified and effective pro-growth coalition including local politicians helped them sell the idea of an expanding facility. Mayors have been the out-front booster of the airport. Henry Ogrodzinski, former president and CEO of the National Association of State Aviation Officials (NASAO), observed, "If the airport doesn't have a 'champion,' it's toast."[24] Formed in 1931, NASAO represented the various state agencies concerned with aviation. North Carolina and the city of Charlotte have benefited from airport champions who have significantly impacted the political discourse. While the next chapter will discuss Charlotte Airport advocates, a brief summary of the intersection of local politics and the airport appears below.

AIRPORT AND CITY POLITICS

Airport politics is a confluence of local economic aspirations, federal nudging, and airline instability. A book about Charlotte's airport and city politics must also review the linked histories of airlines, equipment and route changes, and incessant mergers. Expansion is further linked to federal airport policy. In each case, politics served as leverage to make airports relevant, and relevancy required constant expansion. The airport's success made it a magnet for economic development and partisan intrigue, particularly regarding the distribution of city patronage.

In my earlier work *Politics of Urban Personnel Policy*, I distinguished between grand and petty patronages.[25] For instance, grand patronage for airports includes high-level benefits and jobs—lawyers, consultants, and building contractors. Petty patronage usually includes low-level positions, wage laborers, and temporary jobs. In the old days, connections with political parties and officeholders secured people city jobs. Now, however, applicants obtain jobs in city departments by taking an examination. Petty patronage disappeared with the introduction of the merit system. This trend was consolidated with the decision in *Elrod v. Burns* (1976) holding that low-level city workers cannot be discharged from jobs because of their political party affiliations. Still, employees of professional firms are allowed to feast at the grand patronage bowl. This is especially true for work associated with consulting, designing, building, and evaluating government projects.

The opportunities for grand patronage grew as the airport grew. A city's most important resource is its control over land use. Eminent domain allows Charlotte to control land use around its airport, thus facilitating the facility's expansion. Former city manager Ron Carlee has stated, "[Charlotte's] Airport is one of the city's biggest assets."[26] It followed that Charlotte utilized its land and airports to grow the city. As political scientist Paul Peterson's *City Limits* points out, these resources gain value when used to attract businesses. Business growth acts as a multiplier and attracts residents. The land around the airport must be amenable to airport expansion. The land closest to the airport, but not in landing alleys, is suitable for real estate development. Airport growth is highly dependent on use of eminent domain and access to airport entry roads. If expansion requires more space, the city council must agree to exercise eminent domain. As we shall see in chapter 7, this state of affairs caused some neighborhood backlash.

To offset potential backlash, a city's pro-growth regime seeks ways to compromise and cooperate. Political scientist Clarence Stone's *Regime Politics*, a study of Atlanta, states that progress is dependent on cooperation between the political class and the business elite. Governing authorities in urban politics include political and economic leaders who form a coalition to achieve social production goals. Stone identifies four different types of regimes: caretaking, economic development or growth oriented, middle-class progressive (i.e., liberal goals of environmental protection, historic preservation, affordable housing, etc.), and lower-class opportunity expansion regimes.[27] Charlotte is a prototype of a pro-growth development regime. Despite the usual problems of generational leadership succession and differing social backgrounds, the coalition kept the business leaders and the politicians on the same page. In addition, they recruited airport directors who shared their pro-growth views.

Three elements should be kept in mind when discussing the plight of airports in cities. First, members of the economic leadership class, as exemplified by business organizations and individual business leaders who wrote letters to the mayor, were essential to the growth and development of the airport. Second, national developments concerning airlines affect the city's relationship to the airline carriers and industry. The federal government makes airline policies that have a "ripple effect" on city airport policy. Third, the maintaining and keeping of an airport is analogous to a city's relationship to professional sport franchises. The airport is like a city logo. It is a major gateway representing the city to passengers who are making connections. Therefore, it must look good and be efficient. To keep tenants (airlines) the city must build bigger and better facilities.

Though not widely acknowledged, airlines have preemptive power over cities' airport decisions. Cities seeking economic growth and more nonstop trips are forced to negotiate with airlines. Airlines make demands for technical facilities like runways and terminals. If a city doesn't meet these demands, airlines can reduce services, perhaps by providing fewer nonstop trips and loading travelers on smaller regional jets. Even when cities comply, there is no guarantee that service will continue. In general, airline CEOs have the extremely difficult task of making ends meet. Profit margins may shift from year to year, and as we will see, airlines are quite vulnerable to recession, fluctuating fuel prices, and labor problems.

This review of Charlotte Airport's role in the city's transformation demonstrates that outside consultancy was critical in airport planning and representation. Both city politicians and airport managers use consultants when making decisions. City politicians hire consultants to add legitimacy to the city's choices; outside consultant reports are presented as objective analyses. This type of expert imprimatur is necessary if there is a need for city residents to vote on revenue bonds or if a facility upgrade is indicated. A consultant report can make a case for change, but it cannot separate the politics of Charlotte from the political and economic realities of its residents.

Again, Charlotte's transformation and, indeed, maturation would mean giving up some of its small-town ways and embracing the fast pace of financial capitalism. In 2002 journalist Richard Maschal observed, "Charlotte once debated, in all seriousness, when and if it would achieve 'world class' status. That talk is over, although a growing Hispanic population has made it more diverse. But it remains hungry for recognition and frets about the 'CH factor,' the tendency of outsiders to confuse it with Charleston, South Carolina; Charlottesville, West Virginia."[28] Charlotte has come a long way since 2002, improving its recognition by hosting the 2012 Democratic National Convention. The successes of professional sport franchises have brought even more attention to the city. Now it has embraced its pro-growth reputation, if not global-city aspiration.

A city that advertises its focus on growth competes with other southeastern cities such as Atlanta, Nashville, and Miami. Charlotte also has intrastate competition from cities like Greensboro, Raleigh, and Winston-Salem. Remember, Wachovia Bank and Piedmont Airlines started in Winston-Salem. Aware of the rivalry, Charlotte's pro-growth coalition sought more amenities to drive development.

Most pro-growth cities have what geographer Mark Boyle calls "urban propaganda projects."[29] For example, North Carolina cities like Raleigh and Durham used the Research Triangle to booster their claim of being an intellectual oasis. Such projects are designed to attract investors and new residents, as well as nationwide, and in some cases worldwide, attention. These endeavors at once symbolize the new transformative city of Charlotte and serve as means for endless economic growth. Growth is supposed to be contagious and additive because it brings more people and businesses to the city.

The mission for the Charlotte pro-growth coalition was explaining how the airport would grow the city significantly and provide benefits for all. These benefits included an attractive infrastructure, prestige, and more jobs. More jobs would mean a bigger skyline, stronger neighborhoods, and big-city status. A visible and recurrent project holding the coalition together would help achieve those results. The Charlotte Douglas International Airport was selected as a lead project because it provided a place-promotion function that leaders sought and unlimited opportunities for local boosterism. More importantly, it did not directly threaten any local business interest.

Given these realities and differentiations of living preferences, what do city residents want from their airport? What is the proper role of the airport in Charlotte's economic development? Unfortunately, there is no annual polling of residents' sentiments about changes in the city. The city's demographics and the power of its government have changed dramatically since the 1960s. While the white-dominated business elites are still in place, now they often have to engage in what Clarence Stone calls social production—that is, they seek the cooperation of rising minority politicians.[30] By cooperating, elected politicians influence economic decisions. Several southern cities such as Charlotte, New

Orleans, and Atlanta have had black mayors, city councilpersons, and state legislators and congresspersons. In other words, the pro-growth coalition had the acumen to anticipate the interest and political preferences of minority residents. They supported minority candidates. The new politics of the city of Charlotte should mirror the changing demographics of the city, and this is where social production matters. Leaders from all sections of the community must be in constant communication and exchange ideas in order to keep the city's image intact.

Charlotte is not a city that continues to question itself or survey its residents' preferences. Although some citizens know the names of the mayors and city managers, many don't know the names and committee assignments of their council members. Charlotteans continually redefine their notions of a "good place to live." The "politically conscious Charlotteans," even urbane ones, may not be well informed about their local government or the division of responsibility between the county and the city. City residents seem satisfied that garbage is collected, traffic lights are working, crossing guards assist their schoolkids across the street, and police arrive when called. They don't think about the airport unless they want to travel or the local media covers massive flight cancellations. And as long as airport parking remains relatively inexpensive, they do not raise questions about the airport management. The fact that the city council meets weekly to discuss city problems and mayors often work long hours attempting to solve problems is often taken for granted. Accordingly, residents seem amenable to the pro-growth coalition's claim that the airport effectively attracts business development.

AIRPORTS AS BUSINESS MAGNETS

The metro Charlotte area is currently home to six Fortune 500 companies. The Bank of America ranks number one, followed by Duke Energy, Nucor, Family Dollar, Sonic Automotive, and SPX (an industrial supplier of infrastructure equipment). Although Charlotte is also a big health care provider (Carolinas Healthcare System), the city markets itself as the second banking center of the United States. The aforementioned Bank of America is headquartered there. Though headquartered in San Francisco, Wells Fargo has more employees in Charlotte after its takeover of Wachovia. Together, Wells Fargo and Bank of America employ more than thirty thousand city residents. The Charlotte Chamber of Commerce claims, "A total of 248,547 people are employed by company headquarters in the Charlotte region. Spending by those companies and their employees supports an additional 281,102 jobs. These total 529,649 employees and the businesses that hire them have $67 billion total economic impact on the Charlotte region."³¹

Owing to the BMW plant in nearby Greer, S.C., the metro Charlotte area has the largest concentration of German-owned businesses. Moreover, the Charlotte–Gaston–Rock Hill metro area is home to 1.4 million people. Thus, cities like Charlotte are no longer just feeder cities for the roaring Northeast and big cities in the West. Charlotte is now a destination city seeking more people, business, and tourists, which the pro-growth coalition needs a "good" airport to attract. No local organization recognizes this challenge more than the Charlotte Chamber of Commerce.

THE CHAMBER OF COMMERCE AND AIRPORT POLICY

A key member of the pro-growth coalition is the Charlotte Chamber of Commerce. The chamber has been an unabashed, consistent, and critical booster of Charlotte Douglas Airport's growth and expansion over the years. As Prof. Bill McCoy asserted in 2007, "We [Charlotte] are a place that aspires to big things. And the Chamber is often the most vocal tub-thumper in staking out those claims."³²

The Charlotte Chamber of Commerce sought to advance the interests of the business community starting in 1870. In 1917, the chamber campaigned to build economic assets in Charlotte by procuring Camp Nathanael Greene, a World War I army camp that would later play a role in the development of the city's airports. In the twenties, Charlotte had the slogan Watch Charlotte Grow. Clarence O. Kuester of the Charlotte Chamber of Commerce was dubbed Booster Kuester and Mr. Charlotte.³³ Starting out as a traveling salesman, called a drummer, Kuester became the chamber of commerce's paid executive in 1921 and worked there until his retirement in 1948. He would also play a role in the development of the municipal airport. In 1931 Kuester was one of the city leaders, along with Mayor Charles E. Lambeth, to welcome famous female flier Amelia Earhart to Charlotte. As the next chapters will show, he was active in the city airport politics. Two months before his retirement in April 1947, he was part of a film at the Charlotte Plaza airfield that advertised the city.

Chris Mead, senior vice president of the Association of Chamber of Commerce Executives, entitled his book *The Magicians of Main Street* after local chamber of commerce organizations. They sometimes make things appear and disappear. Although the Charlotte Chamber of Commerce is a voluntary nonprofit organization, it has impacted airport politics since the 1920s. In 1927, a

U.S. Chamber of Commerce study celebrated local chambers' air traffic promotion efforts in 134 cities.³⁴ Chris Mead asserts, "Chambers of Commerce . . . sometimes operated as an aristocracy lite, a restraining, senate-lite, calming influence on the body politic."³⁵ Sometimes the Chamber operates quietly behind the scenes. At other times local chambers are openly proactive about economic and business issues. Again, Mead notes, "Chambers of commerce often functioned as the venture capitalists and entrepreneurs of civic life. If a camel is a horse created by a committee, then these business organizations generated more than their share of dromedaries."³⁶ Journalist Jack Claiborne's *Crown of Queen City* notes that a 1960 editorial in the *Charlotte Observer* acknowledged the role of the chamber: "Charlotte is run, primarily, and well, by its Chamber of Commerce. . . . We are pleased to acknowledge its bossism and to wish it continued health."³⁷

The *Charlotte Observer*, the city's main newspaper, often cites the chamber of commerce as the voice of the business community. In general, the newspaper and media petitioned the business leadership for comments on every economic project. When the city elected two businessmen mayors (Stanford Brookshire and John M. Belk) associated with the chamber in the 1960s and 1970s, it was rumored that the chamber actually ran the city. This subtext persisted because of the chamber of commerce's linkage with economic development projects. Thus, the chamber has clarified its role over the years. In 1980 the *Charlotte Observer* published the organization's purpose: "The Greater Charlotte Chamber of Commerce believes that a rewarding quality of life for all of our citizens is dependent upon the existence of a buoyant local economy, one that draws its strength from the competitive enterprise system and a dynamic regional economy. The purpose of the chamber is to work for the attainment of those conditions that will foster and advance a favorable economic environment in the greater Charlotte area."³⁸

The Charlotte Chamber of Commerce is aware of its public profile and has worked hard not to appear in total control of fellow pro-growth coalition members. Research for this book suggests that this attitude was not prominent. This disclaimer was made despite the fact that leading businesspersons associated with the airport have served on the chamber's board over the years. The chamber of commerce's active Aviation Committee makes recommendations to the city. In 1960, chambers of commerce produced a multicounty proposal called "Advantage Carolina" that argued for metro Charlotte to achieve even greater glory in the twenty-first century.³⁹ Calling for a regional approach to economic development, the proposal further stated that the chamber of commerce was again trying to redefine Charlotte's reason for being. The city had shifted focus from gold mines to railroads, from cotton manufacturing to trucking, and finally from distribution to banking and financial services.[40]

As we will see, the Charlotte Chamber of Commerce's Aviation Committee has been intimately involved in the construction and governing of the airport. Aside from board members' personal and business interest in the airport, David Dawley, Robert Stephens, and David Stephen suggest other motivations for promoting such projects: "Chamber board members also receive indirect economic benefits through enhanced learning, board and community interactions, networking, and increased visibility. Service on the chamber of commerce board avails an individual to the cumulative attainment of higher level needs and to the indirect benefits mentioned above. For a local businessperson, there are few, if any, volunteering alternatives for achieving both psychological and economic benefits."[41]

The economic development or pro-growth coalition of Charlotte has linked the airport's expansion to the city's and region's overall economic development. Making Charlotte Douglas Airport an airline hub with international flights required the cooperation of the chamber of commerce, business leaders, mayors, the city council, the congressional delegation, and sometimes state officials in the two Carolinas.

The same media that sought the chamber of commerce's position will sometimes take an advocacy role. Especially in the case of the newspapers (the *Charlotte Observer* and the former *Charlotte News*), the media played a significant part in the airport's early development. The public received most of their information about the airport from the newspaper. As we shall discuss, the newspaper tracks the airport's overall progress, and it reports the activities of the Charlotte City Council and the Airport Advisory Committee. Airlines are national entities that attract the national press. But local press must also keep up, because what happens in one city will affect others. The *Charlotte Observer* has been particularly good at reporting the airport director's political statements and actions. This book will evaluate the *Charlotte Observer*'s record on airport issues.

The political history of a city tells just one story. Several other histories exist—social, economic, racial, neighborhood, and, yes, airport history. Charlotte combines many interacting stories and developments. The following chapters explain the intersection of the federal government, the airline industry, the pro-growth coalition supporting the development of the Charlotte Douglas International Airport, and the overall economic development of the city.

Chapter 1 examines the early history of Charlotte Municipal Airport. As historian Janet R. Daly Bednarek argues in her comparative study of city airports, politics played a critical role in the development of most such facilities.[42] Before World War II, Charlotte began transitioning from a textile center into a nascent banking one. Moreover, the history of the city airport was linked at the intersection of federal regulatory policies and largesse. The technological development of the airplane drove the infrastructure for takeoffs and landings. We will see how the politics of infrastructure continues after the entity has been built. This chapter also highlights individuals that Henry Ogrodzinski called the airport "champions." This work identifies who did what, how, and why.

Chapter 2 links postwar Charlotte with the history of airplanes and airline carrier development. All airports are subjected to the "ripple effects of technology"—that is, changes in aircraft design, speed, and noise. Charlotte's airport grew because it reacted well to technological change. These related elements proved critical to Charlotte's economic development and to Charlotte Douglas's status as the fifth-busiest airport in the nation. While the growth of the airport often paralleled the population increases in the city, at other times it preceded demographic changes.

Chapter 3 examines the impact of airline deregulation and its ripple effects on airlines' financial stability and fares. This chapter shows how members of a local pro-growth coalition can be reduced to bystanders when federal airline policy preempts local interest. Deregulation changed how Charlotte's airport did business with the large carriers and start-up discount airlines. This chapter also links 1970s banking deregulations and mergers to changes in the architecture of financial capitalism. These changes took place as the nation and the city of Charlotte underwent racial and social deregulations. In the latter case the pro-growth leaders enabled social change.

Chapter 4 gives the reader a more detailed look at the process of passenger loading and disembarking. It reviews the intersection of airport management, expansion, and development. As an enterprise, municipal agency is faced with a variety of financial and managerial challenges. In a postindustrial economy, poor management of local infrastructures like airports can signal airlines and outside investors to stay away.

Chapter 5 analyzes the role of airport directors and consultants in Charlotte's economic development. Unlike some political histories, this chapter delves deeply into the management responsibilities of airport heads. Charlotte airport directors were both operational executives and promoters of the transformative city. In addition, they were divided into two types—locals and outsiders. Directors' recruitment and supervision highlights the role of the city council and the city manager. This work also discusses the elasticity of administrative discretion accorded airport directors and the boundaries of consultancies.

Chapter 6 traces local politicians' reactions to the airport developments on the city's quest for economic growth. Making the transformative city brought officials to the intersection of the nascent postindustrial economy's needs and the business leaders' ambition. The apparent intersection of city and airport politics is found in revenue bond campaigns and elections. Furthermore, the airport tells a story of entrepreneurship by directors and high levels of boosterism by the Charlotte Chamber of Commerce. Political scientist Clarence Stone calls the dominance of a city by business interests a "corporate regime." Yet the visible and invisible role of the city's mayors became critical to the success of the airport and its tenants—the airlines. These roles were revealed, in part, in papers of former mayors and in interviews. Interestingly, city councilpersons were players in airport politics, especially in the allocation of grand patronage. In addition to hiring the city managers, selecting consultants, and awarding construction contracts, the council remained a key participant in the allocation process.

Chapter 7 concerns the Charlotte City Council and its oversight responsibilities. As we saw in chapter 2, the interaction of the mayor and members of the city council was critical during the inception of the airport. This chapter discusses how modern-day council members interact with the city manager, airport directors, and the overall economic strategy of the city. The council's leverage lay in its authority to use city revenue bonds to build the airport. Managing conflicts between residents and the airport constituted the other part of the council's responsibility. To do so, the council had to address issues ranging from zoning to the environment. Given the nature of the airport infrastructure, the grand patronage the city council allocated matters. All these recurrent issues affect the transformative city.

Chapter 8 examines the state of North Carolina's attempt to remove the airport from city control and turn its management over to a regional authority or commission. With this turn of events, Charlotte found its future as the transformative city at a critical juncture. The takeover plot failed, but it showed how Charlotte rallied its agency after its ethos was under attack. Equally fascinating was how the failed takeover failure revealed cracks in what had been a solid pro-growth coalition. Local interest had diverged as the demographics changed. Chapter 8 is also a story of state encroachment, city responses, personalities, corporate interest, courts, and partisan politics.

The final chapter reconsiders the airport's growth and Charlotte's future as a transformative city. The airport has made Charlotte a global financial middleweight, but it has also brought new challenges to the city.

CHAPTER 1

Textile Charlotte Learns to Fly

THE STORY OF FLIGHT IS essential to understanding how aircraft's changing technology and multiple uses impacted American cities' locations and functions. When modes of transportation change so do the relationships between cities. The city of Charlotte grew because the distance between cities and towns shrunk, and its own role as a commercial center increased. This early transition occurred because Charlotte had a competitive transportation advantage. The underlying questions are as follows: Why did a small textile town such as Charlotte want to grow? Was it solely because of the uncertainty of textile markets?

MIT management professor Jay Wright Forrester's seminal book *Urban Dynamics* argues that cities attract resources, businesses, and residents to grow.[1] Obviously, the city of Charlotte began its growth journey because its leaders apparently feared stagnation and wanted to join the intercity competition. As this chapter will suggest, the city grew because city boosters inveigled the public and pushed the politicians to accommodate change.

The chapter delves into the history of the airplane as it paralleled the story of Charlotte and often interacted with its growth. We will discover how Charlotte decided to create a space for a municipal airport, then debated the airport, built it, lost it, and recovered it. This chapter also tells a story of the rise of airmail, the fledgling airline industry, and the men who fought to bring air travel to the Queen City. In many ways, Charlotte was an unlikely place for the development of an airport. The city is located in the middle of the American hinterland, and its economy was based on textiles and agriculture. Furthermore, Charlotte was a city with deep southern traditions and laws.

At first glance there seems to be no relationship between textile Charlotte and airport Charlotte. Historian David Goldfield recalls the work of Daniel A. Tompkins, an early owner of the *Charlotte Observer*, the *Charlotte Evening News*, and Observer Printing House, as the 1880 builder and owner of cotton mills in the area surrounding Charlotte. By 1905, the wider city trading region had "half of the looms in the South," enabling it to challenge New England for textile manufacturing supremacy. As a result, rural Carolina residents began moving to Charlotte. Goldfield observes, "Local capital financed it for the most part. That is how Charlotte got into the banking business. The progenitors of Bank of America and Wachovia originated as groups of well-heeled farmers and merchants raising money, obtaining a bank charter, and lending out funds."[2] No one at the time envisioned Charlotte bankers as lenders for more than the textile industry. The first flight occurred in 1903, and a local airport, opened in 1937, would allow bankers to lend money and do business throughout the state of North Carolina and eventually the world. A closer look reveals a clear transformation in which the pro-growth Charlotte coalition evolved from its textile development moorings to its decision to promote the building of a municipal airport.

Building a municipal airport is a complex phenomenon surrounded by politics at all levels of government and subject to rapid technological evolutions of airplanes. Airport directors had to deal with federal grants-in-aid, changing federal laws, competition among airlines, and mergers of airlines. Yet Charlotte Municipal Airport made the journey from a small feeder landing space to a hub for international travel.

As we suggested earlier, the history of airplanes and pilots recounts the story of famous Americans and world-changing events. Telling the daring story of flight helped sell this type of travel to the skeptics. However, convincing the public that cities needed a municipal airport was more challenging. The business leaders of Charlotte assumed this task with the support of elected officials and local newspapers like the *Charlotte Observer*, *Charlotte News*, and *Charlotte Post*. Together, they played a critical role in the development of airplanes, airplane makers, and airport construction. Starting with the rise and fall of the Wright brothers, the print media of that era treated the development of flights and landing spaces as a colorful spectacle with endearing characters.

FLIGHT STARTED IN NORTH CAROLINA

On December 17, 1903, Orville and Wilbur Wright flew the first airplane at Kitty Hawk, North Carolina, about 370 miles from Charlotte. This short first flight climbed 10 feet, traveled 120 feet, and landed in 20 seconds. Subsequently, the Wright brothers were covered like celebrities. In 1904, the *Charlotte Observer* first reported the Wrights' flying feat as a "claim"; a reporter stated that both Wrights claimed to have flown twice from the Kill Devil Sand Hill in Dare County, North Carolina. The article further commented on the brothers' feat: "From the beginning we have employed entirely new principle of control, and as all the experiments have been conducted at their own expense, without assistance from any individual or institution, we do not feel ready at present to give any pictures or detailed description of the machine."[3]

When the Wrights switched their flying experiments to Dayton, Ohio, the *Charlotte Observer* remained skeptical. Under the headline "Wright Brothers Try Again," a 1904 article reported that "secrecy was maintained about the test and few witnessed it."[4] In 1908, the *Observer* called them the "mysterious 'Wright Brothers'" and observed, "They have given no public demonstration in Europe of the powers of their aeroplane."[5] At the time, the possibility of passenger flight by lighter-than-air vehicles fascinated many travelers. The German makers of the Zeppelin, a type of rigid airship, claimed that their vehicle would be first to accomplish this feat, eventually carrying up to one hundred passengers. In 1910 the Zeppelin was able to provide the first passenger service.

Meanwhile, the Wright brothers continued to refine their winged aircraft. Indeed, the *Charlotte Observer* gave the brothers due recognition after their heavier-than-air aircraft worked and they received medals from the Aero Club of America. Doing its journalistic duty, the *Observer* also reported the crash of the Wright plane a month later.[6] Once a machinist's dream, airplanes now stood at the beginning of a major transition in travel.

History shows that the Wright design gave way to several more efficient ways to lift, fly, and land aircraft. In 1910 magician and escape artist Harry Houdini flew his French biplane over Australia, a land area almost the size of the United States. Yet at the time, few knew that the airplane would allow humans to fly around the earth in cylinders and that intercity travel would take hours rather than days. Making this travel transition was not easy. Building airplanes, training people to fly them, and using aircraft for more than air shows for the curious required an imaginative vision. Building an aircraft industry and making pilots more than daredevils required local air travel advocates, supportive publicity, and more resources. As we suggested earlier, the more difficult task for flying enthusiasts and promoters was convincing cities that such machines could land regularly at designated and permanent runways. As we shall see, the media also played a role in this debate about the public accommodation of airplanes and the role of municipalities.

CHARLOTTE, THE TEXTILE HUB

In the first decades of the twentieth century, American railroad companies had a virtual monopoly on intercity travel and the delivery of mail. Many cities like Charlotte were rail centered with multiple connections to other cities. Although an intercity trip would take time and maybe several train changes, a traveler could go anyplace in the nation on a train, where food and even luxury accommodations were available. It is understandable that some dismissed airplanes as attention grabbers but not real competition for the intercity passenger trains. In 1914 the *Charlotte Daily Observer* proclaimed that forty-three trains carried mail in and out of the city. This traffic facilitated the city's claim of being a regional banking city. The paper made the article's subtitle a brag: "Wherein Charlotte Enjoys Unexcelled Facilities in [a] Banking Way."[7]

With its eighteen thousand people, Charlotte was now the largest city in North Carolina. It had become an epicenter of railroad freight due to its heavy investment in textile production and cotton mills. In fact, Charlotte was also becoming the largest textile center in the South. In 1905, Pres. Theodore Roosevelt came to the city and said, "I rejoice in the symptoms of your abounding prosperity. I am here in a great center of cotton manufacture."[8] Historian Mildred G. Andrew reports that the city was home to 17 mills. Within these mills were 3 million looms, 125 spindles, and 6,000 operators. Andrew also finds that "the average raw cotton trade in Charlotte came to $1.2 million per annum."[9] In 1928 the *Charlotte Observer* studied 250 plants, branches, and agencies in the city and found that the annual volume of business represented more than $200 million. The paper further elaborated on this state of affairs:

> Not only does Charlotte surpass all other cities in the gross volume of business done through its textile connections, but it has a long lead over other cities in the number of textile plants operating as well as in the number of large machinery, dyestuff, and supply agencies handling their entire southern business through Charlotte offices. The majority of the large textile machinery and dyestuff corporations of the United States and England which operate in the south have southern headquarters in Charlotte. And no other city in the entire south can claim half so many southern branches.[10]

Along with garment- and furniture-making companies, these were the traditional southern industries that required semiskilled workers, often from rural North Carolina and western South Carolina. Charlotte was growing, but it was still a southern city dominated by the textile industry elite. Some Charlotteans had to be curious about how this type of travel would change their lives and what place it would assume in a textile industry city.

As Charlotte was gaining visibility as a textile center, the airplane was still in its developmental stage. Citizens had read about the Wright brothers, but few of them had flown. In 1912, Thornwell "Thorny" Andrew, an auto mechanic and self-taught pilot, recorded the first flight in Charlotte when he flew a Curtiss Jenny over the old fairground. Yet skeptics abounded, and travelers and shippers would prefer railroads for several more decades.

In a debate about airline noise and railroads, Gerry Bunn states, "If one builds 500 miles of high-speed rail track, you commit to 500 miles of continuous noise, irrevocably despoiled countryside and ever-increasing maintenance costs. Three miles of runway comes with almost five miles of reducing noise—but that is the extent of your investment, and the world is your oyster."[11] For cities, the investment in air travel was more than a simple takeoff and landing runway. Rather, it demanded total commitment. Rails and buses require one stop inside cities. The old joke was that a chicken contributes (eggs) to breakfast, whereas a pig makes a total contribution (bacon). So the attitudes of city leaders made the difference for an airport.

WORLD WAR I AND FLYING

After their use as military weapons during World War I, thinking about the utility of airplanes changed. Despite airplanes' success in combat, Americans doubted they could be used to ferry intercity passengers. Yet Europeans were not so hesitant to admit planes' utility, and they moved quickly to manufacture aircraft. To keep up with their European opponents, the U.S. Army established an air corps unit and trained more soldiers as pilots. One of the army's training bases, Camp Greene, was located in Charlotte. In addition, World War I spurred Congress to invest in private airplane production.

Airplanes were slowly shifting away from their stage at air shows and becoming a part of the American military complex. Pilots, with their leather flying suits and helmets, were not just daredevils and war heroes. After the war, the nation had no major air carriers but a surplus of trained aviators and pilots, some of them employed by air shows. Charlotte had its own air stunt man, Ben Huntley. A traveling air show called the Thrasher Brothers Flying Circus featured Grant Thrasher, an ace of American stunt pilots. His brother Bud Thrasher would climb out of planes and "hang by heels from struts of the plane. He would sometimes pick up a handkerchief from the ground."[12]

A way to make profit was needed to entice private investment in carrier business. History shows that the federal government promoted air travel as a quick and efficient way to move the mail. Competition among airplane owners and entrepreneurs for the airmail business led to the development of better airplanes and eventually led to the creation of airline companies.

Like most cities, Charlotte found that the world wars changed the context of flying. Larger aircraft opened up the possibility of passenger-oriented aircraft. And the idea of air travel all started as a way to move the mail faster to cities. To understand this process, it is important to review the history from before Charlotte Airport was a physical entity. We will start with a review of airlines as mail carriers.

AIRMAIL AND AIRLINES

On May 15, 1918, the United States commenced airmail service with six converted U.S. Army Air Service Curtiss JN-4HM aircraft ("Jenny" biplanes) from World War I. The race for airmail was on, and the *Charlotte Observer* told readers, "You will be able to write to any city in the United States and get a reply with 36 hours by airmail."[13] By November, the U.S. postmaster general reported, "The present airmail service is [a] 100 per cent success. Its further extension, accomplishing a saving in time and a great benefit in emergency business operations is assured."[14]

On November 25, 1918, the *Charlotte Observer* published an opinion essay entitled "Coming of the Airplane." It asserted that "an airplane depot or landing place in Charlotte" would be built by the next Thanksgiving, and it claimed that the route had been mapped. In addition, the newspaper had gotten a letter from the Aerial League of America pledging its cooperation with the city in procuring airmail. The *Observer* urged the leadership of the city to work with the league to get airmail and a landing space. Then the essay went further, suggesting that people would buy airplanes and airplanes would sidetrack both automobiles and railroads. Finally, the paper supported the idea of an air depot or landing place and made a fascinating prediction: "This is a proposition which The Observer believes should secure the instant attention of the people of this city. The establishment of an airplane-landing place is one of the assured developments of the future. . . . It is a safe prophecy that in the days to come Charlotte will be known as a city of aerodromes for planes to land on and depart from, and Charlotte is quite sure to be called upon shortly to take up consideration of establishing the institution of this kind for mail service."[15]

On November 26, 1918, Charlotte mayor Frank R. McNinch received correspondence from the Aerial League of America suggesting Charlotte was a possible landing place for airmail delivery. McNinch approved of the idea and appointed a committee to handle all matters of the airmail delivery:

> I am enthusiastic over the prospect, and I will be glad to join in this movement for the establishment of this proposed services—a quicker means of transporting important mail. The scheme itself appeals to me and I think this city is entitled to the service if the route is established by the government. The part the airplane

will assume in the conduct of American business in the near future will be of vast importance.... I cannot believe other than that an extension of this service would be not only practicable but profitable.[16]

The leaders of Charlotte's public utilities, the cotton mills, and textile mills echoed the mayor's enthusiasm for getting airmail deliveries. Mobilization had begun for airmail and a landing space. The *Charlotte Observer* reported endorsements from business leaders ranging from cotton manufacturer spokespersons and local retail merchants.

THE ROARING TWENTIES

In 1920 Charlotte was a small city of fewer than fifty thousand people. In 1921 some of these Charlotteans began listening to WBT, the city's first radio station. Life in the Queen City was changing, but the onslaught of postwar prosperity did not have the dramatic economic impact it had on larger cities like Chicago and New York. Yet the advent of the nationwide consumer economy spurred demand for new technology. Americans had money and wanted to buy things (e.g., automobiles and refrigerators) and go places (e.g., embark on intercity travel). Business was expanding and faster communication was necessary. Congress's enthusiasm for airmail delivery was building. Cities around the nation were vying for airplane landings and designating landing strips for the mail. In Charlotte, Cannon Airfield became the landing spot for most of the airmail. Aero Club of America, started in 1905, promoted aviation and issued licenses to pilots. In 1929, four part-time fliers and businessmen started the club's Charlotte chapter. They bought a licensed used airplane and overhauled it, then flew in and out of what was then called Charlotte Airport.[17] Also in 1929, Charles E. Lambeth, then a World War I lieutenant junior grade in the Naval Air Service, became the first president of Charlotte Aero Club. Lambeth later worked as a real estate developer and became the mayor of Charlotte (1931–1933). In other words, members of Charlotte's business community were among an elite group of fliers.

It is important to remember that the city of Charlotte was in the process of restructuring its government in the twenties. It was also a relatively small city led by a Democratic Party–dominated aldermanic system allied with the cotton and textile industries. Small southern cities like Charlotte had most of the challenges of the Old South. Poverty and poor schools and race relations made its residents provincial, and the myopia of agrarian economic leaders and textile manufacturers often overshadowed city politics. This combination of factors restrained the city's development. Thomas Hanchett's book *Sorting Out the New South* argues this point convincingly.

Charlotte was not yet the progressive city that consultants would later inveigle it to become. Nevertheless, southern Democrats leading Congress, the same politicians who promoted racial segregation, would join forces with their northern counterparts to promote the idea of airmail. Congress passed the Kelly Airmail Act of 1925 that allowed the U.S. Postal Service to create the competition for airplane owners and carriers to carry domestic mail. Many southern congresspersons voted for the airmail bill.

In 1926, Congress passed the Air Commerce Act providing money for air navigation. This was essentially a federal policy decision to foster the commercial development of aircraft. The law also established the first set of airline safety rules and created the Aeronautics Branch in the Commerce Department. This measure allowed for more coordination and support for carriers. Writing in the *Journal of Air Transportation*, Randy Johnson further explains the act's effects:

> The passage of the Air Commerce Act in 1926 brought about bureaucratic reorganization in the Department of Commerce and the transfer of the lighted airway system and 17 radio stations from the Post Office to the newly created Aeronautics Branch. Within the Aeronautics Branch maintenance for the airways systems fell to the Airways Division. Research and development came under the Aeronautics Research Division and it was within this division that the NBS expanded its research responsibilities. Development, construction and maintenance for aeronautical telecommunications now rested in one administrative agency—the Aeronautics Branch.[18]

Congressman Clyde Kelly of Pennsylvania led the congressional effort to get more letters and packages on airlines. Delivering mail between cities within a day proved a major breakthrough and selling point for the public. It was also clear that there was money to be made in carrying the mail and providing financial stability for airlines. In 1928, the first foreign mail act was passed, initiating the global connection and indicating the need for bigger local airports.

In 1928, engineer E. P. Goodrich reported the following statistics for growing numbers of airports to the Commerce Department. The United States was home to 864 operating airports and airplane landing fields. Of these, 207, or 24 percent, were owned by municipalities. Goodrich further reported 3,000 additional unequipped emergency landing fields.[19] Charlotte had to wait another nine years to get its municipal airport.

Meanwhile, the state government involved itself in the regulation of fliers and airport construction, and the state of North Carolina entered the flying business. On January 20, 1929, attorney and flier Robert A. Wellon convinced the Mecklenburg representatives to sponsor a bill that would make it possible for cities to use city land for airport purposes. Authored by Wellon, the bill aimed to appropriate money to maintain the airport, and it provided for the municipal government's use of eminent domain to get land for an airport. The bill also penalized pilots who flew drunk. Although the Eighteenth Amendment (Prohibition) and the Volstead Act of 1920 made getting a drink difficult, they did not stop people from imbibing.

PROGRESS DURING THE DEPRESSION

The twenties were a growth decade for most cities. For its part, Charlotte experienced a 78 percent increase in population. In 1924 Charlotte was chosen as a location for a Ford assembly plant, a facility that was a small step away from textiles. The factory also represented the city's nascent industrial and commercial aspirations. In 1927 Charlotte was the center of textile manufacturing territory outside New England. The region featured 770 mills and over 10 million spindles.[20] In 1928 *Charlotte Observer* reporter LeGette Blythe wrote about the city's journey to becoming a big-time retail center with banks. This rising skyline was impressive, but it would be stretching the imagination to call the two blocks of South Tryon Street "Charlotte's Wall Street."[21]

Even so, the textile mills were at their peak. In addition, as an emerging center of banking and distribution, Charlotte attracted new residents. Rural people fled to join the city's eighty thousand inhabitants. And more people meant more need for entertainment. In the 1930s, the public was fascinated with air shows and the barnstormer era. Johnny Crowell, the manager of Cannon Airfield and one of the city's best-known pilots, started flying in 1922. He piloted all types of planes and performed stunts including the "hands off." For this feat, Crowell would fly a modified plane from takeoff through landing with his hands tied outside the cockpit.[22] Other stunt pilots were eager to come to Charlotte as well; famous stunt flier Freddy Lund traveled to the city in 1931.[23]

The city of Charlotte underwent the economic travails of the Great Depression like the rest of the nation. In 1929 the Ford assembly plant, along with other businesses, closed. Mayor Lambeth's administration (1931–1933) witnessed bread lines in the city. Air shows provided a diversion from the economic reality of unemployment and failed businesses. Yet the momentum for the development of airplanes remained relatively steady. Presidents Hoover and Roosevelt supported airmail delivery and the growth of the airplane manufacturing. Indeed, the nascent airline industry grew during this period.

On April 2, 1930, Eastern Air Transport delivered the first airmail to Charlotte and encountered what the *Charlotte Observer* called a "wildly enthusiastic throng" of thirty thousand to fifty thousand people. Clarence O. Kuester, "Charlotte's Booster," was there to meet the airplane, as was Mayor Baxter. Under the headline "Thousands See First Air Mail," the *Charlotte Observer* reported, "Roaring out of the darkness of the south, Gene Brown, intrepid flier of night skies, last night officially christened Charlotte as an air mail stop when he brought the first air mail into the city and landed gracefully."[24] Historian Mary Kratt notes that the aircraft carried twenty thousand pieces of outgoing mail, but she also acknowledges that "many people still thought the airport was a harebrained idea and much too far out of town."[25]

AIRMAIL FOR CHARLOTTE

On December 10, 1936, Eastern Air Transport officially inaugurated airmail service. Postmaster General Walter Brown flew to Charlotte in a Curtiss Condor, an eighteen-passenger biplane, and Mayor Wilson and Clarence O. "Booster" Kuester attended the ceremony. Capt. Thomas B. Doe told the audience that Eastern Air Transport wanted Charlotte to be a junction point for eastern lines heading southward from Jacksonville. Mr. Brown informed those present that the U.S. Post Office was spending $20 million annually to promote aviation. He asserted,

> Aviation in the United States must become self-supporting. You people of Charlotte and the Carolinas should support this tremendously important enterprise of the government and I bespeak the most liberal support by the public of the service the Eastern Air Transports inaugurating today.
>
> ... The primary purpose is not so much to expedite the movement of letters but to build up civil aeronautics so that in the event of a national emergency our nation will have the factories, the airports, the other physical facilities and some trained personnel. We cannot keep up this financial assistance for aviation indefinitely.[26]

Brown's point was that the nation was still in the midst of the Depression. The subtext of his message was that Charlotteans should support local leaders who supported airmail and the facilities that made pickup and delivery possible. To continue this major breakthrough in mail delivery, municipalities needed to assume more of the related cost. Yet in 1930, Congress passed the McNary-Watres Act. This law attempted to reduce the maximum payment to airlines and also required airlines to get route certificates. It was passed in the wake of the Great Depression and during the Hoover administration's struggles to restore the economy.

Despite the pending economic collapse, the airlines were thriving as more cities and towns wanted airmail. Just as carriers were beginning to make a profit, a scandal broke out concerning an attempt by U.S. postmaster Walter Brown and airline executives to divide the airmail routes among the big carriers and reduce competition. The *Saturday Evening Post* claimed that Brown knew what he was doing: "The McNary-Watres Law made him virtual dictator of the airmail lines. Using this power Brown cracked the heads of the big operators together, ruthlessly froze out the shoestring lines, using trick provisions in the law, brought the industry out of quasi-anarchy and forced it, against its will, into passenger flying."[27] This was one of the first development crises for the airline industry and for those who hoped to get a landing space in their cities.

Postmaster Brown tried to calm the situation by calling a conference to resolve the growing route problems resulting from struggling airlines' efforts to game the system. On May 20, 1930, he invited the heads of the airlines to what journalists called the "Spoils Conference." The charge under discussion was that airlines friendly to the Hoover administration got contracts, but this was subsequently refuted.

If anything could be called an airline financial growth setback, it was the scandal around the Spoils Conference. The end of the twenties saw the stock market crash and the onset of the Great Depression. Economic dislocation and instability swept the nation and devastated growing cities like Charlotte. After President Hoover left office, the new Roosevelt administration attempted to get the airlines out of the mail business. In February 1934, Roosevelt signed Executive Order 6591 canceling all mail contracts. He then ordered the U.S. Army Air Corps to fly the mail. Aside from causing serious financial problems for the airline industry, this proved to be an impractical policy alternative. Airmail returned to commercial carriers two months later, and the *Saturday Evening Post* called the Roosevelt solution "the first great blunder of his Administration."[28] The old routes were opened for bidding and the existing carrier received all of them.

Four years later the airmail scandal also triggered a Senate investigation. Alabama senator Hugo Black (later a Supreme Court justice) led the investigation. No senators from the Carolinas were present for the questioning, but John C. Taylor was a member of the House investigation hearings, which made several recommendations to the president and Congress. In June 1934, Congress passed the Air Mail Act of 1934 designed to regulate the airmail business and remove some of the participants in the Spoils Conference from airmail delivery. The law provided that airlines could not be in the manufacturing and mail business at the same time. Airlines like Northwest Airways and United Airlines changed their names, in the former case to Northwest Airlines. United Aircraft and Transportation Company split into three parts: United Air Lines Transportation Company, United Aircraft Manufacturing Company, and Boeing Aircraft Company.

Furthermore, the act made the U.S. Postal Service responsible for awarding airmail contracts. It also authorized the Interstate Commerce Commission to set the rates for airmail contracts and the Bureau of Air Commerce to monitor the routes and equipment. More monitoring of equipment was the reaction to a disastrous rollout of military planes in which several pilots died. Although what happened in Congress seemed far removed from Charlotte, the nascent Eastern Air Transport, the primary airmail delivery service for the city, was one of the airlines forbidden to bid for contracts. Eastern Air Transport Incorporated subsequently reorganized itself and was renamed Eastern Air Lines. Four years later, Congress passed the Airmail Act of 1938. This measure stabilized the airlines by establishing mail rates for them.

Meanwhile new aircraft were evolving technically and in terms of speed. Reduced travel time was one of the salient features of new airplanes—airline promoters argued that these flying machines could go anyplace in less time. In 1927, Charles Lindbergh made his historical solo flight across the Atlantic Ocean. He was in the air for thirty-three and a half hours and traveled more than one thousand miles, sometimes in bad weather.[29] This flight's significance lay in its reinforcement of the idea that air travel was the carrier of the future. Now, airplane manufacturers only needed to make a plane that hauled passengers and turned a profit.

Americans were sold on faster mail delivery, but selling them on air transportation would take a few more years. Remember that most Americans did their intercity travel by rail. The nation had an array of privately owned passenger train services that carried presidents, corporate moguls, movie stars, and ordinary Americans. It would take years to get citizens to travel in cylindrical machines heavier than air. It would take even longer to convince taxpayers that their cities needed to buy land and set it aside for air transportation. Airport construction as an economic imperative for city development and growth had not yet become a believable narrative.

While private individuals owned airplanes and cities had airfields (sometimes grassy fields), few airports were owned, designated, and managed by municipalities. Cities would not commit land for what were called municipal airports until sixteen years after the Wrights' first flight. As historian Howard Stussman points out, "From the Wright brothers' first flight until after World War I, any mowed swath in a field of alfalfa, a level pasture or a 1,500-ft stretch of compacted cinders qualified as a runway. Add a gas pump, a wooden loading ramp and a shed, and the airfield became an 'airport.'"[30] Fliers may have thought that better airports were clearly necessary, but many city governments did not believe that municipalities should build them.

The presence of an airport implies the existence of scheduled flights. Here, however, is where the definition of "airport" gets fuzzy. In 1914 the first scheduled flight took place between cities in Florida. On November 20, 1919, the first plane landed in the city of Tucson, Arizona, producing the claim that the city was the nation's first municipal airport. (This assertion is disputed as College Park, Maryland, cites itself as the first airport in the world, dating from 1911.) Note that all of these landing locations were in place before the 1925 Air Mail Act. Interestingly, Bisbee-Douglas (1943) in Cochise County, Arizona, considered itself the first international airport.

In 1927, Pan Am Airways became the first American airline. In 1929, the Sunbelt city of Atlanta bought the old Chandler Field and renamed it Atlanta Municipal Airport. This purchase will perhaps go down as one of the most important decisions in the city's history. The field's acquisition would eventually make Atlanta the regional city of the southeastern United States and allow it to overshadow other southern cities like Birmingham and Charlotte.

Claiming status as the city with the first airport was not as important as the decision by local economic leaders to follow through on federal incentives. Cities would build airports in the middle of the great economic uncertainty of the Depression. These projects were part of Pres. Franklin Roosevelt's efforts to get the country working again and to develop the relatively economically stunted south. Such policies helped the city of Charlotte to recover from the Depression.

AIRMAIL AND CHARLOTTE AIRPORT

In the early twenties, Charlotte's political leadership was not fully convinced that the city needed an airport. City officials desired airmail delivery, but many felt the airplanes could land at the various privately owned airfields. Some politicians did not believe that city government should have to fund an airport of its own. Once the business community got behind the "let's build a municipal airport narrative" in the late twenties, public attitudes began to change. In 1927, airport champion E. G. Griffith of the Charlotte Chamber of Commerce asserted, "Charlotte must wake up or be left behind in the advance of progress. Instead of taking it seriously, people here are referring to it as absurd. The city government should open its eyes and take more interest in the establishment of an airport than it has demonstrated."[31]

Griffith conceived that it would be expensive to build an airport on the rugged land of Charlotte. The *Charlotte Observer* sought an outsider's view of why a municipal facility would be so essential to the city's future. Thus, the paper quoted airport expert Harold D. Dennis, who had been associated with the Georgia-Florida Airways. Dennis provided an infrastructure rationale for a municipal airport. For him, a municipal airport was as vital to a progressive community as a "faucet to a waterpipe."[32] As Dennis asserted, "To delay the construction of a municipal airport is only a handicap to that city from a transportation viewpoint, an advertising factor and an announcement that Charlotte is behind times."[33]

Political pressure for a municipal airport began to build. In 1928, the *Charlotte Observer* headlines read, "Aid for Airport Expected Soon After Operations Start." However, the city council was in a catch-22, and it stated that Charlotte couldn't legally make any appropriations for an airport until it was a functioning municipal property. Hence it would become "municipal necessary."[34] Airports were not yet seen as necessary.

As early as 1929, a delegation of Charlotte businesspersons went to Washington to persuade the Commerce Department to add Charlotte to the New York and Atlanta mail route. The delegation was led by W. S. Creigton, manager of the traffic department of the Charlotte Shippers and Manufacturers Association; E. G. Griffith, president of the Charlotte Airport Corporation and chair of the Charlotte Chamber of Commerce Airport Committee; and Clarence O. Kuester, business manager of the city's chamber of commerce.[35]

This group may have heard or read the Commerce Department report written by Col. Clarence M. Young, assistant secretary of commerce for aeronautics. The department stated that 1 million flights were made during the first half of the 1930s. Of this group of passengers, 984,800 were involved with air travel. Another 208,357 were passengers on regular scheduled flights.[36] These statistics strengthened the case for cities to join the air travel network. More importantly, this type of government report helped local airport promoters make their case for city-owned airports. Clearly, more ordinary people were flying, and a municipal airport would not replace privately owned airports. People who owned private planes could still use privately owned airports.

PRIVATELY OWNED AIRPORTS IN CHARLOTTE

The original privately owned Charlotte Airport was also called Cannon Airport. Its geographic coordinates were described as 35.24 North / 80.89 West (northwest of downtown Charlotte, about three miles from what is now Charlotte Douglas International Airport). Cannon Aircraft Sales and Service Inc.

started as an aircraft dealer and flight school in North Carolina in 1934. Charlotte aviator Johnny Crowell managed Cannon Airfield, which was built from the remains of Camp Greene, a former World War I–era army training base. The airfield had three asphalt and gravel runways, one extending southwest and southeast and another north to southwest and northeast, 2,300 feet by 300 feet each. The third runway measured 2,700 feet by 100 feet. Two metal hangars were also present at Cannon.

In April 1930, Eastern Air Transport delivered the first airmail to Charlotte, and it landed at Cannon Airport. However, the field was also open on weekends for air shows and pilot training. Eric Carnes observed in December 1930, "Cannon's problem was that it was somewhat hemmed in & had gravel runways, and when the airlines started talking in the late 1920s about coming to Charlotte they decided Cannon was inadequate."[37] Besides, pilots complained that the gravel runways created rocks that chewed up their propellers.

While Charlotte Municipal Airport was being built, other fields or airports like Rockenbrough, Willow Grove, Delta, and Carpenter Airfield served as landing places for aircraft. It is not clear when these airports closed, but some continued to operate alongside the building of the new publicly owned airport, which would be known as Charlotte Municipal Airport.

THE RISE AND FALL OF CANNON AIRFIELD

The Charlotte Chamber of Commerce held a $3,000 mortgage on the airport at that point in history, and on April 15, 1931, the chamber's members announced that they wanted to sell it. They were trying to dispose of the mortgages "in order to complete the raising of a fund of $9,000 by the corporation to meet obligations."[38] Clarence O. Kuester, the executive manager of the chamber of commerce, argued in 1931 that the city needed to own a municipal airport. Charlotte was one of three cities that had airmail but did not own an airport. Kuester urged a favorable vote on the proposal to allow the takeover of Charlotte Airport from its stockholders. Unless it took over the airport, he argued, the city "would not be successful as far as passenger and mail travel."[39]

Meanwhile the private airfield called Charlotte Airport Inc. went into receivership. To save the airport, the facility's supporters called for a revenue bond on the ballot. However, there was not much citizen enthusiasm about this idea. Airmail was now in peril. In May 1932, the chamber of commerce publicly expressed its frustration with voters. Chamber president J. Luther Snyder asserted, "The Chamber of Commerce has done all it could, but it has reached its rope's end. It is now up to the people of Charlotte to act if they want an airport for the city."⁴⁰ The *Charlotte Observer* quoted H. A. Elliot, vice president of Eastern Air Transport, as saying, "It is against our policy to come to the aid of airports along our lines. The moment the lights are turned off at the airport, our mail plane begins skipping Charlotte."⁴¹ In order to continue receiving airmail, the city faced a choice between providing financial support for an existing private airport or building a city-owned one.

The idea of fast airmail was not enough for residents to buy into the idea of a city-owned airport. Widespread unemployment during the Depression meant that the public wanted jobs. A writer for the *Saturday Evening Post* recalled,

> The city's businessmen began to move in on the depression shortly after its arrival. They began with unemployment. What moved them was not the social gospel but self-interest. The relief bills were getting too big for their pocketbooks. Through a committee of the Chamber of Commerce they began to do, in 1930, what the Federal Government had not yet got around to doing, acting on the assumption, since politically repudiated, that unemployment is not a relief but an employment problem, they instituted a program to match the available jobless with the available jobs.⁴²

To this end, Charlotte business leaders needed to motivate and mobilize the citizenry. The unemployed had to be encouraged to become politically active. Accordingly, city government structure had to be changed to stimulate citizens' interest and to highlight the mayor as the city's chief salesperson. The people would vote for politicians to whom they could speak and relate. Ben Douglas was one such man.

MOBILIZATION FOR A MUNICIPAL AIRPORT

Historian Janet Bednarek concludes, "The period between 1929 and 1933 . . . represented one in which cities began to work out their relationship with their local 'municipal' airport. . . . Arguments in favor of public ownership, however, became stronger and more common."⁴³ The Charlotte Chamber of Commerce, the vanguard of the pro-growth coalition, was one of the fervent promoters of a municipal airport.

In 1934, the city of Charlotte decided to elect a mayor separate from the city council. This change allowed the mayor more visibility while keeping the council-manager form of government. Benjamin Elbert Douglas, a thirty-nine-year-old undertaker, ran against incumbent mayor Arthur H. Wearn and two other candidates. Douglas won the runoff against Wearn by 670 votes,⁴⁴ becoming the first mayor elected separately under the council-manager city government on May 8, 1935. A true airport champion, he served from 1935 to 1941. In addition, he actively promoted the idea of a municipal airport during his time in office and continued to do so after leaving city hall. Douglas asserted, "I started the Airport. People said, what's the use. We've got one. But Connor [Cannon] Airport runway was only 3,000 feet. long. Churches, schools, libraries are nice but to build a community you have to have water and transportation. I felt we had to have it."[45]

The same man who pushed for a bigger and city-owned airport for Charlotte was afraid to fly. The mayor admitted this fear publicly when he stated that he was more afraid of getting in an airplane than fighting for an airport. He said, "Like a lot of other people, I was actually afraid to fly, even though I knew it meant so much to the people to have air travel here."[46] Mayor Douglas had the full support of the Charlotte Chamber of Commerce in his quest for a municipal airport. Former mayor Charles Lambert, Douglas's predecessor, was now the chamber's president. Indeed, it was Lambert who presented the city council with the case for purchasing land for the airport. The business community wanted airmail for the city, and Eastern Air Lines was described as "anxious" to make Charlotte a stop between Washington and Atlanta.[47]

August was the month of citizen mobilization. Paul B. Eaton, president of the Charlotte Aero Club, began writing to the actors in the unfolding airport drama. He publicly released a letter from Howard G. Baitty, the state engineer for the Federal Public Works Program. Therein, Baitty assured Eaton that the Works Progress Administration would complete airport runway grading and other necessary tasks. Baitty stated, "We shall welcome an application for this purpose."[48]

Five potential sites for the airport were examined, but only three of them seemed appropriate. These three—Statesville Road, Wilkinson Boulevard (located near Gastonia), and Hoskins sector (rear for the Hoskins drug store)—had been surveyed for the airport and were available. The decision was made to locate the airport on the two hundred acres of land on Statesville Road, about six and a half miles from Charlotte. Charlotte real estate man Brandon Smith stated that the land could be purchased for about $13,500. It would provide enough space for three runways—3,400, 4,500, and 5,000 feet long.

Once the Charlotte business leaders decided to go forward with a municipal airport, they, along with politicians and opinion leaders, had to mobilize the citizens. Convinced that airmail was the wave of progress for the future, members of the pro-growth coalition entered the campaign for the revenue bond. The coalition knew that average people were fascinated by air shows and the role of the airplanes in World War I. The task now was to get the residents to vote for revenue bonds to buy the land for the airport.

In 1935, the Charlotte Exchange Club voted unanimously to work with the Charlotte Junior Chamber of Commerce to rally support from voters. Bomar Lowrence headed the get-out-the-vote effort, whose goal was to contact 5,000 of the 6,142 residents registered to vote for the revenue bond. This was a special election. It would entail a vote against registration, and a total of 3,072 votes for the bonds would be a victory. In other words, if the registered voters did not vote, their abstention would be counted as a "no" vote. The *Charlotte Observer* noted as much: "All persons who are registered in this special airport bond election who fail to vote next Tuesday will be counted as having voted against the bond issue."[49]

Meanwhile, Mayor Ben Douglas was reassuring residents that the airport would be built at no cost to taxpayers. Voters would only be supporting the city's purchase of land located at Juneau Station on the main line of the Southern Railway. This location was then about six and a half miles from the city of Charlotte proper.

During the mobilization campaign, the state of North Carolina was also recruited to support the mayor and the pro-growth coalition. Capus M. Waynick, chair of the North Carolina Highway Commission, stated that he would "probably authorize" the construction of a hard-surface highway from Wilkinson Boulevard to the proposed airport. He made no firm "commitment," but he would give the idea "his sympathetic attention."[50] These comments preceded the fall elections. Jack Wynne of the U.S. Bureau of Commerce sounded an alarm.

> I have had a number of conferences with John Small in regard to the situation in Charlotte and in conditions of Charlotte are considerably involved. I understand that the owners of the port have a mortgage of about $100,000 on the property that they want the city to assume, but on the other hand the city charter does not permit investment of public funds in an airport. With that being the situation, I do not know what can be done.... We are ready to make a grant through the Works Progress Administration on municipally-owned airports, but cannot spend government money on any others. Moreover, the Post Office department is very anxious to have the large planes stop at Charlotte, but the situation is well known, in this respect.[51]

In addition to these statements, the federal government began planning for a positive vote. It was also announced that the U.S. Commerce Department had dispatched bureau inspector Maj. E. M. Haight to oversee the planning for an airport. Haight was also expected to supervise the construction work.

With all these positive indicators in place, it became the mayor's responsibility to educate the public. Citizens were expected to both vote and pressure their council representatives to carry the project forward. The local media followed Mayor Douglas's lead and reported his public comments. Douglas also solicited the *Charlotte Observer* to publicize the upcoming revenue bond. He encouraged citizens to vote early so that the city would have votes in the ballot box. In addition, Douglas claimed that the airport's proposed construction would provide nine months' work for two hundred unemployed Charlotteans. As the city was still in the midst of the Great Depression, this was good news—any talk about jobs would receive serious attention for the citizenry. Mayor Douglas contended that defeat of the revenue bond would force the Charlotte City Council to provide for needy citizens during the winter months. He asserted, "This will probably result in a substantial increase in the tax rate."[52] The mobilization campaign was ultimately successful and the pro-growth coalition victorious. Of 6,100 registered voters, 4,583 voted for the bond and 1,150 against it.

WPA AND AIRPORT BUILDING

Historians debate whether World War II or the New Deal resuscitated the national economy. As it put Charlotte residents back to work, the New Deal was manna from Washington. The Works Progress Administration (WPA) was one of the agencies of Pres. Franklin D. Roosevelt's New Deal program. Led by Harry Hopkins, the WPA had a budget of almost $5 billion, and it employed 3.5 million out-of-work Americans who built everything from parks to bridges. Roosevelt's strategy was to put the unemployed back to work and not rely on a free-market turnaround. This Keynesian economic strategy of pump priming (i.e., governmental funding of public works jobs to put money in workers' hands) had its conservative critics. In fact, Democratic senator Josiah W. Bailey of North Carolina was one of the New Deal's chief detractors.[53] Yet the state of North Carolina accepted the WPA, with its patronage that generated jobs. George Coan, mayor of Winston-Salem, became North Carolina's WPA director.

From 1935 to 1943, the WPA constructed much of what is considered early built infrastructure in cities. In Charlotte, the Mecklenburg WPA was led by regional director John Grice. Mr. Grice stated, "We have conferred with city officials concerning using WPA funds for a Charlotte Airport. In my opinion a municipally owned airport is the No. 1 project in which the city should interest itself at the present time."⁵⁴ David M. Rea had been an engineer with the North Carolina Highway Department. He later became Grice's assistant for projects and planning, and he ultimately took charge of the airport's construction. Charlotte Municipal Airport was one of the WPA's biggest projects. Its closest rival was the proposed stadium at Independence Park. During a debate about the stadium, Grice had to assure citizens that the facility would be funded.

Mayor Douglas got the Charlotte City Council to vote to accept the WPA funding to build the airport. The first airport bond for $50,000 was approved by the city council. The WPA granted the city the funds, and the council used the funds to buy the land for the airport. Construction on the airport started in 1934 and was finally completed in 1937. With a $200,000 grant from the Works Progress Administration (WPA), the construction began. As one of the largest projects for the WPA in the city, it also brought federal funding and new people to the city. It was reported, "W.P.A. funds accounted for $323,889.47. This was combined with an investment of $57,703.28 from the City of Charlotte. Of this money, $143,334.96 was paid in salary to the workers on the site."⁵⁵

On March 1, 1936, voters approved the bonds and they were sold to pay for improvements—a terminal and a hangar. The U.S. Department of Commerce assigned Maj. E. M. Height as inspector for the airport. He was given an office in city hall. In his annual report to the city council, city manager J. B. Marshall stated, "Actual construction was started on November 27, 1935 and air service began on May 17, 1937. Sponsored by the City of Charlotte at the cost of $57,703; and by the state with a bridge and highway cost $34,461; and with the Federal Government furnishing $323,889 in labor and material, the present field represents a total expenditure of $416,054."⁵⁶

In the thirties, construction was a slow process. Although the WPA allotted $15,000, it would take two years to build a shelter and to turn on the beam. Mary Kratt, one of the first writers to record the building of the airport, reported on the WPA completion of the facilities, stating, "When W.P.A. construction ceased in June 1937, the new Charlotte Municipal Airport boasted an administration/terminal building, a single hangar, beacon tower, and three runways—two 3000 feet long landing strips and one 2500 strip each 150 feet wide."⁵⁷

Reports of the airport's actual cost vary. H. G. Trotter, who authored a history of the airport, indicated the total cost was $802,237. The WPA contributed $638,100, the city $84,240. Charlotte bought the land for $50,000 and $30,000.⁵⁸ The Civil Aeronautics Administration then appropriated it. On May 17 the Charlotte Municipal Airport opened, and Eastern Air Transport made its first flight to the new facility.

CITY-OWNED AIRPORT BUT STATE CONTROL?

After the construction ceased, the political intrigue began. The municipal airport was no longer a fantasy of Charlotte leaders; it was now a visible part of the infrastructure. On May 11, 1937, the North Carolina General Assembly session of 1937 established a nine-member Charlotte Airport Commission. The state appointed six members—Hugh E. Campbell, C. P. Street, and John C. Erwin among them. The Charlotte City Council appointed three members. On May 15, 1937, the commission appointed Maj. V. L. Nash, a retired army officer and district manager for the WPA, temporary manager of the Charlotte Airport. The first chair of the Charlotte Airport Commission was former councilman William States Lee Jr. John F. Boyd and former mayor Charles E. Lambeth were announced as commission members. Robert Lassiter, another commissioner, served as chair during the army takeover of the airport.[59] A reporting of these individuals' actions indicates that the pro-growth coalition sought to restrict those who made decisions about the airport to its supporters.

In November 1937 the city's relationship with the airport was challenged by a suit testing the constitutionality of spending $5,000 in tax money for the upkeep of the building and grounds. The city council appointed members to the Charlotte Airport Commission to operate the new facility. During its first year of operation, Kratt reported six daily flights from Charlotte Municipal Airport. By 1938, the number of daily flights had increased to eight.

Despite the turmoil in the national economy, the city of Charlotte had a working airport that was slowly demonstrating its utility. The task now was to make it a department of municipal government. In 1945 city manager R. W. Flack followed his annual report by appointing D. M. Rea, who had been the chief engineer for the WPA, the first permanent airport director. The Charlotte Municipal Airport was now operational, and the city of Charlotte was in the airport business. In the 1940s, the city council agreed to sell land on North Graham Street between Fifth and Sixth Streets to buy eighty-two additional acres adjacent to the airport. This transaction was necessary because the previously appointed commission refused to use its surplus as a loan for the land. The city council leased eighty-two acres to the airport, and the *Charlotte Observer* later quoted Mayor Douglas as saying, "This is the proudest day of my life."[60]

As noted earlier, Eastern Air Transport had been delivering mail to the city of Charlotte. Eddie Rickenbacker, a famous World War I flying ace, led the new Eastern Air Lines, which made Charlotte Municipal Airport one of its hubs. The airline was able to make a profit out of flying by using the DC-3 Eastern. In early days, the DC-3 had a sleeper (i.e., a reclining seat that could become a bed) for long flights. After the war Eastern replaced the DC-3s with the Lockheed L-1049, the "Super Constellation." Here we see how airplane technology and glamour was used to attract public support.

Eastern Air Lines used a Lockheed Electra to fly from Atlanta to Charlotte. Atlanta councilman John L. Wilkinson and his wife were passengers on that inaugural flight, and Wilkinson brought with him a letter from Atlanta's mayor to Mayor Douglas, who was hospitalized at the time. The first flight also carried fifteen thousand letters to Charlotte. Historian Janet R. Daly Bednarek observes that the DC-3, a propeller-driven airliner that could reach speeds of over two hundred miles per hour, was "immediately popular" and "made it possible for airlines to make money from passengers only, thus making the airmail subsidy less important."[61]

In 1938, Congress reorganized the government's role in airline development. In June of that year, President Roosevelt signed the McCarran-Lea Bill establishing the independent Civil Aeronautics Board (CAB). This measure transferred the regulation of airlines from the Bureau of Aeronautics in the Department of Commerce to the CAB. CAB assumed responsibility for monitoring airline safety, and it also began the process of setting fares and routes for carriers. This restructuring was a part of Roosevelt's overall reorganization plans.

CHANGING TECHNOLOGY OF AIRCRAFT

In retrospect, the early airplanes were simple to operate and maintain. Yet the rapid development of engines, cockpits, and fuselages meant that airports had to upgrade themselves. Airport management had to learn this new technology in order to communicate with airlines. Speed became the mantra of aircraft development—there always seemed to be a new aircraft capable of embarking on longer flights and hauling larger cargo loads. For example, when air-cooled engines replaced water-cooled engines, they generated more horsepower and enabled aircraft to increase their speed to 110 miles per hour.

As suggested earlier in this chapter, airmail was the flywheel of airplanes and aircraft development. Aircraft companies like Boeing grew as airmail delivery grew, for larger loads required bigger airplanes. In 1925, the Boeing Model 40 was built to deliver the mail. On July 27, 1928, the Boeing-built Model 80 made its maiden flight carrying twelve passengers. The 80A increased passenger load to eighteen. In 1933, Boeing introduced the Model 247 all-metal twin-engine monoplanes for United Airlines. United thus had an advantage over competitors, and it had the capacity to fly planes on one engine.

New engines and aircraft required sales marketing techniques. Aircraft manufacturers, like automobile makers, employed many workers. The manufacturers also used an enormous amount of metal, plastic, and glass products in the production process. As it became obvious that making new aircraft was not enough, manufacturers began hiring lobbyists in Washington to promote their airplanes and industry. The federal government also encouraged airlines to continue to upgrade their fleet. Presidents and Congresses have facilitated air travel and the airline industry since the twenties. Regardless of political party, presidents have been in the forefront of air transportation policy. During the Great Depression, for example, President Hoover was a great supporter of the expansion of airline traffic. Johnson observes, "When Hoover's Presidency ended in 1933, he left an industry that had grown under his policies. This industry had continued to expand even during the depression and had been transformed from flying the mail in single-engine, open-cockpit aircraft without radios to one that had begun passenger service in multi-engine, instrumented aircraft capable of electronically communicating and navigating through weather and at night."[62]

As was discussed earlier in this chapter, the Air Mail Act of 1934 prohibited manufacturers and carriers from being the same corporation. The Douglas Aircraft Company was founded in 1921, and it developed its DC-3 in 1936. The C in DC stands for "commercial." This was the plane Eastern Air Transport used to start its flights to Charlotte. In further developments, a decision was made on May 23, 1937, to install a radio beam that would help planes land in inclement weather.

In 1938, the famous Boeing 314 Clipper, the largest aircraft of its time, was developed. It carried ninety passengers and opened the way for international flights. In the same year, Boeing developed the first pressurized cabin aircraft (Model 307 Stratoliner), which allowed planes to fly at altitudes of twenty thousand feet and avoid some weather problems. These were important technological changes, but few could imagine what changing the power train (engine) of aircraft would mean for cities and their airports and passengers.

JET ENGINES AND AIRPORTS

The replacement of propeller-driven aircraft with jet engines changed the paradigm of flight and airports. In the late 1930s, Frank Whitter of the United Kingdom and Han Von Ohain of Germany developed the first jet engine. Von Ohain's model flew in 1939, Whitter's model two years later. World War II accelerated the development of the jet engine; these motors would allow aircraft to fly faster than their propeller predecessors.

When aircraft design changed, it often produced a "ripple effect" on airports. Cecil Brownlow agreed when he stated in 1957 that the introduction of jets caused a "chain reaction of costs and problems for airlines, airport operators and government agencies."[63] Airports must accommodate new aircraft. As Brownlow stated, airports needed to update the traffic control system, expand the terminal facilities, institute a new system of ticketing, and build new runways and more maintenance facilities. Faster airplanes made more noise and needed long runways and parking spaces. They also needed mechanists who kept abreast of engine changes. In other words, these technological changes meant more jobs unrelated to Charlotte's textile industry.

In 1940, Charlotte's population reached one hundred thousand, making it one of the largest cities in the South. But the Depression continued, and the war in Europe was expanding. The Roosevelt administration allotted over $3 million for Charlotte Airport. This sum was in addition to $1 million the WPA was to spend improving the facility for military use.

In 1941, Charlotte's airport supporters attempted to put another infrastructure revenue bond before the public. William States Lee Jr. led the second bond election, and the measure was defeated by 198 votes (1,354 to 1,749).[64] Mayor Douglas was reportedly disappointed—this was the first citizen backlash against airport expansion. Voting against the bond issue was yet another way to remind city leaders that the Depression remained a reality in Charlotte.

THE ARMY TAKEOVER OF THE AIRPORT

The Depression continued, but the clouds of war were gathering in Europe. President Roosevelt and Congress began making contingent preparations for war. In 1941 the old Ford assembly plant's seventy-six-acre site was sold to the U.S. Army. The army subsequently started the Quartermaster Corps Depot, a processing and supplying center for the pending war.

The Roosevelt administration also considered local airports that the New Deal helped fund and build to be a logical place to train pilots in case the United States entered the European conflict. Cities did not resist such takeovers. Indeed, many lobbied Washington to assume control of their airports because they knew the federal government would improve the infrastructure. After taking over Charlotte Douglas Municipal Airport, the U.S. Army named it Charlotte Army Base. The formal ceremony surrounding the new army base airport was one of the largest in the city's history. Fiorello H. La Guardia, the New York City mayor and folk hero, addressed a crowd of ten thousand at the event, telling the audience that Adolf Hitler was challenging the nation. Mayor Douglas expressed concern with the army's takeover of the airport and feared similar interference with Connor Airport, the private landing field in Charlotte.[65] Seven months later, on December 7, 1941, America was attacked by Japan. The nation entered World War II.

On January 22, 1942, Charlotte Army Base was renamed Morris Field Air Base in honor of army major William C. Morris, a North Carolina native and World War I pilot. The Morris Field airport started with two short runways expanded to a width of three hundred feet. The runways were also lengthened (the east–west runway to 3,065 feet, the north–south runway to 5,175 feet, and the northeast runway to 5,000 feet) and paved with asphalt. In order to train pilots, the army developed a control tower. In addition, the government built over one hundred barracks, hangars, and other facilities at the base.

The Morris Field Airport was fenced off from the public for security purposes; townspeople could not view the base until 1943. Morris Field brought soldiers from all over the nation to Charlotte. Many of them had never been to the South before, and after training, they went to war against the German and Japanese armies. After the Allied victory in World War II, the U.S. Army had little use for Morris Field.

THE MORRIS FIELD CONVERSION

After the war ended in 1945, the United States had accumulated surplus military equipment and training bases. Cities and states then began to negotiate to keep the war surplus. Charlotte was one of the cities asking for the return of its airport, which had been leased to the army. The city council and Mayor Baxter negotiated with the War Asset Administration, and it was determined that sixteen federal agencies had to approve the reacquisition of the airport and its buildings. By late January 1946, city leaders had cleared fifteen agencies and only needed approval from the Surplus Property Board (SPB). The board was quoted as saying that it was moving forward with "all possible haste."[66] Mayor Baxter stated that the Reconstruction Finance Corporation (RFC) would make the final approval.

One of the hitches in the negotiation was what to do with Morris Field's housing and medical center building. The question was whether the buildings had a high salvage value and whether the cost of restoring the property was too high. The surplus property administrator concluded, "If the restoration of the property to the city approximates the salvage value of the buildings, the government may be relieved of its responsibility of restoring the premise by transferring the buildings thereon to the city in consideration of release from its obligation."[67] Thus, the government was obligated to restore the premises. The Army Corps of Engineers in Atlanta bore responsibility for deciding whether to relinquish Morris Field's buildings to the city of Charlotte.

The army engineers' delayed decision owed to the telephone strike. However, the corps finally agreed, and the Surplus Administration SPA amended the lease and transferred the title of the housing (Stonewall Jackson Homes) to the city without cost. Charlotte received 1,261 acres of land and a $5 million gift as a result. Senator Bailey of North Carolina headed of one of the committees concerned with the disposal of surplus government property after World War II.

Charlotte was the one town in the nation that indicated it could not accept the surplus property on a permit basis. Instead, the city wanted a title.[68] Special city attorney Edward Hanson negotiated the deal, with assistance from Sen. Joe Blythe and Rep. Joe Ervin, both members of the congressional delegation.

The RFC drafted a deed transferring the property to the city. When the *Charlotte Observer* reported on the negotiation, chamber of commerce president Roy Palmer objected to the bargaining process. Mayor Baxter wrote a confidential letter explaining the city's position of obtaining clear title to the field and the barracks. The letter further pointed out the airport would be returned to the city for one dollar.[69] Since Charlotte was not declared a war industry city, it lacked the authority to build any houses. Like most postwar cities, Charlotte was also undergoing a housing shortage. Returning veterans and war production workers wanted to live in cities.

After the Mead Act of 1946 passed Congress, funds became available for temporary housing in shortage areas. Mayor Baxter asked the Federal Housing Agency in Atlanta for funds for Charlotte's ex-servicemen. Some members of the community wanted the housing to be built by private investors. Under this arrangement, the city could lease the land to the investors and provide the capital to build the housing. Charlotte's housing department could manage the housing, but the rent would go to investors. The city was not willing to enter this arrangement because it could jeopardize the return of the airport. The dispute over how to handle the housing on airport land then became part of the mayoral campaign between Mayor Baxter and Coleman Roberts, chairman of the Citizen Emergency Housing Committee. Mayor Baxter won the election, but the housing dispute, cost, and expansion continued. Writing in the election year, Lynn Bollinger concluded,

> Local officials understandably take pride in the impressiveness of the airport constructed during their regime. Yet they too seldom feel adequate responsibility concerning the future since they cannot be held accountable if costly operations result during later years. The pride which local leaders may take in creating a

monumental facility is therefore not sufficiently counterbalanced by incentives for economy. . . .

To this natural feeling of pride is added the tendency of many local leaders to be overly optimistic regarding their community's future expansion as a focal point of trade and commerce. Excessive and uneconomical airport plans too often result.[70]

SUMMARY

Charlotte grew as a textile center because it met what economist Edwin S. Mills calls the two fundamental conditions necessary for economic centralization.[71] A place for production must have a low transportation cost and a capacity to achieve an economy of scale. Charlotte had the advantage of having workers that lived close to the mills. Textile manufacturing is more efficient when carried out on a large scale.

After World War I the winds of textile manufacturing change were stirring. The Depression was a wake-up call for the business community. Cautioned by growing intercity competition, those in the nascent pro-growth coalition knew they had to find a new economic angle. Flying had been started in the city with the assistance of the Charlotte Chamber of Commerce, and it acted as the vanguard of new transportation modes. Airmail changed the dynamics of local businesses and proved critical for the development of the city-owned airport. For one, businessmen could send messages outside the city quickly. They could also advertise their products more broadly and grow their businesses outside the confines of the city proper.

No one could have predicted that the era of textiles and furniture making would come to an end. Textile elites were still leading the city's business community, but they supported air travel, a city-owned airport (a city takeover of airmail and passenger services from private airports like Cannon Field), and emerging industries. In a study of three other cities, historian Douglas Karsner concludes, "Local boosters tirelessly campaigned for increased airline service that they believed was vital to the continued economic growth of their cities. Their efforts were reminiscent of nineteenth-century city boosters fighting to obtain railroad routes. These twentieth-century boosters also worked to attract businesses to the airport environment."[72]

As will be discussed in chapter 3, Charlotte became the second banking capital of the nation, explaining why journalist Rick Rothacker calls it "Banktown."[73] Ironically, the seeds for banking had been planted early in the city's history. Rothacker states, "Charlotte's reputation as a financial center took a major leap in February 1927 when the Federal Reserve Board in Washington approached the creation of a branch office in the city."[74] The Federal Reserve took this step ten years before the city completed its municipal airport. Charlotte was still a mill town, and few thought it would be anything else.

However, the decline of the cotton mills, textile industry, and passenger trains and the centering of the banking industry made Charlotte the "transformative city." It is understandable that textile mill owners and furniture makers were not among the drum majors for the parade for a new transportation mode (airlines). They were busy moving products that were not suitable to be carried by small airplanes of the time. Thus, these businessmen stood on the sidelines until they were convinced that airmail would facilitate financial transactions across the nation. The nascent banking industry recognized the meaning of the new transportation mode; bankers were among those whom political scientist Robert Dahl called the "new men."[75] These individuals came from the real estate, retail, and banking industries, and they began assuming leadership of Charlotte public affairs. Chapter 6 will discuss how these new men changed the structure of city government. Indeed, the chamber of commerce openly supported candidates for mayor.

Charlotte was able to build its new airport with the assistance of New Deal largesse. In the late 1930s New Deal financing surpassed local funding for airports.[76] Shortly after the Charlotte Airport was built, the federal government commandeered it for military training for the pending war. The nascent airline industry benefited from the Zeppelin rigid airship's failure (i.e., the 1937 Hindenburg disaster) and the pending world war. World War II was a boom time for Charlotte. The city's military encampment brought with it new people, including some Yankees.

What a difference a war makes—World War II transformed the United States' role in the world and consolidated its industrialized economy. America, emerging as a nation of heavy metal production, saw cities in the Northeast and Midwest grow. These cities had a location advantage over southern cities like Charlotte; the South had few heavy metal enterprises aside from the steel mills in Birmingham, Alabama. At the end of the war, few could have predicted that air travel would eliminate some aspects of manufacturing cities' location advantage. Similarly, few could have foretold Charlotte's shift from textile manufacturing to banking. Nor did the pundits predict that Charlotte's city-owned airport would be so critical to that transition, and that structural change in the city government structures would make more mayors airport "champions." In the next chapter, we will see how quickly the pro-growth coalition shifted its economic attention and tackled uncertainties of the airline industry, airport expansion, and federal government regulation of air travel and airports.

CHAPTER 2

Postwar Years and the New Airport

AFTER WORLD WAR II, CHARLOTTE began discarding its textile cocoon and making the slow transition to another economic conduit. The city became the "nerve center" of the slow industrialization of the state. Once a large textile mill community, Charlotte was "a textile-influenced community."[1] Charlotte's dismantling as a major center for cotton mills began before the war as the city's large mills succumbed to mergers and acquisitions. By 1946, one of the major mills, Chadwick Hoskins, was sold to a company in Rhode Island. Johnson Mill Company was also acquired by an out-of-state company, and some smaller mills were literally abandoned. Change was afoot and economic dislocation was inevitable. When certain types of work disappeared, Charlotteans had to have experienced some angst. Who would hire the children of mill workers? In 1957 Don Oberdorfer of the *Charlotte Observer* began to sound the alarm about the changing economy. He noted that thirty-eight mills had been liquidated in the last five years. A chart accompanying his reporting shows that 7,395 textile workers from the Carolinas were affected by the closures between 1952 and 1956. Oberdorfer attributed the changes to modernization and mergers.[2]

Perhaps no one knew at the time that Charlotte was undergoing a profound economic transformation. Nor might anyone have known what the "transformative city" would look like. How could a tiny airfield built during the Great Depression and once occupied by the U.S. Army be the major facilitator of this transition? Did anyone realize that the new employers would need a different type of talent than displaced mill workers?

This chapter traces how the local pro-growth coalition reacted to the airport developments during Charlotte's quest for economic growth. The origins of the transformative city can be found in the intersection of the needs of the nascent postindustrial economy and the ambitions of business leaders. City politics and the airport's growth needs apparently converged in revenue-bond politics and elections. The airport's development also tells the story of the decades of entrepreneurship by airport directors, changes in the airline industry, national events, and high levels of boosterism by the chamber of commerce. It all started when the U.S. Army had no more use for Morris Field and returned the airport to the city of Charlotte.

CONSOLIDATION OF CITY AIRPORT CONTROL

On May 20, 1946, the War Assets Administration returned the airport facilities' hangars and barracks to the city of Charlotte. The abandoned army-conscripted airfield had made several improvements in the municipal airport's infrastructure. Mayor Herbert Baxter had gone to Washington and met with airport planners, and he told the *Charlotte Observer* that the airport needed an extension of 2,250 feet to handle big airplanes and cargo ships. He further stated, "As a matter of fact, we are lucky to have an airport that will require little improvement to get in shape. If we get the Morris Field land and equipment, the greatest part of our needs will be satisfied."[3] Yet in 1946, Charlotte voters defeated the $200,000 bond for the airport. This setback occurred five years after the 1941 bond defeat. Clearly, the pro-growth coalition needed to work harder to convince voters that airport expansion was in their best interest. However, all was not lost; 1946 would be a decisive year for municipal airports. The federal government came to the rescue of struggling local facilities.

On May 13, 1946, Pres. Harry Truman signed the Federal Airport Act, which committed the U.S. government to providing additional regulations and funding for airports. The act supplied an annual fund of $75 million for this purpose. This meant the $500 million in grants would be paid over seven years, while airports like Charlotte's were required to issue bonds to finance the rest of the building cost. Airports also had to meet Civil Aeronautics Administration (CAA) standards for location and infrastructures. In addition, the act stipulated that all tax money the local government collected for the airport had to be spent on operations and maintenance. By the beginning of the next year, big-city mayors were complaining about the CAA's intention to spend more money on smaller airports like Charlotte's. Mayor Ed Kelly of Chicago wanted more money to relieve congestion at airports. The CAA wanted smaller airports to encourage general aviation. *Time* magazine summarized the situation:

> In its final regulations, announced last week, CAA gave way a little. It agreed to pay half the cost of projects up to $5,000,000. The Federal share will then decrease 5% for each additional $1,000,000, down to a minimum contribution of 20%. Despite this change, $36,000,000 of the $45,000,000 which CAA has to spend this fiscal year will be spent on 800 small airports. Reason: CAA's proposed expenditures on larger projects must be submitted to Congress two months before the beginning

of the fiscal year—and the Federal Airport Act was passed too late for CAA to comply this year. It looked as if nothing much would be done about dangerously overcrowded commercial airports for another year.[4]

Also in 1946, Eastern Air Lines started flying the DC-4 and the Lockheed L-649. The airline was able to carry more passengers and cargo, and the improvement in passenger airlines stimulated more business and a postwar boom. More airplanes were taking off and landing at municipal airports. The downside of the air travel boom owed to the fact that some flights were landing near residential properties. Homeowners complained about the engine noise and attempted to sue their cities for property depreciation.

However, the U.S. Supreme Court held in *United States v. Causby* (1946) that landowners do not control the airspace above their property. At a certain height, the space belongs to everyone. Therefore, landowners cannot make trespassing claims on airplanes or airlines. This case involved landowners in Greensboro, North Carolina, but it would apply to homeowners near Charlotte's airport. The ruling was supportive of local airport politics, but as we shall see in chapter 7, conflict between homeowners and the airport would arise again.

More changes in airport politics would come with the state airport commission's return of Charlotte Municipal Airport to the city of Charlotte. State oversight of the facility was deemed redundant. Thus in 1946, the Charlotte Airport Commission, appointed by the state of North Carolina, resigned as a body and recommended the airport become a city department. Commissioners also recommended that the city appoint an Airport Advisory Committee. The resignations were formally accepted May 21, 1947.

THE POSTWAR TAKEOFFS

With help from the federal government and the courts, the city of Charlotte had control of the airport's future. The pro-growth coalition wanted the airport to grow into a multicity takeoff platform. This would allow passengers to fly to more cities and more businesses to locate in Charlotte. On June 25, 1946, the city council sought a new certificate under Section 401 of the Civil Aeronautics Administration Act of 1938. H. B. Campbell, attorney for the city, made the case. Campbell stated, "Charlotte has been the pariah among cities in regard to air service."[5] The city was the center of a variety of industries such as cotton, textiles, finished goods, lumber products, and chemicals. Therefore, Campbell declared, "Charlotte wants, needs and demands air service to all points of the compass, to balance its scale of supply and demand, but it is imperative that air service be accorded which will open direct passage to Chicago and the west beyond."⁶ The CAA granted the certificate, thereby allowing Eastern Air Lines to schedule more flights at the airport.

The postwar period saw growth in Charlotte's economy and the airline industry in general. In 1953, journalist Thomas E. Mullaney predicted that commercial flying would become a billion-dollar industry within three decades.⁷ This prediction was possible because William M. Mashland had commanded the first round-the-world trip by a commercial aircraft ten years earlier. Air travel was now the key to the growing international trade. Cities would be the beneficiaries if they could gear up for the new levels of takeoffs and landings. Ergo, they would need to build larger airports.

A NEW AIRPORT TERMINAL

More flights would mean more passenger traffic, and the terminal would then serve as the face of the city and reflect its transformation. It would be part of the "dress up imperative" necessary for the population's continued growth. This strategy was in addition to the city's aggressive annexation policies discussed earlier.

In 1947, the Charlotte Chamber of Commerce published a pamphlet extolling the city's growth and claiming that it had reached a population of one hundred thousand. According to the brochure, 69 percent of Charlotteans were white and 99 percent were native born. Although the city now had only seven cotton mills, it had 287 different factories. The Alwin Manufacturing Company was still making furniture inside the city. The nascent banking industry now had two national banks, two state banks, and four industrial banks. Eastern Air Lines had fourteen planes flying in and out of the municipal airport. In addition, three privately owned airports were located nearer to Charlotte's center.⁸ For the chamber of commerce, Charlotte had reached its goal as the center of regional industrial development in the Carolinas. Since the 1930s, Mr. Kuester, the manager of the Chamber, had played a major role as an airport booster.

In his last interview in 1948, "Booster" Kuester predicted that Charlotte's population would reach a quarter of a million. He also admitted, "I do not have graphs and charts—I only use my imagination and hope in making this prediction."⁹ A year later, some Charlotteans had their imagination stretched further as television broadcasting became available with WBTV. By 1950, the city's population had grown to 134,042, increasing 33 percent since 1940. In 1954 the city and county government formed the Charlotte-Mecklenburg Planning Department in response to this growth. It was designed to manage zoning problems, historical districts, and transportation. However, it had no responsibility for the airport.

A city with potentially a quarter of a million residents needed an airport terminal that could accommodate that type of traffic. In the fifties, President Truman supported airport development and signed an extension of the 1950 Airport Act until 1958. The law covered runways, but the local government would be responsible for terminals and equipment. In 1951, the city of Charlotte decided to build a new terminal that was to be completed in 1954 at the cost of $1.3 million. One half the money would come from the FAA and the other half from airport revenue. The Cannon Endowment, established by Joseph F. Cannon Jr. to further aviation in Charlotte, provided the money for the planning. The city created a separate planning committee to oversee the development of the airport.

When the new airport was completed, it provided comfort for passengers and a new face for Charlotte. The new airport terminal was a 1,600-acre complex with two fully lighted runways, a parallel taxiway, and one fully instrumented runway for bad weather. Moreover, the terminal had terrazzo tile, a rubber floor, air-conditioning, and two coal-burning stoker-fed boilers. More importantly, the structure had three levels of floors—for ticketing, baggage, and administration offices. Finally, the terminal featured 173 upholstered seats and a public observation deck.

The idea for an airport terminal had been around since 1951. On January 27, 1954, Samuel Hair of consulting firm Gotch and Crawford surveyed the airport facilities and concluded that their location was good, and the new terminal would be excellent when completed. "Probably the old terminal building retarded traffic development somewhat," he stated.[10] Hair recommended that Charlotte seek aggressively new authorization for service between Northwest and Southeast. Hair also supported Delta's proposal to provide services at the airport. On July 10, 1954, the new terminal was formally dedicated. The same year, the city named the airport after former mayor Ben Douglas. Douglas continued promoting the airport after leaving office; in fact, he spent the rest of his life doing so.

The airport grew as Charlotte became a major location for banking headquarters. In 1950, H. G. Trotter of the *Charlotte Observer* wrote "Air Service for Charlotte Has Had Phenomenal Rise," a review of the airport that was three broadsheet pages in length. He reported that in nineteen years Capital Airlines, Piedmont Airlines, Southern Airlines and Eastern Air Lines had come to Charlotte. In August 1950 Southern Airlines committed to fly at the airport. Capital Airlines, a pioneering low-cost airline, had been there since December 5, 1947.

Piedmont, headquartered in Winston-Salem, was added February 20, 1948. Piedmont had provided pilot training during World War II, and it had the only overall certified engine capacity between Washington and Atlanta. Piedmont grew out of Carmel City Flying Service that had been flying in North Carolina since 1940. In addition to Charlotte Municipal Airport, there were four other airports in the city: Cannon, Plaza, Delta, and Brockrough.

In 1951, during Mayor Victor Shaw's administration, the runway was extended from 5,000 square feet to 7,500 square feet. The first passenger terminal, measuring 70,000 square feet, was built in 1954. That year, the airport was also renamed Charlotte Douglas. In 1956, Delta began service, and Capital and Southern Airlines subsequently became tenants. The city of Charlotte had changed dramatically during the Shaw era, for Samuel Lubell asserted in 1951, "Today, Mayor Victor Shaw judges that at most civic gatherings scarcely one of ten persons is native."[11]

In 1958, Congress passed the Federal Aviation Act. In part a reaction to fears of midair accidents, this law established the independent Federal Aviation Administration, now known as the FAA. The Federal Aviation Act also transferred responsibility for safety regulation, air navigation, and traffic control to FAA. CAB retained oversight of route and fare regulations.

BECOMING A MIDSIZE CITY

By 1960, Charlotte's population reached 200,000 (201,464), in part due to a 1959 annexation under a new state law. Annexation surrounding the community doubled the city's population during Mayor James Saxon Smith's administration. Despite the civil rights movement and other social turmoil of the late fifties and sixties, the airport kept expanding. In 1960, Eastern started its DC-8 service out of Charlotte. In February of that year, the chamber of commerce sought legislation allowing the city of Charlotte to spend tax funds for capital improvement at the airport. Focused on meeting the new needs of the expanding jet age, the chamber established the Rogan Committee, headed by Airport Advisory Committee member J. P. Rogan, to determine whether the facility should be operated by an authority.[12]

In 1961, the city of Charlotte protested the CAB's proposed route changes. Charlotte had its Washington attorney James Verner object to proposed changes to Piedmont's north–south routes. These new routes would exclude Charlotte. The *Charlotte Observer* noted, "This presents the threat that Charlotte's role as a 'feeder' airport for North Carolina would be reduced, and hence Eastern or Delta might have to chop flights through the city."[13]

In 1970, the Federal Airport Act was repealed. Pres. Richard Nixon signed the Airport and Airway Development Act of 1970 and the Airport and Airway Revenue Act of 1970. Title I of the new airport and development law provided $250 million annually for the "acquisition, establishment, and improvement of air navigational facilities," and security equipment over a ten-year period. Title II created what was popularly called the aviation trust fund, financed by an 8 percent tax on domestic passenger fares. It also imposed a three-dollar surcharge on passenger tickets originating in the United States, seven cents per gallon on gasoline and jet fuel, a five percent tax on airfreight waybills, and an annual registration fee and charge per pound for aircraft.

These two acts changed the way airports were designed and funded. The Airport and Airway Revenue Act created funding for the airport's capital development. The new user tax applied to aviation fuels, tickets, cargo, and general aircraft use. In addition, this new law even taxed international departures. As a result, the federal government now had a fund to use as an incentive to make cities grow their airports. The federal government would make a 90 percent grant for airports, and local communities would raise 10 percent to match. Also under the new law, the Department of Transportation was required to publish the National Airport System Plan.

As the federal, state, and local governments changed their postures toward the airline industry, cities had to build bigger airports with longer runways. Meanwhile, the development of airplane carriers paralleled that of the airports. Charlotte Douglas Airport would be in the middle of the rise and fall of Piedmont and Eastern Air Lines, both of which were critical to the airport's development and expansion. Piedmont's and Eastern's history underscores what Charlotte Douglas had to do and how its management teams sold their plans to the city government.

EASTERN AND PIEDMONT AIRLINES

In 1940, Thomas Davis brought Carmel City Flying Service and changed its name to Piedmont Airlines. Piedmont was headquartered in Winston-Salem, North Carolina, and Davis led it from 1943 to 1983, when Bill Howard succeeded him. Howard then began passenger service to Charlotte Douglas. Charlotte became a Piedmont Airlines hub and in turn promoted the growth of the airport. In 1948, passenger service began from the Carolinas to the Ohio Valley. In the 1960s, the airline evolved from using its DC-3 to flying jets.

Jerry Orr, who became the airport director in the late 1980s, acknowledged the close relationship between Charlotte Douglas and Piedmont. Orr stated,

"We always had the feeling that if we got in trouble, Piedmont would at least be sympathetic. If we had miscalculated costs, or inadvertently left out of our rates something they should be paying, we had relations where we could ask them and straighten it out."[14]

Because of its success at Charlotte, Piedmont Airlines decided to expand into two other hubs in Dayton, Ohio, and Baltimore-Washington International Airport (BWI). In tracing Piedmont's development, historian Walter R. Turner sees the airline's expansion as the work of two men, Dick James and Bob McAphin. Dick James convinced CAB to allow the airline to make cross-connecting flights though Charlotte. Bob McAphin, the schedule manager for Piedmont, created a system that allowed passengers to move through the South without using Eastern flights out of Atlanta.[15] Turner summarizes the overall strategy.

> The Howard-James-McAphin strategy planned to begin adding flights at Charlotte in 1979. The goal was to originate flights at points within a three hundred-mile radius of Charlotte, including all North Carolina cities the airline served, some West Virginia cities, Roanoke and Norfolk in Virginia, Charleston and Myrtle Beach in South Carolina, and Tri Cities [Bristol, Kingsport, Johnson City]. These flights would connect nonstop to Charlotte and then continue to a long-range destination.[16]

At Piedmont's peak in Charlotte and before its merger with USAir, over five thousand of its employees were based in the city. Piedmont played a major role in the airport's growth, and director Orr suggested it was a symbiotic relationship. Orr called the airline "home folks."[17] Although Eastern Air Lines was not a home state carrier, it had similar impact on the development of Charlotte Airport.

For an airline that started out with the unlikely name of Pitcarn Aviation, Eastern Air Transport (Eastern Air Lines) emerged as the high-profile airline of the sixties and seventies. Capt. Eddie Rickenbacker, Eastern's famous leader, bought the airline for $800,000 and made it the dominant carrier on the East Coast. Headquartered in Miami, it became the largest airline in terms of passengers. In 1962, Eastern Air Lines started jet service at Charlotte Douglas Airport. It was the same year the nation endured a flight engineer strike affecting thirty-five flights into the city. The resulting serious unemployment at the airport reportedly cost Charlotte $1 million. Eastern Air Lines resumed partial service on August 23, two months to the day after 374 members of the Flight Engineers' International Association went on strike.

Charlotte Airport director Orr recalled that the airlines began using DCs and wanted a north–south runway extended from 5,000 to 7,800 feet. An extension was clearly indicated, as Charlotte voters approved a $12.6 million airport bond referendum for that purpose in 1962. Eastern Air Lines opened the first unit terminal that same year.

In 1962, Eastern Air Lines endured another strike that cut into airport revenue. Somewhat recovered in 1965, the airline started using the DC-9, which became its standard equipment. Eastern also became the biggest carrier at Charlotte Douglas in 1965, and Atlanta served as one of its major hubs. By 1968, there were a hundred flights a day at Charlotte's airport. The first enclosed concourse was built by 1969. As a result, Charlotte Douglas had achieved status as a mini-hub for the Southeast.

In July 1966, all the major carriers were hit by a strike of the International Association of Mechanics. At Charlotte Douglas Airport the strike affected 59 local flights and 1,000 workers. In addition, it grounded 50 of the 72 daily flights out of Charlotte.[18] Reporter J. A. C. Dunn advised air travelers to take a "stagecoach" on their next trip, adding, "Douglas Airport gave you an off-balance feeling Friday. Hardly anybody was there which was strange for a Friday afternoon, and the few people who were there seemed to be in the wrong place."[19]

After the strike, Piedmont Airlines continued to bring people from small towns and cities to Charlotte. In 1969 the airline moved into a designated concourse. Piedmont was now the most important feeder airline at Charlotte Douglas Airport, which was continuing to grow as a backup complex to the Atlanta Airport.

GROWING AIRPORT FOR A GROWING CITY

The late sixties and midseventies were a time of increasing city growth. Charlotteans elected elite businessmen Stan Brookshire and John Belk as mayors. Both had been president of the Charlotte Chamber of Commerce, and both were respected in the business community. Jack Claiborne's book *Crown of the Queen City* examines how the chamber planned and supported Brookshire's mayoral run. The decision was made in the office of Brookshire's college classmate with a group that included the chamber of commerce's finance chairman and twenty other chamber members.[20] In 1969 members of the same small chamber group made the case for Brookshire's successor John Belk. Belk had served on the Airport Advisory Committee (AAC) and was the son of William H. Belk, founder of Belk Department Store. John Belk was elected in 1969 and he served until 1977.

Much of the Charlotte skyline was built during the Belk administration. In addition, the runways at Charlotte Douglas were expanded during Belk's tenure.

In 1968, the city of Charlotte adopted a plan for a new terminal and a fully instrumented ten-thousand-foot parallel runway. Further annexations expanded the city population at this time.

By 1970, the city's population stood at 241,474 residents. This growth formed the central argument of the city of Charlotte's petition before the CAB to open up the airport to Delta and United Airlines. The city took exception to a CAB examiner's report that supported no change in service at Charlotte Douglas. The city attorney stated that the purpose of the brief before the CAB was to "break Eastern's virtual monopoly in the Queen City." Despite Piedmont's presence, Eastern Air Lines had dominated air traffic at Charlotte Douglas. The pro-growth coalition understood the change was needed both to allow the airport to grow and to hook up other airlines' service to other cities. It was a two-and-a-half-year legal struggle joined by nine airlines and the chamber of commerce. According to city leaders, the scheduling and services Eastern Air Lines provided were not flexible enough. Besides, Eastern Air Lines continued to have labor problems with its pilots. Eastern Air Lines' management opposed the brief because awarding routes to other airlines at Charlotte Douglas would put Eastern in directly competitive routes with other carriers. That would cost it $15 million a year. The CAB rejected Eastern's argument and stated, "We find that Eastern will suffer little or no diversion in the Chicago and Miami market because of the growth of traffic to those points."[21] The pro-growth coalition had won again.

MORE AIRLINES, A 1950 TERMINAL

In 1971, airport director Josh Birmingham completed an environmental study supporting the need for a new ten-thousand-square-foot parallel runway. In 1973, the airport awarded Odell Architects the contract to design a new terminal building. The existing terminal was only twenty years old, but Charlotte Douglas and the city had outgrown it. An attractive and modern terminal would draw more flights, and the facility would be a new face of the city as Charlotte Douglas Airport grew as a hub. Obviously, no growing city wants a reputation for having an airport with inadequate runways and an ugly terminal. As sociologist Mark Gottdiener observes, "The best of the new airport spaces foster a contemplative atmosphere that massages fears rather than forcing passengers to confront them. With a strong sense of place and an increasing mixture of malls, hotels, entertainment facilities, workout rooms, chapels, and upscale dining, the best of the new air terminals are places in which people can spend considerable time, despite the ordeals of boredom, layovers, and canceled flights."[22]

In 1974, the federal government agreed to construct a new air control tower at the airport. Susan Jettson reported that the National Airport Operators Association had classified Charlotte as the flight-origin point for residents of the eleven-county Metrolina area. It was considered the "fastest growing airport in the United States."[23] Josh Birmingham agreed, stating, "I don't know of any way you can stop this kind of growth short of cutting off your arm. Douglas Airport is the most vibrant contributor to the growth of Charlotte Mecklenburg."[24] In 1975, the unimpressed voters rejected a $55 million referendum for the new terminal by a vote of 17,133 to 14,654. The failure of the vote was related to changing city politics and the hubris of the pro-growth coalition. The bond vote and its political implications will be discussed in the next chapter.

Throughout the history of aircraft, the occasional accident remained the bane of operations. The development of airplanes and air travel was highly related to safety concerns. Airline crashes punctuated the development of air travel. In 1941, company CEO Eddie Rickenbacker was among the survivors of an Eastern Air Lines crash in Atlanta. The same year, Carole Lombard, a famous film actress, was killed on a TWA flight. In the forties, the deadliest crash involved Eastern Air Lines Flight 410 and resulted in fifty-three deaths. Two years later, another Eastern Air Lines plane crashed, and fifty-five people died. The equipment for both flights was a DC-4.

In 1974, DC-9 Eastern Air Lines Flight 212 from Charleston, South Carolina, landed three miles short of the runway and killed seventy-two people. The crash was judged the result of pilot error. Understandably, the shock of airline crashes created more anxiety among the flying public. Established in 1967, the National Transportation Safety Board (NTSB) investigated the causes of accidents, ranging from weather and engine trouble to pilot error. After every accident, the NTSB produced a report that attempted to explain what happened. Finding a cause serves to reassure passengers. These incidents did not deter the Charlotte pro-growth coalition from advocating the airport's expansion. Aircraft manufacturers promised to make safer instruments and equipment, and full confidence in air travel was eventually restored.

In 1978, Charlotte elected its first pilot mayor, Kenneth Harris. Mayor Harris sent a letter to the CAB endorsing Eastern's proposal to buy National Airlines. He wrote, "Because Eastern has demonstrated to Charlotte that it is a good corporate citizen and has shown an interest in developing third level commuter airlines for smaller markets, I feel our support of Eastern in acquiring National is warranted."[25] Such correspondence was common for mayors; letter writing is a low-cost enterprise that grows out of their role as chief city salespersons. At the time, few knew the complete story of Eastern's internal dynamics and deregulation's impact on it and other legacy airlines.

THE FLYING EIGHTIES

The Airline Deregulation Act of 1978, discussed in detail in the next chapter, changed airline policies and fortunes. Deregulation benefited Piedmont Airlines, which made fifty-three flights a day from Charlotte Douglas in 1981. This total surpassed Eastern Air Lines' forty-nine flights. William Howard told the *Charlotte Observer*, "We've sold Charlotte as a better, easier and quicker alternative to Atlanta."[26] Piedmont Airlines grew as a result of airline deregulation. In Charlotte, it went from boarding four hundred passengers a day in 1978 to ten thousand a day in 1985. The *Charlotte Observer* further quoted Gene Mercer, chief of the Federal Aviation Administration (FAA), as saying, "Airlines have gotten away from direct service [from major city to major city] and gone to a hub and spoke approach." Mercer explained:

> That's why Piedmont chose Charlotte rather than Atlanta. This is happening all over the country. A hub-and-spoke arrangement means carriers schedule flights, so they connect from smaller cities to a larger hub at peak travel hours. This enables a passenger from Hickory, for instance, to connect with a flight to New York at Charlotte/Douglas International with a minimum of effort.[27]

Moreover, Eastern Air Lines continued to grow nationally. Six years earlier (1972), it had bought Braniff Airlines. It also bought Colonial Airlines in order to get into the Canadian market, but this acquisition was not enough to save it. Discount carrier People Airlines, which had a six-year tenure at Charlotte Douglas, began showing signs of financial trouble. It had overreached and expanded too quickly, making for a colorful start but a short run. Such signs of airline instability were not discussed publicly.

In spite of deregulation, some airports, even with new discount carriers, continued to have financial difficulties. In 1982, Congress passed the Airport and Airway Improvement Act giving the secretary of transportation the authority to freeze landing fees charged by airports. The move was designed to improve the management of the air traffic control system and to help airlines.

THE NEW TERMINAL CHALLENGES

Ironically, Charlotte Douglas Airport prospered during deregulation despite the rise and fall of airlines. The city recognized that it needed a new terminal. Consultant Arnold Thompson compared the need for these updates to adding rooms to a family home: "If you're lucky the floor plan of the house will allow you to add on without too much trouble. Or you might have to add the new bedroom off the dining room. Douglas is like the house where the new bedroom has to be added off the dining room."²⁸

Thus, the city voted a revenue bond for a new terminal in 1978. This new facility had been planned since 1971 and had suffered a negative revenue vote in 1975. On the occasion of the ground breaking for the new terminal, former mayor Douglas, then eighty-five years old, asserted, "Don't say 'the airport.' Always say Douglas Airport. I was called enough SOBs to merit that."²⁹ He had been ridiculed when Eastern Air Lines started using a twenty-six-seat DC-2 on routes from Charlotte to New York City. In 1982, a new 325,000-square-foot international concourse was built. The pro-growth coalition had learned from the 1975 defeat of the terminal referendum.

The construction of the terminal was not slowed by the 1978 deregulation of airlines, and airport director Josh Birmingham had been vindicated. He stated, "Seein[g] this thing develop, I will tell you, you just don't get chance to do that but once in a lifetime, and I'm pleased that the lot chose me to do it, that the Lord chose me to do it—or fate chose me to do it here."³⁰ Birmingham, however, had a lot of help. Civil engineer and project director Louis Martinelli worked with Day & Zimmermann, a Philadelphia firm managing the airport construction. Specifically, he coordinated the work of contractors and consultants. About the airport, he observed, "It's not a Taj Mahal. Believe me, we put the money where it would do the most good. I'm talking about maintainability of the airport, energy conservation, and space requirements. I think everybody's going to be pleased with it."³¹ Roy Johnson, the terminal's architect, asserted, "They tell me this is not a record, but this is one of fastest airports ever built.... I think that's a measure of the ability of the city, the airlines—everybody—to work together."³²

Bill Veeder, president of the chamber of commerce, described the new terminal as follows: "This is quantum-leap. It is probably the most significant thing that will happen relative to the future of Charlotte in many, many many and many moons."³³ The new terminal complex was built for $64.2 million. Covering 367 acres, its 339,497-square-foot size was twice that of the old facility. The new structure created nine more gates, bringing the total to twenty-five. Moreover, the new terminal was designed to accommodate three million departing passengers, and it added more than four hundred new parking spaces, thereby putting Charlotte Douglas in the big league of airports. Writer Cassandra Lawton asserted in 1982, "We had what I considered to be a minor league terminal here. Now we're in the major league and everybody benefits."³⁴ The *Charlotte News* reported that fifty thousand people came to look at the "glossy new airport terminal." Indeed, the ribbon-cutting ceremony included the governor, chamber of commerce president, former mayors, AAC members, and many prominent citizens.[35] At its completion, the new terminal was ready to accommodate many more carriers and passengers. In addition to eight commuter airlines, it hosted flights from Delta, Eastern, Piedmont, United, Pan Am, Trans World, and Ozark. In June 1982, People Express would land at Charlotte as well.

RUMORS, MERGERS, AND COLLAPSES

Meanwhile, Eastern Air Lines continued to have its problems. Despite having former astronaut Frank Borman as its high-profile leader, and despite attempting all types of management changes, the airline could not solve its financial and labor problems. Deregulation exaggerated the fiscal environment of the airlines. What was happening to Eastern affected what happened at Charlotte Douglas Airport.

At the end of 1986, Piedmont Airlines had lobbied some of the most powerful people in Washington in its bid for an international flight to London. Both South Carolina senators, Ernest Hollings and Strom Thurmond, wrote supporting letters to the U.S. Department of Transportation.[36] At the time, Senator Hollings was in line to be the new chair of the Senate Commerce, Science, and Transportation Committee. The DOT secretary at the time was Elizabeth Dole, another North Carolina politician and the wife of Sen. Robert Dole of Kansas. At the time, ex-mayor John Belk was chair of the Charlotte Douglas Airport Advisory Committee. Therefore, considerable political clout had accumulated around the issue of Piedmont flights from Charlotte to London. Jack Claiborne states that these flights "legitimized Douglas Airport's claim to be an international airport" so that "Charlotte's national image took a greater clarity."[37]

In 1988, Piedmont suggested it was considering flights to Canada or the Caribbean. At that point, Piedmont had about 500 pilots based in Charlotte but no flight attendants. Both Ozark and Pan Am Airlines began service in Charlotte in 1983. During the Harvey Gantt administration, a new ten-thousand-foot runway was finished. By 1985, Piedmont had 550 pilots based in Charlotte but still no flight attendants. To expand its routes, it bought New York–based Empire Airlines that year.

In 1985, the city of Charlotte offered a $110 million revenue bond with underwriters Smith Barney, Harris Upham.[38] American Airlines, People Express, and TWA began service to Charlotte that same year. People Express was a discount airline that operated from 1981 to 1987. At its peak, the carrier served 100 cities with 115 aircraft, making three flights a day from Charlotte to Newark

International Airport. People Express made big news with its no-frills flights and low fares. The company then acquired Frontier Airlines and regional commuter airline Midwest Britt Airways in 1985 and offered services to cities around the country. In the end, People Express overextended itself and went into bankruptcy. It had to sell its assets to Continental Airlines.

During earlier periods of deregulation, predatory acquisition began to run amok. In 1986, U.S. Airways purchased Pacific Southwest Airlines to build a West Coast presence. American Airlines had bought Air California, and Delta had acquired Western Airlines. In 1987, USAir started providing direct international service from Charlotte to London. In 1990, a new eighty-thousand-square-foot concourse for international and commuter travel was opened at Charlotte Douglas.

In 1986, rumors arose of a possible Piedmont and Delta merger. While these rumors came to nothing, Piedmont merged with USAir three years later. Mergers were thought to facilitate competition with discount airlines at that time. Piedmont had become the dominant carrier at Charlotte Douglas by 1986, carrying 80 percent of its passengers. The airline then announced a $90 million expansion plan with two hundred flights a day. Historian Walter Turner credits Piedmont executive vice president Bill Howard with the vision to make Charlotte a hub.[39] Other rumors during this period held that Eastern Air Lines was in more serious trouble than first expected. Management could not stop the carrier's rapid descent. In 1985, Eastern Air Lines carried a debt of $3.5 billion. The next year, the company's shareholders decided to approve its sale to Texas Air Corporation for $615 million. The strike of 1989 was the dying kick of the airline.

North Carolina Commerce Department spokesman Sam Taylor told the *Atlanta Journal-Constitution* two years earlier, "Charlotte-Douglas International Airport has played a vital role in that city's rise to becoming a commercial center. In Charlotte, the growth of Piedmont Airlines' presence is augmenting statewide efforts to recruit commercial firms such as banks, insurance companies, data processing concerns, and communications companies."[40] Apparently, Atlanta readers wanted to know about Charlotte's ambitions. Uptown Charlotte, the heart of the transforming city, aspired to look like Manhattan—skyscraper-wise. Real estate developer Johnny Harris proved bullish on Charlotte's growth. He noted that the city's attractiveness as a regional hub would provide myriad opportunities and pitfalls for the local development community in the 1990s. Harris stated in 1988, "I don't think we need to be as deeply concerned about unrestrained growth destroying the fabric of our city. We'll never be another Atlanta. We couldn't be, even if we wanted to be."[41]

In 1989 the NCNB Corporation wanted to build a sixty-story office building. The project had the full support of the pro-growth coalition and airport director Jerry Orr. However, the FAA regional office in Atlanta determined that such a building would adversely affect air navigation. The Washington office of the FAA reversed the finding, and Charlotte was on a roll.

AIRPORT AND THE WEATHER

On September 22, 1989, the unthinkable and unexpected happened to the expanding Charlotte Airport. Hurricane Hugo was supposed to hit only the beachfront areas of North Carolina, but it roared into the Queen City with sixty-nine-mile-per-hour winds. The airport closed, and major carrier USAir canceled most of its flights—300 in Charlotte alone, where the airline served 93 percent of passengers. Duke Power Company stated that 90 percent of Charlotte residents lost power. Most of the roofs of Charlotte Douglas's Concourse B were blown off, and Concourse A lost 10 percent of its roof. Concourses B and C suffered water damage, and the jetways experienced wind damage. Repair costs for the overall damage to the airport were estimated at $3 million. Director Orr reported power was restored to "85 percent of the airport."[42] Hugo provided another lesson that inland airports were not immune to Mother Nature.

THE NINETIES FALLOUT AND GROWTH

The nineties were a significant period in American politics and Charlotte mayoral politics. The city elected its first Republican mayor, Sue Myrick, after its first African American mayor, Harvey Gantt. After Myrick the city elected Republicans Richard Vinroot and Pat McCrory. The latter served for fourteen years. Overall, America was reacting to taxes and the growth of big government—the nation spent eight years under the Reagan administration and its antigovernment ideology. Yet the Airport and Airway Improvement Act of 1982 was amended alongside the Airport and Airway Safety and Capacity Expansion Act of 1982. The Safety and Capacity Expansion Act was amended in 1990. In 1992, Congress enacted the Airport and Airway Safety, Capacity Noise Improvement, and Intermodal Transportation Act. In other words, lobbyists for airport expansion were as successful as they had been in previous administrations.

George H. W. Bush, Reagan's successor, came to the presidency during a time of an ascendant neoliberal narrative about the cost of public facilities. This narrative also debated the rising cost of public services. City services were deemed too costly when compared to the private sector. Neoliberals marshaled data urging cities and municipal governments to solve fiscal problems by contracting facilities to private companies. E. S. Savas, a professor and former deputy city administrator of New York City, became one of the gurus of the municipal privatization movement. He made the case for cities to privatize most of their departments.[43] In a 1990 study, author Robert W. Poole cites the Reason Foundation of California's recommendation that the top fifty American cities sell their airports: "Airport privatization would also mean new revenue for the federal government. Just the top 50 commercial airports, operating as private enterprises and earning a nominal 10% annual return on assets would generate profits of $2.35 billion per year. At the average effective federal corporate income tax rate of 26%, there would be $611 million in additional federal tax revenue per year from these companies."[44]

The study Poole references contends that privatization would increase competition among airlines at major airports and generate more tax income for cities. Privatization had one additional benefit: private owners could better negotiate costs with airlines. Such owners would not want to link their airports' fate to one or two major airline tenants. Poole believed that selling the airports would generate a onetime $24 billion windfall for local governments. Private airports would pay $390 million in taxes annually.

At the time of the study, Charlotte Douglas was ranked twenty-fourth among the top fifty airports. Airport director Jerry Orr reacted immediately to the idea of a privatized airport for Charlotte. He disagreed with the Reason Foundation's findings for four reasons. First, he stated, "Selling the airports to private investors would expose each such airport to similar conditions including the possibility of financial failure, bankruptcy and other characteristics of our private enterprise system that cull out mismanaged or unfortunate enterprises." Second, he argued that the current system kept the airport's earnings in-house and allowed it to make "qualitative improvements." Privatization would mean the profits would go to the owners. Third, Orr doubted the foundation's financial figures for Charlotte. Based on its assertion that Charlotte Douglas was worth $394,831,711, Orr observed the following:

> Under a typical analysis a purchaser might want to recover its investment over 10 years, thus the annual profit should be 1/10 or 10% of the purchase price. The purchase price, likewise, would be 10 times the annual earnings.... Under typical investment analysis this suggests an annual "net profit" of about 39.5 million. For FY 89–90 the "net profit" at Charlotte/Douglas International Airport was reported as $6,698,000, which could support a purchase price of $67 million if it was sold.[45]

Orr went on to dispute the claim that the airlines were not paying the airport enough fare money. He asserted that the purpose of an airport is to provide a facility for travelers. The Charlotte Airport provides capital facilities for passengers at no cost to the public. Orr did not believe that lower cost to airlines would attract more carriers to the airport. He concluded, "[The] Reason Foundation assumptions are ill-founded, and its conclusion flawed."[46] The privatization movement was short-lived because its ideas seemed partisan and difficult to implement. Yet the argument about the airports continued, and the optimism of the director was also short-lived.

Charlotte Douglas's management did not anticipate that the next years would be ones of rapid fallout. In 1986, 70 percent of Eastern Air Lines' shareholders approved the Texas Air Corporation's purchase of the company for $600 million, ending its independent status. The airline then lost $44 million in the second quarter. This setback represented a $69.5 million decline from the previous year's profits of $25.5 million. According to the company, its revenue fell 12.3 percent to $1.119 billion. In August, Eastern laid off 186 of its 236 workers at Douglas. The airline had notified the Securities and Exchange Commission that it would lose about $57.6 million that year. In 1985, the carrier made a profit of only $6 million.[47] Simply put, this was not a good business situation for the struggling airlines.

For Charlotte Douglas, it meant that one of most supportive airlines was declining in significance. In 1986, Eastern also reduced its daily flights from fifty-three to twelve. Eastern Air Lines chairman George Robinette was quoted as saying, "It was inevitable. We had been losing money at our Charlotte hub in recent years because of thinned-out passenger traffic. . . . It looks like we're picking on Charlotte, but we are not."[48] Nationwide, Eastern Air Lines laid off 1,500 employees as a part of a $160 million cost-cutting program. In 1991, Eastern Air Lines, so important to the development of Charlotte Douglas, went out of business. It had fallen victim to labor troubles, poor leadership, the rise of discount airlines, and the turbulence of deregulation. The new airlines took over Eastern's routes, but the other major carriers were experiencing fiscal problems.

Other airlines were not immune to changes in ridership and the economy. USAir also cut employees' salaries by 20 percent in an attempt to save $400 million. In 1991, the *Charlotte Observer* reported the airline had about 6,800 employees in Charlotte, 1,600 of them pilots. Citing NCNB economist Dan Friel, the paper said this cut would affect over 1 percent of the metropolitan workforce.[49] The UNCC economist agreed but considered salary cuts better than layoffs. He reminded readers, "USAir is such an important ingredient in the local economy."⁵⁰

At the end of the year, the *Charlotte Observer* reported that the Charlotte Douglas Airport had defied the recession. Its freight loading had increased 12 percent (16.1 million pounds). In addition, a record number of passengers—7.66 million—were using the airport.⁵¹ Charlotte had prospered because of the nature of its economy. Economist John Connaughton told the *Atlanta Journal-Constitution*, "This is a finance, insurance and real estate town. Those industries are not cyclical and will continue to do well in the 1990s."⁵² Faith in Charlotte grew, and USAir decided to close its Dayton, Ohio, hub and make Charlotte and Pittsburgh its primary hubs. USAir offered 370 daily flights, dwarfing the other airlines.

In 1992, USAir CEO Seth Schofield told the Charlotte Chamber of Commerce, "As a major hub, Charlotte will be the recipient over time, of enhanced international service. USAir is a major player here in Charlotte. It's an important partnership: We need you. You need us."⁵³ Schofield made this statement in support of a proposed alliance with British Airways. USAir had lost $1 billion since 1989 and wanted British Airways to buy 44 percent of the company. Because USAir was the dominant tenant at the airport, Charlotte had an obvious stake in these talks. U.S. Airways ultimately survived its financial difficulties.

In 1994, a one-thousand-foot extension for the runway at Charlotte Douglas was completed. This was also the year that Northwest Airlines began nonstop service to Detroit. On July 2, a DC-9 USAir jet with fifty-five passengers crashed into a house near the Charlotte airport, sending thirty-three passengers to a nearby hospital. Again, aircraft safety became an issue for airlines.

Nineteen days later, Congress passed the General Aviation Revitalization Act. Signed by Pres. Bill Clinton, the new law reduced the liability of aircraft manufacturing companies. Under the act, the companies were not held accountable when aircraft parts were eighteen or more years old at the time of an accident. Obviously, this reduced the cost of liability insurance for manufacturers. Aircraft manufacturers had previously argued that such insurance reduced their production rate and export sales. President Clinton also signed an executive order making air traffic control an independent unit within the FAA called Air Traffic Organization.

In 1998, the economic situation in Charlotte changed dramatically, and the city became what Rick Rothacker calls "Banktown."⁵⁴ NationsBank of Charlotte acquired Bank of America in the largest acquisition of its kind at the time. Hugh McColl became CEO of the merged banks, known as the new Bank of

America. Mr. McColl, an ex-marine who kept a plastic grenade on his desk, became one of the leaders of Charlotte's economic elite. He profoundly impacted the city's development—his bank built one of the city's most impressive buildings, dubbed "Taj McColl."

McColl retired in 2001, and Bank of America gained access to the U.S. Northeast when it acquired the Fleet Bank of Boston. This purchase also made Bank of America one of the largest financial institutions in the nation. The bank would later acquire major investment company Merrill Lynch, thereby consolidating the city of Charlotte as a major international financial center. The city's increased international profile then made an international airport more essential. Charlotte Douglas began by expanding its runways and increasing its number of gates from sixty-three to eighty-two. In addition, the airport started to build fifteen thousand parking spaces to be completed in three years. Other changes to the facility included moving the commuter airlines from Concourse D to the New Concourse E so that passengers would not have to board outside. Finally, work on a new nine-thousand-foot runway was to begin in 2000. In other words, the airport was gearing up for the turn of the century.

THE TURN OF THE CENTURY

In 2000, the nation was rattled by the so-called Y2K problem—the prospect that computers could not transition into the new century. It was anticipated that a computer bug would cause errors in dates and other data. The city of Charlotte grew alarmed because it was the nation's second-largest banking center and its airport was the second-largest hub in the southeastern United States. However, history shows that not much happened during the Y2K crisis. First Union chief Ed Crutchfield called it "a big yawn," and Bank of America officials stated, "We've seen nothing."[55]

Although computer-dependent aircraft and the air travel industry experienced no glitches in their computers, the recession created low demand for travel.[56] The financially troubled USAir and United Airlines unsuccessfully attempted a merger in which United would pay $11.6 billion. The two airlines' leaders hoped to solve USAir's continuing financial problems in this manner. Such a merger would have been the largest in airline history, and it would have profoundly affected the airport.

Charlotte was now USAir's busiest hub, with 102 nonstop destinations. While USAir was the largest tenant at Charlotte Douglas, it had high labor costs associated with its mergers with other airlines. Delays and pilot retirements also plagued USAir, and fare wars prevented it from making a profit until 1995. In 2000, the *Charlotte Observer* article cited these points and noted, "U.S. Airways' cost per seat-mile was 12.9 cents last year. This was a whopping 42 percent higher than the average for its leading competitors. Even a higher revenue per available seat mile—12.96 cents for U.S. Airways vs. 9.75 cents for its leading competitors—melts away under the glare of those higher expenses."[57] Obviously, the airline was in financial trouble. Words like "merger," "restructuring," and "bankruptcy" were being discussed. The *Charlotte Observer* then quoted University of Chicago economist Prof. Sam Peltzman:

> That's a danger signal. It's ominous to have a carrier like U.S. Airways struggling in this kind of environment. U.S. Airways has a problem with costs. Its costs are higher than other carriers similar[ly] situated, most obviously Southwest, which flies short hauls and has a considerable cost advantage. . . . U.S. Airways has reduced its costs, but not enough. It's also unusually leveraged. A lot of its operating cash flow is going to pay interest.[58]

Despite the support of Charlotte's elected officials, Mayor Pat McCrory, Governor Jim Hunt, Charlotte Chamber and some members of the North Carolina Congressional Delegation (Sen. John Edwards being an exception), the merger with United failed to get the U.S. Justice Department's support. South Carolina Gov. Jim Hodges also declined to support the merger. In July 2001, the merger was rejected. The airlines had not made the case. There were simply too many questions about whether the merger would reduce fare prices at Charlotte Douglas. The Justice Department concluded that a merger would reduce competition across the nation.

THE IMPACT OF 9/11

The world of air travel and aviation underwent a major political and safety transformation on September 11, 2001. That day, a group of terrorists hijacked and flew American Airlines Flight 11 and United Airlines Flight 175 into the World Trade Center in New York City. Terrorists hijacked yet another plane, American Airlines Flight 77, and crashed it into the Pentagon in Washington, D.C. And United Airlines Flight 93 was diverted when passengers rushed Al-Qaeda hijackers onboard and crashed the plane in Pennsylvania. All these acts changed the entire narrative about airlines, passenger safety, and security. Over three thousand people died and over six thousand were injured. Eight of those individuals worked for Wachovia and Bank of America. All air traffic was terminated after the attacks. Rothacker reported that Wachovia president Ken

Thompson had to "hastily" hire a limousine to get back to Charlotte.[59] In addition, passenger traffic decreased and caused layoffs at airports. Over a month later, Mayor Pat McCrory appeared on C-Span confirming air traffic's importance to Charlotte as a "job generator" and encouraging people to fly again and not have a "bunker mentality."[60] The nation had to be reassured that flying would be safe again and that terrorists would be punished. Pres. George W. Bush asserted as much as he stood on the ruins of the World Trade Center and promised retribution.

To ensure passengers' safety and deter terrorists, Congress created the Transportation Security Administration (TSA) to assume responsibility for boarding and overall security at airports. In 2003, the TSA was moved to the new Department of Homeland Security. Air travel around the world changed as a result of these measures. Like other facilities, Charlotte Douglas was transformed into a fortress where passengers were searched before they entered the boarding area. Uniformed security agents checked identities and wielded full-body scanners. They also inspected every passenger's luggage, sometimes with the aid of dogs. Once through the security checkpoints, passengers disappeared from the view of their family and friends, who were denied entrance to the boarding areas. Travelers then returned to a regular routine boarding process, but they were restricted in what they could bring on planes. For example, a bottle of water or wine was no longer permitted. Furthermore, a no-fly list was created to prevent certain individuals from boarding airplanes. Once they entered airplanes, passengers rode with air marshals and with undercover agents who scrutinized their behavior.

In 2005, yet another financial fallout was pending. Four of the six legacy airlines were in the early stages of bankruptcy, and Delta and Northwest Airlines were teetering on the edge of bankruptcy. Most airlines were cutting staff and trying to find ways to save money. For its part, USAir decided to merge with American West to survive. Journalist Rick Newman reported on this move, which was considered a triumph for USAir.

> For all the whooping, however, the coup at U.S. Airways has not been bloodless. Through bankruptcy, U.S. Airways furloughed more than 7,000 pilots, mechanics, and other union employees. Both companies combined have shed an additional 1,200 management jobs. The layoffs have especially hurt Pittsburgh, where there is little left, besides a minor hub, of an operation that was once large enough to justify a multibillion-dollar new airport. To U.S. Airways survivors, that's a better outcome than total liquidation would have been. "We didn't want that," says Al Crellin, operations director for both the old and the new U.S. Airways, "because

of all the employees and the families." As business has improved, U.S. Airways has hired back about 65 pilots and 200 flight attendants.[61]

In an interview with the *Charlotte Observer*, USAir CEO Doug Parker speculated about the future of air travel: "The industry will figure out a way to be profitable. We will adapt. The industry we end up with, though, is not one that anybody's going to like. It will have fewer seats, fewer flights to fewer markets. It will become more like before deregulation, when it was more of a luxury good than something people are used to using as a way to get around the country. That's certainly not what we're in favor of, but that's where we'll end up, I fear, if oil prices stay where they are."[62] Even during all these changes, Charlotte Douglas Airport continued to expand its runways. MATE, an Alpharetta, Georgia, engineering company, was contracted to pave a new parallel runway and taxiways. The members of Charlotte's pro-growth coalition were true believers, and they now had a larger stake in air travel.

SUMMARY

Despite the reassurance offered by USAir CEO Mr. Parker, the situation for airlines and airports did not return to what it had been before deregulation. The sorting out of airlines—including legacy airlines—would continue. Some cities resisted becoming an "airport city." Writer H. McKinley Conway points out that many towns were unaware of problems associated with air isolation. He concludes that these cities were "silently permitting themselves to be closed out of the nation's airways."[63] For Conway, this decision had an economic impact on these cities and contributed to congested larger airports.

Charlotte, which Conway does not mention, had already decided to become an airport city. Business leaders knew the city could not continue to grow as a textile center; technology, synthetic fiber, and the globalization of the textile industry (China and India) had rendered Charlotte's economy outmoded. In fact, looms all over North Carolina were closing. Charlotte had never been a major player in the passenger railroad business. Yet it declined rapidly in that regard too as the nation constructed the interstate highway system and cars became affordable for short trips.

The federal government had abandoned the passenger railway business and put its subsidies in the airline industry. In 1961, the U.S. Postal Service partially forsook the railroad industry by delivering its first-class mail via trucks and airplanes. To stay current with changing industries and survive economically, Charlotte had to become an airport city. With air travel, the city's residents and businesses were better able to move around the nation and the world. Unexpectedly, the history of Charlotte Douglas was also determined by the plight of the airline industry and which airlines were merged. Charlotte's mayors had to support proposed mergers when the airport's future was at stake. As we saw in the review of airport history, every decade presented different problems.

Furthermore, Charlotte Douglas had to react to changing federal airport policies. The airport has benefited from federal funding since the existence of the WPA and the takeover by the U.S. Army. The army built the first full version of Charlotte Douglas, and federal largesse helped fuel its continuing expansions. Charlotte Airport's history suggests that policies made by Congress and the airline industry drive municipal facilities. Local municipal boosters supported the aforementioned expansions. Hugh McColl asserted, "The airport was a critical component for economic development. It was a driving force." Former mayor Sue Myrick once said of Piedmont's impact on Charlotte's economic development, "Large corporations began to look at us not just as Charlotte, N.C., but as a city where they move their headquarters and go anyplace in the world easily."[64]

In 2015, U.S. Airways merged with American Airlines to become the new American Airlines. As a hub for the new, larger American Airlines, Charlotte Douglas International Airport took on yet another transportation role. Simply put, evolving from being a hub for Eastern Air Lines to Piedmont Airlines to U.S. Airways to American Airlines was a technological and managerial journey. The airport is now in the international customs and security business. This change also demonstrated the nexus between technical and political aspects of airports. Former city manager Ron Carlee described the growth of the airport from its "mom and pop beginning to big Wal-Mart" status.[65]

Charlotte Douglas International Airport developed within the context of city politics and federal regulations. In the next chapter we will see how members of Charlotte's pro-growth coalition were reduced to bystanders during the airline deregulation era. However, these individuals acted as enablers in social/racial deregulation.

CHAPTER 3

Charlotte in an Era of Deregulation

AS WE SUGGESTED IN THE last chapter, Charlotte's pro-growth coalition has supported the city's economic aspirations during several uncertain periods. However, this solid support provided little help when the federal government decided to encroach on the air travel market and interrupt city ambitions. Any type of preemptive state and federal actions against local government can be unsettling. Accordingly, the politics of federal regulation and deregulation can be a tricky business, particularly when it upends settled municipal policies. A "transformative city" must be alert to this possibility, and it often has to anticipate policy changes.

The city of Charlotte's politics are located in the nexus between state and federal government policies. Federal and state policies trump city-enacted ordinances. Cities have no standing in the U.S. Constitution, but they are not absolutely powerless. This axiom holds true for social policies (e.g., race relations), environmental policies (e.g., aircraft noise), and economic policies (e.g., air travel and banking). In some cases, city politicians are reduced to spectators and bystanders. Thus, they depend on the media, lobbyists, and the state's congressional delegation to act as a sentinel for oncoming federal policies. Oftentimes a policy may appear innocuous but make a profound and unexpected impact on a city and its government.

In most air travel policies, the federal government has a long history of preempting local government actions. This is especially true for national air travel regulations and international open skies. In the latter case, the federal government makes bilateral agreements with other countries regarding scheduling and pricing of international flights. Subgovernments like cities are bound by those decisions. As an emerging global city, Charlotte has a stake in those policies but can do little to influence them. Yet the city and its airport are obligated to react to both national and international airline regulations.

This chapter reviews the impact of the nation's overall deregulation schemes as yet another aspect of the "ripple effects of technology" on Charlotte's politics and economy. As previously suggested, advances in aircraft technology such as jet engines forced airport upgrades. Charlotte was required to invest more and expand the airport. While this action attracted more flights to the airport and more residents and businesses to the city, it also imposed costs. The federal government's decision to deregulate airlines affected the industry's financial stability. That choice also destabilized passenger fares and airport planning. Furthermore, deregulation changed how the airport did business with the large carriers and discount airlines. Several discount airlines were formed, and several of them obtained gates at Charlotte Douglas. Over the years, however, some of these start-up airlines were winnowed out.

The airline deregulation of the 1970s coincided with a later banking deregulation. Removing restrictions on both of these industries would profoundly impact Charlotte. In addition, there existed an unrecognized intersectionality of the deregulation of racial policies, airlines, and, later, banking. While these events seem unrelated, they were critical to the making of the new Charlotte.

AIR TRAVEL AND THE OPEN SKIES

The skies over the United States belong to the American people, and it matters what happens in this space and who uses it. To regulate or not regulate has never been the question. Like all vehicles that carry humans, rules and regulations for airplanes are necessary. And the safety of such vehicles is the government's business. With the advent of flying machines, self-proclaimed pilots operated with relatively little oversight and regulation. However, as more airplanes took flight and the purposes of flying expanded to include commerce, passengers, and military defense, rules had to be made. As we saw in the last chapter, the federal government's involvement in flying and airports began in the 1920s. Politicians at all levels of government wanted to know who could fly, what could fly, and where flying machines could land, among other things. Local governments first dictated where airplanes could land before municipal airports existed; cities restricted the landing fields and helped operate air shows. The North Carolina legislature entered the regulation business by restricting pilots from flying while drunk. But it was the federal government that played a large regulatory role in air travel.

The federal government got into the air travel business by organizing and subsidizing airmail as a part of its responsibility to promote interstate commerce. Creating the airmail system and supporting the growing airline industry were not initially seen as signs that the federal government intended to micromanage this new marketplace. A case was made for allowing the nascent airlines to take their chances in the marketplace. Since the airline companies were trying to make a profit, it was first thought that the government should not decide what they would charge for services and which routes they would service.

In this new marketplace, well-run companies were supposed to thrive, while poorly run companies would fail. Indeed, some small airlines were winners and others losers.

The airmail scandal of the 1930s found the budding airlines trying to game the airmail system. The Spoils Conference did not solve the situation. Therefore, the federal government (i.e., Roosevelt administration) decided to intervene so that some cities and towns would get airmail and air travel. Without congressional intervention, many cities may have had to wait for decades for airmail service and even longer for scheduled passenger service. Air travel quickly became too important and political to allow the market to determine policy. The "let-the-market-decide ideology" lost a lot of credibility with the collapse of the nation's economic system and the start of the Great Depression.

Ultimately, the federal government decided to intervene in all aspects of economic activities. The new economy was designed to be a mixed one of government and markets. Additionally, the federal government started a tradition of grants-in-aid to airports, national air travel planning, and operations of the air traffic system. Airline regulation started in late 1930s and peaked in the late 1970s. In order to understand the building of the airline industry and its impact on city airport policies, it is important to review the case for regulation.

THE CASE FOR REGULATION

A variety of advocates claimed that federal airline regulation would prevent a corporate monopoly that would threaten democracy and free choice. Lack of competition in any marketplace will drive up prices. The airline industry was accused of rigging the system to prevent outsiders from competing in a growing industry. Supporters of airline oversight cited the Spoils Conference as an early example of a failure of self-regulation. For years the so-called legacy airlines dominated the skies. Farewise, small companies could not compete with them. High airfares made air travel unavailable for most Americans, and several small cities did not have air travel connections. Accordingly, regulation was supposed to stimulate competition, keep fares reasonable, and provide services to underserved parts of the nation. In February 1978, the Government Accounting Organization released a study concluding that passengers would have saved between $1.5 and $2.0 billion if CAB had not regulated airfares. Passengers embarking on interstate travel in large states not covered by CAB enjoyed fares that were 30 to 60 percent lower than regulated ones.[1]

Proper regulation of the airlines would eliminate the uncertainties of the marketplace and preserve competition. Such regulation could also prevent costly management errors and job expenses. Some optimists even suggested that regulation would correct market imperfections, reconciling consumers' interests with the airline industry's growth ambitions. Universal norms could eliminate abuse, improve public regard for the industry, and allow Congress and its designated agency to oversee airlines more closely. Once rules were established, Congress could determine if they were being implemented. An independent regulatory agency (i.e., CAB) was formed with the intention of eliminating partisan influence on the industry. As a side benefit of regulation, the government was to develop and employ its own civilian airline experts. The government would also protect passenger rights. Integrating the nation's air transportation was essential for national economic development. In effect, regulations addressed several public policy issues.

Since the beginning of airlines, the federal government has continued to define and refine its role as arbiter of interstate transportation and international commerce. As Charlotte Airport's history demonstrates, the federal government has been critical to understanding what an airport is, what it can do, and why. Because of its preemptive powers over the states and cities, the federal government could standardize the rule-making process. The federal government also had the resources to make development grants. Fascinatingly, airline-regulating policy has been for the most part bipartisan. Democratic and Republican lawmakers share a similar interest in airline regulations. The inclination to promote these rules is related to airlines' centrality in modern transportation. Granted, airline carriers employed a world-class lobby operation at the congressional level; however, it was passengers and voters who often prompted action by Congress. As previously discussed, presidents from both political parties signed new airport development laws.

THE PROCESS OF REGULATING AIRLINES

The history of air travel can be traced back the 1926 Air Commerce Act, which the airplane industry prompted Congress to pass to promote commercial air travel and traffic rules. Political leaders understood that the federal government was the only level of government that could effectively set safety standards. The Aeronautic Branch of the U.S. Department of Commerce was the first air travel enforcement agency. In the 1930s, few Americans owned and flew private planes, and most cities did not have a municipal airport. As the federal government sought to grow aircraft manufacturing, the airline industry, and general aviation, it therefore encouraged local government to establish landing fields.

Local booster organizations encouraged cities like Charlotte to keep up with modern trends in intercity air transportation.

The Aeronautics Bureau of the Department of Commerce controlled the development of the air travel industry in the twenties and thirties. In 1936, an early system of air traffic controllers was established. In 1938, Congress passed the Civil Aeronautics Act that took the aeronautics unit out of the Department of Commerce and made it an independent agency called the Civil Aeronautics Authority. It also created the Civil Aeronautics Board and the Civil Aeronautics Administration (CAA).

CIVIL AERONAUTICS BOARD

The Civil Aeronautics Board oversaw aircraft and pilot certification and suspension. Regulation of airways, control towers, and other navigational facilities was the responsibility of the Civil Aeronautics Administration (CAA). The CAA's formation was the first attempt to bring order to a loose group of airline companies in what might be called an unregulated state. Before the CAA was created, four bureaus carried out much of the oversight of airlines: the Bureau of Aeronautics branch, the Bureau of Air Commerce, and the Bureaus of Air Mail and the Interstate Commerce Commission. The fragmentation of oversight agencies created accountability and planning problems for the growing airline industry. Reasoning at the time held that safety requirements and commerce had to be standardized and located in one regulatory agency. Another incentive for change was that all parts of the nation wanted and needed to have air travel, and a single federal agency was thought to be the way to achieve this goal.

As the airline industry grew, more Americans depended on it for intercity and world travel. People who could afford to fly were abandoning the railroads. However, with more passengers came more complaints, and safety also became a larger issue.

In 1940, the federal government split the Civil Aeronautic Agencies into the Civil Aeronautics Administration (CAA) and the Civil Aeronautics Board (CAB). The CAA was charged with aircraft control, aircraft certification, safety, and airline industry development. The former was returned to the Commerce Department.

The Civil Aeronautics Board (CAB), now an independent agency, was charged with air safety and investigating accidents. It was also charged with keeping the airline industry solvent. In 1940, the CAB expanded its powers to control takeoffs and landings at airports. This new regulatory presence grew after the

Depression and the war in Europe; some wanted the government to regulate airlines more directly. After the nation formally entered World War II, aircraft development became a priority, local airports were conscripted, and new cadres of pilots were trained.

In 1946, Congress expanded the CAA's reach and provided it with a federal aid program to develop city airports. In 1970, Congress created the U.S. Department of Transportation. The CAB subsequently became a part of this department and changed its name to the Federal Aviation Administration. The National Transportation Safety Board assumed the accident investigation responsibility of the CAB. The CAB was then left with regulation of routes and fares.

The original purpose of the CAB was to keep fares low to entice the public to fly and to maintain airline substantiality. CAA regulations allowed airlines to get 12 percent returns on flights that were only 55 percent full. Free-market economists attacked this cost-control measure and advocated more market-driven dynamics they believed would be more consumer friendly. The 1974 oil embargo and inflation during the Ford administration created an environment that demanded Congress rethink the CAB's mission.

The CAB differed from most government administrative agencies. First, the agency had a board rather than a single appointed head. Additionally, it performed all three functions of government—executive, legislative, and judicial. The president could not remove CAB board members except for just cause. Congress constructed the agency to be independent and to promote competitive fares and routes. This 1938 policy forming the CAB was made before Charlotte Municipal Airport got its footing as a facility. Three years later the Charlotte Municipal Airport was taken over by the U.S. Army.

For over forty years, the CAB did its job determining routes and setting fares, profoundly impacting airlines and airports as a result. The board could determine what type of aircraft could land in specific cities. Cities like Charlotte had convinced the CAB that their airports could handle new aircraft. Historian Janet Bednarek summarizes the CAB's powers: "CAB determined which airline or airlines served which city. It restricted competition on flights between the nation's largest cities, but also guaranteed flights to the nation's smaller cities. Cities wishing for expanded air service had to woo not just the airlines, but the CAB as well. Cities threatened with diminished service could also plead their case to the CAB, as it could require an airline to serve specific cities."[2]

Airlines were able to stabilize their financial foundations and agree on which carriers would serve which cities. Like most regulatory agencies, the CAB had its critics. By the end of the Vietnam War, airlines had become big business. Like several regulatory agencies, the CAB came under attack and became the subject of administrative reform.

In the 1970s, a strong case was made to deregulate the airlines. The President's Advisory Council on Executive Organization Commission, which later came to be known as the Ash Commission after its chairman Roy Ash in 1971, represented the general growing displeasure with independent regulatory agencies. The Ash Commission claimed these organizations lacked accountability and coordination. In addition, the commission recommended merging the ICC, the CAB, and the Federal Maritime Commission into a single agency—the Transport Regulatory Agency. (The first Hoover Commission's Task Force Proposal of 1949 had also suggested ending independent agencies.) Some critics argued that independent regulators were not amenable to changes in presidential leadership and, more importantly, in public opinion. In 1950, the CAB received eighty applications to start new airlines.[3] Processing these documents took too much time, and critics thought the CAB was too bureaucratic and fares were too high. The two regulating agencies also had a personnel turnover problem. Experts were leaving the CAB to work for airlines. Regulated disputes often landed on the court docket rather than being resolved by the regulators and the regulated. In 1975, the Gerald Ford administration wanted to deregulate the airlines, but the relevant bill never got out of committee. Academics were also making the case that regulatory agencies were too amenable to co-optation.

CHANGING CHARLOTTE BY DEREGULATIONS

A case could made that the transformative city of the twentieth century was made possible primarily because of the deregulation of the airline industry and banking. If one reads closely, one can see the parallels of social and institutional deregulation; the arguments were strikingly similar. Deregulation should increase efficiency (i.e., dismantle antiquated laws), reduce social and financial costs, and improve the overall welfare. This was the case made by those seeking to deregulate what happens in the skies. The argument began in the realm of ideas about how to make government more efficient and how to use the marketplace to reduce the cost of goods and services.

In *The Politics of Deregulation*, political scientists Martha Derthick and Paul Quirk suggest that deregulation resulted from a politics of ideas.[4] The sixties were a time when social scientists, particularly economists, began assaulting the regulatory policy status quo. Regulation is what governments do. They also create agencies to implement regulatory policies. Academics began to question settled ideas, laws, and agencies. With respect to agencies, the seventies were an era of government deregulation of air transportation.

THE ACADEMIC ASSAULT

In the fifties, academics began to identify most independent regulatory agencies as ineffective bureaucracies. As early as 1952, famous political scientist Sam Huntington suggested that all regulatory agencies were amenable to capture by the industries they regulated (i.e., captive theory). The regulators and the regulated interact incessantly with each other, creating opportunities for groupthink. In 1955, social scientist Marvel Bernstein made a different case with his life-cycle theory of agencies. An agency attracts reformers and crusaders when it is young. As the agency grows older, the crusaders leave after fighting in courts. Simply put, public agencies get old and become institutionalized. As these organizations mature, they opt for keeping alive rather attacking the status quo. By 1963, Gabriela Kolkhoz had produced the "original intent theory" suggesting that many agencies had veered away from the original purpose of the congressional legislation. For some political scientists, co-optation was inevitable. These scholars warned that regulatory agencies couldn't resist becoming supplicants of the regulated groups.

Economists joined the debate by claiming that regulation itself inhibits competition. For them, the CAB had become too paternalistic toward the airline industry. In fact, the agency would not allow an airline to fail. The CAB could not decide whether to maintain competition among airlines or preserve airlines. As the board was successful in the latter undertaking, many poorly managed airlines stayed in the air. Moreover, the CAB's policies did not keep fares low—many ordinary Americans could not afford to fly. In other words, the CAB lost its rhetorical argument with its critics about protecting consumer interests.

ADMINISTRATIVE REORGANIZATION

In 1958, Congress passed the Federal Aviation Act, which transferred some of the missions of the CAA and CAB to a new agency, the Federal Aviation Administration. The FAA would control all air traffic. Twenty years later, the CAB was abolished, and airlines were allowed to decide their own routes and ticket prices. In theory, any entrepreneur with financial resources, aircraft, and gate rents could start an airline. Although Democratic president Jimmy Carter did not campaign on this issue, he saw himself more as a regulatory-reform president. President Carter promoted the idea of airline deregulation, and with the help of Congress he was able to sign the historic deregulation bill. The bill's passage represented bipartisan consensus at its finest. Indeed, almost all of the House Democrats voted for the measure (368 to 8), and in the Senate the vote tally was 83 to 9. To understand why this support was so overwhelming, it is important to examine the context of this major reform.

Although there was no strong citizen demand for it, Congress characterized this regulatory decision as an attempt to protect Americans from real ticket-fare exploitation. A famous textbook in public administration asserts, "Regulation of the economy is in fact political, brought into existence by public demand for protection of consumer interest."[5] For example, without the CAB's efforts, the government would not have been able to keep airline service for small communities.

Throughout airline history, airline lobbyists have helped write the CAB regulations. In other words, politics has often overwhelmed the regulators and undermined regulation's original intent. Over the years, CAB regulation tended to foster monopolies. Monopolies are often disposed to slackness in service quality and unwarranted cost increases. This may explain why passenger complaints found space in local newspapers and letters to elected officials.

COMPLAINING ABOUT AIRLINES

Under the CAB regime, airlines were relatively insulated from public accountability. Complaints arose regarding airlines' large-market biases, service cancellations, and escalating fare increases. Airlines created the hub system to reduce costs and service small towns with few potential passengers. Although airlines like the hub system, its inconvenience for passengers produces incessant complaints. The *New York Times* asserted, "For years it has been a favorite joke among weary air travelers in the Southeast: When you die, they say, you do not go directly to heaven or hell. First, You stop at Atlanta to change planes."[6] Regulation came to the South, but it was not enough to change airlines' behavior. Under CAB regulation an uneven development of airports and scheduling practices became more obvious. By the middle of the 1970s, air travel had become so important to the national economic system that the federal government needed to take further action.

The nation was divided between those who believed deregulation could solve airline problems and those who believed the federal government had obvious and compelling stakes in its most important transportation sector. For the latter individuals, airlines could not be trusted to make wise market decisions. Some claimed that airlines had become arrogant and treated passengers as they pleased and with impunity. For example, carriers' general policy was to overbook flights, as there were always late or absent passengers.

In 1976, consumer advocate Ralph Nader was bumped from an Allegheny Airlines flight. His consequent suit against the airline went all the way to the U.S. Supreme Court. Because Allegheny had not notified Nader and thus misrepresented its service, the airline was liable for overbooking flights.[7] This case prompted the CAB to launch a two-year study of the airline booking procedures. Based on the study, the CAB then ordered increased compensation for bumping.

Charlotte Douglas International Airport was and is a part of a large flying network, so it had a stake in the deregulation process. Since the military and commercial system shared a common navigation system, national security issues arose.

In the 1970s, economists promoted the idea that regulating airlines and routes drove up prices for consumers and allowed airlines to thwart competition from smaller or start-up airlines. As stated earlier, the federal government had played a critical role in the development and sustainability of airlines and had done so while increasing its regulatory mission. For forty years, the Civil Aeronautics Board set the fares, routes, and schedules for all interstate air travel. Yet widespread dissatisfaction among the passenger class endured. Both conservative and liberal opinion leaders supported deregulation.

CONGRESSIONAL RESPONSE TO PASSENGERS

Few people had ever heard of Alfred Kahn, a Cornell University economist, before Pres. Jimmy Carter appointed him head of the CAB. Professor Kahn was among those economists who had long advocated deregulation of airlines. Their rationale for deregulation was that it would stimulate more competition among carriers, which in turn would supposedly promote better service and cheaper tickets. Almost immediately upon taking office, CAB chairman Kahn stopped the review of most fares. That opened airlines to fare competition. Kahn also went on record as supporting the abolishment of the CAB and the elimination of his job. Economist Gary McDonnell suggested that the demand for deregulation was the result of the politics of ideas. He concluded,

> This process may have been necessary to bring about regulatory reform, but it was not sufficient to bring about complete deregulation—that is, freedom of entry and pricing as well as the eventual elimination of the CAB. The industry's inability to lobby with a unified effort, reflecting little perceived net benefit from regulation,

was in effect the ultimate precursor to deregulation. The complete deregulation of entry and pricing was not the sole result of ideas generated by academic critiques (the politics of ideas) but rather was an unintended consequence of a process that revealed little expected value from continued economic regulation.[8]

Congressional hearings were held, speeches were made, and deregulation's supporters prompted Congress to pass a bill eliminating the power of the CAB. On October 24, 1978, Pres. Jimmy Carter signed the Airline Deregulation Act.[9] As stated earlier, the bill garnered overwhelming support. Reform had the enthusiastic backing of Sen. Edward Kennedy, a famous liberal and Democratic Party icon. Proponents of the bill, including the National Association of Counties, Common Cause, the American Conservative Union, Ralph Nader, and the American Association of Retired Persons, were able to overcome earlier airline opposition.[10] During the final debate, the Airlines Transportation Association (ATA), the most powerful air travel lobby, did not testify against the bill.

The stage was now set to test the notion that contestable markets create competition promoting lower prices and improved services. Economists argued that creating a contestable market required more airline providers and more varied fares. Economist Laurence T. Phillips makes the case succinctly.

> Airline deregulation is premised on the belief that city-pair markets are contestable; that is, a potential entrant could, almost effortlessly, replicate along all relevant dimensions (cost, service, product variety, etc.) the operations and performance of established firms. Further, the theory of contestable markets rests on the assumption that a firm which enters a market can, if market conditions change, exit that market at a relatively low cost. If high levels of concentration at large hub airports make it more costly for potential competitors to establish operations and develop economically viable route networks, either because of a potential entrant's inability to secure sufficient traffic or because of strategic actions taken by incumbent firms to disadvantage potential rivals, then competition among air carriers will be less vigorous than it would be otherwise.[11]

Becoming a hub was essential to Charlotte's economy. In the late seventies, Charlotte Douglas had become a hub for Piedmont Airlines; the airport director had signed long-term leases in order to stabilize Piedmont's growth. In addition, promoters like the Charlotte Chamber of Commerce persuaded voters to support a 1978 referendum on revenue bonds.[12] The success of the 1978 vote allowed the airport to plan for a new terminal, which was crucial to accelerating the facility's expansion. In the late seventies and early eighties, Piedmont Airlines had little competition. Start-ups and smaller airlines could not contend for its ridership. Using Charlotte as a hub, Piedmont changed its image as a regional airline, buying Eastern Air Lines' twelve gates and increasing its number of daily flights to 185. Piedmont became a major player in other regions of the United States as a result.

The *Charlotte Observer* published dueling editorials on this topic. Sen. Edward Kennedy noted that the only competition among airlines before deregulation concerned food quality and stewardesses' uniforms.[13] Edwin I. Colodny predicted that deregulation would result in a concentration of airlines. The largest airlines in the 1970s—American, United, TWA, Eastern, and Delta—would "whomp any other airlines if they want to."[14] Obviously hindsight about deregulation is better than foresight.

DEREGULATIONS AND CHARLOTTE DOUGLAS AIRPORT

Although the impetus for deregulation had to come from the federal government, all airports in the United States, regardless of governance and management structure, were affected by airline deregulation. Although some economists remained enthusiastic about this development, its impact on airline hubs like Charlotte Douglas was mixed. What works in economic models does not always work in reality. Legacy airlines were exposed financially, and carriers began terminating services to unpopular destinations. Although Charlotte was a hub, it was not exempt from airline cutbacks. Charlotte businessman Richard A. Klein complained immediately about the declining number of flights at Charlotte, asking, "Is anyone lobbying for us?"[15] Delta decided to stop flights to New York City, and it also moved many direct flights out of Charlotte and put passengers on shuttle aircraft to Atlanta. Other airlines were limiting their service as well. After the only nonstop to Houston was canceled, Klein wrote another letter to the airport director. He inquired, "What can we citizens do to go to bat for better air service in Charlotte?"[16]

Even after deregulation was causing disruptions, economists kept the faith. Many of them believed the economic models simply needed more time to work. The *Charlotte Observer* criticized such economists, admitting in an editorial that it had misjudged deregulation's impact on the city.

> We were wrong. After a flurry of innovation—introduction of the hub and spoke system, intensive use of peripheral airports, no-frills service and entry of small new competitors—unexpected patterns started to emerge. Through control of reservations systems, in which size conveys substantial advantages; through frequent-flier kickbacks, which skim off the profitable business traveler; and

through monopolistic domination of hubs, which offer a limited supply of takeoff and landing slots, big airlines were able to absorb or destroy most of their small competitors and some giant rivals. The number of airlines has shrunk since the mid-1980s.[17]

Ironically, deregulation helped some of the major airlines at Charlotte Douglas Airport. Piedmont, the airport's biggest tenant, originally opposed deregulation. However, the airline's leadership quickly realized that the company might fare well with such changes. William R. Howard, Piedmont's president, stated, "First of all, we weren't going to win that battle. We were operating the right airplanes [and] we were a low-cost airline. It seemed to me that there were a lot of reasons why we should not fear being gobbled up."[18] Indeed, Piedmont became a gobbler, using its Charlotte hub to create landings in more cities. During that time period, Piedmont serviced 129 flights out of Charlotte. The success of the Charlotte Douglas hub then encouraged Piedmont to establish another hub at Baltimore-Washington International (BWI). In that above-quoted interview with the *Washington Post*, Howard was optimistic and bullish about the expansion and future of the airline. Even so, Piedmont merged with USAir four years later.

In 1979, the United States Conference of Mayors surveyed the nation's mayors about the number of air carriers at their airports. Charlotte Douglas hosted four carriers and eight commuter airlines at the time. Mayor Knox asked airport director Josh Birmingham to respond, and Birmingham reported that deregulation had decreased the number of certificated carriers and flights but increased the size of aircraft. When asked about deregulation's overall effect on Charlotte Douglas, Birmingham answered, "Commuter operators increase and cause overcrowding of ramp and terminal."[19] He also reported an increase in airfreight traffic. In an interview with the *Charlotte Observer*, Birmingham said, "Anytime that we lose any services to a city it concerns us. However, especially with deregulation, they are taking airplanes that heretofore have been marginal money-makers, and they're putting those planes on routes that are money-makers. I understand why they do that."[20] Charlotte Chamber of Commerce researcher Jerry Hendricks agreed and stated, "The whole airline industry is in such a state of flux because of deregulation. The CAB (Civil Aeronautics Board) itself anticipated there would be many, many small and middle-sized cities losing service."[21]

Since federal government grants had inspired and funded most of these airports' growth, cities like Charlotte depended on these incentives for expansion. The pro-growth coalition welcomed the federal funds because they supported its economic aspirations.

Nationwide airport expansion underwent four phases. David NewMyer, a professor of aviation management, calls the initial period the expansion period. The industry grew from thirty large carriers in 1978 to 105 in 1985.[22] Charlotte Douglas had to increase its number of gates and enlarge its ramp space. The city of Charlotte was certainly among the Sunbelt cities adjusting to these new landings, and the increased demand made its role as a hub more salient.

These new demands and the hub-and-spoke network allowed Piedmont Airlines to grow beyond the Southeast. To establish gates in the Northeast, Piedmont purchased Empire Airlines in 1985. Piedmont also expanded connections with several commuter airlines, including Brockway, CCAir, and Henson. Commuter carriers brought more passengers to Charlotte Douglas and then redistributed them throughout the rest of the nation.

David NewMyer identifies the second phase of airlines development as consolidation. This period lasted between 1986 and 1988 and was exemplified by eleven airline mergers and sixteen buyouts, the latter of which included the regional and commuter airlines. NewMyer calls the third period of development the concentration phase. He found that the four largest carriers accounted for 60.4 percent of the traffic in 1988. This represented an increase from 52.5 percent in 1978.[23] For Charlotte, this phase saw the merger of U.S. Airways and Piedmont. Piedmont, the so-called "hometown airline," was consumed by emerging giant U.S. Airways. At Charlotte Douglas, the new U.S. Airways began to receive the special attention that Piedmont previously had. Some analysts did not expect large airline companies to buy smaller ones. As Gesell and Sobotta assert, "The industry had become more concentrated than before deregulation!"[24]

NewMyer's fourth phase of deregulation is called globalization. In 1987 this phase began the internationalization of airlines, as business and travel are no longer limited to the United States. Charlotte Douglas started international nonstop flight in the 1990s, when British Airways and Lufthansa rented gates in the airport. To adapt to the demand for international flights, Charlotte Douglas created customs and immigration check stations. In August 1990, Lufthansa Flight 448 landed at the completed $22 million international concourse.

The final phase of NewMyer's typology is called realignment. This phase was prompted by the terrorist attack of September 11, 2001, after which passenger demand dropped. The safety scare and continuing financial instability put several legacy airlines in jeopardy. Up-and-coming U.S. Airways bought American Airlines, and Delta Airlines brought Northwest Airlines, giving routes to Asia. The entire operation of Charlotte Douglas Airport changed as a result. American Airlines is now the dominant carrier at Charlotte Douglas, and Delta flies most of its long-range passengers to Atlanta before flying them to their destination. In effect, deregulation and the terrorist attack had a mixed effect on the airport hub and the city plans for expansion.

THE CONTINUING FALLOUT OF DEREGULATION

The winds of change started four years into the post-deregulation era. The airlines' initial reactions were to cut services to small communities and reduce the quality of in-flight treats. Carriers also lowered fares. Layoffs and service cuts were so rampant that some airline unions urged Congress to repeal the Airline Deregulation Act. As this did not happen, airports and airlines had to adjust to the globalization phase of their development.

Like most hubs, Charlotte Douglas found its resources stressed after deregulation. The *Charlotte Observer* admitted after the opening of the 1982 terminal that deregulation had ushered in one of the most turbulent eras in the history of the airline industry. Journalist Bill Arthur concluded, "Deregulation brought additions and changes, especially from a liberated Piedmont, which increased its space in the new terminal from four gates to twelve. Five gates were added to the original construction plan. Piedmont took three more from other airlines."[25] Many more passengers land in Charlotte en route to another destination. American Airlines is able to predict fixed costs at Charlotte Douglas; Delta and United have few gates at the airport.

Eight years after deregulation, Eastern Air Lines was seen as an unexpected loser. The *Charlotte Observer* asserted, "Eastern Airlines was running fine in Charlotte until it tripped over a surging competitor and a five-syllable word: deregulation."[26] Remember Eastern Air Lines played a critical element in the growth of Charlotte's airport. In 1986, it announced it would cut daily flights from Charlotte from fifty-three to twelve and cut its payroll by one hundred employees. In Charlotte, a smaller Piedmont Airlines headquartered in Winston-Salem, N.C., upstaged Eastern Air Lines. In a few years, Piedmont, once considered a feeder airline, became the dominant carrier at Charlotte Douglas Airport. As we discussed above, the deregulation of airlines encouraged Piedmont to spread its wings and rent gates in several cities. Moreover, the airline had 187 daily flights of out of Charlotte. Piedmont was in the right place to take over as Eastern gave up gates and declined in route significance.

As we suggested earlier, Charlotte Douglas Airport's development and expansion were at the center of Charlotte's overall economic development. However, Charlotte's becoming an airline hub came at a cost for city residents. The promise of low fares was the major selling point for deregulation; however, airfares at Charlotte Douglas remained higher than at other airports in the state. Airfares did not respond to marketplace competition. A 1990 study by the U.S. Department of Transportation cited Charlotte as one of the hub cities paying 18.7 percent higher airfares. The study concluded, "Not all travelers and markets have enjoyed the same level of benefits. Passengers departing from or traveling to some highly concentrated hubs pay high fares. And while hub-and-spoke operations have fostered industry efficiency, they have also increased airport congestion."[27]

The intuitive solution to the fare problem was renting gates to discount airlines. In line with economists' theories, more airlines should generate competition and drive down fares. Charlotte did accept discount airlines, but several questions remained: Did long-term slots or gate leases with legacy airlines limit start-up airlines from coming to the Charlotte Airport? Would more airline landings and takeoffs at peak times create congestion problems? Would a congestion-based fee reduce the landings at peak hours? Remember that Piedmont Airlines expanded its flights at Charlotte Douglas Airport after deregulation.

Writing in 1983, Stephen E. Creager noted that deregulation created a scarcity of slots at airports in high demand, thereby causing congestion. Creager even suggested that the FAA auction off some slots. He concluded, "In a deregulated airline industry, there must be much greater reliance on airports to ensure competitive performance of the industry."[28]

In the 1960s, U.S. Airways had 34,000 employees in the city as the airline was near bankruptcy. After the decline in air travel after 9/11, the airline had to lay off 1,700 employees. These layoffs did not stop a further slide in the airlines' fortunes. The instability of U.S. Airways had serious implications for the city of Charlotte.

LINKED FORTUNES OF AIRLINES AND THE CITY

Cities who live by air travel can die by its absence. In 2002, Charlotte mayor Pat McCrory commented on the linkage between the airline and the city's future: "The departure of the city basketball team [the Charlotte Hornets went to New Orleans] pales in comparison with the troubles at U.S. Airways. This year Charlotte's biggest economic development issue is the future viability of U.S. Airways."[29] The mayor hinted at mothballing the terminal to keep the airport viable. Yet without the terminal, Charlotte Douglas would lose its status as a major hub. Airport director Orr was more direct about the significance of the airport's hub status: "The hub brings companies to Charlotte and keeps them here. Without the hub, we would be the 49th-largest airport in the country."[30] Indeed, hubs have produced a more efficient airline system and helped support airports like Charlotte Douglas.

Robert Crandall, former CEO of American Airlines, wrote a *New York Times* editorial asking the federal government to rescue his industry. He set forth a variety of justifications for this request: "Our airlines, once the world leader, are now laggards in every category, including fleet age, service quality and international reputation. Fewer and fewer flights are on time. Airport congestion has become a staple of late-night comedy shows. An ever-higher percentage of bags are lost or sent to the wrong airports. Last-minute seats are harder and harder to find. Passenger complaints have skyrocketed. Airline service, by any standard, has become unacceptable."[31]

Despite what looked like chaos in the air travel industry, deregulation still had its true believers who supported their point with data and essays. In a 1990 article in the *New York Times,* Clifford Winston and Steven A. Morrison, coauthors of *The Economic Effect of Airline Deregulation*, wrote,

> Based on our calculations, the number of effective competitors at the route level has risen from an average of 1.5 in 1978 to 1.9 in 1988. This means that today only 17 percent of passengers travel on carriers that control more than 90 percent of the traffic on a route. In 1978 the figure was 28 percent. At the same time, 17 percent of passengers fly on carriers that control 20 percent or less of the traffic on their routes—up from 7 percent in 1978. Fewer carriers, yes, but they are competing with one another more often. Our calculations also show that throughout the decade deregulated fares have been below regulated fares by an average of 18 percent. This amounts to average annual savings for travelers of roughly $6 billion, calculated in 1988 dollars. But while fares have declined on average under deregulation, the spread of fares has increased. In 1978, less than half of 1 percent of travelers paid more than twice the average fare. In 1988 the figure was nearly 4 percent. In 1978 only, 10 percent of travelers paid fares less than 80 percent of the average. In 1988 more than 25 percent did.[32]

Winston and Morrison divided passengers into the categories of business and pleasure. While they conceded that business travelers paid more to fly than pleasure travelers did, they maintained that deregulation had been a success overall. Although deregulation had caused some dislocations, few people in the industry wanted to return to the pre-deregulation days. The post-deregulation decades saw growth in air travel, and lower fares attracted more passengers. However, the 2001 terrorist attack of the New York World Trade Center interrupted the democratization of air travel.

Journalist Joe Nocera agreed that airlines suffered low passenger loads due to the fallout from the 9/11 attack. He also noted that overall aircraft fuel costs rose from $16.8 billion to $50 billion between 2000 and 2012. The 2008 recession compounded the financial instability of airlines and cities. Quiet panic resulted as many airlines decided that mergers were the way to go. The big airline merger involved Delta buying Northwest Airlines, the pride of Minneapolis. At present, we are in a period of mega-airlines. Nocera concluded,

> The first decade of this century was, if anything, even tougher. First came 9/11. . . . What did consolidation give the airlines? Pricing power, as it's called. As the number of airlines dwindled, so did the number of routes and flights, as the airlines concluded that their health depended on cutting back the number of seats they offered. That's why when you fly today, the plane is likely to be full; there are simply fewer flights available. And that's also why airlines have been able to raise prices: Demand hasn't slackened nearly as much as supply has.
>
> What the American airline industry is today is an oligopoly, with two dominant carriers. The government could have attempted to prevent such an outcome when the Delta and United merger were announced.
>
> . . . And oligopolies, by their very nature, are anticompetitive. But it's a little late to be complaining about oligopolies.[33]

THE OVERALL IMPACT OF DEREGULATION

Airline deregulation had a tremendous impact on Charlotte Douglas International Airport and many other airports. Since 1978, 82 airlines have filed for bankruptcy and over 140 have closed their gates and sold their assets (e.g., Midway Airlines). When legacy airlines began to shut down, jobs disappeared, and the promise of low fares proved evanescent. The 1978 Airline Deregulation Act created new carriers, but it also exposed those flying giants with few resources. Economists had speculated that airlines would make money once they were free to compete; however, the industry lost over $10 billion. Although some fares decreased, so did the quality of service. "File, merge, or die" became the mantra for airlines.

The early eighties, specifically the years from 1980 to 1983, were rough for an airline industry facing rising fuel prices and decreasing demand. Moreover, routing options for Charlotte passengers had to be expanded. The fear about small communities losing service did not realize itself quickly. A study made five years later found that while some direct-flight services had been terminated, commuter airlines replaced the major carriers. Commuter airlines were still connected to Charlotte-type hubs.³⁴ CCAir was cited as a success as it was connected with Piedmont.³⁵ Over time, small North Carolina towns were able to get services.

In 1992, Sen. John McCain of Arizona stated, "The promise of deregulation has turned to ashes in our mouths, literally. We must find a way to reverse the recent, disturbing trends in the airline industry that threaten competition and its benefits."³⁶ The previous year, Bernard Wasow had stated in a *Charlotte Observer* editorial entitled "Airlines Are In a Tailspin," "Let us deliberately put into place the elements of a new regulatory system: further regulation of reservation systems, price or quantity limits to monopolistic practices at hubs, price or quantity limits to scheduling during peak-load hours, the elimination of kickback schemes." Wasow also advocated auctions of takeoff and landing slots. He wanted the airlines to be better at cost management than "bakeries or variety stores."³⁷ The city of Charlotte had stretched itself to accommodate the airlines. Now it was the airlines' turn to make changes. Lawyer Peter C. Carstensen made a similar argument:

> A special barrier to entry into some important markets is a lack of gates and landing slots. These two essential inputs are relatively fixed in quantity at any time. If the supply at an airport is fully committed, a potential entrant only can enter if it acquires facilities and landing rights from an existing firm. Even when the total is not fixed, it may be hard to find landing slots or acquire a set of gates so located that the new entrant can be an effective competitor, particularly in light of the hub and spoke integration that is essential for efficient operation.³⁸

Charlotte Douglas did not reverse its policy of limited landing slots. The fallout from airline deregulation continued, and exclusive landing patterns were institutionalized. Airline mergers helped consolidate a hub-and-spoke route system. Hubs were useful for airlines because they permitted more direct flights into Charlotte. This system in turn increased the number of seats filled on each flight. Full aircraft are hypothetically more efficient and cost effective. Yet according to a U.S. Department of Transportation study, this system created a "pocket of problems."³⁹ Indeed, the U.S. Airways hubs concentrated market power in Charlotte. This development led to a fare increase for passengers.

Although deregulation was considered the harbinger of low fares and discount airlines, the debate over the 1978 deregulation reform law's sufficiency continued long after its passage. Washington think tanks disagreed openly about the efficacy of deregulation. In 1990 the Economic Policy Institute found no or little effect on fares and services. In contrast, the Brookings Institution provided evidence that deregulation had worked.⁴⁰ Deregulation may have worked for some because the eight largest airlines accounted for 90 percent of the traffic. In the 1990s, American, United, Northwest, USAir, Texas Air (Continental and Eastern), Trans World, and Pan Am dominated the airways. Yet many of these airlines did not survive the decade.

People Airlines was the most famous discount airline, but despite the hoopla, it lasted only five years. Eastern and TWA Airlines subsequently went bankrupt. Delta Airlines merged with Northwest Airlines, United Airlines with Continental Airlines, and U.S. Airways with American Airlines. Southwest Airlines bought the struggling Air Tran Airlines for its gates in cities it did not yet serve. Timothy Vowles finds that the Southwest Effect had mixed results. Reduced fares in multi-airport regions yielded no increase in passenger traffic, and airlines kept their fares high at their hubs.[41] In 2001, there were fourteen major domestic airlines in the United States. As of 2015, there are now just four major airlines—American, Delta, Southwest, and United. Together they control about 87 percent of the domestic market.

Charlotte Douglas International Airport was affected by these changes. Some modifications enhanced its position as a hub, and others resulted in the loss of airline competition at the airport. American Airlines continued its domination at Charlotte Douglas. Passenger fares remained higher than at other North Carolina city airports, but this did not affect the growth of the banking industry. Banks were at the tail end of a deregulation sequence that had started after the 1970s. The arguments for reforming banking were similar to those for airline deregulation.

DEREGULATION PARALLELS IN BANKING

Banking started in Charlotte the same way it did in most cities. Banks grew because they provided safety for the savings of ordinary people. The money pool provided entrepreneurs the finances to create businesses and to conduct a variety of financial transactions. In Charlotte's early days, the bank's money was used for agricultural and textile mill development. Union National Bank was founded in 1908, and the Charlotte branch of the Federal Bank of Richmond opened nineteen years later. In addition, the McFadden Act of 1927 allowed more concentration of financial activity within states, and it also permitted banks to acquire banks in other states. In reaction to the Great Depression, Congress passed the Glass-Steagall Act of 1933 prohibiting investment speculation involving banks. The act also established the Federal Deposit Insurance Corporation (FDIC) to provide insurance for bank depositors. This restored confidence in banking and prevented depositor runs on the banks.

World War II changed the nation's industrial structure and accelerated Charlotte's release from its textile moorings. The war's end marked growing recognition, at least for the business elite, that the extant economic base of the city was not sustainable. Banking was seen as the wave of the future. In 1957 American Commercial Bank was formed. In 1959 twenty-four-year-old banker Hugh McColl came to Charlotte from Bennettsville, South Carolina, and found a rather lifeless town. He stated, "Charlotte was a boring town. You could fire a shotgun down the street and not hit anyone. People kept saying Charlotte is a good place to raise a family. It was a Southern Baptist town. You could not buy whiskey by the drink. There was no live music. Yet it was great place to raise a family in 1950 and even today but not for everyone. Some people [blacks] had a millstone around their necks. They were living in a theoretically separate but equal town."[42]

In the late fifties, local banks began to merge. American Trust and Commercial National, the bank that young McColl joined, started a merger mania that would characterize Charlotte's emerging banking industry. Banking was welcomed as the city's new business, a turnstile for new types of talented immigrants and social change.

Journalist Rick Rothacker chronicled the rise of banking in Charlotte, relating a story of smart young bankers pushing the merger envelope. In 1958 Union National Bank merged with First National and Trust Company to form First Union. The new bank headquarters were moved from Asheville to Charlotte. In 1973 thirty-two-year-old Edward "Ed" Crutchfield became president of First Union. In 1974 thirty-nine-year-old Hugh McColl became president of NCNB. Both men assumed leadership of their banks during the stock market crash and the so-called stagflation recession of 1973–1974. The two men met the challenge of leading their institutions through a period of change and regulation.

Just as the year 1978 changed airlines, it also changed the way banks operated. In general, the late seventies were a turning point for Charlotte banks. In 1978, the U.S. Supreme Court held in *Marquette vs. First of Omaha* against state usury rate ceilings. Congress later passed the Depository Institutions Deregulation and Monetary Control Act of 1980 that increased deposit insurance from $40,000 to $100,000. The new law also promoted a phaseout of interest rate ceilings on deposit accounts.

After Pres. Ronald Reagan took office, Congress passed the Garn–St. Germain Depository Institutions Act of 1982 that deregulated thrift banks. In 1983, North Carolina passed the Reciprocal Interstate Banking Act, known as Article 17, that promoted acquisition of banks in other states. In 1989 Congress passed the Financial Institutions Reform Recovery and Enforcement Act. Bank mergers were now possible if approved by federal and state regulators. This major change in North Carolina banking history laid the groundwork for the growth of local banks. By 1985 Edward Crutchfeld, now chairman of First Union, had made a series of acquisitions. Acquiring out-of-state banks was also a strategy used by NCNB's McColl.

During Pres. Bill Clinton's administration, Congress passed the Riegle-Neal Interstate Banking and Branching Efficiency Act of 1994. This act repealed part of the McFadden Act and allowed banks to open branches across state lines. The inception of regional banks facilitated the connections among interstate business communities. First Union then acquired First Fidelity in 1995.

Rothacker stated that Hugh McColl, president of Bank of America, "got part of the credit for the bill after cultivating a relationship with Clinton."[43] Free from restrictions on interstate banking and branching, Charlotte banks could now do business in any state.[44] Two years earlier, McColl had made the now-famous statement "Let the strong take over the weak so that we can move forward."[45] In 1998, NationsBank of Charlotte merged with Bank of America. The following year, the Gramm-Leach-Bliley Act repealed the Glass-Steagall Act of 1933 prohibiting banks from mixing banking and investment. Banking was on a roll in the eighties and nineties; large banks were acting like airlines, buying and merging with smaller ones. At the same time, Charlotte was growing rapidly and finally getting the recognition the pro-growth coalition craved. When Crutchfield retired in 2000, his bank had assets over $200 billion. When McColl retired a year later, Bank of America was a major national bank. Indeed, the early part of the decade was a heady time for American banks.

The nation's largest banks were in the international investment banking business—selling exotic instruments such as derivatives. However, these exotic investment instruments collapsed, and the nation went into the worst financial crisis since the Great Depression. Caused in part by the subprime mortgage scandal, the Great Recession of 2008 sent shock waves throughout the entire banking industry. Bank of America and Wachovia were not immune. In 2008, Congress passed the Emergency Economic Stabilization Act designed to steady banking by providing more capital for the banks. In October 2008, the federal government injected $125 billion into nine major banks and increased deposit insurance to $250,000.

In 2008, Wachovia announced a $393 million first-quarter loss and cut dividends. Bank of America bought Countrywide Financial, a major mortgage lender. Also in 2008, Wells Fargo bought Charlotte-based Wachovia Corporation for $15.1 billion, making it a superbank. Bank of America brought Merrill Lynch, the world's largest management corporation, the next year.[46]

During the President Obama administration, Congress passed the Dodd-Frank Wall Street Reform and Consumer Protection Act of 2010. With this reform law, the federal government acted to regulate the investment industry, protect consumers, and stabilize the airline and banking industries. In the process, it secured Charlotte's position as the nation's second-largest banking center.[47]

Some would argue that the seventies were also a time of social and racial deregulation. The previous decades of civil rights activism had a profound impact on Charlotte.

RACIAL DEREGULATIONS

As was suggested earlier, in Charlotte, like most southern cities, housing, schools, neighborhoods, and friendships were segregated by race. In this, the city was like most others in the South, a region that had long been racially regulated. Though Charlotte was not the quintessential segregated city, it followed most of the South's discriminatory practices. On May 17, 1954, the U.S. Supreme Court declared separate-but-equal schools unconstitutional, emboldening civil rights organizations and accelerating the black civil rights movement in Charlotte.

The civil rights movement reached Charlotte Airport that same year when four black leaders were denied service at a restaurant.[48] The city council referred the case to city attorney John Shaw, who declared that the nondiscrimination clause in the lease contract only applied to persons in transit.[49] Cases like this one prompted Congress to pass the 1964 Civil Rights Act, which outlawed discrimination in public accommodations, and the 1965 Voting Rights Act, which outlawed discrimination at the ballot box. These could be seen as deregulation of rigid southern racial policies. The 1971 *Swann* case on school desegregation was a turning point in Charlotte's history. However, it did not reverse racial patterns that had been in place for years. In a review of the 1970s, *Charlotte Observer* reporter Bill Arthur highlighted a variety of successes and challenges for Charlotte but concluded, "Desegregation of our schools was Charlotte's toughest problem and most significant event of the '70s—its most remarkable achievement."[50]

Charlotte's iconoclastic journalist Harry Golden, who published a small newspaper called the *Carolina Israelite*, attacked Jim Crow laws and southern traditions with satire. Sit-ins and protests by young people began to undermine what was once considered sacrosanct. Racial regulation laws (Jim Crow laws) that kept minorities on the bottom of the economic ladder were being declared illegal. Clearly, new social and racial deregulation policies were indicated. Social deregulation is defined as changing practices and social customs by replacing laws and changing attitudes and social relations. These social changes brought with them changes in local politics and agendas.

Southern cities like Charlotte, once considered relatively economically undeveloped, grew in part because they abandoned social regulation. This change came at a time of growing recognition, at least among the economic elite, that a change in racial relations was required for Charlotte to enter the mainstream economy. For the young and growing banking industry, this modification was imperative. Mayor Brookshire's public statement and actions on race relations made it clear that elites' opinion had changed. As was pointed out earlier, the national media celebrated Charlotte's attempt to rid itself of its segregation legacy. By 1983 the city had elected its first African American mayor, Harvey Gantt. At first glance, it would appear that changing social relations had little if anything to do with the airport's growth. A closer examination uncovers elites' recognition that a progressive reputation would give Charlotte a competitive advantage in attracting businesses. This image worked for Atlanta in the 1960s, when its motto was "The city too busy to hate." Charlotte could be the city in which school integration worked. As was suggested earlier, Charlotte took some of its marketing cues from Atlanta's success.

Social change was in the air in the late seventies and the early eighties. The airline industry may have thought it was immune to social change, but it was wrong.

SUMMARY

The black civil rights movement facilitated the remaking of Charlotte's social structure. In the 1960s, the federal government further deregulated southern race relations by passing the 1964 Civil Rights Act and the 1965 Voting Rights Act. In 1978, the federal government deregulated air travel routes and fares. The story of Charlotte Douglas Airport cannot be separated from the ripple effects of technology. Advances in aircraft technology obliged the airport to expand. Charlotte was required to invest more financial resources into the airport. In turn, the airport benefited by having more flights, leasing more gates, and attracting discount airlines and related businesses. In the 1980s and 1990s, the federal government began deregulating banking, thereby providing a catalyst for local banking industry expansion. These events may seem unrelated, but they were critical to Charlotte's transformation. Each deregulation event took place in its own political time. In order to become a new Charlotte, the city leadership had to change its southern image and gain national recognition as a progressive city. Although they never linked change explicitly to banking and airport developments, city politicians knew an image change was imperative.

Charlotte, like most hub cities, found itself in the middle of airline deregulation's consequences. Airports had relied on long-term leases to retain airlines and to stabilize expansion. The demise of the airline-friendly CAB compounded airlines' financial instability. Ten years after the deregulation law, Tom Eblen reported, "Since deregulation, annual airline industry profit margins have averaged a slim 0.7 percent, compared to 4.5 percent for other U.S. industries."[51]

The nation saw the entry of discount airlines and a brief period of lower fares. In 1978 there were 272 million airline passengers. As a result of deregulation, 447 million people flew on commercial airlines.[52] While discount airlines were a brief hit, legacy airlines merged over time and purchased the airline start-ups. The more successful Southwest Airlines and JetBlue Airlines survived, but even they have been forced to grow or risk being taken over. At present, the battle for gates continues. There are fewer airlines, but economic uncertainty still haunts them.

Airlines are like fish in the sea—the big ones eat the small ones. Mergers are a central part of carriers' legacy and economics. Indeed, eleven mergers and sixteen acquisitions occurred between 1978 and 1984.[53] Since they are not good at profit-making and fiscal strength, airlines consolidate for growth and temporary stability. The contested environment of airlines is full of tension between the desire to compete energetically and the allure of merging and becoming bigger. As history shows, no airline is immune to the merger mania.

The year 1978 seems so far away. Journalists still reference the Airline Deregulation Act when writing about the decline of start-up airlines. We now know that legacy air carriers did not fare well in the new contestable environment. Remember that Northwest, Continental, Eastern, U.S. Air, Trans World, and Pan Am are all gone. Discount airlines proved trendy for a few years, and they bought cheaper aircraft and hired nonunionized workers. The stronger airlines weathered the deregulation storm by outmarketing the newcomers and making some smart and timely pricing policies.

Even so, bankruptcies and mergers created a variety of planning problems for airports. No one predicted the current level of concentration, and pricing continues to be a problem. Yet the "pocket of problems" is deeper. Airlines reacted by building a series of hub-and-spoke systems that allowed them to control most of an airport's resources. However, not all airports enjoyed the same level of success.

Discount airlines have responded by creating catchy television ads and prohibiting travel sites from listing their prices. Southwest Airlines has a better frequent-flier program than some of the larger airlines. However, discount airlines still make a limited number of landings, and they often require passengers to change planes in areas located opposite to their designation. A Charlotte passenger may have to fly to Baltimore or Chicago Midway to go to New Orleans.

Airline deregulation was a brief win for passengers, who now have fewer carriers for travel choices. Dissatisfaction with airlines has increased, and it is compounded by new fees for the premium seats, baggage fees, and the rise of self-ticketing. More importantly, a hub-and-spoke system will likely stay in place because it works for airlines. For southeastern passengers traveling outside hubs like Atlanta and Charlotte, the days of nonstop flights are disappearing. The politics of these cities cannot change this fact, and airlines will continue to search for new revenue sources.

Racial and social deregulation was a long-term victory for the city. It prompted African Americans to enter politics and provided more overall economic mobility. It also helped develop Charlotte's cosmopolitan image. Generally speaking, banking deregulation went too far; related transactions led to the 2008 recession, the fallout from which hurt Charlotte banks. It may take years for the city's two major banks to fully recover. Moreover, the deregulation demonstrated that assets have to be organized to survive, compete, and grow. This was especially true for the city's biggest economic asset, the airport. The next chapter will examine how the city organizes this resource.

Hugh McColl (*right*) and
Johnny Harris (*below*)
(courtesy of *Charlotte Observer*
and Hugh McColl and Johnny Harris)

Clarence O. Kuester
(courtesy of UNCC Library and Betty Kuester)

Mayor Ben Douglas
(courtesy of UNCC Library)

Left to right, Bill Nebel, W. S. Creighton, Mayor Charles Lambeth, Amelia Earhart, and Clarence O. Kuester
(courtesy of *Charlotte Observer*)

Jerry Orr, Josh Birmingham, and Lou Martinelli
(courtesy of *Charlotte Observer* and Charlotte Airport Department)

CHAPTER 4

Organizing the City's Greatest Asset

IT IS IMPORTANT TO REMEMBER that airports are not stand-alone built systems. Instead, they are products of changes in their political and economic surroundings. Equally important is the fact that technological breakthroughs can overrun the capacity of airport buildings and runways. Planned obsolescence is not a part of the planning for an airport building; however, technology forces change and additions. No group is more aware of this fact than airport managers. They are constantly responding to local politicians, health emergencies, strikes, and civil rights demands, as well as the rise of terrorism.

Thankfully, all these management demands and challenges are met out of passengers' sight. Understandably, air travelers often go in and out of city airports without paying much attention to their locations and structures. For these individuals, the airport is a just a place to park, rent a car, or get directions. Air travelers are less likely to know how an airport is organized or who runs it. Some may not care about the politics underlying airport management and development. Many just know that their local airport is the starting point connecting them to the rest of the world.

North Carolina is home to ten public airports, four of them international airports with incoming carriers that fly outside the United States. Regional airports connect flights from small cities to the various airline hubs. The hubs, like Charlotte Douglas International Airport, collect passengers at one place and reroute them to their destinations. In other words, Charlotte's airport acts like an aeromobility facilitator for the state, the region, and the world.

Aeromobility today is restricted only by cost—flying is available to anyone who can purchase an airline ticket. A Charlotte resident can board a carrier at Charlotte Douglas International Airport, make one connection in Chicago O'Hare International Airport, and land in Tokyo's Narita International Airport in sixteen hours. The Internet connects these airports, but they have different management and governing structures. They also have different terminal designs, concession offerings, and organizational cultures. These differences reflect the politics of airports and the context of their relationships to the host economies and cities. Aside from being places where tickets are collected and passengers are accommodated, airports also control the transportation of cargo, maintain aircraft, and provide safety and security. In most large cities in the world, airports are at the axis of the economy and as such are exchange platforms.

As a result, most travelers are temporary denizens in airports, people who spend their time waiting, eating/drinking, and passing through security lines. University of North Carolina economist John D. Kasarda has coined the term "aerotropolis."[1] Kasarda and Greg Lindsay define an aerotropolis as "an airport-integrated region, extending as far as sixty miles from the inner clusters of hotels, offices, distribution and logistics facilities."[2] Hence, airports are more than places to enplane and deplane. They are subcommunities with an organizational culture and routine.

In addition, airports are communities defined by uniformed workers, who perform a variety of jobs to make passengers feel safe and comfortable. After 9/11, airports became places where security remains ever present. Both uniformed and plainclothes security officers check for potential terrorists and disoriented or ill passengers. Furthermore, computer monitors are as widespread as uniforms; passengers read monitors that route or organize them by concourses and gates. This is not to suggest that all airports are equally efficient or architecturally pleasing. Some airports are unsightly "front doors" to their cities. Poorly managed and unattractive, these facilities are caricatured as detention centers that briefly detain Americans in transit.

Since most intercity travelers can now afford flights, all classes of Americans interact in airports. With the democratization of air travel and cheap flights came a corresponding decline in food service and legroom. Quick flights made onboard food service unnecessary, and stretch-out spaces gave way to more seats. Some passengers understandably compare traveling on airplanes to riding the bus; people who used to travel by bus can now fly. Finally, air travel, except for first class and business class, is a socially leveling experience. Frequent fliers, tourists, and occasional fliers share the same space. Waiting for a flight provides a people-watching opportunity. And passengers rarely dress formally to board an airplane.

Moreover, as a part of their advertising and marketing schemes, most airlines now encourage the flight crew to greet and thank passengers. Since airlines basically have a captive clientele, it should follow that their flights are full, and their profits break records. This is not the case, as they continually go bankrupt and merge to stay afloat. Part of the reason for this paradox is that the airline industry is an uncertain business. Although most carriers employ normal management models, the business is so sensitive to the national economy and fuel prices that its profit margins are quite uneven. In addition, airline employees are heavily unionized. Cost fluctuations and mismanagement pushed many of the so-called legacy airlines such as Eastern and Pan Am out of business. Fuel costs, debt services, and union contracts are soft bellies of airline management.

At first glance, airline mergers seem unrelated to local politics and airports. Closer consideration reveals that airlines need city politicians and local business leaders to make the landings and takeoffs more effective and plausible. Carriers need city mayors, the most visible elected officials, to back them. Mayors' backing often takes the form of supporting letters regarding airline issues such as mergers, international flights, security, Federal Aviation Administration (FAA) rules, and the U.S. Department of Justice.

Airlines may also solicit a state congressional delegation to intervene with the FAA and the U.S. Justice Department. Because of the city's growth, economic development ambitions, and the airline industry's uncertainty, Charlotte and the airlines benefited from a symbiotic relationship. During North Carolina's attempt to take over the Charlotte Airport, discussed in detail in chapter 8, the U.S. Justice Department was considering the merger of U.S. Airways and American Airlines. The Charlotte Chamber of Commerce publicly endorsed the merger. Chamber president Bob Morgan told the *Charlotte Observer*, "The Charlotte Chamber of Commerce believes the merger of U.S. Airways and American Airlines will further advance our ability to attract new companies and create jobs for the local economy."[3] Travel analyst Henry Hartevelt stated that the connection with American Airlines would help the city's future growth in international markets such as Latin America and Asia. Mike Boyd, an aviation analyst, concluded, "If this merger goes away now, Charlotte unfortunately would miss out on a lot of future growth."[4] The airlines ultimately merged and became the new American Airlines.

Postindustrial cities cannot insulate themselves from the uncertainty of the air travel industry. All rumors of a merger are taken seriously because they could create instability for the airport. Bankruptcies and mergers are a part of airline history, and they have profoundly impacted airport development. A running joke among airport watchers is that a group of investors will borrow some money, start an airline, and get a few gates and routes. But after a year or two, a larger airline will buy the newcomers. This joke may be lost on outsiders, but mergers are what airlines do. Carriers are not inclined to compete for the most affordable fares or for staff; they can simply buy out the competition. Moreover, mergers are not simply a matter of repainting airlines, changing the uniforms of the crew, and putting up different signs at gates. This complicated process often involves differences in organizational culture and union contracts, as well as changes in fares, schedules, and the number of nonstop flights. Such alterations are developmental challenges for local airports.

Airports like Charlotte Douglas International are linked to the airlines' financial plights. Although carriers enjoy a near oligopoly regarding prices, their business is still a turbulent one. The capital-intensive airline industry requires considerable investment in equipment, labor costs, and fuel. Good leadership and timing may not be enough for success. As airlines often overreach and misjudge passengers' preferences, they must adjust to changing conditions by manipulating schedules and modifying the size of aircraft and routes. As I suggested earlier, airlines are also very vulnerable to labor management strife, which journalist Thomas Petzinger's *Hard Landing* suggests creates chaos in the industry. The graveyard of airlines is full of once-distinguished carriers.[5]

In order to understand the plight of airlines one must appreciate the leadership sages of the industry. Airline CEOs are among the nation's leading corporate celebrities. Their colorful history includes stars such as Eastern Air Lines' Eddie Rickenbacker, Continental Airlines' Frank Borman and Frank Lorenzo, American Airlines' Doug Parker, and Delta's Edward Bastian. As airlines seek the best and the brightest to lead them, air carriers continue to recruit a panoply of highly regarded managers.

Yet leadership alone cannot overcome the political context of the industry. Airports exist in an environment of mergers and changes in federal air travel regulations. Therefore, airports have to change as airlines change. Unlike air carriers, airports are obligated to be welcoming and to be seen as stable institutions. Their funding sources include landing fees, gate rentals, and multiple concession retailers. Well-managed airports often look like malls featuring all types of conveniences for travelers, but they are designed to efficiently manage the maintenance, takeoff/landing, and security of aircraft. Passengers are often oblivious to the politics holding airlines and airports together.

Most passengers are unaware of aircraft manufacturers' role in making air travel policy. Air travelers are also unaware of the lobbying and air travel politics in Congress. The airline lobby (e.g., the Air Transportation Association—ATA—which is one of the most successful Washington interest groups) has been around since the creation of airline regulation. In response, Congress has afforded the airline industry a near monopoly in intercity travel. Laws regulating airports exemplify this policy bias by providing incentives to these facilities (e.g., the Airport and Airway Development Act of 1970 and the Airway Revenue Act of 1970, amended in 1976 and 1982). All of these laws redound on local politics. Cities must accommodate new laws by making political adjustments involving land use and access roads. City council agendas often feature applications for available federal category grants; city bureaucrats rarely encounter a grant that they would not investigate and perhaps apply for. In other words, local politics concerning airports often provides a reaction to federal airport policy. In the case of Charlotte, federal airport expansion policies matched the city's economic development agenda.

In general, few city residents are aware of the political context of local airports. They may not know the names of any given facility's chief executive officer. Fewer residents are aware of airport technocrats' struggle to evade political oversight and accountability. Claiming federal mandates, airport directors seek to protect themselves from city hall oversight. Still fewer individuals realize that airlines play cities against each other in much the same way professional sports franchises treat their host cities. Airlines may terminate nonstop service and rearrange flight schedules at will. Most passengers who board small regional jets with major airline logos are unaware that the major airlines neither own nor operate these aircraft. Most passengers just want to reach their destinations and enter and exit airports quickly.

THE ORGANIZATIONAL CULTURE OF AIRPORTS

Airports have to be understood within their organizational context and therefore separated from their images in popular culture. Since the invention of airplanes, flying has become a part of the popular culture. Celebrity pilots like Amelia Earhart, Charles Lindbergh, Howard Hughes, and Capt. Chesley Sullenberger epitomize the courage, vision, and heroism of flying. Even after more than a century of existence, air travel retains some of its adventure, glamour, and fascination—so much so that Hollywood has made it a recurrent theme in filmmaking. A trilogy of movies concerning airports was released in the 1970s. The plot of *Airport 1970* involves attempts to keep the airport open during a snowstorm, and the subplot centers around a suicidal bomber trying to bring down a Boeing 707. Throughout, the movie explores issues such as airline operations, noise pollution, and employee relations. The second installment in the trilogy is *Airport 1975*, a disaster movie involving a Boeing 747-100 whose pilots are killed when a small plane crashes into the cockpit. A helicopter subsequently inserts a new pilot into the plane so that it can land.

The later film *Airport '77* takes a different angle. When a private Boeing 747 carrying rich people transporting expensive art is hijacked, the survivors are stranded on an island in the Bermuda Triangle. Perhaps the most amusing of these movies was entitled *The Terminal*. This film tells the story of a man without citizenship in any country who is trapped in an airport resembling New

York City's John F. Kennedy International Airport. These movies are fantasies, and they do not represent what most Americans encounter when they go to airports for intercity and foreign travel. The reality is that airplane rides have become rather dull.

Charlotte Douglas International Airport's operations may never match the drama of airport movies. But as we saw in the previous chapter, the airport became a jewel in the crown of the Queen City. Obviously, the real airport's internal dynamics are rarely discussed. Why isn't the story of this immobile infrastructure constantly appearing on the front page of the *Charlotte Observer* or serving as a regular lead-in for the local evening news? The city of Charlotte built the airport and is obligated to maintain and upgrade it. Earlier chapters outline how federal and local politics influenced the airport's growth and maintenance. It has been suggested that hub airports like Charlotte Douglas are job multipliers and magnets for businesses and people. If so, why the relatively low media profile? The fact is that safe takeoffs and landings are rarely newsworthy.

For the public, airport growth seems fine as long as it is self-sustaining. However, history suggests passenger traffic reflects the economy, and the air travel industry is amenable to cycles of management disequilibrium. Accordingly, management of the city-owned airport had to keep pace with the "ripple of aircraft technology." Aircraft have come a long way since their invention. The enclosed cockpit, more elaborate instrumentation, passenger accommodation seating, and jet engines are just a few of the changes made in these flying machines. Just as early media commentators considered airplanes attention-grabbing gimmicks fit only for carnival and air shows, many manufacturers deemed the piston engine the technological ceiling for aircraft. Therefore, earlier airport planners believed that all a pilot needed was a clear, straight runway to land and take off. This may have worked for the early landing fields, but with the advent of passenger service more infrastructure was needed.

As I have suggested, sophisticated and permanent airports with hangars, terminals, and repair shops were necessary once scheduled passenger service became profitable. Airports had to develop into passenger friendly facilities—travelers need more accommodations than places to sit and wait on a flight. Thus, the terminal as we know it became essential to the air travel industry. Moreover, the invention of the jet airplane changed what airports were required to do to accommodate these new aircraft. Bigger and more powerful aircraft need longer and longer runways.

This chapter examines the financial and management operations of Charlotte Douglas International Airport. Like all airports, Charlotte Douglas was required to stay current with the federal government's regulations and the airlines' expectations. Accordingly, the federal rules play a significant role in airport management. This chapter will investigate how Charlotte Douglas emerged as a hub. Richard de Neufville and Amedeo Odoni state, "Hub-and-spoke network structures allow airlines to serve many origin-destination (O-D) markets with fewer flights, requiring fewer aircraft departures that generate fewer 'available seat-kilometers' (ASKs) at lower total operating costs than a complete point-to-point route network."[6] Hub status entails creating more gates, modifying boarding areas, and upgrading concessions and security.

THE ROLE OF THE FEDERAL GOVERNMENT

In chapter 2 I discussed how the federal government got involved in the technification of aircraft. I also describe how regulations mandated changes in airports' construction to accommodate these ever-changing aircraft. Starting with the U.S. Department of Commerce, the Civil Aeronautics Board, and then the Federal Aviation Administration, the federal government promulgated more and more regulations for airport operations. Because Congress mandated a national plan for airports, airports were not allowed to remain static and outdated. They had to meet standards and plan for the future. A written plan includes collecting data and making predictions about ridership. Consultant companies specialized in producing attractive local plans. As we shall see in chapter 5, the use of consultants expanded the grand patronage of city politicians.

Aircraft accidents, hijackings, and terrorists also changed what airports needed to do to protect air travelers. Accordingly, these incidents created more regulations and report writing. As we saw in the history chapter, the federal government often awarded airports grants to build towers and runways. Aside from a series of category grants available to airports, changing aircraft models promoted the sophistication and technification of airports. Airport managers and city officials had to stay alert. The federal government made funding offers that local airports like Charlotte Douglas could not refuse.

The growth of technology in aircraft, runways, and aircraft control towers transformed airport managers into technocrats. Indeed, as aircraft became more sophisticated, serving them promoted a division of the staff into those with essential and nonessential status. Accordingly, the more technical the aspects of accommodating airlines and passenger transition, the more management believed some issues did not need to be cleared by the city manager and city council. Consequently, the staff began defining operational issues as technical ones. Members of the city council were socialized to accept these technical issues as beyond the scope of the council's work. Yet the staff had to keep the elected politicians in the loop. As we shall see in the chapter on local politics, some changes in airports created political problems.

Inevitably, the technical requirements of airport operations overlapped with local politics. Nevertheless, airport decisions were presented as infrastructure imperatives that did not include raising taxpayer costs and concerns. Over the years, this narrative of technical issues served the interests of those who wanted to nurture an inattentive host community. For example, citizens were never involved with airport leasing practices. Before deregulation, the practice of signing long-term leasing agreements with airlines prevented new carriers from coming into the airport. Questions that should have been debated include the matter of whether Charlotte Douglas's managers made leasing agreements with tenants such as U.S. Airways and Eastern Air Lines and included allowing them to block competition from other airlines.

Leasing policies are at the core of airports' existence. Yet the media and the city council hosted no open debates about this critical issue. Noncompetition clauses were permitted before deregulation. Yet legacy airlines retained their financial advantage during deregulation, in part because little public debate addressed their relationship with their host airports. This circumstance can be explained to an extent by the airport's budget relationship with the host city.

THE STRUCTURE OF CHARLOTTE DOUGLAS

Charlotte Douglas International Airport is a municipal enterprise agency (i.e., a city agency funded by user fees), and it is expected to be self-sustaining. The city of Charlotte's three entrepreneurial agencies—the Charlotte Water Department, Charlotte Area Transit, and Charlotte Douglas International Airport—are all expected to be self-supporting. Their budgets are segregated from the rest of the city budget. In fact, these agencies perform a countywide service and operate on fees. As reported earlier, the airport has needed the city of Charlotte's general obligation bond prowess to fund expansion. Such bonds can be sold at low interest rates. Expansion always entails indirect cost. Like most city agencies, Charlotte Douglas has to stay within its budget. The task for such an agency is to keep current with cost challenges and make a profit to cover pending expenditures. Charlotte Douglas is not unique in facing this task, for the financial challenge is related to the structure of American airports.

Airport managers face different challenges based on the ownership of the airport. The type of ownership defines the airport's relationship with local politics. For example, airports are owned and managed by twenty-four major cities (e.g., Miami International, Chicago O'Hare, Denver International). These facilities are involved in municipal politics. The state of Maryland operates Baltimore-Washington International Airport (BWI), and the state of Hawaii operates Honolulu International Airport. State-owned airports allow managers to bypass local politics. Of the twenty-two airport authorities, the most famous are Boston Logan International Airport (Massport), Dallas / Fort Worth International Airport, and Seattle-Tacoma International Airport. Airport authorities resemble special districts, a type of independent regional subgovernment authorized by a state. And in one case, an interstate compact is involved. The Port Authority of New York and New Jersey operates three airports—Newark International Airport, John F. Kennedy International Airport, and LaGuardia International Airport. In the case of the Port Authority of New York and New Jersey, the interstate compact is authorized by Congress and comanaged by the States of New York and New Jersey.

In the case of Charlotte Douglas, a municipal airport operating under a council-manager form of government, airport directors report to the city managers and the city council. In addition, both city managers and airport directors are relatively insulated from electoral accountability. The mayor cannot appoint or remove the airport director. The city's elected officials serve on a two-year election cycle. In an elected strong mayor-council government like Atlanta's, the mayor hires and fires the airport managers.

As was discussed in the history chapter, the city of Charlotte built the airport in the late 1930s and began full operation of the facility after World War II. Although Charlotte Douglas does not receive operating funds from the city, money flows between the city and the airport. Indeed, the airport has to pay for all city-furnished services, including the use of Charlotte-Mecklenburg Police Department. The airport's revenue comes from landing fees, terminal concessions, cargo space, and parking. As explained below, the airport landing fees are subjected to federal regulations. Concession fees depend on the market traffic and passengers' buying preferences. Comfortable browsing is also critical for selling passengers food, drink, and other things.[7]

A 1979 report to the Charlotte City Council includes a preface acknowledging the airport's role as a self-sustaining enterprise. The report also describes how the airport planners should work with the Finance Department to make its capital improvement program financially sound.

> Although managed as a department of city government, the airport receives no tax revenues and must depend on airport operating revenues to defray operating

and capital costs. As a consequence, the airport must be operated as a business. Operating expenses must be programmed within available revenues and capital improvements must be funded from existing revenues or future earnings. Planning for capital facilities must then include planning for the financing thereof. Increasing use of air transportation for both business and private purposes over the last ten years has combined with the aging of existing facilities so as to require extensive capital improvements at Douglas Airport.[8]

REVENUES AND FEES

Unlike the two other city entrepreneurial agencies, Charlotte Douglas International Airport is considered a job multiplier and magnet. This unique function supports its reputation as a revenue maker, not a revenue taker. Under former director Jerry Orr, the airport gained a national reputation as a low-cost airport. Such airports are coveted by airlines seeking to constrain operating costs. Indeed, the current and bigger tenant American Airlines, formerly U.S. Airways, has always had a large stake in the low costs associated with Charlotte Douglas. During the debate about the merger of U.S. Airways and American Airlines, aviation analyst Mike Boyd stated, "But this much is clear, with or without a merger: Charlotte Douglas is one of the world's cheapest airports for airlines to operate. Charlotte's cost-per-enplanement is 96 cents and is expected to remain below $1 through 2017, according to credit rating company Fitch Ratings. That compares to $9.65 at Philadelphia International Airport, another U.S. Airways hub, and $6.59 at Dallas / Fort Worth."[9]

The questions are whether the airport income is sufficient and what the indirect costs to taxpayers and nonusers of the airport are. Indirect costs are those costs not directly related to airport functions, that is, administrative costs related to airport employees being, in effect, city employees. Ordinarily, aeronautical revenues come from landing fees and cargo. Aeronautical income has never been sufficient to cover the entire operating cost of the airport. Table 2, which became available in 2015, shows the 2014 revenues and expenditures for Charlotte Douglas Airport. The information in this table concerns just one year and does not summarize trends.

This table also shows the shortfall in the passenger fees and contract facility charges. Parking and concession revenues offset these deficits. Most passengers are usually unaware that the hot dogs they buy subsidize the cost of aeronautical operations. As a hub, Charlotte Douglas is a temporary landing spot for connecting and layover passengers. Since food is no longer available on short flights, layover passengers will buy foods at concession stands. Parking and contract

Table 2. Revenues and Expenditures, 2014

	Budget	Actual	Variance—Positive (Negative)
Revenues			
Terminal Area	$29,632	$33,609	3,977
Airfield	17,534	22,644	5,110
Concessions	51,495	52,890	1,395
Parking	36,814	40,824	4,010
Passenger Facility Charges	29,893	59,526	29,633
Contract Facility Charges	3,819	10,009	6,190
Other	35,327	27,772	(7,555)
Investment Earnings	3,025	4,841	1,816
Total Revenues	207,539	252,115	44,576
Expenditures			
Operating	129,716	116,831	12,885
Nonoperating	15,239	14,777	462
Total Expenditures	144,955	131,608	13,347
Revenues Over Expenditures	62,584	120,507	57,923
Transfers In			
Airport Debt Service	24	24	—
Airport Capital Projects	762	762	—
Total Transfers In	786	786	—
Transfers Out			
Airport Debt Service	64,304	52,520	11,784
Airport Capital Projects	37,317	37,317	—
Total Transfers Out	101,621	89,837	11,784
Revenues and Transfers Over (Under) Expenditures and Transfers	$(38,251)	$31,456	$69,707

Source: "City of Charlotte, North Carolina Airport Operating Fund, Schedules of Revenues, Expenditures and Transfers—Budget and Actual (Non-GAAP Basis) for the Year Ended June 30, 2014 (in Thousands)," p. 151, http://charmeck.org/city/charlotte/Finance/Documents/FY14%20CAFR.pdf.

services are a different matter; they are fixed and predictable. In researching fifty-nine U.S. airports from 2002 to 2010, Yap Yin Choo finds strong evidence of cross subsidization from non-aeronautical revenue to aeronautical charges.[10] He states, "Non-aeronautical revenue is undeniably an important stream of revenue for airports, as on average, it accounts for slightly more than 50% of total revenue for most large and medium airports. This revenue is income generated from food and beverages, retail business, parking, car rentals, and other concession revenues. Depending on the type of agreement with airlines, airports can make use of this source of revenue to cross-subsidize aeronautical revenue."[11]

Clearly airports cannot survive on aeronautical income alone. Indeed, federal regulations limit their landing fees. Hence, there is a need for airports to find creative ways to get revenue. In this situation, Charlotte Douglas is like other airports competing to provide highly visible amenities. The facility's rocking chairs and potted plants are part of selling the airport as a place to land and relax. In 2010, *USA Today* quoted Sean Broderick of the American Association of Airport Executives (AAAE) as follows:

> As recently as 10 or 15 years ago, airports were more like utilities with one customer: airlines. And it was the airlines that were responsible for getting customers and taking care of them. Now, airports play a huge role in generating their own income and providing amenities and services that airlines no longer provide. In markets where travelers have some choice, airports are getting aggressive about competing for revenue and market share. Airports are looking for revenue under every stone. So, it's not just parking and concession fees they're after, but passenger facility charges, too.[12]

Remember that Charlotte Douglas International Airport, like most municipal infrastructures, has a high level of sunk cost in the facility. Through its revenue bonds, Charlotte invested heavily in the airport's built environment. The quality of the facility is important, serving as a marketing tool for the pro-growth coalition and the city in general.

Although an airport is considered a monopoly with a captive clientele, it has to charge "reasonable fees." Otherwise, it potentially obstructs the flow of interstate commerce. Regulation of interstate commerce is a federal responsibility, and airports that accept federal construction subsidies are bound by pricing constraints.[13] This was the holding in *Evansville-Vanderburg Airport Authority District v. Delta Airlines* (1972). However, the U.S. Supreme Court upheld the reasonable passenger head taxes the local government imposed for air travel.

The airline industry responded to this ruling by creating a narrative in which local governments should not charge high fees that would put a financial burden on the airlines. Moreover, the industry argued that such fees could not be used for anything other than airport development. In response to the Evansville case, Congress passed section seven of the Airport Development Acceleration Act of 1973, commonly referred to as the Anti–Head Tax Act.[14] The act prohibits states and cities from levying and collecting a tax, fee, or head charge of any kind on individual air passengers or airlines. Congress defines what is a reasonable fee. Explaining the limits of user fees, Stephen Creager states, "User fees which provide revenue greater than that needed to recover the cost of maintaining airport facilities and debt service charges are unreasonable."[15] Airports can only charge landing fees that are required for operating and maintaining the facility. In other words, the airlines got Congress to protect them from being local airports' main source of revenue.

Since most American intercity traffic is by air, it could have been argued that the public should be willing to pay higher passenger fees for better services. This, however, is not the case, as passengers prefer lower fares. Accordingly, airports have to rely on non-aeronautical income to keep the terminal doors open. During the Orr era, the operations of Charlotte Douglas enjoyed a reputation for being low in cost.

Revenues and operational efficiencies seem to be related, but the challenge for airport management is achieving a balance between the two. This is the great test for any airport. In 1993, the management at Charlotte Douglas investigated paying for improvements with a three-dollar tax on every departing passenger. This plan was obviously difficult to implement, but several airports like Charlotte Douglas had such a tax. The city council would have to approve the measure. In addition, longtime airport director Jerry Orr was concerned about passenger backlash and its impact on U.S. Airlines. He explained why Charlotte Douglas would charge three dollars if it decided to levy the tax: "If you're going to make somebody mad, you may as well get the maximum benefit. A $3 tax in Charlotte would raise more than $27 million a year. It is viewed as a potential funding source for an additional runway, which has been in the airport's long-term plan."[16] In the end, the tax was not approved.

The preferred solution to raising more revenue was building larger airport terminals and installing more runways and parking spaces. This would ideally attract more carriers and passengers to the terminals. However, more carriers put new demands on the airport facilities.

MORE AIRPLANES, MORE CONGESTION

The 1978 Airline Deregulation Act reopened the ongoing controversy about general aviation. Sharing the runways with private planes is not one of airline pilots' and the airline industry's favorite topics. Restricting private planes' access to the airport is partly political and partly managerial. As early as July 1967, Airport Advisory Committee (AAC) chair John C. Erwin went so far as to suggest building another airport to relieve the congestion at Charlotte Douglas. The problem was that the county fairground had taken over the old Brockenbrough Airport. In addition, industrial expansion had caused the closing of Carpenter Airport. The question was where to locate an airport reserved for private planes.

Charlotte Douglas Airport director Ross Knight suggested using a consultant to find a solution. He first estimated consultants would cost $30,000. The city council decided to support a consultant study if the fee was reduced. Now the cost was $12,000.[17] In September, the council approved J. D. Griener Company of Baltimore to perform the assessment, which was also necessary to fulfill the FAA deadline for a new master plan expectation. The AAC made the case for general aviation before the consultants. Knight wanted Charlotte Douglas to keep the passenger service, airfreight, and charter and corporate aircraft. A new airport would only handle small private planes. A smaller airport that would accommodate general aviation was never built.

General aviation air traffic became more active with the growth of private luxury jets for corporate leaders, wealthy people, and celebrities. Some no longer fly commercial, and these incoming and departing flights put new stress on facilities and personnel. Private aircraft land at the adjacent Wilson Center, a full-service fixed-base operator (FBO). Private and passenger aircraft use the same runways in some cities. In Charlotte, this is not the case.

SAFETY AT AIRPORTS

Airports have become bigger, and their architecture often borders on the surreal. The high-ceilinged space is designed for movement of large crowds of people. Yet there is a required herding dynamic in airports. In addition, the facilities can alienate some passengers. In 1978, *New York Times* essayist William Safire wrote, "No longer is an airport a place just outside of town to which travelers run to catch a flight. We are in the era of the Airport World—flying Clockwork Orange—an eerily quiet, climate-controlled series of cantilevered concrete caverns. Molded plastic chairs stare at coin-operated television sets; doors careen open by themselves; escalators never stop, and conversations never start."[18]

It is debatable whether modern airports resemble the 1971 dystopian sci-fi film *A Clockwork Orange*. These buildings possess a distinct ambience, but passengers do arrive in a variety of fashion getups. Coin-operated televisions and telephones have been replaced by individual cell phones providing everything from phone service to video games. Passengers converse on their phones but not with one another while waiting to board or once they are on the airplane. Modern travelers' main interest is safety, not socializing.

Safety has always been an issue with air travel. There was a short era of hijacking, but the terrorist attack on 9/11 changed everything about flying. Airports installed cameras and X-ray equipment, employed screeners, and checked all passengers for weapons and explosives. Some passengers are individually searched, and others were monitored. Dogs also search for explosives. No-fly lists prevent certain individuals from boarding aircraft, and air marshals (trained law enforcement officers) ride on certain flights.

The threat of terrorism has created not only a new fear but also a reconfigured airport. The recurring incidence of terrorist attacks created the need for more police and security presence. Agents from the TSA serve as screeners for most airports, and Charlotte Douglas is also patrolled by officers from the Charlotte-Mecklenburg Police Department. As mentioned earlier, incidents ranging from medical emergencies to unruly passengers that require police action always occur at airports.

Making airports into minifortresses has added to the cost of maintaining the facilities. When there is an incident, the immediate reaction is to plug the loophole to make enplaning and flying safer. However, these security additions have become permanent items on an airport's budget. Passengers have to be assured that they are safe on the ground and in the air. This explanation is, in part, why airport expansions are so much a part of local economic development and city image.

EXPANSION OF CHARLOTTE DOUGLAS AIRPORT

Airports are not "fields of dreams." If you build them they (airlines) may not come (lease gates). Cities have to add more incentives. First, local business leaders must demonstrate business acuity and make a case for continual population growth. Moreover, city politicians have to remember that airlines may treat the Charlotte Airport like a host city for a professional sports franchise. If the city does not maintain a first-class airport, it could lose flights and other related business to other cities.

A first-class airport is supposed to be a testimony to a first-class city. Remember this is a marketing tool for economic development. City leaders would not want visitors to say that Charlotte is a nice place with a shabby airport. However, building an airport is a highly technical matter involving runway lengths, noise abatements, and environmental considerations. Airports need specific equipment and aircraft specialists. Airlines are by definition more complicated than modes of ground transportation such as buses, cars, and railways.

Charlotte Municipal Airport started as a gravel runway, but subsequent runways had to be built to exact specifications. And runways must be kept ready for all types of weather and aircraft. Occasional changes in takeoff and landing requirements for aircraft make expanding and rebuilding seem like an endless process. Accordingly, the quality of the infrastructure of an airport is critical to its operations. In addition, the federal government through the FAA regulates airports and defines how they are built. Federal funds provide the majority of money for expansion, and this fact acts as an incentive to build airports and keep them updated. Even after the Charlotte Airport became Charlotte Douglas International Airport, the staff, the pro-growth coalition, and the city council had to continue selling the facility's expansion. To do so, the pro-growth coalition could call on the airline industry and its ability to buy new aircraft and upgrade in-flight amenities. After all, airline companies are major stakeholders in airport appearances—airports are places where passengers enplane and deplane.

AIRPORTS AS ENPLANING ORGANIZATIONS

In a hub city such as Charlotte, the issue was how to justify expanding an airport serving a high percentage of connecting passengers who may never step outside the terminal. Pro-growth leaders are aware of this situation, but they consider it important to keep the city in the conversation about air travel. Doing so may make it easier to market the city to new businesses. Accordingly, airports are obligated to accept some of the airlines' terminal ideas.

Travelers' priority is finding their flight gates. Passengers are quietly evaluating the airport, and like most things in America, airports are ranked in terms of passenger satisfaction. In 1930, writer Wyatt Brummitt stated, "Americans pay gladly for transportation and for service, but they do not enjoy paying for discomfort or inconvenience."[19] Surveys about passengers' airport satisfaction rank terminals and other facilities. Some city airports have been described as "third worldly"—that is, they have old hangars and outmoded terminals. A pro-growth city does not want this reputation.

In terms of architecture and design, some American airports are not as modern as those in Persian Gulf nations. Yet for passengers, the airport is the first step in traveling elsewhere. Travelers arrive at airports and depart from them. Flight attendants will welcome passengers to a city like Charlotte, tell them the local time, thank them for traveling with the airline, and advise them to check the monitor for connecting flights if they have not reached their final stop. Passengers will find themselves in a concourse or long hallway with signs indicating the location of restrooms, retail shops, and baggage and ground transportation. A few airports (e.g., Atlanta) greet new arrivals with welcoming messages from the city mayor. Other cities seem uninterested in the passengers and offer little information.

Aside from knowing the Transportation Service Agency (TSA) checks their identity, luggage, and ticket, passengers may be otherwise unaware of the federal government's role in air transportation and airports. However, most Americans were alerted to the federal role at airports when Pres. Ronald Reagan fired over eleven thousand air traffic controllers. Led by the Professional Air Traffic Controllers Organization (PATCO), these employees went on strike. To the surprise of the public, the Reagan administration won this battle. PATCO was decertified and bankrupted. Air traffic workers then created a new union organization and denounced the strike tactic. This incident demonstrates the primacy of a free-flowing air travel system.

Airlines want airport management to concentrate on passengers and landing facilities. In order to stay current, Charlotte Douglas had to build concourses to accommodate passengers and gates. In 1975, a consultant predicted the airport would be boarding 3.1 million passengers in 1992. By 1985, passenger load had reached 2.9 million, demonstrating the need for a new concourse. In 1985, the Charlotte City Council approved $2.9 million for the new concourse with a proposed thirty-seven gates. Airport manager R. C. "Josh" Birmingham stated, "Personally, I don't see how we can keep up this level of growth." His deputy director, Jerry Orr, agreed, asserting, "We think the new concourse will be adequate." Orr responded, "I think it [the passenger growth rate] is going to level off."[20]

However, it did not. Charlotte Douglas Airport continued to redesign and upgrade itself to meet the demands of new aircraft, security needs, and passenger demands. Yet the cost of enplaning at Charlotte Airport had to be kept low in order to be competitive with other cities. And low cost should not be at the expense of a passenger-friendly airport.

TIMES ARE A-CHANGING AT THE AIRPORT

As we suggested in the history chapters, the city of Charlotte has come a long way in developing and redeveloping its airport. Charlotte Douglas International Airport is an example of how a city-owned airport can promote economic development. A new terminal built in 1982 put the facility in the major league of air travel. Airports' importance is ranked by the number of passengers they serve. Passenger services have changed, as have those who use the airport. Historian Julie M. Fenster elaborates on this point.

> In the ancient days of our own times, flying was actually glamorous. Passengers dressed up for a flight. But gradually through the years, members of the flying public had to accept the fact that they were no longer personages. Long before

security concerns added extra rules, passengers were turned into nonentities by the airports and airlines. Service personnel learned to excel at condescension, a contradiction in terms that left a trip through an airport as something to be endured. And endure it I did, but barely, before a flight in late July. In fact, by the time I reached the gate I wanted to go home. But with requisite obedience, I settled into a seat in a fixed row of chairs like those at every airport, as sturdy as an I-beam and just as ergonomic.[21]

Flying does not exude 1950s glamour anymore. Air travel is now opened to most low-income individuals, and enplaning begins with providing easy access and affordable parking for most passengers. The expansion of parking facilities at Charlotte Douglas is related to its growth as a hub. At this writing, the airport is in the process of building more open-air and closed parking near the terminal.

Providing for taxi services is a part of the politics of airports. Cities handle the services in different ways, sometimes requiring cabs to be licensed to operate at the airport. A meter supposedly measures services. The city council sets rates. Additionally, many cities have a fixed cost for taxi service from the airport to the downtown areas. In some cases, like Cleveland's, only designated cabs are allowed to take people directly from the airport into the city. Most airports allow all types of taxis to bring passengers to the airport, but only contracted taxis can pick up passengers at the airport. Charlotte employs the latter method. Taxi contracts are an important element in the financing of airport facilities. Accordingly, then, the cab contracts have been a controversial issue.

Deciding who gets these contracts is a political issue because it is a form of grand patronage (cab companies are owned by middle-level businesspersons). The issue goes back to the midfifties. In 1956, the Airport Advisory Committee recommended that the Yellow Cab Company be the facility's exclusive takeaway cab company. The company agreed to pay the city $6,000 annually, and a percentage of the take tied to increased traffic at the airport. Al Quinn, then the airport director, supported the idea because cabs could take passengers anywhere in Charlotte for one dollar.[22] Taxi contracts will continue to be an issue before the Charlotte City Council. Since there is no light-rail service to the airport, a traveler is instead forced to drive or take an inconvenient bus service.

DIFFERENT PASSENGERS, DIFFERENT SERVICE

The overall purpose of the airport is to get passengers on and off airplanes. Yet what looks like a simple task is often a complicated one. Organizing passengers in the seating areas and then preparing them for boarding requires effective queues, and airlines have different methods to facilitate boarding and seats. In 1959, Frank Der Yuen invented the jetway or passenger boarding bridge. This enclosed moveable connector allows passengers to get into airplanes in all types of weather. Jetways also facilitate disembarking. These bridges added to the cost of operating airports and increased the airline parking problems at airports.

While passengers are in the airport, it is the responsibility of airport management to take care of them. In the past, providing clean restrooms and pay phones all over the airport seemed to be enough. Today, airports must provide places for passengers to charge their cell phones in comfortable seats. Another mandate for today's airports is providing travelers a smoke-free facility.

Charlotte Douglas has endeavored to make itself comfortable. In 1997, the airport introduced old-fashioned rocking chairs for passengers. This gesture elicited a humorous reaction from Julie Fenster. She asked, "Rocking chairs in an airport? A bastion of nineteenth-century domesticity as an antidote to twenty-first-century regimentation?"[23] Fenster continued,

> It is certainly a step in the right direction. To see them, and the lucky people contentedly rocking away in them, was heartwarming. Maybe the warden doesn't hate us after all. Rocking chairs, I have since learned, first made an impact in the Charlotte airport, where they were supposed to be part of a temporary exhibit about the traditional front porch. Passengers insisted that they remain after the exhibit left. Since then the idea has been adopted at other airports. Possibly hooked rugs, an Autoharp, and a calico cat at every gate will be next.[24]

Charlotte Douglas ranked third out of thirty-six airports in a 1998 passenger satisfaction survey by Plog Research Incorporated. In a 2000 survey of twenty-nine airports, Charlotte Douglas was tied for sixth place in a passenger satisfaction ranking. This more recent survey was conducted by J. D. Power, and it asked 6,500 passengers about gate areas, ease of travel to and from the airport, check-in and security procedures, retail outlets, and baggage claims. Director Orr was not satisfied with Charlotte Douglas's ranking, saying, "Sixth place just isn't good enough. We usually finish higher. We've got to tighten up here, turn up the wick."[25] By 2015, Charlotte Douglas Airport lost its top ranking by J. D. Power and was ranked eleventh among large airports. It earned 734 out of 1,000 points in the survey.[26]

Airports require specialized landing and takeoff platforms centered around aircraft, but their waiting rooms should be passenger-centered environments. Basically speaking, there are several types of airport users. The business elite and celebrities rarely use commercial airlines. If there is only one airport, they use the airport for parking and maintenance. Regular airport clientele usually consists of locals who want to go from one city to another. Airports also serve tourists and visitors who spend time with relatives or at the local entertainment sites. Finally, airports accommodate business travelers (bean counters, salespersons, and construction workers) who move from one facility to the next.

Layover passengers are a final consideration. A well-run airport hub must be able to accommodate each group separately. As historian Bednarek points out, food sales went up as the airlines cut back on food on the planes. She calls this phenomenon the "malling of airports."[27] The locals just want to catch a flight, and they probably ate before they left home. They are less likely to buy food, clothes, or items from the bar. Tourists are the customers shopping for souvenirs and clothes, and in some airports these are priority passengers. Also, in some cases (e.g., Miami, Las Vegas, New Orleans), some of the city income depends on these passengers. Such visitor cities want passengers to return. Business travelers with economy tickets rarely get special treatment, as they are considered transient. Airlines, however, cater to first-class passengers with separate waiting lounges.

Layover passengers are different clienteles. They will not leave the airport, and during the time before the next flight, the facility has an opportunity to supply them with food and drink. This group of travelers needs to be impressed with good maintenance, food, and bars. Historian Walter Turner describes the significant change at Charlotte Douglas with the new terminal for Piedmont Airlines. Wayne Tucker, the Charlotte station manager, told Turner that seeing the new terminal was like "moving into a new house with all new furniture." Turner concludes, "The move to the new terminal in 1982 gave the airline an enhanced image—its one hundred daily flights that year included nonstop jet service to New York, Denver, New Orleans, and Cincinnati."[28]

Over the years, airports evolved from nondescript waiting areas to full-size malls with retail-service areas providing everything from restaurants and new suitcases to rental cars and ATMs. Passengers frequenting these full-service establishments also enjoy Wi-Fi access, a necessity for business travelers.

Airport managers face the challenge of accommodating the passenger's comfort, meeting airline equipment requirements, and providing airline security. In other words, the successful airport creates a culture of reassurance. Passengers must be assured that their trips and accommodations will be as quick as possible and cause little stress. In fact, air travelers are encouraged to expect a good flight. A 2012 study by Adams D. Steven, Yan Dong, and Martin Dresner argues that "market concentration moderates the relationship between satisfaction and profitability for U.S. airlines. Airlines that operate in concentrated markets have fewer incentives to satisfy their customers than airlines that operate in more competitive markets."[29]

In an empirical study of airports and innovations like self-check-in kiosks, the X-ray, social media, and microhotels, James K. C. Chen, Amirita Batchuluun, and Javkhuu Batnasan find that safety or the perception of safety trumps other parts of airport accommodations. These scholars identify a strong positive relationship between customer satisfaction and customer value of the airport.[30] Further analysis of their findings identifies the security check as the most influential customer satisfaction factor. This result is consistent with previous studies. Passengers are willing to be patient during security-related airport service procedures, which they expect to provide a travel experience of better quality, reliability, and safety. Traveling by air is sometimes considered a life-or-death experience; many accidents can happen in flight. Therefore, passengers also are more likely to be satisfied with their increased safety despite any related inconveniences. Chen further concludes, "The next influential factor on customer satisfaction was airport accessibility. As a result, the airport environment was revealed to be the most influential dimension of airport service quality, which was followed by access, dining and immigration/customs, which was supported in this study. Unlike with previous studies, this study found that terminal facilities did not influence customer satisfaction."[31]

Again, Charlotte Douglas Airport is a great bargain for airlines because of its low enplanement costs. For example, five years ago Choo found that the airport's 2010 "cost per enplanement for Charlotte Douglas was US$2.82 but cost 8 times more at New York JFK airport US$24.17."[32] Surely that cost gap has widened over the years. Overall, Charlotte is one of the cheaper cities in which to conduct air travel, maintain a hub, and house airport employees. Table 3 shows Charlotte's ranking among the southeastern U.S. airports included in the top fifty airports nationwide. The table also shows the increase in southeastern airports' passenger enplanement since 2002.

Charlotte's high passenger loads result directly from its function as a hub for U.S. Airways, now American Airlines. Many passengers never set foot outside the airport terminal. In effect, they have been through Charlotte but not to it.

THE EMERGENCE OF CHARLOTTE AS A HUB

An airline hub is a location where airlines concentrate flights and organize air traffic and passenger redistribution. The hub concentrates equipment, communication, and personnel in one facility. Regional airlines or feeder airlines can arrange and print tickets for airports where they have no gates. Smaller airlines

Table 3. Ranking Among Southeast U.S. City Airports

Airport	2005 Rank	2015 Rank	Percent Change in Passenger Load
Atlanta	1	1	16.8
Charlotte	18	8	55.1
Miami	16	11	38.4
Orlando	12	14	12.6
Tampa	27	29	−1.6
Nashville	42	35	19.3
Raleigh/Durham	45	39	5.0

Source: Adapted from U.S. Department of Transportation, Bureau of Transportation Statistics, Table 1-44 Passengers Boarded at the Top U.S. Airport, 2015.

and airplanes can off-load passengers into larger systems. Critical to airlines' development and operation, the hub system was built as a response to the 1978 deregulation of airlines. This topic was discussed in chapter 3.

In the 1980s, Charlotte Douglas had two major carrier airlines—Eastern and Piedmont. By 1985, Piedmont was a rising airline in the region. After starting with only 30 daily flights, it eventually offered 177. Yet a consultant, Evan Futterman of Howard, Needles, Tammen and Bergendoff (HNTB), found that Charlotte Douglas Airport was operating at about 60 percent of its capacity.

Eastern Air Lines started takeoffs and landings in Charlotte in 1926 and ended them in 1991. Despite its several famous CEOs, the airline could not solve its cost difficulties, aircraft overreach, safety violations, and labor problems. Eastern also tried to compete with Delta in the Atlanta Airport. In 1991, Eastern Air Lines went into bankruptcy. As was suggested in chapter 2, Charlotte Douglas had bet heavily on Eastern, a heavyweight in the eastern United States. The airline had been an American institution since the thirties, and at its peak, it had several flights out of Charlotte Douglas.

As we discussed in chapter 2, Eastern Air Lines and Piedmont Airlines made Charlotte Douglas Airport their hub for destinations in the southeastern United States. U.S. Airways started as a small airmail service and grew into a major carrier that took over many flights to the Southeast. In 2001, William

Douglas Parker became CEO of America West. A member of the so-called young "Brat Pack" that gained fame for saving America West from bankruptcy, Parker merged the airline with U.S. Airways in 2005 and became CEO of U.S. Airways. After failing to merge with Delta, United, and Continental, he successfully merged with American Airlines in 2013. As CEO of the newly merged carriers, Parker moved the staff into the new American Airlines headquarters in Dallas. Meanwhile, Charlotte Douglas had increased its number of gates. At one time, American Airlines had only two gates, and these were used by American Eagle, a regional airline for American Airlines. In 2015, the merger of U.S. Airways and American Airlines was completed, affording the new carrier several gates at Charlotte Douglas Airport.

In keeping with the theory that signing higher passenger loads to long-term leases would minimize costs, airlines were able to increase passenger loads on flights to and from the airport. With more passenger loads, carriers like American Airlines were able to offer more frequent flights. Locating passenger transfers at one place allows the airline to use larger aircraft and make higher profits. At one point, Charlotte Douglas Airport handled 6.5 percent of the airline passengers and relied on connecting passengers for 75 percent of its traffic. Currently American Airlines offers approximately 640 daily flights to 140 destinations around the nation. In 2013, the airport had $820 million in bonds outstanding for expansion, including a new seven-thousand-space parking deck. Expansion creates more gates, which in turn allow the airport to accommodate more aircraft and passengers.

GATES AND MORE GATES

Building gates was more than a matter of bricks and mortar. Rather, these projects were major investments and a gamble. Throughout the airport's history, speculation about the necessary number of gates endured. In the pre-merger days, Winston-Salem–based Piedmont Airlines announced a major expansion for Charlotte Douglas. The carrier planned to build a $42 million maintenance, training, and parts facility at the airport. Piedmont also spent another $15 million to add six more gates to Concourse B. Mayor Harvey Gantt considered this move significant, stating, "It's a facility that will have a major impact on Charlotte, the airport and jobs."[33] The project created four thousand jobs in Charlotte by 1988. The cost of the Piedmont gates would exceed $90 million and be financed with voter-approved North Carolina bonds. Piedmont also bought the eight Eastern gates in Concourse B. Director Birmingham stated of the purchase, "It just shifts development from one end of the airport to the other.

They're actually building the same thing."[34] Charlotte Douglas was growing rapidly and becoming a major hub for the airline. When asked whether Piedmont would move its headquarters from Winston-Salem to Charlotte, Chairman William Howard answered emphatically, "No, no no and no."[35] He may have reassured Winston-Salem residents, but their city would never be a real competitor for faster-growing Charlotte.

While infrastructure expansion is not infinite, strategic management is critical to an airport's success. Slot or gates control is the most promising asset. In 1985, the Charlotte City Council voted to start planning for a third concourse. In 1986, twelve gates were built in Concourse A to serve Delta, Frontier, JetBlue, Southwest, and United. Concourse B and C had sixteen gates and served American Airlines. Concourses A and C were expanded in 1987. Concourse D's thirteen gates were considered the international gates, and Concourse E served American Eagle with thirty-eight gates.

Dealing with gate applicants after the 1978 Airline Deregulation Act is a challenge for airport directors. After deregulation, Charlotte Douglas built a ten-thousand-foot parallel runway. In 1989, Piedmont merged with U.S. Airways, and the new airline signed a twenty-five-year lease with the airport. The third international terminal would open later in April 1989. Again, the facility was renamed Charlotte Douglas International Airport because it carried international cargo. However, in a 1982 article, *Charlotte Observer* reporter Kays Gary asked, "Is Charlotte putting on airs with 'international' label?" Quoting the Raleigh *News and Observer*'s editorial, Gary asserted, "Charlotte is an exception to the state motto, 'To Be Rather Than to Seem.'"[36] As the editorial pointed out, there were no international passenger flights from Charlotte to another country, no immigration and customs operations, and no currency exchange.

In 1986, the Washington firm of Howard, Needles, Tammen and Bergendoff produced a twenty-year master plan for Charlotte Douglas International Airport. The plan called for 4 runways, 4 concourses, 63 gates, and 10,500 parking spaces. These improvements would entail a 1,000-foot runway extension. They also required obtaining 323 acres of land adjacent to the airport and changing the airport entrance road.

In 1990 an 80,000-square-foot international concourse (Concourse D) was built at the airport. U.S. Airways (now American Airlines) added new D gates to its existing leases; they will expire in 2016. In 2002, Concourse E was open with 32 gates. U.S. Airways subsequently began international nonstop flights. In June 1991, a 23-member Airport Capacity Design Team, composed of federal and state experts, produced a report entitled "Charlotte/Douglas International

Table 4. Designated Gates in 2015

Concourse	Number of Gates	Tenants	Opening Year
A	12	Delta, Air Canada, JetBlue, Southwest, United, ViaAir	1986
B	16	American Airlines	1982
C	18	American Airlines	1982
D	13	Lufthansa InselAir	1990
E	38	American Eagle	2002
Planned Concourse	25		

Airport Capacity Enhancement Plan." The report "warned" that delaying development of a new 10,000-foot runway parallel to the existing one on the facility's west side would impede the airport's growth. The runway would cost $27 million, and federal funds would assume $20 million of that cost. Fliers would save 30,000 hours a year in delays as a result.

Jerry Orr, Charlotte Douglas's director, agreed the second priority was the extension of 7,845-foot Runway 36—right on the airport's east side. This 1,000-foot extension would save $13 million a year in flight delays. Leonard Griffs, FAA assistant administrator for airports, asserted, "You are at the pulse of what's happening; unless you properly plan for the future, someone will pass you by."[37] As the Airport Capacity Design Team was aware of the environmental impact of more plane landings at Douglas, "it recommended a study of relaxed noise rules for newer, so-called Stage III jets, which have quieter engines than older models."[38] In 2005, America West Airlines merged with U.S. Airways. Table 4 shows Charlotte Douglas's array of gates and their opening years as of 2015.

SUMMARY

The metanarrative of Charlotte Douglas International Airport is that it facilitates economic development in the Charlotte metro region—that is, Metrolina. It helped make Charlotte the "transformative city." As the airport is a self-sustaining organization, its directors do not get publicly involved in municipal or state budget battles. Concessions, parking, and taxi contracts are Charlotte Douglas's primary sources of revenue. The facility's indirect costs (e.g., security costs) to the city are difficult to calculate. There is no systematic way to capture that figure.

Federal law prohibits the use of airport revenues for nonairport purposes. Unlike the Port Authority of New York and New Jersey, Charlotte Airport cannot mix funds with other revenues to pay for other municipal operations. Simply put, it cannot divert airport revenues into municipal coffers. Ironically, this narrative was among those used to promote the idea of regional authority for the airport, which will be discussed in chapter 8.

The gate problem remains an issue since it inhibits competition and hence brings higher fares. Although the Government Accounting Office (GAO) recommended a lottery system for gates, that is unlikely to be implemented. The leasing practices stabilized the airlines and the airport. However, further expansion will facilitate Charlotte's journey into the complex world of capitalism. City businesspersons need nonstop trips to obligatory landing cities like Washington, D.C., New York, Los Angeles, and Chicago. Airlines need to know what the passenger load will be in order to determine what type of aircraft to use in the hub cities. In the case of the new American Airlines, its competition is with Delta and Atlanta. Meanwhile, the leadership of Charlotte Douglas Airport was granted more independence and discretion to ensure the airport worked well as a low-cost hub.

With the assistance of federal mandates and pro-growth leaders, the expansion of Charlotte Douglas International Airport continued. Airport managers became more technocratic to stay current with FAA orders, advisory circulars, regulations, and now TSA regulations. As the airport became a technocracy, its leaders could not afford to ignore local politics. Recurrent problems such as construction costs, airline industry uncertainty, and security concerns often overlap with state and local politics. Yet the airport is a fixed place that needs to be able to respond to unexpected and unwelcome pressures.

The September 11, 2001, terrorist attacks changed the way all American airports handled security. Charlotte Douglas, like most airports, was not designed to thwart terrorists. Now some passengers are seen as potential threats. The introduction of the TSA involved more personnel operating on the airport floor space. These new security measures also changed who does what, when, and how at the airport.

The next chapter examines the evolution of airport leadership. Airport directors played a variety of roles in airport management and city economic development. Yet studies of city airport development barely mention these individuals' names because they are hired help. While directors are the day-to-day management people, they can also influence what the pro-growth coalition decides to do.

CHAPTER 5

The Pro-Growth Coalition and the Hired Help

CHARLOTTE'S PRO-GROWTH COALITION PRIDES ITSELF on knowing where it plans to take Charlotte economically. Given the limits of the council-manager form of government, discussed in the next chapter, and the fact that the city does not have the specialized staff to conduct policy studies and create a plan, consultants are needed. Different consultants work on different projects. Unlike consultants, airport directors have to implement plans. For the city, the challenge is to find good help. The ideal candidate would be a man (no women have yet served as airport director) who could manage the exigency of a busy facility, lead the airport expansion, and sell it to the public. Hence, the appointment of an airport director is a very important political decision, because this person will serve multifaceted roles. Managing one of the city's biggest assets is a difficult task because the airport is a large facility with a budget of over $140 million and a staff of 450 regular members of the city civil service. In addition, the airport hosts 18,000 employees, including airline workers, custodians, concession staff, and federal employees. As discussed in the last chapter, Charlotte Douglas has a 1.8-million-square-foot terminal building with 5 concourses and 96 gates.

The aviation director's job is not just a facility management position, In addition, the incumbent serves as the public face of the airport. Aside from speaking on behalf of airport employees and overseeing the airport's role in the overall city development, the director is expected to speak to a variety of community groups. As we shall see, the personality of the director matters. The city manager, the business community, and the city political leadership interview and vet candidates for this job. Outside applicants must prove their true belief in the inevitability of Charlotte's growth—after all, it is the "transformative city." Local candidates must demonstrate commitment to this goal while working at the airport. Leading one of the city's most important promotional and economic developmental assets requires a high level of salesmanship, networking capacity, and entrepreneurial ability. Also, incumbents must understand that the aviation director is hired help and can be removed fairly easily.

This chapter will examine the role of outside consultants in the planning and promotion of airport expansion. It will also discuss the history and tenure of airport directors. Directors take a variety of traditional management and leadership roles, and Charlotte Douglas Airport's history suggests that these leaders fall into the categories of insiders and outsiders. Each director impacted the facility's image and expansion. Obviously, the political atmosphere during which directors served impacted their tenures. As discussed in chapters 2 and 3, Charlotte Douglas International Airport developed in response to local and national economic and transportation policies. Aviation directors had to work within the city's overall economic environment. Although somewhat insulated from elected officials, airport directors could not safely ignore them.

THE POLITICAL USES OF CONSULTANTS

One of the most interesting aspects of airports' political expansion is their use of consultants. As stated earlier, consultants often write airport master plans. Richard de Neufville and Amedeo Odoni conclude, "Master plans rapidly become obsolete. Airport operations frequently have to junk the ultimate, 20-year vision of the master plan after only a few years."[1] The authors also state that plans are "sometimes 'dead on arrival' due to their inflexibility."[2] Yet once a crisis is identified or a solution is debatable, all sides hire a consultant. These professionals circle municipal problems like hawks looking for prey, and they are quick to provide immediate assistance. Bruce W. Fraser's article "Consultants to the Rescue" outlines why businesses seek consultants. Quoting Jan King's "Business Plan to Game Plans," Fraser elaborates on four common situations requiring outside assistance: "1. a high level of expertise is needed, but the company cannot afford to pay an employee who has such knowledge and skills, 2. needs, generated by growth or external market forces, are only temporary, 3. problems have become so acute that they require immediate response, 4. problems are of such a broad institutional nature that they defy internal response."[3]

Examples of the need for high levels of expertise are scattered through the post–World War II history of Charlotte Airport's development. In 1961, the Airport Advisory Committee recommended to the city council that J. N. Pease & Company be engineers for the first year of a five-year capital improvement project at the airport. This $250,000 job would expand and repair terminal aprons (areas where aircraft park and load). Director Quinn told the council, "Our apron won't stand another winter."[4] Pease got the job in October, but he did so for a payout of $133,750.

In 1961, Quinn had hired New York consultant firm James C. Buckley, Incorporated to arrange a financial plan for the airport.[5] The company recommended that the airport sell bonds to expand services—a new terminal and runway additions. In addition, the firm suggested that $7.3 million be spent between 1962 and 1970, and it called for a more centralized management system. The city of Charlotte would sell bonds for $4 million of the aforementioned $7.3 million. Moreover, the Buckley firm advised improving Charlotte Douglas's accounting procedures and increasing the rent. The rental agreements predated Quinn's tenure at the airport, and the city manager had supported the aforementioned rent increase. After Quinn resigned, Tom Rafferty was hired. A *Charlotte Observer* reporter greeted the new airport manager with the headline "Al Quinn's Successor on Hot Seat."[6] Clearly, the new manager was obligated to respond to these problems.

In 1973, the airport employed A. G. Odell Associates to design a new terminal. Odell was a well-known local firm that had done the architectural work for the Charlotte Coliseum and the civic center. The Airport Advisory Committee also recommended the company to the Charlotte City Council. However, local architects objected to the contract, and some councilpersons raised questions about it. Yet former mayor Ben Douglas, then chair of the AAC, supported Odell. He stated that while the ten local firms with the capacity to design the terminal were invited to make a bid, only seven of them responded. The council voted six to one to award the contract to Odell. Local firms subsequently refused to comment for "fear of never getting jobs."[7]

Throughout the history of Charlotte Douglas, consultants' two main consumers were the airport directors and the city council. Consultants were hired for expertise and for cover. An old saying asks, "Why do politicians read the Bible?" The answer is that they read it for enlightenment and justification. Usually the employer, the city, knows what it wants to do, and the consultant's job is to create a spiral booklet with the words and statistical justification/support for the policy. If an airport runway extension narrative needs support, the first step is to hire a consultant. If the city council decides to debate an issue, council members hire a consultant to outline the options. The result is a relatively quick analysis confirming what the politicians want to do. Presented in a bound copy, this consultant's report includes background information and references to the plight of similarly situated airports. It is not unusual for report writers to assume a neutral position and simply lay out options for the director or the city council. Yet there are also expected justifications for expansion.

SELLING AN EXPANSION

Airport management promoted airport facility upgrades as a technical problem. When an improvement was needed, the airport director would encourage the city council to hire a consultant to perform a study. Referrals to consultants increased as the airport grew. In 1975, the Charlotte Airport sought a runway extension, and consultants confirmed the need for a ten-thousand-foot runway costing $23 million. Their report stated that expansion would only cost Charlotte taxpayers $1.3 million. Surrounding neighborhoods objected on environmental grounds and filed a $75 million suit against the city. Additionally, the new runways would require relocation of Berry Hill Elementary School. Community leaders ultimately rejected the move.

Interestingly, the *Charlotte Observer* joined the fight against expanding the airport, sending a team of reporters to carry out an independent investigation. These journalists concluded that the new runway was not needed. First, the newspaper disputed airport management's claim that traffic was expected to increase 122 percent between 1970 and 1985. Reporters cited an FAA study finding half that increase. As the additional traffic would come mainly from general aviation, the *Charlotte Observer* suggested that building a small airport nearby would solve that problem.

Second, the *Charlotte Observer*'s investigative reporters disputed the claim that a longer runway would allow airlines' jets to fly longer distances nonstop. The authors stated, "No airline has any definite plan to fly anywhere that it can't go now," and they indicated that if airlines needed to reach additional destinations, "either existing runway at Douglas could be extended to the necessary length."[8] Third, the *Charlotte Observer*'s study did not accept the stated need for more sophisticated landing instruments. The current Category II could be incorporated into Douglas's existing runways. In June, federal judge James Bryan McMillian issued an injunction against building the runway.

Airport manager Josh Birmingham disagreed with the *Charlotte Observer*'s findings, asserting, "The study conclusions are subjective and not supported by the weight of the evidence."[9] This dispute opened the airport managers to more public criticism and scrutiny, meaning that this time the consultant report was not enough.

In 1975, the airlines needed a terminal, not a runway. Orr considered this point in Charlotte Douglas's history its "low water mark."[10] Director Birmingham asked his assistant Jerry Orr if it would be possible to build the terminal for less than $55 million. According to Orr, the Odell design would not have supported a hub. Birmingham, Frank Newton, and Orr then worked "under the radar" to redesign the terminal.[11] Orr recalled, "They worked 12 hours a day to design the terminal. They were able to create a plan to move the program. With the aid of consultants, we redid the environment statement to support the runway. The Admiral knew all properties' representatives. It was a heck of negotiation. We were upfront. We answered questions honestly. Three things were important to us. It was a win-win situation."[12]

In June 1976, work on the terminal was resumed. A separate Charlotte Chamber of Commerce study conducted that year supported the extension of the runway. In its position paper entitled "The Need for Affirmation Action on the Expansion of Douglas Municipal Airport," the chamber of commerce argued, "Calls on city government move aggressively to complete the present phase of the airport expansion and to continue to expand facilities and services as appropriate to best serve the needs and demands of Charlotte and the regions."[13] In a letter to Mayor John Belk, the chamber stressed the word "aggressively."[14]

The 1978 pro-growth mobilization for the $47 million revenue bond referendum involved a multifaceted approach. Supporters brought back consultant Arnold Thompson, who had made a series of predictions about airport growth in 1975. In the *Charlotte Observer*, Thompson admitted his earlier growth estimates were too high, stating, "What you will find is the whole industry, the airlines, the manufacturers, the FAA and the consultants were wrong [for 1975]. The airlines are always changing. Something is always changing. It's just the nature of aviation that there will be change."[15] Thompson continued, "I think it's to Charlotte's advantage to be building as soon as possible. I would rather err on the side of being ahead of time."[16] He argued against patching the twenty-five-year-old terminal, citing the traffic jams in front of it as evidence of its "wrong configuration" for planes and its failure to conserve energy.

The *Charlotte Observer* provided citizens an opportunity to react to Thompson's advice and object to the expansion. Jo Ellen Wade of Steele Creek Community Association stated, "I am continually amazed at the comparison between the projected growth for Douglas Airport by airport officials and the actual growth."[17] For Wade, an expanded airport would bring more noise and air pollution. In an article entitled "The Sour Note in Terminal Choir," the *Charlotte Observer* quoted the lone dissenter in the city council, Don Carroll. He thought a stand-alone June referendum bond vote would have bad timing, and he believed the council had done a poor job of studying the project. Moreover, Carroll raised doubts about using the city's general obligation bonds for the project, suggesting that the money be spent on parks instead. Airport terminal proponents offered Councilman Carroll an opportunity to nominate three people for the campaign committee. He refused, and the campaign went on without him.

According to Jerry Orr, Eastern Air Lines played Greensboro against Charlotte.[18] Greensboro obviously lacked Charlotte's potential population capacity.

However, building a hub in Greensboro could change the competition between the cities. As Charlotte won out in the end, Piedmont and Eastern Air Lines became the dominant carriers at Charlotte Douglas. The airport accommodated these airlines, and their presence was necessary to expand the airport.

Once the airlines had settled at the airport, airline executives began to make new demands. The airlines needed a better terminal for parking groundside. The airport was able to meet these demands, but the director had to convince the airlines that the city had limited financial resources. Then the story behind these negotiations took an interesting twist.

Director Birmingham described his team's approach to negotiating with the airlines: "[Negotiators for the city wore the] shabbiest suits I have ever seen in my life. One man had a cigarette burn on his pants."[19] Roy Callahan, the city's financial consultant, wore a black serge suit shiny from wear. Callahan told Birmingham, "The sartorial slumming was deliberate: lawyers jockeying for position. No one wanted to look like he has any money."[20] The tactic worked, as the airlines allowed the airport managers more time to expand parking and to build a new terminal. In 1982 the new terminal opened.

Three years after the new terminal's construction, it became clear that yet another expansion was needed. A consultant, Evan Futterman of consultant firm Howard, Needles, Tammen and Bergendoff, was hired to make the airport's case to the Charlotte City Council and the public. The resulting report recommended a major upgrade and concluded that Charlotte Douglas was operating at about 60 percent capacity. Consultants suggested expanding Concourse A and constructing a new concourse. They also argued that an upgrade of the terminal would facilitate the growth of Piedmont Airlines, the largest airline at Charlotte Douglas. Ironically, Evan Futterman stated, "Charlotte is almost Piedmont territory. We don't forecast another [airline] having a major hub here."[21] Members Howard, Needles, Tammen and Bergendoff did not predict that Piedmont Airlines would merge with another airline, which would change the shape of the airport.

In 1987, consultants updated the master plan and suggested a $187 million expansion. This upgrade was necessary to continue the airport's growth of the airport for the next twenty years. It was predicted that passenger traffic would increase 300 percent by 2005. New runways, gates, and parking spaces were needed to prepare for this eventuality. While the entire upgrading enterprise was needed for technical reasons, the chief beneficiary would be the city itself. In sum, consultants' reports are part of the selling process, and the airport director worked closely with consultants in all cases.

THE OFFICIAL AIRPORT DIRECTORS

Officially, the manager of Charlotte Douglas International Airport is the director of aviation in the city's Airport Department. As suggested earlier, the airport has not reached acropolis status. Yet every decade since the 1940s has seen expansion. The pro-growth coalition has covered the facilities' external challenges, but it has left the day-to-day operations to the professional staff. At first glance the primary function of an airport seems relatively simple: get the airplanes safely into the air, provide safe landing runways and taxiing, and assist passengers with wheelchairs/ticketing/boarding, concessions routing, baggage, security, arrival/departure traffic, and parking lots.

A closer look reveals a very complex facilities-coordination process. The federal government manages the air traffic system and passenger screening. The airlines take care of the scheduling, maintenance, baggage, and gate personnel. Contract companies handle passenger assistance, concessions, and janitorial services. Conflicts with these services arise incessantly. Although these seem to operate in parallel universes, airline disruptions can offset airports' daily routines. Passengers rarely notice the services unless there is a breakdown of these activities. A day at the airport normally looks seamless.

A further examination of the airport's day reveals daily operational complications including late flights, weather problems, union grievances, and passenger mishaps/misconnections, as well as other types of emergencies, security breakdowns, and air traffic delays. Dull days are rare in airport management. Airport employees are expected to present a can-do persona. They seek to convey the notion that they are in control, and they encourage passengers not to worry because they will get safely on the plane. Flight delays and cancellations are the airlines' fault.

At most airports, internal dynamics between the inside terminal personnel and outside tarmac workers are present. Yet these employees may be unaware of one another's schedules or specific routines. The people who work on the tarmac (air traffic personnel, baggage handlers, food and fuel vendors, and aircraft mechanists) and those who work inside the terminal (security personnel, restaurant workers, baggage personnel, gate agents, and passenger assistants) are relative strangers.

Yet there is also a hierarchy of who does what and where. Traffic personnel can regulate parking and taxi services. Baggage personnel are usually only seen through the window. If a mechanical problem occurs, the maintenance workers must give permission for a plane to fly. Security personnel have the power to stop people from flying without proper identification or with restricted carry-on items. Food servers and other vendors, passenger assistants for the disabled, and janitors are equal in terms of their relation to passengers. Gate agents have more authority when dealing with seat assignments, rescheduling, and flight overload/bumping. In the terminal, gate agents have control over pilots and crew briefly before enplanement; they identify themselves before boarding the aircraft. Once in the air, however, the crew takes charge.

The organizational culture of airports looks relaxed but is based on rigid rules and symbols designed to reassure passengers that flying is safe, clean, and enjoyable. To this end, terminal staffers follow different schedules and organizational commands to avoid conflicts. Pilots and copilots are selected by bids, and they often do not personally know each other. Flight attendants are based in cities but fly to other cities with regularity. At-large airports' different staff members are usually complete strangers.

The architecture and airport environment are designed like a pinball table to route and reroute passengers without being invasive. Passengers expect anonymity, cheerful employees, and respect. Few travelers want to make friends in the airport or on the airplane. The terminal staff responsible for passenger accommodation take action simultaneously but parallel to one another. A situation like that in the 2004 movie *The Terminal*, in which Tom Hanks's character spends months in Kennedy Airport and makes it his own world, is pure fiction. Charlotte Douglas International Airport is too small for that to happen, and its staff is too alert.

AIRPORT DIRECTORS AS MANAGERS

The airport director job is prestigious because Charlotte Douglas is an airline hub where a major airline, now American Airlines, does a lot of its connecting flight business. The position is also esteemed because Charlotte is a pro-growth city, one that is constantly changing and attracting new businesses and people. Being the chief operations officer and liaison to the city manager, a department head under the city council, requires significant managerial and political agility. Agility is necessary because the pace of change is relentless, and the demands of airline industry change continually. Directors must also find ways to maneuver within the maze of local politics, the ambitions of local business elites, and the changing technology.

Managing an airport entails more than keeping the physical plant up to standards, clearing taxiways/runways, and making the terminal passenger ready. Managing an airport is like juggling a variety of disparate demands, crises, and rules. Municipal airports have a complex reporting and accountability system. The city-owned facilities are located on city property and are amenable to city ordinances, yet they are subjected to a variety of federal and state mandates and rules. Irate passengers, pushy airline executives, and weather-related inconveniences are expected, but the manager must never let these things undermine the airport's reputation. As we saw in chapter 4, managers cannot absolutely stay out of local politics. Rather, they must engage in politics without seeming to do so. Directors also inherit the policies of their predecessors.

The record shows that insider and outsider airport directors are recruited for different reasons. The careers of insider directors Josh Birmingham and Jerry Orr are highlighted here because of their critical roles at crucial moments in Charlotte Douglas's post–World War II history. Like Birmingham, Jerry Orr was also a consummate salesman, but he had different styles. Finally, this chapter includes a brief discussion of the hiring of Charlotte Airport's current director, Mr. Cagle. In all cases, directors engaged in role taking.

TYPES OF ROLE TAKING

Management professor Henry Mintzberg's classic book *The Nature of Managerial Work* outlines the various roles of the organizational chief executive officer (CEO). Mintzberg discusses the stresses of being a day-to-day manager, including the position's concomitant time management problems. As stated earlier, quiet weeks at the airport are unusual. The director is expected to perform several tasks, some not explicitly defined in the job description.

The earlier discussion of airport history notes that directors were expected to be proactive in their jobs. Starting with David Rea, who took personal action against wild dogs on the airport grounds, directors were expected to take quick on-site decisions and carry out long-range planning for airport growth. They could take internal action without first consulting the city manager. When Josh Birmingham talked about his job, he reminisced about its fluid nature; he attended many meetings and talked to a variety of people.

Aviation directors are also allowed considerable administrative discretion. Aside from being the public face of the city Department of Aviation, the airport director represents the facility in meetings with the airline staff. Such responsibilities make up what Mintzberg calls a figurehead role. Throughout Charlotte Douglas's history, directors are the only individuals associated with the airport whose names make the newspapers. The exception was the airport's Birmingham era, when Orr was often quoted in the newspaper.

Obviously, the airport director takes a leadership role for his subordinates.

Although civil service rules govern a majority of the director's staff, he remains these employees' supervisor. Workers expect him to make decisions and assign responsibilities. As stated previously, airport directors are liaisons with the community and the city council. The figurehead, leadership, and liaison roles are what Mintzberg calls interpersonal roles.

Directors also act as monitors by collecting information for the development of the airport. They are obligated to stay current, and they are required to understand a variety of federal and state laws, regulations, and circulars. The airport director is also expected to disseminate information to subordinates. As the chapter on airport history suggests, the director is the spokesperson for the airport and is expected to communicate with the media and the public. Since Charlotte Douglas had no annual report, management transactions and proceedings were found in Airport Advisory Committee minutes. The airport director's disseminator and spokesperson roles are what Mintzberg called information-processing ones.

Most of all, the directors of Charlotte Douglas Airport were expected to be entrepreneurs—they were tasked with finding new ways to make operations income. Orr's tenure is considered the model for this role. All directors are crisis managers who tackle safety/security issues, weather issues (hurricanes and storms), and other maintenance emergencies. Airport directors are also resource allocators who authorize the uses of the facility's funds. Finally, directors participate in negotiations with airlines and concessions vendors. Mintzberg associates these duties with decision-making roles.

In general, directors of American airports are expected to be at the center of the aerotropolis. Their job descriptions may just define their administrative responsibilities, such as managing the terminals and making contracts with vendors. But in reality, airport directors resemble de facto mayors running a small city. They lead a staff that serves the airline carriers, concession vendors, and taxi/shuttle contract workers alike. This centering of directors in airports holds for both traditional or partisan cities as well as progressive or reform-oriented cities.

In each case, the office of airport directorship works best when political supervisors trust the incumbent. In Charlotte, the airport director's immediate supervisor is the city manager. The manager works for the city council and is expected to make the council aware of the various transactions of the airport. For its part, the city council expects the director to manage the airport in the public interest. Council members expect a director to be accountable, trustworthy, and competent. The assumption is that if the director is found to exhibit none of these qualities, he or she will find it difficult to lead one of the city's most important economic assets, the airport. Once that trust is gained, the city council is comfortable affording considerable administrative discretion to a director. This doesn't mean that a director must be *sans peur et sans reproche*. Such managerial discretion is accorded to all semi-independent city agencies that operate on fees. Given these expectations, directors must have speaking and communication skills.

PUBLIC SPEAKING AND COMMUNICATING

Although the general public is the audience for directors' presentations, the most attentive audience is the pro-growth coalition. Accordingly, an airport director must have the acumen to understand local politics. Reporters often blame the bureaucracy for airport failures and mishaps, and directors must control the information and impose their own interpretations on a given set of circumstances. In service of this goal, successful leaders usually construct "citizenry-specific" messages to promote acceptance of airport management's interpretations of events. Doing so requires certain rhetorical skills that will resonate with the airport's "attentive public." This attentive public includes the media, frequent fliers, and neighborhood groups.

The constituencies of a director are the airline industry, the political establishment, and the business leadership or economic elite. An effective director must comprehend and meet the needs of both the audience and the constituency, and communication is essential to establishing an understanding relationship between these groups. In other words, the director's characterization of airport events is the essence of effective airport management.

Communication between an airport director and his supervisors, the city manager and city council, is also important. However, a third party, the media, can complicate it. Obviously, it would not be prudent for a director to alienate the media; an unsupportive press may challenge, ignore, or misinterpret a director's messages. As the principal storytellers and intermediaries between directors and the public, print reporters at the *Charlotte Observer* played an important part in promoting Charlotte Douglas's expansion. Initially, colleagues in television and broadcast media limited their interest to accidents and weather delays. The 1975 television forum on the revenue bond election was an exception.

This research suggests that directors faced a series of political events amenable to a variety of interpretations. Directors had to be able to respond quickly, directly, and cogently to a potential negative media frame. Sociologist William Gamson and his associates define framing as "a central organizing principle that holds together and gives coherence and meaning to a diverse array of symbols."[22]

If the director successfully frames airport events, alternative explanations will have little chance of gaining public credibility. When directors lose the framing contest and fail to promote future plans, they are left defending airport failures against alternative explanations. Given the array of possible alternative explanations, a reporter can seize the opportunity to challenge the director. And because directorships are defined by events, performance evaluations are an ongoing process.

In addition, the political and economic time during which an individual serves as director matters. Leaders will encounter lulls and periods of hyperactivity. Some events such as airline mergers are more important than others (e.g., weather problems), and a director can often count on the public remembering the most recent occurrences rather than the earlier ones.

In addition, media coverage of an airport is involved in discourse about political life in the city. Coverage is designed to resonate with the majority of viewers and readers, so it is not news when all the planes land safely at the airport. Accidents, security breakdowns, and weather delays constitute news. When and if the airport director's interpretation can be folded into that discourse, everything runs smoothly. Airport coverage is then positive. When the director's views don't fit, problems emerge. These issues are not insurmountable, but they require time and energy to offset the media's negative interpretation. When the 1975 revenue bond vote failed, airport staff took three years to recover. The Birmingham team's recuperation spanned his tenure as director.

TURNOVER AND DIRECTORS

Airport directors from the outside are perhaps more aware than their insider counterparts that they are hired help and can be replaced. Although the city manager cannot remove an airport director on a whim, directors nonetheless exist on a perpetual job bubble. Accordingly, many try to stay out of the newspapers and maintain a low profile. Some do not consider Charlotte the end of their professional career—indeed, a young director may want to move on to larger facilities in Chicago or Atlanta. Leaders enhance their professional reputations by performing well and effecting airport growth. Hence, ambitious directors are aware they are being monitored within the network of directors.

Airport directors may not be as turnover prone as Charlotte-Mecklenburg school superintendents, but they are nearly as vulnerable. Turnover is often a positive thing; it can bring new ideas and vision to the management of a city airport. The question for a city manager is whether to hire a cosmopolitan (national figure) from outside the city or a local applicant. Each candidate has

Table 5. Managers and Tenure

Airport Manager	City Manager	Tenure	Events
V. L. Nash	A. K. Flack	1945	
David Rea	A. K. Flack	1946–1955	Conversion of Morris Field
Al Quinn	Henry Yancey	1956–1962	Delta landing Buckley report
Thomas Rafferty	William Veered	1962–1967	Mural controversy
Ross Knight	William Veered	1967–1970	
G. Edwin Pietro	William Veered	1970	
Josh Birmingham	Paul Bobo (acting) David Burkhalter O. Wendell White	1971–1988	Runway improvements 1978 revenue bond victory New terminal 1982 Deregulation Act
Jerry Orr	O. Wendell White W. Curtis Walton Julie Burch Ron Carlee	1988–2013	Piedmont merger with U.S. Airways International flights Discount airlines
Brent Cagle	Ron Carlee	2013–present	U.S. Airways merger with American Airlines

advantages and disadvantages. Cosmopolitans are more likely to have accumulated airport management experience and a reputation of good leadership that can be evaluated by a search committee. Moreover, a national search tends to generate many names, and the resulting publicity bolsters the airport's status. Outsiders are also less likely to "go native," meaning they will stay out of local politics and invest time and energy in the airport. However, cosmopolitans are also more likely to leave for an attractive outside offer.

Locals—that is, directors recruited from the existing staff or other departments in the city—are more likely to have some political connections and friends in the community. They have already gone "native." And once they become entrenched, it may be politically difficult to remove them. The clear advantage of hiring locals is that they offer long-term consistency and predictability. The problem with such managers is that they lack leadership experiences elsewhere. Because they have never worked in another facility, they rely on the history of the local airport. Local hires are also more likely to use their connections to politicians and business leaders to advance the airport. This could be an asset when dealing with local media and airline executives. Table 5 lists the Charlotte Douglas directors, the Charlotte city managers, and the events that occurred during their tenure.

As this table also shows, there was considerable overlap between the airport directors and the city managers. Some airport directors achieved more political distance from city managers than others because of turnover. Director Orr and Birmingham are examples. Because locals have local support, they have a better chance of achieving a long tenure and an opportunity for leadership. However, cosmopolitans did make an impact on the airport, for many of the early directors were outsiders.

THE EARLY DIRECTORS

Charlotte has a long history of recruiting airport directors, including most of the early ones, from outside the city. As noted earlier regarding the airport's history, the city appointed Maj. V. L. Nash the facility's first temporary director. The army operated the airport from 1941 to 1945. Nash was a bridge manager to city control during that period. In June 1946, city manager R. W. Flack announced that David Rea would remain the engineer in charge. Nash and Rea were part of the 1930 WPA construction of the Charlotte Airport. They could be defined as maintenance managers, and in Flack's view, this type of leadership was all that was needed at the time. The city manager then advertised the job and claimed that a dozen candidates applied. This level of interest is understandable because the salary was $5,000 to $6,000 a year, currently equivalent to $87,072. Flack ultimately hired no one and stated that he would add management of the airport to his duties.[23]

The decades after World War II saw Charlotte undergo a fundamental demographic transformation. Per the 1950 census, the city population grew to 134,042, increasing 32.8 percent since 1940. The army base had put Charlotte on the map for some veterans. It was a rising city in the U.S. Southeast.

It became clear to city leaders that Charlotte Douglas Airport could not be run effectively from city hall. The airport needed a full-time director at the facility. City manager Flack decided to officially appoint David M. Rea the first director of Charlotte Douglas. Rea, the former assistant and the engineer in charge of construction for the airport, had been acting manager without the title. Flack told him in a letter, "Your duties are to include maintenance, leasing property, collecting rentals, etc. You will have general supervision over the entire project and be responsible for the enforcement of all rules and regulation governing the enterprise."²⁴ The appointment letter is interesting because it reminded Rea that Charlotte had a formal Department of Aviation under the supervision of the city manager. The letter also stated that Rea's appointment had received the endorsement of John C. Erwin, C. P. Street, and Hugh Campbell. Five days into Rea's tenure, a miniscandal broke out.

City officials decided to sell fifty-two old Morris Field buildings to twenty individuals. The *Charlotte Observer* reported that some of the buildings were sold for prices ranging from $2.30 to $302.60. Also according to the newspaper, twenty-nine houses were sold. Flack and Rea challenged the word "houses" and said these structures were storage sheds, tool shacks, and clapboard structures. The problem for the city manager and airport director was that few people knew of the sales because they had taken place at an "impromptu auction." The *Charlotte Observer* noted, "If all these purported 'houses' were the six-by-six variety somebody got gypped."²⁵ Besides, home-seeking veterans did not know about the sale, and those who did know about it were nonveterans needing materials to build homes. Some building materials were even sold to real estate promoters with eyes for a bargain. The *Charlotte Observer* ended the article by observing, "But 'tempest' or not. The teapot was still bubbling last night and it seems highly probable that when the next cups were filled veterans will get the first sip."²⁶ The airport housing scandal was embarrassing, but it signaled that the city finally owned the facility.

Rea's remaining tenure as director was not newsworthy, but Rea was an interesting character in his own right. After Morris Field was returned to the city, some soldiers who had been stationed there abandoned their pet dogs. These "wild dogs of the airport" created packs and would run onto the runways and after light aircraft. In response to this danger and embarrassment, Rea would go after these dogs with his gun.²⁷ Rea remained director for nine years. He died in November 1955.

In 1956, Henry Yancey replaced Flack as city manager. The Charlotte Aero Club and the Airport Advisory Committee supported Yancey's plan to hire a professional manager and conduct a nationwide search. Yancey asked the city council to raise the manager's salary from $6,000 to $7,500 to attract a professional candidate for the job. Four months after Rea's death, Al Quinn was recruited as the city's first professional airport director. He served in the job from 1956 to 1962 and arrived in Charlotte as its economic development was taking off. During Quinn's tenure, the U.S. Census count of the city's population grew to 201,564, a 50 percent increase over the 1950 population. Quinn also came to Charlotte when its pro-growth coalition was gaining strength and its economy was relatively stable.

Quinn had been a chief engineer with the Civil Aeronautics Administration at the Atlanta Airport for twelve years. He had earned an electrical engineering degree from an Ivy League school, Columbia University, and he had also been a consultant with Lockheed Aircraft in Marietta. Quinn received a substantial amount of publicity because he was forty-two years old and had a wife who was also a pilot. He claimed that one of his neighbors was Charlie Woolman, president of Delta, and that Delta wanted to start service at Charlotte Douglas. Quinn further claimed that he had taken a pay cut to take the position as manager of the airport. He predicted, "Charlotte, in 10 years, should be one of the top 10 airports in the United States. . . . Competitive airline service offers the best public service and with Delta and Eastern and others Charlotte will have the best."[28]

In 1961, Quinn hired New York consultant firm James C. Buckley Incorporated to craft a financial plan for the Charlotte Airport. The firm recommended that the airport sell bonds to expand the facility with a new terminal and added runways. Consultants also suggested that the airport spend $7.3 million between 1962 and 1970, and that it develop a more centralized management system. Of the $7.3 million, the city of Charlotte would sell bonds for $4 million.[29] In addition, James C. Buckley's members suggested improving the airport's accounting procedures and increasing its rent. The various rental agreements predated Quinn's tenure, but while city manager Yancey had supported an increase in rates.

Obviously, Quinn was an airport expansionist. Part of his attraction to the job was his grand ambition for Charlotte Douglas. He stated early in his tenure, "A big part of an airport manager's job is to find new sources of revenue. . . . We're growing. But remember, as we grow, we must spend money to expand. Like the $10,000 for the new Delta operation."[30] While Quinn was director of Charlotte Douglas, the FAA sent Congress a master plan for 465 new airports, including Charlotte's. Quinn told the *Charlotte Observer* that he doubted the city would get any money. He likened the process to putting your name in a pot and hoping it would be drawn. "That doesn't mean you will get any money," Quinn told the newspaper.[31]

During Quinn's tenure, a pilot for the Jewel Ridge Coal Corporation filed a lawsuit against the airport director and the city of Charlotte. The pilot claimed that his plane was heavily damaged because of a faulty runway—in the absence of warning signs, his aircraft crashed. A judge dismissed the suit against the city but held against Quinn as the airport's operation officer. Quinn was ordered to pay the plaintiff $15,000.[32]

Charlotte Observer reporter Alex Coffin calls Al Quinn's tenure "controversial."³³ When Quinn announced his resignation as airport director, city manager Veeder announced that the next manager would not be a current staffer. Quinn claimed that he quit because of the low salary, which was $9,100 at the time. He disclaimed any friction between himself and city management.

The *Charlotte Observer* noted a problem between Quinn and the city council concerning his salary. According to Coffin, pressure to remove Quinn had been building. City manager William Veeder expressed surprise that the Charlotte Aero Club had honored Quinn as "Airport Man of the Year." Veeder in fact asserted, "[Quinn] hasn't done anything to deserve the honor."³⁴ Indeed, Veeder said that he should have gotten the award for getting rid of Quinn.

The problems associated with the Quinn years did not deter Veeder from pursuing another national search. Rather, he stated that he would "try to find the best man with the experience for the job."³⁵ In February 1962, Veeder announced that the Charlotte Douglas Airport expansion would be delayed for a year. Tom Rafferty of Long Beach, California, was then selected from a nationwide pool of applicants. Nevertheless, the *Charlotte Observer* reporter greeted new airport manager Rafferty with the headline "Al Quinn's Successor on Hot Seat."³⁶ The new manager was obligated to respond to these problems.

This period witnessed efforts to pass a new revenue bond for the airport. Headed by Robert Alander, the Charlotte Chamber of Commerce's Bond Promotion Committee led the drive for new revenue for the airport. The $12.6 million effort was essentially a bond for water and sewers. Again, the strategy was to emphasize the fact that the bond would be retired by airport fees and not new taxes. The majority of the $8.1 million was designated for water and sewers, and only $1.5 million was set aside for the airport. Another $3 million was to be used to buy an expressway right-of-way. Ultimately, the revenue bond was successful.

In 1962, the Airport Advisory Committee and airport manager Thomas Rafferty recommended that Wilmington consultancy John Talbert and Associates be awarded an engineering contract at the airport. Rafferty told the Charlotte City Council that the company's consultants were specialists and came highly recommended for a $100,000 fee. This was a small part of a multimillion-dollar job partly funded by the Federal Aviation Administration. Another of the Talbert firm's qualifications was that it had a former member of the FAA on staff. Wondering why a local firm did not get the job, some members of the council began to challenge the recommendation and give preference to J. N. Pease and Company of Charlotte. Although two council members claimed politics was involved, they also stated that, "all things being equal," they should consider the local company.³⁷ Mayor Brookshire admitted that Talbert had an office in

Charlotte and that Pease was a local firm. However, the Talbert firm got the job. The council's challenge of recommendation was an opportunity for members to show symbolic support for local companies.

Rafferty was also director during the conflict over the controversial airport mural. In 1964, artist Charles L. Sweitzer proposed the five-foot-high, two-hundred-foot-long, ten-panel *Charlotte 220 History Mural* depicting Mecklenburg's more than two centuries of industrial progress. Endorsed by the Airport Advisory Committee and the city council, the work was to be a gift to the airport. Rafferty stated, "The great number of people who come through the airport will get a quick review of Charlotte's history."[38] He further noted that the thirty thousand people who passed through the airport each month would see the waiting-room mural.[39] In the end, Sweitzer's mural was not installed. It was proposed in the middle of the civil rights movement, and its subject was considered demeaning to African Americans.

Rafferty's tenure at the Charlotte Airport also coincided with the Eastern Air Lines engineer strike. He served as aviation director from 1962 to 1967 and left Charlotte Douglas to take the airport directorship in San Antonio.

In June 1970, city manager Veeder hired G. Edwin Pietro to be airport director. When he was appointed to the position, Pietro held a degree in air transportation engineering from Purdue University and had amassed twenty-five years' experience in the airport management field. He had been assistant airport director in Indianapolis after spending six years as manager of New Castle County Airport in Wilmington, Delaware. Pietro had also served twelve years as an airport director in Indianapolis. During his tenure at Charlotte Douglas, the city of Charlotte applied for a $4.5 million airport expansion grant. The money would pay for land acquisition. The early seventies were an interesting period for the "transformative city." Although the U.S. Census showed that the city population had grown to 241,420, Charlotte itself had only grown by 19.8 percent. In addition, the airport did not expand much, and Pietro lasted six months in the job. Dick Datty was appointed interim director after his departure.

After another six months, Ross Knight replaced Datty. Knight, a U.S. Naval Academy graduate and navy pilot, was chosen from a pool of forty applicants. His previous twenty-six years of experience included consulting on airport problems for Airports Operation Council International. At the time of his appointment, the forty-nine-year-old Knight was a "Jet Age airport manager."[40] He had also made positive remarks about the tenure of Thomas Rafferty.[41]

Knight served as director in the initial stage of the airport's $57 million expansion. The new concourse opened on November 22, 1969, and provided six enclosed waiting rooms and a snack bar. Also during Knight's tenure, the airport created a new parking lot with over five hundred spaces in front of the terminal. The facility's parking meters were replaced with automatic entrances with attendants.[42] Problems with small planes at the airport subsequently created new pressure on Knight, who asked the council to hire a consultant to conduct a study. At the same time, the city turned down an offer to buy Carpenter Airport, then located about five miles from Charlotte Douglas.[43] Knight served as airport director from 1967, when he started his tenure by hiring J. E. Griener Company of Baltimore to create a master plan for the facility, to 1970, when he died from a coronary in June.

The short tenures of Pietro, Datty, and Knight might have contributed to the idea of hiring someone from the Charlotte community as airport director. In an article concerning former director Knight, the *Charlotte Observer* pointed out that city manager William Veeders had set the "pattern of recruiting established professionals, many of them non-Charlotteans."[44]

THE RISE OF LOCAL MANAGERS

In April 1971, acting city manager Paul Bobo informed the press that he was considering acting aviation director Richard L. Beaty and assistant director Robert Covington "Josh" Birmingham for the position of permanent manager at Charlotte Douglas. Beaty did not live in the city and did not meet the job's residency requirement. Though interested in the opening, he would not comment publicly on a move to Charlotte.[45] In the meantime, the city council had resisted appointing an outsider to the office. Council members wanted a resident city employee to take the helm at Charlotte Douglas. As a result, forty-eight-year-old Birmingham, a Charlotte civil engineer, was named airport manager. Birmingham was a local college graduate (Belmont Abbey College) who had started to work for the city in 1948. The first local to head Charlotte Douglas since David Rea, he assumed his duties when eighty flights traveled to and from Charlotte Airport. Birmingham soon earned a reputation as the man behind the scenes.

In an article entitled "Airport Administration Satisfied Working Behind the Scenes," a former mayor was quoted as saying, "We picked him because he got along with people so well."[46] Birmingham defined the main elements of his job as follows: "Mostly paperwork, mostly liaison with the city management, mostly with the advisory board, most liaison with the Chamber of Commerce. [There are] a lot of liaisons with civic groups wanting presentations on airport development. Last year, me and my staff probably gave two or three of those a week."[47]

Like his predecessors, Birmingham advocated linking the city's economic development and the airport's: "I don't know of any way you can stop this kind of growth short of cutting off your arm. Douglas Airport is the most vibrant contribution to the growth of Charlotte-Mecklenburg.... The airport is the front door to this area. It is the first thing potential investors see when they come to visit. And its service is the first thing they ask about."[48] Charlotte became even more public about its growing and changing economy in the 1970s. In a 1975 article on the evolution of the city economy, Ken Clark asserted that Charlotte was not a one-industry town. He stated, "Today this city's bank deposits exceed Atlanta's. There are more trucking firms here than in any other city besides Chicago. Our network of highways is strategically important. Three hundred trains a week and 150 airplanes a day make stops in Charlotte."[49]

Hugh McColl, president of the city's largest bank, North Carolina National Bank (NCNB), also deemed growth essential. *Fortune* magazine reported that McColl lived by the creed "Once you stop growing, you start dying."[50] The decade from the 1970s to the 1980s was indeed a boom period. In 1980, the city grew 30.7 percent and reached a population of 315,474. Charlotte did not exactly double its growth since 1970, but it nonetheless became large enough to garner the airline industry's attention. For airlines, more residents meant more potential passengers.

In 1973, the airport employed A. G. Odell Associates to design a new terminal. Since Odell had done the architectural work for Charlotte's coliseum and civic center, the Airport Advisory Committee also recommended the company to the city council. However, local architects objected to the contract, and a councilperson also raised questions about it. Even so, former mayor Douglas, then chair of the AAC, supported Odell. Douglas stated that while ten local firms with the capacity to help were invited to make a bid, only seven of them responded. The council voted six to one to award the contract to Odell. Local firms refused to comment for "fear of never getting jobs."[51]

Birmingham was a longtime Charlotte resident who knew people in the government. He could talk to them and vice versa. Such was the case during the 1980 exchange between Birmingham and Mayor Knox concerning the Civil Air Patrol's (CAP's) tenancy at the airport. Birmingham's letter provided the history of the CAP and argued the fact that the organization had occupied three old World War II buildings since 1950 and had paid a $1.00 leasing fee. In 1967, that fee increased to $1.50. In 1974, the Charlotte City Council voted to allow CAP to remain in those buildings at a low rate. Colonel Bonderrant of CAP had requested the buildings be rent-free until action by the city council.

In October 1974, Birmingham wrote assistant city manager L. P. Bobo and stated his desire to continue the $1.50 monthly fee. The CAP, a civilian auxiliary of the U.S. Air Force, refused to pay the rent for its facility on the airport campus. Birmingham then asked CAP to move to a more permanent facility connected with the North Carolina National Guard. Birmingham made it clear that the present facilities at the airport were prime commercial locations and that he wanted to develop the space as a "revenue generator for the airport."[52] An outsider might not have been able to make the final deal, in which the CAP was moved to a different part of the airport complex.

In many ways, Josh Birmingham was the prototype of an insider director. He came to the job with no fancy degrees or previous airport leadership experience. Thus, he literally learned on the job. Bill McCoy, a professor and the former head of the University of North Carolina at Charlotte's Urban Institute, described Birmingham as "the epitome of the smooth, professional businessman, who fit right in with other business leaders of the community."[53] Described by a friend as having "no ego," Birmingham guided the airport through the 1974 crash of Eastern Air Lines and the 1975 and 1978 challenges of airline deregulation. Remember, when he took the job the airport serviced 80 flights a day, and when he retired in 1988, the facility serviced 426 flights a day. Birmingham had served for seventeen years, during which time the airport had to change its racial policies. He survived the rejection of the 1975 revenue bond proposal, and he led the airport during the planning and building of the main 1982 terminal at Charlotte Douglas. Birmingham also mentored Jerry Orr, who became his assistant manager in 1980.

Josh Birmingham, for whom the city of Charlotte named a parkway, could also be described as a consummate technocrat. Although the city manager directly supervises the airport director, history reveals a variety of political relationships between the city managers and directors. Birmingham was already native. Jerry Orr, also a local, was a Birmingham successor.

THE ASCENDANCY OF JERRY ORR

The long and illustrious career of Jerry Orr is a study of entrepreneurship, vision, and political acumen. Former city manager Ron Carlee said as much in an interview.

> I will give Mr. Orr credit for the airport being grown to the magnitude it is today. The way it was grown, I doubt that anyone could have done this other than Jerry Orr. He had an entrepreneurial skill and had developed relationships with very financially weak airlines, Piedmont and USAir. He figured out a way to give them a base of operation at lowest cost possible and that ultimately enabled them to survive.... I give him a lot credit for growing it. I don't think anyone else could have done it.[54]

The story of Charlotte Douglas International Airport after the late eighties is the story of the career of T. J. "Jerry" Orr. Orr joined the airport staff in 1964 and was appointed manager in the winter of 1988, while Charlotte was undergoing a demographic change. The 1990 Census reported a 25.5 percent increase in the city population (395,934). By 2000, the population rose to 540,828, another 36.6 percent increase. In 2010, Charlotte's population reached 731,424, increasing yet another 35.2 percent. Orr would be leading a fast-growing airport for a developing city.

Orr learned his craft by watching and supporting Birmingham. The two worked closely with each other during the failure of the 1975 revenue bond and the building of the new 1982 terminal. In 1980, Orr became assistant director of the airport. Eight years later he was selected to be director over eighty-five other candidates from around the nation. Orr oversaw both 160 city employees at the airport and a budget of $31 million. As previously mentioned, during his tenure, the transformative city increased in population 25.5 percent in 1990 and 36.6 percent in 2000. In 2010, Charlotte's population grew to 731,424 or 35.2 percent. In effect, Orr's tenure spanned three decades of population growth. Changing demographics made the job of selling airport expansion much easier for the airlines and for the citizens of Metrolina.

During his twenty-four years' tenure as aviation director, Orr had both supporters and critics. Supporters pointed to his long-term vision for the development of Charlotte Douglas. In interviews conducted for this book, people associated with the airport repeatedly used the word "vision" in reference to Director Orr. It follows that Orr was a man people listened to and learned from.

Bill McCoy and architect Michael Gallis met numerous times with Orr. Gallis developed a presentation called "the Silk Route" that used history to show how trade linked the world together. McCoy stated, "Jerry Orr was interested in this concept as it might apply to the Charlotte Airport.... These discussions eventually led to a plan, which has been realized in the last five years or so."[55] Michael Gallis recalled,

> Jerry kept the airport low cost. Charlotte has the lowest percentage of O&D [origin and destination] passengers of any hub in the U.S. It was around 30% as opposed to every other major hub that had over 50% of its passengers either enplaning or deplaning in Charlotte. He knew he had to compete on price. He was committed to having the lowest price airport. Jerry was one of the few who could understand the global vision. Jerry had a large vision and at the same time was involved with small details. Jerry could be aware of minute details. Usually detail people are not visionary people. Jerry was both. This is what made Jerry unique.

He understood global air travel and how Charlotte fits into the world. He could tell a contractor that the waterproofing between the precast concrete panels in the parking garages was not installed correctly. Everyone knew Jerry Orr. He could relate to everyone from a ditch digger to [an airline executive]. He could communicate with everyone.[56]

Leaders with vision can see things that don't exist and find ways to make them happen. In 2001, Orr saw potential for monorails or people movers that would connect the Charlotte Douglas terminal with the Norfolk Southern Railroad.[57] These transportation systems were not built, but Orr understood that travelers needed a quick way to get to the airport. Orr also grasped the benefits of being a larger hub before others and found a way to make it happen. He pushed the idea of an airport as an accelerator for regional economic development. With a 169-employee staff and a $31 million budget, Orr took a small airport and made it into the nation's sixth-largest one. Former city manager Carlee described Orr's action as turning a "mom and pop store into a Wal-Mart." Orr also developed the facility's Air Cargo Center and facilitated the emergence of the airport as a hub for U.S. Airways. Historian Walter R. Turner characterizes the transition from Birmingham to Orr.

> The airport's leadership transition was smooth. Orr quickly established a close working relationship with USAir, which was initially skeptical of the Charlotte hub. Despite a series of financial and leadership changes, USAir has continued to expand the Charlotte hub. In 1997, the year the airline changed its name to U.S. Airways, it closed maintenance bases in Winston-Salem and Greensboro and moved most employees from those facilities to Charlotte. In 2004, the airline downgraded its hub in Pittsburgh and expanded its hubs in Charlotte and Philadelphia. U.S. Airways has maintained its Charlotte-London flights to the present, with assistance from British Airways during the mid-1990s.[58]

In 1996, the Government Accounting Office (GAO) identified Charlotte Douglas as an airport whose leasing policy inhibited competition. One of Charlotte Douglas's advantages over other airports was cheap leasing deals. Leasing arrangements with Piedmont Airlines allowed the carrier to develop a larger hub in Charlotte and expand its reach into new cities. Of course, such deals also limit competition. Discount airlines did not have access to gates; instead, they had to go to great expense to sublease gates from Piedmont and USAir. The lack of competition meant that most passenger traffic at Charlotte Douglas was with U.S. Airways. As a result, Charlotte residents paid higher fares.

On the one hand, airport gate leasing discouraged competition and allowed struggling in-house airlines to survive. On the other hand, the airport signed long-term leases with the big airlines because it needed to arrange its own long-term planning. Leasing represented an investment for both the airlines and the airport. Long-term leases were also necessary for airlines for airport expansion.

In addition, concession vendors prefer long-term leases because they help them sign long-term contracts. Leases are negotiated by airport managers and are considered moneymaking and operational matters. This is not to say that concession leasing is free of city politics. Technical operational requirements are considered outside city politics.

Orr's critics claimed that he ran the airport as if it were his personal business. Often the city manager and city council members were out of the loop—the airport was Jerry's world. Orr's personalized style of management generated employee loyalty but alienated some critics. As we will see later, Orr was one of the actors that initiated the state's attempts to take over the airport.

The Orr administration presided over new international flights to Europe, Mexico, and Latin America. Charlotte Douglas had four runways and a main terminal divided by five concourses with a total of eighty-five gates. While Orr was at its helm, the airport was considered the eleventh-busiest facility in the nation, serving over thirty-eight million travelers and hosting ten different airlines. In effect, thousands of passengers passed through Charlotte Douglas International Airport every day without ever setting a foot outside the facility.

With that record of success, Orr assumed a sense of personal ownership over Charlotte Douglas Airport. Understandably, his supporters believed that he helped make the airport a strong city asset. Orr earned considerable trust from the business community, several mayors, and city managers. The disposition of the privatization proposal and taxi contracts demonstrated the confidence Charlotteans accorded to the director.

In 1991, Orr had to defend the airport against rising criticism of general aviation, which was said to be in decline at Charlotte Douglas. Private and corporate jets claimed they were being "squeezed" out by big airlines. As a result, pilots for these aircraft had to use regional airports. Orr challenged the numbers and the methodology used by private pilots. Despite achieving a level V rating as a business, Orr claimed that an effort was made to accommodate general aviation.[59] Through June of that year, 32,798 general aviation flights came through Charlotte Douglas—a 22 percent decrease since the previous year. Orr attributed the decline to the recession.

For his battle for expansion and support for airlines, Jerry Orr became one of the most high-profile and revered airport directors in the nation. In 2010, the

International Air Transport Association honored him with the prestigious Eagle Award for Best Airport in the World. This award was based on the airport's low costs, low debt, and solid service levels. Ed McMahan and Ned Curran, the chamber of commerce's chair of economic development and chair of public policy respectively, wrote an editorial praising Jerry Orr's efforts toward improving and promoting the airport.[60] According to McMahan and Curran, the airport was a "defining factor" in companies' decision to relocate to and expand in Charlotte. They further noted that Jerry Orr had been an effective leader for over twenty years, stating, "We support Mr. Orr's management and thank him for his service to our community."[61] Former Mayor Vinroot and John Belk received a similar comment when British Airlines made its inaugural flight from Charlotte to London. The head of British Airlines offered uncommon praise for Orr's leadership, telling them, "Your city has the best airport manager in America and one of the best in the world. The other one is in Dubai."[62]

In 2010, the IRS extended its audit of some of the airport bonds. Charlotte's city finance department and its counsel, Parker Poe, found that the airport had commingled funds from bonds issued in 2004. As a result, the city issued new guidelines restricting Director Orr's administrative control over Charlotte Douglas's finances. In 2013, Orr asserted that he did not think the accounting problems were a "big issue," stating, "Essentially, what we did was in the accounting process we co-mingled some money that was taxable bond money and non-taxable bond money."[63]

Jerry Orr also understood the ambitions of the state house politicians and the interests of the surrounding counties. Charlotte's changing demographics raised certain officials' concerns, and in the new environment of activism, an airport director had to bargain and compromise. The pro-growth coalition also needed to be reassured. Orr's ability to deal with multiple levels of government made him attractive to airline executives and the chamber of commerce. In effect, Jerry Orr spoke their language.

The more Orr behaved like a businessman and the more success the airport enjoyed, the more independent he became. He dealt in power rather than profit from the airlines. Power came with making Charlotte a low-cost hub, and Orr invested his career in building a business-friendly airport. By granting favors and accumulating IOUs, Orr was also able to overcome the structural limits of his position. His type of leadership seeks to maintain or increase the position stock of power. For him, a good director had to be a bold problem solver and a big deal maker. Given his acumen, Orr survived as the airport approached the turn of the century and then headed into the first decade of the twenty-first century.

Orr's staff structure reflected his management style, for he related directly to his assistant directors without a deputy director. As in most organizations, staff usually adjusts to a leader's idiosyncratic working structure. This was the case with holdovers from Birmingham's leadership of Charlotte Douglas.

In general, Orr defined his position as part manager and part entrepreneur, and he also proved himself a power broker who was willing to take risks. He gambled in lending his support to a proposal for a regional authority for the Charlotte-owned airport. As evidenced in chapter 7, however, he could not control the consequences. In the end, Orr's attempt to replace city ownership with a regional authority was his undoing. In 2013, Orr resigned the aviation directorship, and Brent Cagle was appointed acting director.

THE APPOINTMENT OF BRENT CAGLE

Brent Cagle had worked for Orr for a year as assistant aviation director, administration and finance. Prior to that, he had worked as a budget analyst for the city of Phoenix, and he had also put in five years' service as deputy aviation director for Phoenix Sky Harbor International Airport. Cagle's master's degree in public administration from Texas Tech University involved training in organizational behavior, human resources, planning, and budgets. His studies further taught him the proper boundaries between policy and administration. As Cagle's management style differed from Orr's, he reorganized the senior staff.

By Cagle's own description, he has allowed his subordinates to speak directly to local politicians, including members of the Charlotte City Council, as long as they keep him in the loop. Cagle also maintains that he respects his assistant directors as experts.[64] Like a city manager, he sees himself as a policy expert willing to be publicly available and politically open, and a leader able to manage what is now a mega-airport and infrastructure. Like his predecessors, he has to relate to airline executives, concessionaires, and passengers. Cagle also has the same outside speaking obligations as former directors. Yet passengers, airlines, and elected officials continue to criticize airport environment and policies. David Gillen makes the following observation:

> Whether airports are operating efficiently involves three types of measures. First, are airports operating on the lowest cost function for their size, traffic composition and range of products? Second, are airports operating on the correct point on the lowest function, meaning are they pricing efficiently? Third, are airports

moving ahead in integrating technology whether imbedded in capital (runway or terminal), labour, governance or systems to ensure continued cost efficiency? The empirical evidence has concentrated on the first measure and only recently has research explored the second measure. The third measure has not been explored.[65]

Again, Charlotte Douglas continues to operate at a low cost for its size. The airport still retains a relatively stable financial foundation, and its facilities are lively and offer a variety of concessions. Long-term parking fees are relatively low, but they continue to rise with the addition of new parking facilities. In addition, Charlotte Douglas is amenable to expanding its facilities and building more runways. As of this writing, the airport is undergoing a billion-dollar development process to upgrade buildings and put Charlotte in the middle of a nationwide airport hub competition. Olga Johnson concludes, "Airlines' inter-urban competition becomes especially important in times when the industry is in transition. A new solution, the hub-and-spoke, offered new possibilities and deregulation directly led to entrepreneurial activism by city governments and local business interests."[66] As long as outside directors promote the interest of the pro-growth coalition and airport expansion, there will not be conflict.

As stated earlier, the business community in Charlotte is the biggest beneficiary of the airport's development. Alan Altshuler and David Luberoff conclude, "What competition means for American local governments, above all, is striving to make themselves attractive to private investors." Some of the projects discussed can best be described as "the gifts that keep on taking."[67] A well-managed airport is one of the best selling points in the business community's effort to market Charlotte as a location place for companies.

SUMMARY

As pointed out earlier, municipal governments' use of consultants is a time-honored practice. Throughout the history of Charlotte Douglas, consultants produced plans for the facility's expansion and for many of the city's other economic activities. Consultants are a part of the nationwide municipal grand patronage community. They know how to impress and flatter city leaders, and they can offer services as easily as sending an email. Grand patronage is one of the few types of patronage available to city leaders. By its nature, the council-manager form of government has small mayoral and council staffs that make it dependent on consultants when large projects are discussed and large costs are involved. When such patronage is offered to outside firms, it is only questioned if a local firm can do the job. Obviously, local firms are at an advantage with plan implementation and facility construction. Consultants' professional counterparts are the operations managers of the city.

Like school superintendents and city managers, airport directors are part of an emerging public sector managerial class that operates Charlotte's municipal service institutions. Most airport leaders take their jobs with a view toward making a positive impact in Charlotte. They come to town as professional public administrators, and they are also in the business of professional reputation making. Outsiders who become airport directors know there are other airports out there. These individuals are evaluated locally as well as nationally. A more interesting dynamic is the relationship between the airport director and the city manager. Writing for *Public Administration Review* in 1958, Karl A. Bosworth made the case that a manager must be a politician in order to do his or her job.[68] Though outside airport directors are also policy makers, they must be careful not to be seen as publicly preempting elected officials' actions. They are both members of a growing national urban managerial class, and again, there is always another job. Local airport directors have fewer options and dig themselves into local politics, generally getting more done. The success of any airport director is a matter of the "political time."

Each director's tenure was somewhat limited by the decisions of his predecessor. Airport heads have to deal with the consequences of those decisions while attempting to put their own stamp on the facility. In addition, directors are expected to deal with ongoing political events and promote Charlotte's economic aspirations. Obviously, outsider and insider directors face different challenges. As suggested in the discussion of the airport's history, the city looked for different types of directors at different times in its economic development. Again, having someone to be the face of the airport is critical. Charlotte chose a local, Jerry Orr, at a crucial time for the city's financial affairs. Orr's tenure marked changes in air travel and profound alterations in Charlotte itself, making it the transformative city. During Charlotte Douglas's early years, city leaders thought outside aviation experts needed to be the face of the airport. The directors who preceded Birmingham muddled through, with Tom Rafferty and Ross Knight emerging as relatively successful outside leaders.

The leadership of Jerry Orr was critical to the airport's success. His long tenure was a testimony to local political support and his own anticipatory instincts. No one interviewed for this book disputed this claim, and several leaders openly praised Orr. Witness these words from banker and civic leader Hugh McColl: "Jerry Orr did a fantastic job. He built an efficient and effective airport."[69]

Indeed, Orr benefited from a reservoir of political trust, and he brought a technical background to the job, as well as an ability to communicate with airlines. He also made the jobs of the city manager and the city council easier. Identifying issues as technical allowed the director the space he needed to make deals with airlines. Yet while Orr knew how to persuade others to follow his lead, some business leaders believed that the region was ready for the "great leap" forward regarding real estate.

Times were changing, and the stakes were larger than the plight of hired managers and consultants. We have seen how city politicians promoted the airport and the goals of the pro-growth coalition. The next chapter will detail the structure of Charlotte's government and explain how mayors and the local pro-growth coalition promoted the airport's expansion and the overall economy.

CHAPTER 6

Meshing City Politics and the New Economy

THIS CHAPTER EXAMINES CHARLOTTE POLITICS as it intersects with the economic growth of the city and its airport. We will see how Charlotte's pro-growth coalition pushed the idea of a "transformative city" into another dimension, and how it linked the narrative of airport expansion to local politics. Chapter 6 examines day-to-day local politics because mayors and council members were more than ancillary players in the city's transformation. Elected officials occasionally put airport issues on the agenda and convinced their constituency of the saliency of airport expansion. However, the forces of expansion did not always suppress objections. This chapter will also discuss the role of airport interest groups and selected mayoral terms. As the previous chapters showed, the structure of government matters. Municipal government changes in response to public demand for representation and in response to administrative capacity overload. As the legendary blues singer Jimmy Reed would say, "Bright light, big city." Charlotte is now a big city. Big city also means big politics, or at least intriguing politics. Who gets what patronage, status, results, and credit, and how?

THE NEW ECONOMY NEXUS

In 1987 Edward Crutchfield, then chairman of First Union, told the *Atlanta Journal-Constitution*, "A young person can come here and not know a soul and not have a pedigree and do well, materially, financially and socially. This is a flat-out hustling business city. That's what makes it run."[1] Many so-called urban experts thought that the Sunbelt was ready to make the "great leap forward," and this potential was recognized in the late 1990s. Journalists Jerelyn Eddings and Jill Jordan Sieden stated,

> The South's political transformation has spanned a generation, running parallel to the region's transition from a dirt-poor agrarian society to a modern industrial one with a growing service economy and a more educated populace. The

percentage of college-educated Southerners rose from 6.9 percent in 1960 to 12.3 percent in 1990. Median family income (adjusted for inflation) rose from $20,228 to $31,940 in 1991, leaving the South still behind the national median but no longer in grinding poverty. At an earlier time, populist Democrats could appeal to poor whites with an anti-rich message, but as parts of the South have prospered, that message has lost its punch.[2]

Becoming a regional economic powerhouse is not without its perils. Some local alarms, including a 1974 *Charlotte Observer* editorial entitled "Nonstop to Hell," sounded during Charlotte's early transition. The editorial warned that Charlotte could develop into an Atlanta-sized airport within eleven years, provided Atlanta could transfer its congestion to Charlotte.[3] In 2002 Richard Maschal observed, "If 'Booster' Kuester came back today, he'd see a city less enamored with growth, with setting records like being the second-fastest-growing American city in the 1990s." He pointed to an Urban Land Institute study finding that Charlotte-area residents drive more than people in all but six other major cities, and that "Charlotteans increasingly worry about sprawl."[4] In 2004 Charlotte stood at the center of the largest consolidated rail system in the United States. Northern Southern and CSX Transportation saw three hundred trains passing through the city each week. The Charlotte Intermodal Terminal links the city to the Port of Wilmington, Delaware. In addition, forty of the nation's one hundred trucking firms do business in Charlotte.[5] With more commerce comes more people and more growth.

For years Charlotteans' cry has been "We don't want to be another Atlanta!" These days, the fate of that city—actually smaller in population than Charlotte, although its metro area is larger—seems closer. Maschal also predicts that Charlotte's I-485 loop around the city could act like Atlanta's I-285 in terms of traffic congestion.[6] In fact, Charlotte is now congested in its southernmost stretch. Yet many city residents welcome growth. In 1990 national real estate developer James DeFrancia asserted, "If Charlotte is an overgrown truck stop, well. Atlanta was once an overgrown peach stand. Look at any metro area that has evolved. They all had modest beginnings."[7]

In a 2006 interview with *USA Today*, Sam William, president of the Metro Atlanta Chamber of Commerce, dismissed any real competition between his city and Charlotte. He asserted, "[There will be no contest] unless they go out there and put Hartsfield on wheels and roll it up the interstate. Our competition is not the Charlottes and Nashvilles. Our competition is Frankfurt and Singapore and Shanghai. . . . The Southeast is a like a great big curved mirror. The focal point of that mirror is Atlanta."[8]

While Atlanta leaders' eyes are clearly on world competition, the city remains the gold standard for ambitious southeastern cities. Some Charlotte leaders openly envy Atlanta's success. For example, Charlotte Chamber of Commerce president Bob Morgan stated during an interview, "The City of Atlanta and Charlotte are similar."[9] Charlotte still has its eyes on Atlanta as a role model, or, more specifically, the pro-growth coalition has its eyes on Atlanta.

Nevertheless, Charlotte politics has become more pessimistic and guarded as we move past the millennium. Why? At first glance, U.S. cities like Charlotte cannot separate themselves from the current global economic system. They are not in the position to stop this process. Indeed, the economic leaders and boosters of Charlotte want their city to have world-class status.

Since the post–civil rights era, Charlotte and its elected leaders have attempted to increase the city's national and international profiles. In 1954, the mayor established the Charlotte City Council's twenty-one-member International Committee to provide advice on foreign affairs and business possibilities.[10] Charlotte boasts no organized opposition to globalization. To this point political scientist Darel Paul observes, "In an effort to sell local residents on the sacrifices of going global—including increased taxation, aircraft noise, inconvenience or simply the transformation of a local identity from familiar, particular and even provincial to unfamiliar, universal and cosmopolitan—globalizing elites make purposive appeals to a remade place-based identity and the value of projecting that identity globally."[11] In addition to changing a city identity, a city must also change its government structure to keep up with changing economics.

GOVERNMENT STRUCTURE AND PRO-GROWTH COALITIONS

Charlotte has demonstrated that it can change its politics by changing its government structure. After the Civil War, the city of Charlotte adopted an elected aldermanic and mayoral form of government. In 1870 the city's population of 4,473 was growing as a result of the textile industry's importance and the phenomenon of rural migration. As was discussed in chapter 2, Charlotte's textile years produced textile-influenced politics. Mill owners got most of what they wanted from the political system, yet limits emerged as their business colleagues looked to diversify the city economy. As early as 1894, nine years before the Wright brothers' flight, textile businessmen like Daniel A. Tompkins established a new pro-growth coalition. Called the Southern Manufacturer Club, its members shifted Charlotte from just a "mill town to a mill supplier."[12] The club became the networking vehicle to promote business, dining, and city politics.

By 1907, Charlotte's population had increased to 22,190. Jack Claiborne traced the development of the Charlotte Chamber of Commerce back to the Greater Charlotte Club's 1915 slogan "Watch Charlotte Grow." This businessmen's group started the early twentieth-century version of the Charlotte Chamber of Commerce with David Ovens as the first president.[13] In 1916 the Manufacturer Club of Charlotte invited Pres. Woodrow Wilson to the Queen City. This group lobbied Wilson and Gen. Leonard Wood to establish an army training base in Charlotte's Camp Greene. Jack Claiborne states, "The Camp proved to be a mighty economic stimulus and touched off a building boom that continued well into the 1920s. As a result, the Charlotte skyline bristled with new skyscrapers, topped by the 21-story First National Bank building, then the tallest structure in the Carolinas."[14]

In 1917, the city of Charlotte changed its government from an aldermanic form to a commission form. It had three at-large elected commissioners heading the city departments of finance, works, and public safety. As the city grew, this blending of executive and legislative functions had its problems—that is, politicians who were not good administrators. In 1929, Charlotte residents voted 4,436 to 2,496 to install a city manager form of government consistent with a national municipal reform movement. Executive problems were then concentrated in the hands of the city manager. In 1934, the city decided to elect the mayor directly. The number of council members increased from five to eleven the next year. At this point, the mayor would be the presiding officer of the Charlotte City Council, and the city manager would be the chief operating officer.

During the 1930s, Charlotte's form of government came under attack. Both Benjamin Douglas, the first directly elected mayor, and James Marshall, the city manager, publicly opposed making another change in government.[15] Carl Abbott sees Charlotte as different than other southern cities in regard to municipal reform. He concludes, "Without organizing a formal committee, the businessmen of Charlotte also staged an electoral counterrevolution against factional politics in 1938 and 1939. The city's business establishment reconfirmed its influence in the aftermath of World War II by ending a short experiment with ward voting and encouraging participation of younger entrepreneurs to help implement its ambitious growth strategies."[16] The pro-growth coalition helped to install a weak mayoralty and councilmanic system that facilitated their interests. Historian James Weinstein agrees, stating, "The very concept of the commission and manager governments—that the city was essentially a giant corporation—served to encourage business domination."[17]

The city of Charlotte is now a council-manager form of government with a separately elected mayor. Mayors and city councilpersons are elected every two years. As we suggested earlier, Charlotte's government continues to evolve. In 1978, a partial victory was won for African American residents who wanted council seats elected by districts. The city council changed from a totally at-large election system to one with seven district seats and only four at-large seats. Although the mayor presides over council meetings, appoints council committee members, and appoints advisory boards and commissions, the mayor's office cannot act alone to make things happen in the city. Aside from lacking exclusive jurisdiction over public policies, the mayor earns a low salary ($24,000) and has little in the way of staff. Mayors do not have executive aides for the various public policy areas.

Although elected separately, Charlotte's mayor and city council share control over the city corporation, with the mayor having the most political visibility. The mayor serves as the presiding official at council meetings and can exercise a veto though not a vote in council. Accordingly, the office does not meet political scientist Jeffrey Pressman's preconditions for effective mayoral leadership.[18] Unlike mayors in Nashville, a similar city, Charlotte mayors do not control policy areas of economic and community development, housing, and transportation. This situation represents a deliberate decision by the powers that be because a weak mayoral form of government makes the route to their goals simpler.

The mayor and the council members hire the city manager, city attorney, and city clerk. Although the city manager is the chief executive over city departments, he or she is usually not the target of citizens' frustrations. Residents still blame elected officials if something goes wrong. This is especially true for the administration of the airport. For example, citizens write the mayor about parking, smoking regulations, and taxi services at the airport.

As we saw in earlier chapters, mayors took the airport seriously. A number of former Charlotte mayors stayed involved in airport politics after leaving office. Ben Douglas and John Belk served on the Airport Advisory Committee after their tenures ended. Douglas, for whom the Charlotte Airport is named, once stated, "Politics is the method by which we live . . . and by which we built this country. There is nothing wrong with it. The more politics in government, the more people's voice is heard."[19] Douglas understood that former elected officials had to remain on the Airport Advisory Committee to protect it from current elected officials and from colonization by an opposition group.

As we shall see in chapter 8, the state of North Carolina's attempted takeover of the airport involved several former mayors. Some supported the action while others opposed it. The takeover attempt also exposed a growing divide within the pro-growth coalition, unmasking a schism between Democratic Charlotte and predominately Republican Mecklenburg County. Republican state legislators who represented the county often voted against the city of Charlotte's interests.

Yet the city of Charlotte and the county of Mecklenburg have a history of cooperation, and they also engage in some functional consolidation concerning police, parks, and school departments. The two entities do not, however, have political consolidation like Tennessee's Metropolitan Government of Nashville and Davidson County. Chris Mead provides a history of the attempted political consolidation between Charlotte and Mecklenburg County. In 1968 the Charlotte Chamber of Commerce published a report entitled "Single Government," but voters refused to adopt the 1971 consolidation referendum. Mead concludes, "Elites perceived that there was relatively little to be gained by merging the city and the county. After all, efficiency measures had been made possible by annexations and functional consolidation."[20] In addition, minority leaders opposed referendums for political consolidation.

Mecklenburg County has a separate county commission consisting of nine members elected on even-number years. Six of these members are elected by districts, and the other three are elected at large. A county manager is in charge of the day-to-day administration of county departments. Meanwhile, the commission conducts elections, inspects buildings, and sets the county budget and property taxes for Charlotte, Cornelius, Davidson, Huntersville, Matthews, Mint Hill, and Pineville. However, the Mecklenburg County Commission does not assert itself in airport policy.

UNDERSTANDING CHARLOTTE'S POLITICS

Charlotte's political story is the tale of an American city that had deferred to its southern history/culture for most of the nineteenth and twentieth centuries but was forced to confront social changes brought on by demographics, technology, and intercity competition. Any city would find it difficult to adjust to these changes. And the demands of rapid adaptation then created new problems for the political establishment and the pro-growth coalition. Understanding changes in Charlotte's politics requires more than a simply chronological accounting of political leadership and events. Rather, such knowledge entails a perceptive appreciation of what political scientist Stephen Skowronek calls "political time."[21] Charlotte elected officials in every generation, if not every decade, have had to negotiate between policies they inherited, policies they find to be settled and not easily changed, and, finally, those that are amenable to change. The task for Charlotte's politicians is determining how to make needed changes with a weak mayoral form of government and an increasingly assertive pro-growth business community.

Accordingly, Charlotte's politics reflect a variety of factors: the city's economy, social history, and government structures, as well as the personalities of politicians elected to office. As with most American cities, Charlotte's government and laws form a political nexus with national events and policies. Obviously, Charlotte's politics change to reflect and react to the city's economic and social transformations.

It is clear that mayors and members of the early twentieth-century Charlotte City Council played a supportive role for the textile manufacturers. Indeed, local banks funded the development of the textile industry. In the twenties, national politics was quite provincial and southern statehouses were dominated by rural interests. Southern cities like Charlotte were mired in provincialism and plagued by anti-unionism, low wages, and weak public schools. The local media owned by Daniel A. Tompkins supported this restricted outlook. Nor was banking immune to these views. This may explain, in part, support for the McFadden Act of 1927 prohibiting local banks from engaging in interstate banking expansion. Why expand? As the twenties were also a time of relative affluence, money could be made with local customers.

Yet the Great Depression changed everything economically and politically. In the middle of the thirties, the structure of Charlotte's government changed from a council-manager government with rotating mayors to a hybrid-type council membership with a separately elected mayor. This move proved critical for the establishment of a city-owned airport to promote the nascent development of the airmail phenomenon. After World War II, recognizable signs emerged indicating that the textile industry alone could not produce or sustain the type of growth that many city leaders wanted. Indeed, in 1944 the Charlotte Chamber of Commerce reversed its stand toward land use planning. It instead endorsed "A Pattern for Charlotte," the first comprehensive plan of housing codes, street design, and zoning. The city council then approved the plan and appointed its first Planning Commission. Claiborne correctly points out that the city needed a plan and supporting data to qualify for federal aid.[22]

The U.S. Army's takeover and return of Charlotte Douglas Airport presented the city with a different set of policy options. The two world wars had created a boom for the local economy. A nonindigenous population began to locate itself in the city. At the same time, local banks continued to merge and expand, North

Carolina changed its banking laws, and the U.S. Supreme Court upheld regional banking compacts. By the 1980s, banking industry leaders began making their impact on city politics. An expanded airport would prove critical to the growth of the banking industry and the city itself. Therefore, such issues intersect with the regular day-to-day politics of the city.

REGULAR DAY-TO-DAY CHARLOTTE POLITICS

Charlotte is not known for its ruckus politics and headline-grabbing municipal politicians. Nor does the city have a history of recurrent political machine politics. National media outlets rarely cover Charlotte's elected officials, and residents often tune out local politics and let the leaders act as they please. How do transformative cities like Charlotte generate such relatively low-profile municipal politics? The answer may be found, in part, in the structure of the government. With its weak mayoral system, council-manager government tends to avoid some of the administrative problems associated with mayor-council government. Although elected directly, Charlotte's mayor plays a major role in the council procedures and decision-making. Separately elected mayors in council-manager government are not unusual. William Hansell cites a 1996 survey finding that 62 percent of council-manager governments had directly elected mayors. This may explain why 3,400 cities use this form of government.[23]

It is not unusual for a city of Charlotte's size to have a council-manager government. Cities with over one million residents, such as San Diego and Kansas City, Missouri, have adopted this system. In 2006, the International City Managers Association (ICMA) found that 73 percent of cities and counties led by council-manager governments hired city managers with advanced degrees such as a master of public administration or a master of business administration. The role of the mayor depends on the personalities, traditions, and recurrent issues associated with the incumbent. An argument could be made that separately elected mayors are more independent than those elected by the city council or on a rotating basis. However, a separately elected mayor is not exactly a separation-of-power system.

The organization of Charlotte's government is a fusion of legislative and executive functions. The mayor is clearly involved in the legislative process, serving as the presiding officer of the city council and appointing committee chairs. Mayors also have a veto over council decisions. The question remains as to whether the Charlotte City Council and the mayor are disadvantaged by their two-year term limits. The mayor seems to be in constant campaign mode. City managers are in charge during crises, but residents often expect the mayor to do or say something at these times. The visibility of the office of mayor inflates the mayor's role as spokesperson for the city.

In 2001, William H. Hansell, president of the ICMA, identified the roles of this type of mayoralty. He stated, "Mayors in council-manager communities fulfill two critical leadership functions. The first is that of consensus building: the mayor coalesces the community's disparate constituencies so that they can work together successfully. The second role is to guide development and implementation of policies that improve community service delivery."[24] The history of the airport confirms the consensus-building role of the mayor. Between 1982 and 1983, political scientist James Svara surveyed five North Carolina cities, including Charlotte, finding that mayors in such governments fulfill a variety of roles. He states,

> The mayor, by virtue of his favored position, is able to tap into various communication networks among elected officials, governmental staff, and community leaders. Although they can and do interact with each other independently, the mayor can transmit messages better than anyone else in the government because of the breadth of knowledge and range of contacts he is likely to have. In so doing, the mayor has a unique potential to expand the level of understanding and improve the coordination among participants in the governmental process.[25]

The mayor's communication network includes a variety of interest groups—city employees, vendors, and constituencies. The nature of the office affords the incumbent the license to ask questions and seek answers. Few interest groups would refuse an inquiry from the mayor. The history of the airport indicates that some former mayors have remained at the center of the communication networks and thus were able to exert some influence on the airport. Yet in some cases, the sitting mayor was only able to act if a window of opportunity afforded itself.

Charlotte's weak mayoral form of government may explain some of the political ambiguity. The most telling explanation might be that the pro-growth coalition has become institutionalized and is able to preempt elected officials' preferences. In other regions of the nation, unions play a critical role in discussions about the future of cities. Charlotte does not have a strong union presence. North Carolina is a "right-to-work" state, and its unions have not been able to build an alternative political narrative to offset the pro-growth agenda.

Another explanation for the dominance of the pro-growth agenda may be the lack of a tabloid tradition. Charlotte newspapers do not customarily publish shocking stories about politicians and business deals. Additionally, residents are not inundated with outrageous claims about the airport. This may explain why Charlotte has retained a small-town impulse and residual old-time southern civility. Finally, the dearth of organized citizen groups opposing unfettered economic development and the airport's expansion is more important for the development of Charlotte's pro-growth agenda than the lack of a strong mayoral form of government.

CHARLOTTE MAYORAL ELECTIONS

Despite the weakness of the mayoralty, competition for the office has always been a highly partisan affair. Democrats have dominated the mayor's office since the early 1900s. As discussed earlier, Ben E. Douglas became the first voter-elected mayor of Charlotte in 1935. In 1977, the city council voted to hold partisan elections, and Republicans elected their first mayor, Kenneth Harris, that same year. The Republican Party then held the mayor's office from 1987 to 2009, electing Sue Myrick, Richard Vinroot, and Pat McCrory. Primaries are common for the Democratic Party candidates. Currently, however, Republican mayoral candidates are selected without a primary. The city still has a relatively strong Republican constituency; Republican candidates continue to appeal to remaining social and fiscal conservatives. Yet while the Republican Party is able to elect members of the Charlotte City Council, shifting demographics limit the party's citywide appeal.

Partisan mayoral politics was on display during the writing of this book. The 2015 primary exemplified the state of the two political parties. When Democrat Patrick Cannon was forced to resign after being convicted of corruption, the Charlotte City Council appointed Democratic state representative Dan Clodfelter mayor. Clodfelter assumed office under the assumption he would not run for mayor, but he changed his mind. Jennifer Roberts and city councilmen Michael Barnes and David Howard opposed him in the primary. Roberts was once the chair of the Mecklenburg County Board of Commissioners. Barnes and Howard were African American candidates. After a relatively low-key campaign in which the minority candidates endorsed Clodfelter, Jennifer Roberts won the Democratic primary. She then defeated Republican Edwin Peacock and became Charlotte's second female mayor. The general election involved televised debates and fund-raisers, but for the most part, it too was a low-key affair.

The local Republican Party is kept alive by a state and national patronage system and contributions from newly politicized conservative activists. Though a minority party in most large cities like Charlotte, the Republican Party tends to be more competitive in other southeastern cities. Despite demographic shifts in Charlotte's population, Republicans have remained competitive for certain council seats. Airport policy is rarely debated despite the city council's major role in community politics. In general, there was no partisanship or debate about the airport. In *City Politics*, political scientists Edward Banfield and James Q. Wilson asserted that local parties do not have concrete programs or platforms in elections.[26] This statement was made in the 1960s, but it still holds true for Charlotte. This is not to say that candidates do not discuss political issues; rather, they usually make statements with high levels of generalizations. Name recognition remains a variable in campaigns.

AIRPORT INTEREST GROUPS

The great political scientist David Truman's *Governmental Process* portrays politics in America as the product of interactions, exchanges, and bargaining among interest groups.[27] National and local interest groups operate at covert and overt levels in all municipal decision-making. In cities these groups concentrate their lobbying efforts on the mayors, sitting city council members, and city managers. Some interest groups maintain a relatively low public profile (e.g., the taxi industry), while others are quite open about their interests (e.g., the chamber of commerce). In all cases these groups work to get elected officials to make policies favorable for their members, companies, and neighborhoods.

There are basically five types of local interest groups concerned with airport policy: (1) local business organizations (e.g., Charlotte Chamber of Commerce and Charlotte City Center Partners); (2) consultants (who write the reports for airport decisions); (3) passenger transportation carriers (taxi and shuttle companies); (4) retail vendors (concession food franchises and retail shops); (5) sponsored citizen groups (e.g., the Airport Advisory Committee).

Individual airlines are not reluctant about representing themselves before elected officials. Airline industries will testify before the city council and write letters to the mayor and city manager. It is not uncommon for all of the basic types of interest groups to participate in fund-raising for elected officials' campaigns. These are also organizations that appear at fund-raisers for city council members.

As the chapter on managing airports will discuss, the serving of airlines is somewhat complicated. A variety of consultancies keep tabs on airports' activities and needs and offer their services to airport management and city councilpersons. These companies present themselves as experts and write reports that allow city council members, a mayor, or an airport director to speak authoritatively on an issue. The narrower the airport issue, the more elected officials want so-called outside consultants to provide advice. As we will see, consultants have a quasi monopoly on comparative airport information. More importantly, they serve as a legitimating mechanism for policies the city wants to promote. Are transformative cities vulnerable to corporate planning and the pro-growth coalition's ambitions? Using Minneapolis as a case study, social scientist Gary Mattson tries to explain why anti-growth cities did not succumb to what he calls the four principles of corporate city planning.

> There are four basic principles that underlie the doctrine of Corporate City Planning, which allows for this pro-business dominance 1. Establish a non-partisan electoral system that allows the business community to dominate municipal governance through so-called good government reform organizations. 2. Discourage the adoption of strong conflict of interest laws under the guise of civic boosterism. 3. Dilute citizen participation by establishing quasi-public agencies or special districts so that public funds can flow to private sector ventures. 4. Foster a philosophy of municipal service privatization so that business taxes are kept low by shifting the costs onto the citizen-taxpayer.[28]

Obviously, Charlotte does not meet the first requirement for such planning. Interest groups organize their game plan based on the nature of the government, and they must colonize the planning process in order to be successful. Without a strong community planning tradition, the city is open to corporate planning. To this point, Charlotte is home to no active anti-growth organization, and the city lacks a strong planning department or tradition. Although the city council and mayoral elections are highly competitive and partisan, elected officials usually keep a low profile. The problem is that both positions involve a quick recall—two-year terms. Over the years, Charlotte has not seen mayoral turnover. City councilpersons are routinely reelected, but former mayor Pat McCrory held office for fourteen years. Two-year term limits for elected officials have allowed city politics to be dominated by what Clarence Stone calls a corporate regime.[29] Historian Tom Hanchett makes this point about the chamber of commerce in his commentary for the *Charlotte Observer*.

> Triumphant in the economic sphere, businessmen also dominated the town's political life. The system of at-large elections and voting restrictions created at the turn of the century continued to limit political participation well into the 1960s, ensuring that only well-financed candidates won office. Civic leaders made no secret of business's influence at City Hall. "Scratch beneath the surface of any government program in Charlotte or Mecklenburg these days and you're likely to find

a Chamber of Commerce Committee," wrote the *Charlotte Observer* approvingly in the 1950s. Charlotte is run, primarily and well, by its Chamber of Commerce, the paper reiterated a few years later. "We are pleased to acknowledge its bossism and wish it continued health."[30]

As this work's history chapters reported, this chamber / city politician relationship started in the twenties and was consolidated during the shift from a textile-oriented economy to a banking economy. The airport's development and expansion were a critical part of this transition. As to conflict-of-interest laws, ex-mayors and former city council members are free to engage themselves in airport policy after leaving office. Therefore, Charlotte meets the second of Mattson's requirements. As to the third requirement, Charlotte has yet to endorse an airport authority. City leaders also do not meet the fourth requirement, as they opposed privatization of the airport. The idea was discussed briefly, but airport director Jerry Orr beat it down. Although Charlotte does not meet all the conditions Mattson outlines, the city's growth is nevertheless a product of corporate planning. In addition, the drum major for that economic planning has historically been the mayor.

HOW MAYORS MADE A DIFFERENCE

Since the 1920s, Charlotte mayors have been at the forefront of the city's airport politics. Despite the fact that the mayoralty is a structurally weak office, individual mayors have used access to the media to make the case for airport development. Remember, earlier mayors were often at the center of the communication networks. They thus had continuous contact with local businessmen and the chamber of commerce. As early as the 1920s, mayors wanted airmail to come to Charlotte and so pushed the idea of airplane landing areas or airports. Nineteen mayors have held office since the inception of Charlotte Airport. As we suggested earlier, mayors never had any operational responsibility for the facility, but this circumstance does not insulate them from the airline industry's solicitations and citizens' complaints. Mayoral papers reveal an active correspondence with the airline industry, citizens, and airport staff.

More importantly, mayors have used their high public visibility to circumvent some of the structural limitations of the office. The media asked them to comment on a variety of city issues, thereby allowing them to create a legacy. Mayors are also more likely than other council members to have more contact with other levels of the government. Hence, Charlotte mayors enjoy higher status than glorified at-large members of the city council. Political scientist James Svara makes an interesting comment on mayors' standing in cities:

The mayor may be involved in external relations and help secure agreement among parties to a project. For some mayors, the promoter role is a simple extension of ceremonial tasks. Others are active initiators of contacts and help develop possibilities for the city. As official representative, the mayor has extensive dealings with officials in other governments and may serve as a key participant in formulating agreements with state or federal officials, developers, and others who seek joint ventures with city government. The mayor may also take the lead in projecting a favorable image of the city and seek to "sell" others on investment in it. This role has contributed to the emergence of the mayor as a central figure in council-manager government.[31]

This has been the case for Charlotte mayors and their relationship to the airport. In the 1930s, Mayor Ben Douglas promoted the idea of a municipal airport, got voters to pass the first airport revenue bonds, and persuaded thirty-five business community leaders to cosign a loan for the airport. The first directly elected mayor and the so-called Father of the Charlotte Airport, Douglas obviously made a difference by promoting the idea of a municipal facility. His efforts to mobilize citizens' support were assisted by the chamber of commerce, the newspaper, and other civic organizations. Former Mayor Ben Douglas recalled, "I sometimes think about it, and I cannot understand it.... But for a man who is not a pilot it seems that I am unusually enthusiastic about aviation. Wouldn't it be nice if we just could estimate what will be the ultimate development of aviation and airports and the place airplanes will play in human life? Charlotte Airport is ideally situated."[32]

Ben Douglas also persuaded the War Department to use the Charlotte Airport as a training base during World War II. According to Jack Claiborne, the army initially agreed to lease the airfield and let the city reserve part of it for commercial use. A group of Charlotte flying enthusiasts subsequently objected and threatened to file a suit. According to Claiborne, the army then became "annoyed" and decided it needed 150 more acres for its training base. However, the city did not have $1,200 to buy the extra land. At this point, Claiborne notes, "the Charlotte Chamber persuaded 35 business leaders to buy the land and make it available to the city."[33]

Initially, some people were unhappy with the deal Douglas made with the army. City attorney John H. Small, working on behalf of the city council, emerged as Douglas's opponent on the deal. He and some members of the city council privately called the deal a "giveaway" to the army. Small also complained that Mayor Douglas had acted unilaterally, at one point comparing him to Hitler.[34] Douglas at one point told the *Charlotte Observer* that the council had fifteen questions about the airport's handover to the army. These questions addressed topics ranging from the location and funding for a proposed new airfield to the army's future plans for the airport. Mayor Douglas responded to his critics by telling the *Charlotte Observer*, "As long as I am mayor, I intend to cooperate with the federal government in this emergency."[35] He announced that the city retained ownership of the airport and would use the new funds to purchase land adjacent to the airport. This confrontation between Mr. Small and Mayor Douglas lasted until Douglas withdrew from his reelection campaign. Judge E. McA. Currie, the "Good Government" (i.e., reform) candidate, would eventually win the election. The city council then appointed John Small to the Airport Advisory Committee, and it was not clear whether his appointment was a reward or evidence of his co-optation by the proairport coalition.

The post-Douglas era was not without its problems. In 1941, voters turned down a $60,000 bond issue. Some of the money would have been used to buy land for another freight facility. There was also a proposal for a general aviation airport near the Catawba River. Although the result was not an outright anti-airport vote, the revenue bond failure was a blow to airport supporters. Former mayor Douglas responded, "We had $390,000 in federal funds that could be used but the issue failed by 198 votes. I thought at the time what a Scotch community this is."[36]

The city airport's supporters survived the interregnum of an army takeover. While the army expanded the runways, used the airfield as a training base, and built hangars and barracks for soldiers, it did not ask Mayor E. McA. Currie to do anything. His successor, Mayor Herbert Baxter, had to deal with converting a military airport into a civilian one.

As the city entered the 1950s, supporters of Charlotte Douglas began pushing for a larger terminal. In 1952 Charlotte mayor pro tempore Phillip L. Van Every broke ground for the new airport terminal while chamber of commerce chair Earl Thompson served as master of ceremonies. Herbert H. Baxter, a former mayor and current Civil Air Patrol commander and city council member, attended the opening. Such ceremonies at airports are also opportunities for airlines to show off their newest aircraft. Eastern flew in its new airplane called the Falcon, which could reach speeds of 270 miles per hour. The new terminal at Charlotte Douglas finally opened in 1954. It was one of Charlotte's great public relations spectacles, a facility fit for a middle-sized city of one hundred thousand.

The fifties were also a time of change. World War II hero Gen. Dwight Eisenhower was elected president. The Korean War ended. In addition, the civil rights movement took a new turn with the Montgomery bus boycott (i.e., nonviolent protest), prompting change in southern social norms and race relations.

Segregated public facilities were nearing their end, and the sixties would also usher in a new federal government stance on the black political franchise.

All these changes would affect the social context of the airport. The Civil Aeronautics Administration announced conditions on future aid to Charlotte Douglas. Federal funds would be given for racially segregated airport facilities such as dining rooms or restrooms.[37] This order did not include the whole building. New political and social challenges also prompted a change in the types of mayors elected. In the past, mayors were connected to the chamber of commerce and the business community, and that association fueled the perception that the chamber of commerce was running the city. This notion first appeared in the 1960s and lasted until the 1980s. Charlotte would undergo the social and economic changes, reflected its citizens' choice of mayors, that would facilitate the growth of the transformative city.

THE BROOKSHIRE TERM

Alex Coffin's *Brookshire and Belk* suggests that these two Charlotte businessmen and mayors significantly impacted the economic development of the city and its airport. Businessman Sanford Brookshire was elected mayor in 1961, and he inherited Charlotte's civil rights initiative and Friendly Relationship Committee. Mayor James S. Smith had established the committee in reaction to efforts at lunch counter integration by Johnson C. Smith University students. Two years into his tenure as president of the Charlotte Chamber of Commerce, Brookshire persuaded the chamber to pass a resolution asking businesses to voluntarily open their doors to African Americans. Thus Brookshire, considered a moderate, is remembered for getting the business community to accommodate the civil rights movement before the 1964 Civil Rights Act desegregated public accommodations. In so doing, he put Charlotte ahead of most southern cities at the time.

In addition, Brookshire created the Community Relations Committee with Presbyterian Foundation director Dr. John R. Cunningham as chair.[38] The twenty-seven-member biracial committee prompted several hotels and motels to accept African Americans in their lodging and dining facilities a year before the 1964 federal public accommodations act was passed. Pat Watters quoted the mayor as saying, "It was a combination of social consciousness, civic pride, and 'economic considerations' which moved Charlotte in the Spring and early Summer of 1963 to desegregate voluntarily its leading hotels and motels, '90% of its restaurants' and its first-class movie theatres."[39] Dr. Reginald A. Hawkins, one of the black leaders that attempted to integrate the Charlotte Airport restaurant in the fifties, called the committee's achievement "a tremendous breakthrough," adding, "This put us well on the road toward making Charlotte an open, democratic city. I'm glad to have been a part of it."[40]

This mayoral embrace of social change was critical to Charlotte's transition from a traditional southern city to a moderate one. Obviously, Congress's passage of the 1965 Voting Rights Act changed southern politics forever. In 1965, Charlotteans elected Frederick Douglas Alexander, the first African American member of the chamber of commerce, as an at-large member of the city council. Author Pat Watters also interviewed chamber president J. Ed Burnside, who noted that the organization had an "extraordinary influence" over what happened in Charlotte. Burnside asserted, "Anything that they back goes over."[41] Under his leadership, the chamber of commerce voted unanimously to recommend racial integration of all Charlotte service businesses.

Brookshire recognized that developing Uptown was essential to the city's image and overall economic development. In 1964 a consultant company asserted, "Downtown Charlotte is not going to be revitalized unless there is a determined effort on the part of both private investors and public officials."[42] Brookshire was also a pro-growth coalition supporter and a strong champion of the airport. During Brookshire's tenure, two concourses were built at Charlotte Douglas, and Eastern Air Lines built a reservation center in Charlotte as well. In 1962, an airfreight terminal was built. In a 1980 special insert in the *Charlotte Observer*, the role of the city's airport in the foreign-trade zone was commended. The airport was designated a port of entry in 1964, thereby allowing it to handle "2,200 entries and . . . $940,000 in duties in 1965 [and then move] to handling 15,600 entries and collecting duties of more than $12 million on imports of $124 million."[43] Brookshire ultimately accepted the consultants' recommendations and supported more expansion of the airport. Coffin reported that J. Ed Burnside, chairman of the chamber of commerce Aviation Committee, and former mayor James Smith led a delegation asking Delta Airlines to expand flights at Charlotte Douglas. Brookshire took the occasion to call the airport "a barometer of city growth."[44]

Brookshire also surprised many with his proposal to turn the airport over to Mecklenburg County. This idea followed a request for a multimillion-dollar bond issue to the city. At that point, Charlotte had a $20.1 million legal bond debt limit, but Mecklenburg County had more legal space and could authorize another $58.9 million in general purpose bonds. Brookshire stated, "Personally, I would have no objection to handing over the total management of the Airport to County government. We have to recognize the fact with the tremendous growth of Charlotte and the region it serves we are hard pressed to keep up the air transportation facilities to meet these growth needs. We in city government are quite aware of our limited local resources."[45]

Brookshire argued that the airport needed and deserved a broader base of support because it served the entire region. He thought that if the county government took the airport over, expansion could proceed more quickly. Admitting that he had not discussed the proposal with the city council or county commissioners, Brookshire expressed desire to do so before giving consideration for a bond referendum. He declared besides that he would rather spend the money on expansion of Convention Boulevard than the airport. While Brookshire did not speak to local politicians about the proposal, it is not clear whether he ran the idea by the chamber of commerce, of which he had been president before becoming mayor. In the end, the proposal went nowhere.

In 1969, the city requested more power to use eminent domain to acquire land near Charlotte Douglas Airport. At that time the areas around the airport were heavily populated, and land banking, the "practice of securing land for possible future development," was indicated.[46] State representative P. Jack Baugh took up the anti-expansion argument, declaring his belief that Charlotte Douglas "was obsolete."[47] Baugh further asserted, "We can't pour money into a terrible facility. We can only expand so far. Sooner or later we're going to have to build a new airport."[48] In 1969, he proposed that Mecklenburg County build a new airport in cooperation with Catawba, Gaston, Lincoln, Iredell, Rowan, Anson, and Cabarrus Counties. He stated, "I think we might get their support and we ought to go after it."[49]

Airport director Ross Knight rejected the idea of a new airport, predicting that it was impossible to know what airports would need in the future. He stated, "By 1990 we're going to have a different concept of flying."[50] Baugh agreed with Knight's point about the changing technology of aircraft. He stated, "Every time they expand [Douglas] it is just money down the drain. They're going to be flying aircraft we didn't even dream of within the next 10 years."[51] The Baugh proposal only needed the airport director to dismiss it—engaging the full pro-growth coalition's opposition was unnecessary. When Brookshire left the mayor's office, John Belk succeeded him.

THE BELK TERM

Even before he became mayor, John Belk was an early supporter of the airport. He was elected mayor in 1969 and served until 1977. By 1970, Charlotte's population had increased to over two hundred thousand residents. The sixties had been a decade of turmoil and protest, one in which Pres. John Kennedy,

Sen. Robert Kennedy, Malcolm X, and Dr. Martin L. King were all assassinated. Richard M. Nixon won the U.S. presidency in 1968 due in part to an anti–school busing platform.

Like most southern cities, Charlotte had racially segregated schools despite the *Brown v. Board of Education* (1954) integration ruling that had come down during Mayor Van Every's tenure. Like other southern cities, Charlotte also had a history of ugliness surrounding attempts to integrate schools (e.g., the 1954 jeering of Dorothy Counts at Harding School). The city's residential segregation perpetuated its school segregation. Accordingly, the city of Charlotte initiated a limited busing program to achieve school desegregation. In 1971, the U.S. Supreme Court held in *Swann v. Charlotte-Mecklenburg Board of Education* that busing was a constitutional remedy for integrating public schools.[52] The so-called Charlotte-Mecklenburg Model for school integration was legitimated, and Charlotte was acclaimed as the southern city where such integration worked. In addition, the idea of integrated schools was folded into the general notion of Charlotte as the transformative city. Indeed, this busing policy enhanced Charlotte's reputation for progressiveness in the late sixties and early seventies.

During Belk's tenure as mayor, airport expansion was high on his agenda. Joe Epley, who ran Belk's first campaign, recalled, "In those days, the Belks . . . and some others really had big influence on what made Charlotte grow. When they needed things to happen, they happened. John could see the big picture a lot better than most people could. He didn't focus on the trivial. He was really big on the airport [and] on making Charlotte nationally recognized as a business center."[53] It was Belk who suggested the city annex the land surrounding the airport. He stated, "It's a matter of guarding against jamming up the airport with too much uncontrolled development."[54] Annexation of the airport and surrounding properties would give the city council the authority to zone the entire area and tax the surrounding communities. Belk's proposal would skip over communities between the city and the airport, and it would need the N.C. General Assembly's approval. Such an approach was difficult since annexation was one of Charlotte's principal means of expanding its boundaries.

The seventies saw a mild backlash against the establishment or the so-called Myers Park Crowd. (Myers Park is an upscale Charlotte neighborhood where many business leaders lived.) Elected in 1971, Councilman James McDuffie led that narrative. In 1973, Mayor Belk, the second mayor who had been chamber of commerce president, had to address the notion that the chamber was running the city. He stated, "Charlotte has shifted. I know when I was president the guys who came back here just after World War II were really involved. Now, just one or two of those former presidents of the chambers are still around. The rest have retired, died, or moved away."⁵⁵ Belk believed that the chamber had drifted away from its previous position of power. For him there was simply not enough continuity of presidents to sustain its political influence. Belk's predecessor, Brookshire, also a former chamber president, agreed that there was no domination by the Chamber. He declared, "When I was elected, I emphasized that the Chamber was not going to run city hall, but we did enjoy a good working relationship."⁵⁶ Mr. C. C. Cameron, the then president of the chamber, agreed and stated, "In past history, the chamber was pretty much the power structure, but over the years there was a change in elected officials and they said 'to heck with the Chamber running the city.' . . . Maybe that pendulum has swung too far. We don't want to run the city. That's not our place, but I would think city and county officials would welcome the free advice of we who are willing to give our time and energy to community problems."⁵⁷ City leaders appreciated the chamber of commerce's support, but they also knew that more federal support was required to grow the city and the airport.

In 1976, Mayor Belk wrote a letter asking Senators Jesse Helms and Robert Morgan to help secure funding for expansion of the airport. After Ken Harris, who ran on an airport-improvement platform, was elected Charlotte's mayor in 1977, he helped put together a $47 million bond proposal for a scaled-down terminal. It should be pointed out that Harris was an active letter writer. For example, he wrote to Delta Airlines' David C. Garrett protesting the elimination of the carrier's two daily flights to LaGuardia (NYC).⁵⁸ Harris wanted to know how the airline could do this after the airport was building a $55 million expansion. W. J. Veeder, president of the Charlotte Chamber of Commerce, also wrote a supporting letter. Yet their communications didn't work, as J. A. Cooper, Delta's senior vice president for marketing, responded and denied requests to reinstate the service.

The biggest contribution of the Belk administration was its support of the referendum on revenue bonds. Although the 1975 airport referendum failed, the former mayor continued to support Charlotte Douglas's growth after leaving office. Belk served on the Airport Advisory Committee for several years. According to Coffin, Belk also challenged his successor, Mayor Ken Harris, to get bond money to build the terminal. In 1978, the voters approved the funding for the terminal. Coffin mentions that "some said Belk was 'miffed' when Gantt could not find a way to keep Belk on the AAC once his term ended."⁵⁹ Coffin also cites the following 1993 comment from Duke Power Company president Bill Lee: "For the last 25 years John Belk has been a driving force in bringing the airport to where it is."⁶⁰ For Belk, the airport had become personal.

THE KNOX TERM

History suggests that Charlotte mayors can act when confronted with airport issues. Perhaps the most important contributions made by Mayor H. Edward Knox (1979–1983) were the changes he made in mayoral political power. He recalled, "When I came in the Mayor had no leverage in the City Council. He could only vote in case of a tie. I need the veto to play a part in the process. We got the veto before the Governor."[61] Knox admitted that he did not use this power—he did not need to use it, as the city politics were relatively quiet and economic development was going well. Early in the Knox administration, reporter Bill Arthur wrote, "At the end of the '70s, a visitor can't mistake downtown. In 10 years, Charlotte has developed a skyline of stone and glass that flashes brilliant orange in the sunset."[62]

The Knox administration was involved with the demand for rezoning Uptown (i.e., downtown Charlotte) to permit more development. Subsequently, the city of Charlotte created the Charlotte Uptown Development Corporation (CUDC), a quasi-public organization financed by a tax on downtown properties. The city council and the mayor appointed the leadership of CUDC, and they planned to make Uptown a prime location for high-rise buildings, hotels, and retail shops. CUDC executive director Michael Schneiderman stated, "We want to give persons reason to come downtown to work, to play and to live." Don Bedwell of the *Charlotte Observer* called the potential development plans a coming "boom time for Charlotte."[63]

Two years later the process of making Uptown an attractive magnet for location for businesses hit a snag. The city asked RTKL Associates, a Baltimore consulting company, to make a study of Uptown. The company suggested that the city zoning laws were too loose to promote concentration in Uptown, and it recommended tightening those laws to permit the area to develop.[64] Charlotte's pro-growth coalition and city politicians succeeded in encouraging growth in its Uptown areas. Visitors see a city's downtown area, which represents the city as a whole. Changing Uptown was critical to the transformation of Charlotte, which now had a population of over three hundred thousand residents. Journalist Don Bedwell acknowledges that Hugh McColl was the power behind Uptown's development.[65]

The new Charlotte Airport terminal (1982) was opened during the Knox administration. When some people wanted to change the name of Charlotte Douglas Airport to Charlotte International Airport, it was Knox who wanted to keep Douglas's name associated with the facility. Knox stated, "I thought it was a symbol. He [Douglas] had a big hand in the development of the airport. He promulgated the airport. I didn't want to lose our heritage."⁶⁶ However, the issue was much debated. Knox broke the tie at the first vote, and the council's later vote was unanimous.⁶⁷ The airport's name then changed to Charlotte Douglas International Airport.

The airport's status as a major employer and a job multiplier was one of the selling points for the facility's expansion. In 1979, the Charlotte City Council wanted to create an Affirmative Action Plan for the airport. To this end, it hired the consultant firm Day and Zimmerman Incorporated to conduct a study of the airport's employment practices. Despite the plan's existence, employment issues at the airport remained a challenge. In the 1980s, the FAA issued a rule that airports had to hire minorities and establish an Affirmative Action Policy 14 CFR Part 152, issued February 14, 1980. Mayor H. Edward Knox had the impression that Section 30 required EEO assurances in existing and future leases. He also believed that the city would be required to monitor the Affirmative Action Plan. Mayor Knox wrote a letter (dated March 27) to Sen. Jesse Helms and other members of the North Carolina congressional delegation complaining about these requirements. Helms responded by acknowledging the problem and promising to look into the matter. While he agreed with Knox's views on affirmative action, he stated, "I see little chance of revoking these regulations through legislative action." And Helms added, "Rest assured, however that I will take every opportunity to call these bureaucrats to task."⁶⁸ In fact, Charlotte was not required to monitor the Affirmative Action Plan but was limited to collecting reports and sending them to the FAA.

The Charlotte City Council had committed to giving at least 15 percent of the money for constructing Charlotte's $60 million terminal to companies controlled and operated by minorities and women. This plan was called the Minority Business Enterprise (MBE). On January 10, 1982, a group of constructors, the assistant city manager and airport project director Louis Marinelli, and assistant manager Jerry Orr met at the Sheraton Hotel to discuss the MBE. Charlotte was taking bids for a $13.7 million contract for the new terminal. Only one local company, R. H. Pinnix Associates of Gastonia, had made an offer, and the city needed three bids to award a contract. No other constructors expressed interest due to the requirements for MBE. The MBE's critics claimed some minority companies were white business fronts. Two days later the *Charlotte Observer* reported that an airport report found no evidence of fraud in airport contracts. The MBE was not being abused, and no evidence suggested that minorities and women were "fronting" or serving as figurehead owners for companies actually owned by whites.⁶⁹

Then in January 1989, the U.S. Supreme Court found that municipal minority set-aside (MBE) programs were unconstitutional.[70] Charlotte city attorney Henry Underhill told the *Charlotte Observer*, "Our plan allows more flexibility than Richmond's. Theirs is pure set-aside. They didn't make allowance for any good-faith effort, and the 30 percent goal was arbitrarily selected." M/WBE director Elizabeth Mills supported Underhill. Charlotte had no "blanket" female or minority goals; instead, goals were adjusted for each contract. Mills allowed that in 1980 "minority firms got just 2.5 percent of the city's construction contracts, or $332,000 of $13 million."[71] In 1988, the M/WBE's share had reached 8.1 percent of the construction funds—$8 million of a $98 million fund. Despite the court ruling against set-asides, the idea of minority participation in construction and services was now a part of the city politics.

Almost two years later, Southeast Airlines began service at Charlotte Douglas. The carrier began to offer low fares, which many believed would increase competition among airlines. Southeast president Tom Kolfenbach asserted, "We hear so often how much low-fare service is needed in Charlotte, but the proof is in the pudding. Now, if people want to use the service we provide, that's great. But we're not going to sit there and bury ourselves flying empty airplanes. It doesn't make sense."[72] Two years later Southeast pulled out of Charlotte, and JetBlue and Southwest Airlines were then pursued. These two airlines are among the surviving discount airlines serving Charlotte. The question is whether discount airlines could make a profit at Charlotte Douglas.

The Knox administration also saw the advent of Pres. Ronald Reagan's administration. Reagan was elected on an agenda of small government and cutbacks of federal aid and entitlements. Yet Charlotte's leadership wanted the city's development to continue unabated by the new federal administration. Officials knew that the pro-growth coalition had to have more private investment. One novelty idea was to issue stock to raise money for Charlotte's development.[73] The point is that the city's pro-growth coalition was very serious about developing Uptown and expanding the airport. This attitude carried over to the Gantt administration.

THE GANTT TERM

In 1980 Charlotte was a city of 314,447 people. Three years later, Harvey Gantt, an African American architect and longtime city council member, was elected Charlotte's mayor. Gantt's victory was a significant breakthrough for the city since it reflected demographic changes—softening racial attitudes and increasing political maturity. That same year, Harold Washington became the first African American mayor of Chicago. Philadelphia elected W. Wilson Goode its mayor a year later. Although Gantt's two colleagues operated with a strong mayor form of government and wielded more executive power than he did, the nation took notice of these rising political stars. Gantt's role was promoting the idea that Charlotte was a cosmopolitan city and assisting in its transformation. He described the mayor's job as follows: "The mayor is like being chair of the board of the corporation. Mayors vote when there is a tie. (I used my veto twice.) It is a small amount of power. There is no executive function. This is a council manager form of government and civil servants are appointed by the merit system. The city manager worked for the mayor and the city council."[74]

While a city council member, Gantt was one of a few black leaders who supported the failed 1975 revenue bond offering that the airport wanted to help build a new terminal. He understood the airport's role in Charlotte's future. He also claimed to have had good relations with Josh Birmingham, the longtime airport director. Gantt was mayor when Charlotte Douglas Airport grew as a major hub; Concourses B and C were added, and Piedmont Airlines made its first nonstop flight to London.

Elected mayor at a time when the national electorate had ideologically shifted to the right, Gantt did not have a sympathetic Democratic administration to make the case for the city. Ronald Reagan was a conservative Republican governor who had been elected president, and his strategy was to rely on improving the national economy—that is, use the market mechanism as a way to improve cities. Although he appointed African American Samuel R. Pierce his secretary of housing and urban development, Reagan did not enact policies directly benefiting cities like Charlotte. Unlike his predecessors, Reagan opposed the expansion of social entitlements at a time when urban poverty was growing, manufacturing was declining in significance, and the world economy was drifting toward globalization.

As the Reagan administration reduced federal funds, it became obvious that cities like Charlotte needed to generate more revenue. State-authorized sales and property taxes were not enough to allow the leap Charlotte wanted to make. As a member of the state committee, Mayor Gantt became an advocate for the city's home rule. He stated, "I want home rule. I want a range of things we can do, from user fees to the possibility of an income tax. We need a piece of legislation introduced that would provide us that flexibility."[75] Gantt got the chamber of commerce to support the tax proposal, but the city did not receive home rule or a menu of local taxes.[76]

Gantt presided over a city that was in the process of Uptown development. CUDC was still operating and skyscrapers, shops, and residences were being developed. First Citizens Plaza (1982), Independence Center (1983), and Charlotte

Marriott City Center (1984) were built during Gantt's term. In a major 1986 study of Uptown mixed-use development, consultants made a case for creating a two-theater performing arts center and a new convention center.[77] Charlotte was also undergoing cultural change, as evidenced by the establishment of Metrolina Theater Association and Opera Carolina. High culture tends to attract people to Uptown, and it was therefore used as a marketing tool. Generally speaking, the Gantt administration was successful. In 1990, Gantt would gain national fame while running against Sen. Jesse Helms.

THE VINROOT TERM

The 1990s saw the population of the city grow to 395,934, a gain of 25 percent over the last decade. In 1991, Richard Vinroot was elected Charlotte's second Republican mayor. In his inaugural address, he declared that residents of Charlotte, as well as of Mecklenburg, Cabarrus, Gaston, Iredell, and Union Counties in North Carolina and York County in South Carolina, are "irrevocably one people." He also said, "The tax burden for services such as public transportation should be shouldered by all."[78] Vinroot had a different view of the airport and its relationship to the city. He elaborated on this outlook in an interview.

> I ran on a theme of regionalism. There are a number of cities and towns in the regions. On my first weekend in office I invited 7 or 8 mayors (Rock Hill, Kannapolis etc.) to dinner. We needed to cooperate and work together.
>
> I made the first outside the city appointments to the Airport Advisory Committee. There was one person from South Carolina and two outside Mecklenburg County. The airport is regional in nature.
>
> Some of the City Council members said you shouldn't have appointed anyone not from Charlotte. I knew how important the airport was to regional development. It was not so much a city airport as it was a regional airport.[79]

In 1992, Mayor Vinroot supported a proposal to expand the Airport Advisory Committee from a city-exclusive body to a regional one. He said, "It is fair to say we're not the city of Charlotte. We are regions of at least six or seven counties covering two states." Vinroot further recalled, "On my first day in office, I got a call from Senator Strom Thurmond. He said, 'Take care of my airport. It is the most important economic development tool in South Carolina, my state.'"[80] Charlotte Douglas handled over 80 percent of all flights in the Carolinas. However, the Vinroot proposal was never adopted.

In April 1995, airport workers found themselves being investigated by the city of Charlotte. In 1992, the city investigated claims that employees had wagered on sports and hired a stripper. It was also alleged that staff in the airport's maintenance department had submitted phony bills and falsified time cards, and that equipment and supplies at Charlotte Douglas had been stolen. At the time, the airport employed 230 people. The investigation provided an opportunity for the city to inspect and change the facility's operating policies.

When Charlotte Douglas employees were under investigation, Wendell White was city manager and Jerry Orr was the airport director. White wanted to hold the airport's management accountable. In contrast, Vinroot strongly endorsed Orr and his team. The mayor stated, "The airport is one of the best-operated in the country, if not the best in terms of efficiency, but if something wrong is going on out there criminally, I'd be very troubled. . . . Any misuse of any public property by anybody is wrong and not to be tolerated by our city."[81] The nineties were a decade of expansion and growth for U.S. Airways. Charlotte Douglas opened Concourse D that housed international flights, and it also erected the bronze statue of Queen Charlotte of Mecklenburg-Strelitz in front of the facility. Also during this period, Charlotte residents found that their airfares were higher than other cities'.

THE MCCRORY TERM

Pat McCrory, Charlotte's third Republican mayor, was elected in 1995. Prior to his fourteen years in office, he had worked for Duke Power Company, the region's largest utility business. Charlotte Uptown Development Corporation (CUDC) head Michael Schneiderman resigned a year after McCrory took office. Schneiderman had served for seventeen years and presided over the development in Uptown, with its skyscrapers, retail establishments, and residents. The twenty-one-person CUDC was then reorganized and merged with the Charlotte Chamber of Commerce's Center Charlotte Division.[82] During McCrory's tenure, two major university studies examined the airport's impact on the city's economy. In 1997 the Urban Institute at the University of North Carolina at Charlotte (UNCC) produced a study entitled "Economic Impact of Charlotte Douglass Airport." According to this report, the airport added $1.6 billion to the local economy and directly provided 322 jobs on a payroll of $9,182,194.[83]

In 2005 the study was updated with the following conclusion: "The total economic impact equates to $9,735,141,708 with $5,162,448,874 of this total in annual payroll supporting 100,716 jobs."[84] The total annual payroll also supports hotels around the airport. As economist John Kasarda predicted, some conferences are held at these local hotels.

McCrory's tenure is associated with the development of the city skyline, light-rail, and green spaces. His legacy includes planning, the Blue Line light-rail, and insisting that developers build sidewalks. Because he was a Republican, he was able to get some of his conservative state legislators to support city projects. Also during McCrory's tenure, the Charlotte banking community underwent a major transformation. NationsBank merged with Bank of America and First Union merged with Wachovia. It was now clear that Charlotte's airport had to have more international takeoffs and landings.

In the midst of these developments, the chamber of commerce restarted its Aviation Committee, an intermittent body that had previously existed for years. Members of the committee are volunteers whose names are not public, and they issue reports and comment on airport policy. In 1996, Airport Advisory Committee (AAC) member Eric Locher questioned the rumor that the chamber was resurrecting its Aviation Committee. He worried about duplication of the AAC's work. Jerry Orr quickly responded as a part of the director reports entitled "miscellaneous discussion," stating, "[The chamber's Aviation Committee] is very much in line with the Aviation Advisory Committee's vision for the airport."[85]

Charlotte realized its ambition of being a major hub. Residents enjoyed the convenience of new nonstop flights, but many did not like the rising airfares for all flights. The General Accounting Office (GAO) stated that Charlotte had the highest ticket prices in the nation. One of the disadvantages of being a dominant hub is that airlines can set high prices because of a relative lack of competition. High ticket prices resulted in passengers' complaints to the media and the Charlotte mayor. Passengers in Raleigh and Greensboro were paying less to travel.

In 1999, Mayor Pat McCrory appointed a ten-member task force to review all aspects of airline service at Charlotte Douglas. The task force, composed of several members of the business community, was headed by Ed Weisiger of Carolina Tractor. Consultants were hired and were expected to report in six months. The city also hired Boyd Group / ASRC Incorporated of Evergreen, Colorado, as consultants. These outside experts concluded that use of Charlotte service was "unfairly dominated by U.S. Airways." They further stated, "Presence of the U.S. Airways hub is a double-edged sword: Because of the high level of service the hub affords compared to a relatively modest local catchment area, and the flexibility that U.S. Airways has in providing competitive responses, other airlines are often reluctant to commit resources."[86] This report did not stimulate a search for low-cost airlines.

The appointment of this committee caused a stir among the airport management and airline tenants. In 1999, airport director Jerry Orr penned "To Hub or

Not to Hub," a response to the task force's establishment. Published in *Connections* newsletter, the essay read thusly: "I often say there are two kinds of cities: those that have a hub and those that want a hub. As we try to position ourselves for the next decade, we need to decide if we can lower our airfares without giving up our service advantage. I am confident the Mayor's newly appointed Task Force, working together with AAC, will help us attain these goals."[87]

Orr regarded the situation as a choice of having or not having a hub. Airlines are at advantage in making a city a hub. When cities like Cincinnati, Nashville, Pittsburgh, and Saint Louis lost their hubs, they lost credit ratings and passengers.[88] In 1996 American Airlines eliminated its hub in Nashville, costing the airport millions of passengers. The city subsequently took several years to recover. As we stated earlier, the business community had promoted the narrative that the airport as a hub was central to Charlotte's economic development. Businesspeople were not prepared to cause any problems for the airlines. Simply put, airlines achieved a short financial turnaround by eliminating hubs, but the problem of attaining lower fares for residents while maintaining low costs for airlines remained. The solution was to recruit discount airlines and create more profit-providing services at the airport.

Vance Cariaga of the *Business Journal* reported that the task force had no plan to contact any low-fare airlines and instead took its case to U.S. Airways.[89] The airlines did survive this public relations challenge of high fares, and the controversy died down. U.S. Airways was also able to start international flights. On April 20, 2000, Mayor Pat McCrory was given a free seat on U.S. Airways' inaugural Charlotte-to-Paris flight. Jerry Orr continued to be airport director, and U.S. Airways merged with American West in 2005.

The McCrory tenure marked a financial takeoff for the Charlotte-based banking industry. First Union bought the Money Store, NationsBank, and also Bank of America. Bank of America bought Countrywide Financial and Merrill Lynch. Wachovia purchased Golden West Financial, which Wells Fargo then acquired. Yet the 2008 Great Recession forced the nationwide banking industry to make an unplanned landing.

THE FOXX TERM

In 2009, city councilman Anthony Foxx became Charlotte's second African American mayor. The idea of privatizing the airport became one of the main issues in the contest between Foxx and John Lassiter, his Republican opponent. Lassiter floated the idea of selling Charlotte Douglas and other assets to private investors in order to lower taxes. Jerry Orr opposed the privatization idea and delivered the city's public response to it. Lassiter was defeated, and the issue was not raised again.

Foxx developed a reputation as an infrastructure mayor. He was a major supporter of streetcars in Charlotte. The vehicles changed the nature of the downtown area and gave it much-needed historic ambience. Streetcars also stimulated economic development. Mayor Foxx got involved in airport politics when he questioned the awarding of taxi contracts. In 2011, Foxx threatened to veto any decision to grant such contracts unless he received "more frequent updates from Director Orr." Orr wanted to reduce the number of taxi companies in Charlotte from twelve to three. He had recommended that one of the contracts go to King/Royal, owned by two Kasmary brothers with felony convictions. Orr disclaimed knowledge of the felonies but still felt the company should get a contract. Foxx then declared in a press conference that he wanted more oversight of the airport contract policies. In addition, he raised questions about the airport's lack of deicing fluid in January, as well as the accident of Delvonte Tisdale, a teenager who took a trip in an aircraft landing gear and died. Foxx stated, "We have to look at moving average. Things have been good for 30 years. I am confident in his [Orr's] leadership. But I will ask for more frequent updates from the airport."[90]

Some considered the McCrory and Foxx inquiries an encroachment on Jerry Orr's turf. Orr had the pro-growth coalition's support, and he stood his ground on most issues. While running for governor, former mayor Pat McCrory told a Rotary audience that "he knew enough to stay out of the way when it came to Orr and the airport."[91] McCrory had apparently learned his lesson after the failure of the task force report on the airport. When Foxx disputed Orr was also able to maintain the airport policy with Foxx over the taxi contract.

These minor disagreements do not undercut the assumption that the mayor is the chief salesperson of the city's economic development despite the office's limited power within the city government structure. Even council-appointed mayor Dan Clodfelter was expected to be the city salesperson. He attested to the rise of the transformative city, saying that Charlotte "wasn't much different than Richmond, Virginia; Birmingham, Alabama; or Nashville, Tennessee" when he arrived there in 1977.[92] Clodfelter asserted, "We never really were a one-horse banking town. What we discovered after 2008 or 2009 was that there was so much more to Charlotte's economy than what the national media said . . . which was that Charlotte was a banking town."[93] As adherents to the pro-growth coalition, the relationship between the elected mayors and the pro-growth coalition has been predictable. Yet it is incorrect to say the mayor of Charlotte is powerless with respect to the airport. As history suggests, it depends on the mayor. In most cases, mayoral influence is only episodically available. The influence of Mayors Brookshire and Belk may have been related to their standing in the business community.

SUMMARY

Despite the weakness of their office, Charlotte's mayors have historically played a critical role in promoting local business leaders. Mayors have been the city's chief spokespeople and salespeople, explaining why the media follows them more than it does councilpersons. An argument could be made that council-manager government has worked so far. Despite the limitations of the two-year term, turnover is not a big problem. Since Charlotte mayors do not have a large staff, they must hire consultants. The lack of financial resources will make the mayor's job more difficult as demographics change; more conflicts and demands will arise. Mayors tend to get reelected if they go along and get along with the pro-growth coalition and refrain from introducing controversial social issues. Obviously, demographics will change what mayors say in campaigns, but mayoral candidates will continue to support the pro-growth coalition's goals. However, Charlotte has demonstrated that it will change its structure if the economy demands it.

As early as the tenures of Frank McNinch, Ben Douglas, and John Belk, Charlotte mayors supported the airport. Douglas and Belk in particular were "champions" of the airport. Mayors attended to other responsibilities as the city transformed itself, and they also supported Uptown's development. In effect, then, no open opposition to the pro-growth agenda surfaced. Each post–World War II mayor contributed to Charlotte's overall development. However, banker Hugh McColl concluded, "The two great mayors were John Belk and Harvey Gantt."[94]

CHAPTER 7

City Council Oversight Style

THE CITY OF CHARLOTTE HAS a mixed representational council system. Four at-large city council members are elected citywide, and voters in districts elect the other seven district members. To be elected as one of the four at-large candidates requires mounting a citywide campaign. District members with defined catchment areas run smaller neighborhood campaigns; their constituency is about one hundred thousand residents. The average salary is $23,860 or $11 an hour, so serving on the city council is not considered a full-time job. A small shared council staff handles constituent casework and correspondence. However, it doesn't conduct heavy-duty research projects. This is one reason the city council uses so many consultants—it simply lacks sufficient in-house expertise. Yet the city council has its own internal dynamics in which different members play different roles. Eight council committees with a variety of citizen advisory committees are associated with the Charlotte City Council. Appointing community activists to a council advisory committee is one of the ways council members reward activists in policy areas.

Charlotte's city council performs a variety of political functions. Aside from formulating and passing ordinances, members complete casework and fulfill representational roles. The council also educates the public and resolves conflicts. Council hearings can be substantive as well as symbolic (e.g., allowing citizens to complain about parking at the airport). Substantive hearings address ballot measures and zoning and rezoning cases. As council members represent a variety of identity groups—race, gender, and neighborhoods—attending community forums is an important part of these officials' job. Although they can question the city manager and airport director, council members can hardly carry out in-depth oversight of the airport. Elected officials have the power to conduct hearings when there is a crisis or a request from citizens. But the latter circumstance rarely arises.

Political scientists Heinz Eulau and Robert Eyestone make an interesting observation about a city council's policy maps, which involve individual council members' perception of a problem, policy position, and policy image.

Policymakers' willingness to set their city on a course of development depends on the content of the policy maps—how they perceive the problems facing the city, what preferences they entertain with regards to policy alternatives, and how they envisage the city's future. In general, it seems that municipal decision-makers' policy maps constitute a consistent whole, although there may be discontinuities and deviations. It also appears, in general, that the various components of the policy map are meaningfully related to the stage or phase of city policy development.[1]

As was suggested in the preceding history of the airport, there has always been a high level of consensus about Charlotte Douglas's utility. Some disagreements about the pace of expansion remain unsettled, but city council members and mayors perform a legitimating function. This is the case with airport policy. The pro-growth coalition needs politicians to nurture an inattentive citizenry or a trusting citizenry. In addition, there needs to be a consensus that the city is heading in the right direction. Using data from a national Social Capital Benchmark Survey, Hunter Bacot labels Charlotte and Mecklenburg County "active market culture." He explains his interpretation as follows:

> Charlotte is easily characterized by its affinity with business leadership and its professional government and rational decision-making processes. Charlotte is a "market culture" driven by its mantra, "Charlotte's business is business." In fact, many of the processes institutionalized by government were adapted from popular business practices. A premium is placed on efficient and effective planning before moving forward with nearly all policies. This market approach is apparently appreciated by citizens as most feel their perspectives are being represented and they trust their government to govern.[2]

Geographers Kevin Cox and Andrew Mair ingeniously label this type of engineering of consent "local redemption of identity." They assert, "Localist ideologies promulgated by the business coalition exploit that feeling of loss by propagating a redemptive sense of identity in which locals as a group are beleaguered and oppressed by the outside world, but can, on the other hand, legitimately demand redress due to their local community's status as worthy and as a paragon of national ideals."[3] Local politicians get elected by telling Charlotteans that the city is being underserved by the national and state government. Charlotteans will get their due by supporting specific candidates.

Making the above case may get politicians reelected, but council members' policy maps are not independent of ongoing policy elaborations. In other words, policy toward the airport is cumulative, and council members inherit their predecessors' policy decisions. Eulau and Eyestone are correct that "policymakers cannot do as they please."[4] They are constrained by the context of city development. There is a high level of agreement about the way to grow a medium-size city into a rising metropolis and about the role the airport should play in that process. To help create and maintain such a consensus, airport interest groups continually lobby airport directors, the city manager, and council members.

In Charlotte, a balance is maintained between the airport's municipal oversight and its financial independence. This balance facilitates the airport leadership's ability to make quick and long-range policy decisions. Political scientist Steve Erie captures this balance in his discussion of local governance of ports and airports in Los Angeles: "Public enterprises are hybrid institutions. Operating as a governmental enterprise that provides collective goods and charge users fees, they function in the dual- and conflicting-arenas of market and democracy. As such, they face the inevitable trade-off between market efficiency and democratic accountability. To achieve market efficiency, public enterprises must be free of interference from rent-seeking politicians."[5]

Generally speaking, Charlotte City Council members stay out of day-to-day operations of the airport. As discussed previously, council members, through the city attorney, objected to a deal that Mayor Ben Douglas made with the U.S. Army during its 1937 takeover of Charlotte Airport. Events surrounding the failed 1975 revenue bond vote caused a major restructuring of the council and facilitated the further political incorporation of African Americans. When the bond was reintroduced, a councilman publicly objected to the 1978 revenue bond proposal. This complaint had no impact on the outcome of the vote, as the bond measure passed.

History shows that the city council does address issues concerning the airport. Usually, individual council members try to exert political influence here and there to help airport contractors or consultants. Concessions and taxi contracts with the airport are very lucrative enterprises, and companies compete for them. As we shall discuss later, the council had intervened in taxi contracts and rates. Whenever contracts are to be had, influence peddling is possible. Payoffs are sometimes suspected when the city council debates contracts.

Generally speaking, influence peddling falls into two categories. The first involves council members who agree to move a project or a proposal for a fee. Usually, these individuals want a client to put money directly into their hands. The other type of influence peddling involves council members who eschew direct payment and opt for indirect remunerations. The first category of peddling is often amenable to law enforcement sting operations designed to catch people committing a crime. The second type often advances projects or names by simply making strategic inquiries to city department heads and signaling them that important economic players will move toward their turf. (Politicians claim, "It is a matter of dropping a hint or asking questions of the staff.") Interest groups often reward these types of influence peddlers by quietly referring work to their law firms and businesses. These types of influence peddlers are less amenable to law enforcement stings and are able to nurture a reputation for honesty.

City laws structure the formal relationship between the council and city managers. The city manager is an employee of the entire council and not a part of the mayor's staff. While job description of the city manager precludes active participation in electoral politics, council politics decides who will be hired for the position. For example, William J. Veeder was hired as city manager in 1959 after a campaign called "the Better Government Four" elected a Republican majority to the city council. Claiborne describes him as a "no nonsense city manager" who brought a new level of professionalism to Charlotte.[6]

City managers are not expected to be political. Rather, they are hired to keep the city working by ensuring that the streetlights are on, police officers are walking the beat, and firefighters are well equipped and efficient. For our purposes, city managers are also hired to supervise the airport director. Charlotte's managers know that one way to create problems for themselves is by alienating members of the council. Although mayors do not directly supervise city managers, they are nevertheless the visible officials of city government. Managers may find open conflict with the mayor and other elected officials counterproductive and career destroying. Accordingly, informal relationships between the two officeholders depend on nuances in the legal provisions and city traditions. Glen Sparrow's research demonstrates that mayors in council-manager governments can take a strong role in administrative policy if they are determined to assume such a role. This is possible if the mayor is popular and has full support from the economic elite.

Since the 1990s, Charlotte mayors have generally enjoyed the full support of the business elite but have had to stay out of government operations. James Svara's 1987 survey of North Carolina's five largest cities identifies four basic types of roles for the mayor—ceremonial, communication, organization, and guidance and promotion.[7] The highest percentage of the mayors surveyed assumed the ceremonial role and considered city promotion as an extension of it. This was the case for Charlotte mayors and airport expansion.

In general, mayors arrive in office during events at the airport. As stated, all mayors and city managers supported the airport, but some were more critical than others to the airport's expansion. Table 6 lists the events in which mayors participated and the names of the city managers in charge.

This table also reveals several overlaps in the tenures of mayors and city managers. Mr. J. B. Pridgen only served seven days after Ben Douglas's victory. He had been associated with Douglas's opponent Charles Lambeth. Managers' terms overlap mayors' because managers are supposed to be nonpolitical administrative staff. The council-manager form of government is designed to separate policy and administration, explaining why no elected officials are appointed acting city manager before a new manager takes office. City treasurer L. L. Ledbetter, city accountant George B. Livingston, and assistant city manager L. P. Bobo have served as acting city managers. This practice allows city officials a smooth administrative transition. The longer city managers stay in office, the better they can anticipate the new mayor's policies because some mayors were former council members. Table 6 also shows that most mayors played a role in major airport events.

The airport director is under the direct supervision of the city manager. This does not mean the city manager is involved with the facility's day-to-day operations. Several city managers held the position during former airport director Jerry Orr's tenure, but he maintained his independence. Orr did so in part because he was a pro-growth entrepreneur and had the support of the business community. As discussed previously, Charlotte Douglas's development facilitated the city's growth. Besides, there were no constant public complaints about the airport's management, and this fact may explain why the city council consistently supported the facility's expansion.

In 1999, the Charlotte City Council unanimously approved a $190 million bond issue to expand Charlotte Douglas International Airport. It had been twelve years since the airport had benefited from this type of expansion, and the bonds funding the improvements were underwritten by Salomon Smith Barney. Planned upgrades included a new concourse with twenty-one gates for commuter aircraft, a fourth nine-thousand-foot runway, and the extension of another runway from ten thousand to twelve thousand feet.

The council's support of this plan was a victory of Director Orr's. Councilman Ron Aulty stated, "12,000 feet was enough runway for a jet to fly nonstop to Asia." His colleague Patrick Cannon, who represented the area surrounding the airport, voiced concern about the resulting noise. He suggested that the five hundred homes near the airport should either install heavy insulation or take a buyout. Cannon stated, "We will have the money to deal with this. If the airport revenues should fail, the airlines will step in and make up the difference. But we are not anticipating this. The airport is very healthy financially."[8]

Table 6. Mayors, City Managers, and Events

Mayors	Tenure	Airport Events	City Managers
Ben E. Douglas (D)	1935–1941	Airport built	J. B. Pridgen J. B. Marshall
E. McA. Currie (D)	1941–1943	Army Takeover Morris Field	J. W. Armstrong
Herbert H. Baxter (D)	1943–1949	Airport return Advisory committee established	R. W. Flacks Henry Yancey
Victor Shaw (D)	1949–1953		Henry Yancey
Phillip Van Every (D)	1953–1957	Terminal opening	Henry Yancey
James Saxon Smith	1957–1961		Henry Yancey, William J. Veeder
Stanford R. Brookshire	1961–1969	Concourse built	William J. Veeder
John M. Belk	1969–1977	Revenue bond issue failed	William J. Veeder, David Burkhalter
Kenneth R. Harris (R)	1977–1979	Piedmont hub / bond for terminal passed	David Burkhalter
H. Edward Knox (D)	1979–1983	Graham Pkwy / New terminal opening	David Burkhalter O. Wendell White
Harvey Gantt (D)	1983–1987		O. Wendell White
Sue Myrick (R)	1987–1991		O. Wendell White
Richard Vinroot (R)	1991–1995	UK nonstop flight	O. Wendell White
Pat McCrory (R)	1995–2009	Task force report	O. Wendell White Pamela A. Syfert W. Curtis Walton Jr.
Anthony Foxx (D)	2009–2013	Taxi contract review	Curtis Walton Jr. Julie Burch
Patsy Kinsey (Acting)	2013	State takeover attempt	Julie Burch
Patrick Cannon	2013–2014		Ron Carlee
Daniel G. Clodfelter	2014–2015	Takeover aborted	Ron Carlee
Jennifer Roberts	2015–	USAir and American Airlines merger	Ron Carlee

This general support for expansion does not necessarily indicate an absence of conflicts between the airport director and city officials. As with most council–city manager forms of government, the city council is the final arbiter of who gets what and how (politically). A decision regarding the minority business program for the airport illustrates this state of affairs. As was discussed earlier, the Charlotte City Council passed a minority business enterprise (MBE) program in 1979 that required a percentage of all airport business opportunities to be directed to minority-owned firms.

In 1986, the Airport Advisory Committee [AAC] endorsed the Host International concession contract for $1.2 million. Under the agreement, minority contractor Veronica Alexander would run the airport shop.[9] Her husband, NAACP president Kelly Alexander, had previously been a member of the AAC, and he publicly denied participating in the decision about the concession. Ten years earlier, and while he was an AAC member, Mr. Alexander had written an editorial supporting the 1978 bond issues. He did so after the failure of the 1975 revenue bond, stating, "[The] yes vote is in the best interest of the black community."[10] In the editorial Kelly Alexander also complained about the fact that only one black person held what could be considered a managerial position. This support may have helped the black community vote yes in 1978.

During the 1986 concession controversy, Alexander stated, "Now that I am off the committee, I am a private citizen, I am a member of a small number of black people in this country who have some knowledge of running of an airport. There is nothing wrong with taking some of that knowledge and using it in a private business venture."[11] Airport manager Josh Birmingham agreed, noting that since Alexander was not on the AAC, there was no conflict of interest. Besides, Birmingham stated, the contract would be with Marriott, not Veronica Alexander.

After losing the AAC recommendation Nasif Majeed, owner of a fast-food restaurant franchise and a subcontractor of Aero Enterprises Incorporated, challenged the AAC's decision and began to lobby members of the Charlotte City Council. Aside from providing for more participation, he claimed his proposal would be a better deal for the city. Under his proposal, the city would receive $1.15 million, $50,000 less than under the Marriot proposal. He also claimed his plan was a better deal because he would be operating 50 percent of the business. Majeed said "[Alexander] is getting 10% of the business [under the Marriott proposal]. I really can't understand their [the City Council's] logic."[12] At the March 25 meeting, the city finally awarded the minority subcontract to Veronica Alexander's Alexander-Motsepe Airport Enterprises, thus demonstrating the influence of the Airport Advisory Committee. In 1989, the U.S. Supreme Court struck down the minority set-aside programs. The city continued its minority program based on goals, not strict set-aside percentages. In 1992, the AAC reported the airport had made approximately $3.5 million in what is now called Disadvantaged Business Enterprises Contracts.[13]

THE ROLE OF THE AIRPORT ADVISORY COMMITTEE

As covered in chapter 2, the state of North Carolina established the Charlotte Airport Commission to govern the airport during World War II. After the war, the commission members resigned and recommended that the airport become a city department. The commission also recommended the establishment of the Airport Advisory Committee to be appointed by the city manager with the consent of the city council.

In May 25, 1946, R. W. Flack, the city manager, appointed three businessmen and community leaders to an Airport Advisory Committee. Aviation advocate John C. Erwin served as chair, and his fellow members were Hugh E. Campbell and C. P. Street. All of them were former members of the Charlotte Airport Commission. The purpose of the AAC was to recommend service improvements and reduce airport noise. After 1946, the city manager no longer selected the committee. The city council now has the final say in appointing committee members. As an oversight committee for the council, the AAC also advises the airport manager. Committee members were initially limited to two successive terms of service. However, the Charlotte City Council retains the power to waive this rule; it allowed former mayor Ben Douglas to serve another term. Douglas had been associated with the airport for over forty years, and it was said of him, "The Airport really is his love and it has been his life."[14] Other former mayors also served on the Airport Advisory Committee, as did businessmen and aviation experts. Yet there was no history of plain citizen representation on the AAC.

After World War II, homeowners living near the airport began to complain about its growth and the related noise the airplanes generated. The airport's neighbors claimed that the noise affected their property values. Residents also noted that some health issues were related to noise pollution. In 1946, the U.S. Supreme Court held in *United States v. Causby* that landowners do not control the airspace above their property.[15] At a certain height, the airway belongs to everyone; therefore, landowners cannot make trespassing claims on airplanes or airlines. Nonetheless, it became obvious to the pro-growth coalition that airport neighbors' complaints would be a recurring problem and that the AAC could serve as a way to manage relations with these complainants. Indeed, the membership of the AAC, which included businessmen and former mayors, needed to recruit ordinary citizens to the committee.

On June 13, 1960, the Charlotte Chamber of Commerce's management study, a subcommittee of the Aviation Committee, recommended that the city council appoint a semiprofessional group to promote the economic utilization for the airport. The subcommittee wanted five members of the AAC to do long-range planning.

On July 11, 1960, the Charlotte City Council expanded the AAC from three to five members. Recommended by the Chamber of Commerce's Aviation Committee, the expanded AAC membership was empowered to conduct long-range fiscal planning. To assist the transition, the three old members were granted extended terms. All the members, including the new ones, were businessmen. Politics also played a role as the council rejected the recommendation to add a member who was not a city resident. One council member was quoted as saying, "I think we can find five good men out of 200,000 in the city."[16] However, guiding the airport into the sixties would require more than boosters' firmness.

The sixties proved to be a decade of airport expansion and aircraft technological development. It was also a decade of citizen protest. Among these dissenters were homeowners who lived near airports. They wanted to stop airport expansion and sued the city for liabilities. In 1962, the Supreme Court extended the Causby liability ruling to locally controlled airports in *Griggs v. Allegheny County*.[17] This decision changed the liability narrative for cities so that growth now seemed to have legal limits. Nevertheless, the expansion of airports like Charlotte Douglas continued.

The AAC was not designed be a purely citizen-oriented committee.[18] Instead, it evolved into a group that facilitated airport operations. As Charlotte Douglas International Airport expanded, the consequent increase in flights and noise created a need to pacify homeowners near the airport. The city council and the airport directors recognized early on that citizens' voices needed to be heard. They also recognized the need for a political balance between special interest groups and neighborhood representatives. When Harvey Gantt was mayor he attempted to acknowledge this process. He stated, "We went through laboriously talking about each person, what or who they represented."[19] Over time, the AAC added women and African Americans to its ranks. In 1992, Neighborhood for Airport Change organizer Sue Friday was elected chair. The Airport Advisory Committee and city manager are expected to be the liaison for the city council. In the long run, however, the AAC performed its primary job of promoting airport expansion.

AIRPORT GROWTH AND EXPANSION

As we saw earlier, the pro-growth coalition and the airport managers they hired have made development their mission. The airport directors' role will be discussed in chapter 6, but it is important to understand why these individuals were selected. Al Quinn was hired because he promised to grow Charlotte Douglas. His successor, Thomas Rafferty, also advocated growth. They both knew that more runways and airplanes would create noise. Airport director Birmingham responded to the consequences of airport development as follows: "I don't think there's anything wrong with the growth. I don't know where these questions about our growth are coming from. That's a policy issue the elected officials will have to decide, and you definitely have to be guided by what the community wants. But from where I sit, Charlotte is not at the point of needing restrictions on its airport growth." Birmingham asserted that the airport had handled the noise problem in the "proper way."[20]

Piedmont Airlines spokesperson Ken Carson backed up Birmingham's comments and confirmed Charlotte Douglas's importance as a hub. Bill Millett, senior vice president of the Charlotte Chamber of Commerce, supported the overall pro-growth theme. He stated,

> As close as we've been able to come to quantifying it is to say that the airport is some factor in at least 80 percent of the companies that locate here. It is our trump card.... We want to make sure that economic development is taken into account by the city council as much as the other issues raised by the neighbors. It is a matter of great interest and considerable concern to us. If the talk is of no growth or putting what we consider unreasonable limitations on that growth, then you'll have an argument.[21]

This important exchange between the reporter, airport director, Piedmont Airlines spokesman, and chamber of commerce representative demonstrated the resolve of the airlines and city officials to support airport growth regardless of noise concerns.

In 1969, the AAC and the city council advocated a new terminal for Charlotte Douglas. They based the recommendation on a consultant report by Peat, Warwick, Livingston Company. The consultants suggested that the extension be completed in four stages. The first stage would be a 6,100-foot runway paid for with airport revenue. The second stage was a new terminal estimated to cost $25 million. The third stage would involve an even longer runway. Consultants concluded that the airport expansion proposal would cost $40 million to $45 million. John C. Ervin, Airport Advisory Committee chair, predicted that Charlotte Douglas would become an even larger hub. He stated, "If we let the airport go to pot, Charlotte is going to die."[22] This effort failed and neither the airport nor the city of Charlotte went to pot. The pro-growth coalition continued to campaign for a new terminal.

In 1985, the city council approved a $115 million bond issue that West Charlotte community groups opposed. Sue Friday, chair of the Dixie-Berryhill Neighborhood and a member of the Airport Advisory Committee, stated, "I'm hesitant to use the term blank check, . . . but that's what it looks like."[23] Friday also objected to the 1986 master plan, declaring, "There's not much in this report for the west side."[24] Nor did the plan address the noise issue.

Despite the opposition of the Westside community, the AAC approved the 1986 twenty-year master plan for Charlotte Douglas Airport. Howard, Needles, Tammen and Bergendoff of Washington designed the plan. The firm had met with neighborhood residents in November to discuss their concerns over noise, but the plan went forward regardless.

In February 1987 the city council passed a resolution that charged the AAC with an expanded mission allowing Charlotte Douglas International Airport to grow "to its maximum potential to foster economic development in Charlotte."[25] *Charlotte Observer* reporter Kathleen Curry lamented the maximum growth policy espoused by the consultants for the airport master plan update. But she reminded readers that airport managers could interpret this resolution as a mandate "to be as big as they can be."[26] Indeed, she indicated that Charlotte Douglas could grow into one of the nation's largest airports.

> No one predicted the boom, and no one challenged it. City councils have happily embraced what the airport has asked for. They didn't have to look far to see the effects. On the Billy Graham Parkway, perhaps, where million-dollar office parks give new life to the Westside. Or in the city's tax coffers, filled by revenues from development backers say was drawn by the airport. In December, the council approved without debate $165 million in terminal and maintenance expansion—$75 million of which will be taxpayer-backed bonds—three times the initial terminal cost.[27]

Curry predicted that more growth would create a problem of scale. More growth meant more airplane takeoffs and landings. These, in turn, meant more noise pollution. Therefore, the anxiety of airport neighbors would also grow.

The city council decided that two members of the new expanded AAC, now numbering nine members, would come from the Westside neighborhood. Located near the airport, the neighborhood had organized around the noise issue.

The council wanted to create a balance of business leaders and citizens. Thus, the council appointed Westside activist Sue Friday to the AAC.[28]

In 1989, the Airport Advisory Committee also appointed a twelve-member Neighborhood Task Force to improve relations with the surrounding communities. Over the years the AAC has evolved from a purely advisory committee to a more visible citizen committee. Though the group was not designed to challenge airport decisions, its members have criticized and questioned the director's agenda. As we will see in this chapter, the chairman of the AAC acted against the interests of the city government.

However, the method of appointing this citizen advisory group may explain the committee's relative political impotence. Membership on the committee is obtained through a self-application process. A citizen can simply get an application from the city clerk's office and return it. The council then makes the final decision on the committee's composition. Appointments were made based on the applicant's ability to assist the directors and city council. Some people gained membership because they knew the history of the airport. Others were members of the pro-growth coalition, and still others supported council members. Over time, citizens' complaints created the call for a so-called citizen seat.

The real civic contribution of the AAC is its ability to publicly support an airport policy issue. One such issue was the AAC's encouragement of fees for off-site rental cars and other airport-dependent businesses. The airport management endorsed the idea, but the Charlotte City Council refused to back it, thereby angering the AAC chair. Sue Friday stated, "There is no reason for us to waste our time. If certain council members have already obligated their votes, they should have the courtesy to tell us."[29] The decision to delay caused former mayor Eddie Knox, who represented the people who would have to pay the fee, to storm out of the room. Council member Stan Campbell, chair of the transportation committee, denied that the council had chosen not to support the proposal. He asserted, "Their action to adjourn based on somebody who thought they heard something from somebody who thought they knew something is responsible. Why they would take a lawyer's word for anything, I don't know."[30]

Airport management continued to support the issue of fees. In November 1992, the AAC voted unanimously to recommend the fees for hotel couriers and shuttles, as well as for off-site rental cars and parking. Jerry Orr asserted, "They compete for the same passengers. They're currently paying the airport nothing for having access to those people."[31] As we will discover later, such fees are a critical part of the airport budget.

LOCAL POLITICS AND THE AIRPORT ENVIRONMENT

Noise is a problem for all airports, workers, and their surrounding communities. Obviously, as the airport expanded its runways, it also had more take-offs and landings. "Noise contours" refers to the level of noise created by these flights. In 1979, the airport added the north–south runway that diverted some of the noise from the Westside. In 1985 Charlotte Douglas's average day-night noise level was seventy-five decibels, while "a plane taking off can register between 90–110 decibels."[32] Consultants assured nearby residents that new runway noise "would be insignificant."[33] Yet the din became the focus of intense debate among city politicians, businessmen, and residents.

Residents claimed that aircraft noise lowered property values, and thus the city had spent $5 million to settle 230 lawsuits by 1985. Airports use noise-reducing devices to minimize these problems. However, this technology costs facilities millions of dollars to install, and it also results in the loss of many jobs (since the discontinuation of production would result in layoffs). In 1985, residents asked consultants about the proposed fourth runway at Charlotte Douglas. The consultants met with eighty Charlotteans who had been on the Airport Master Plan Advisory Committee. The issue of noise was clearly related to expansion, which was considered critical to Charlotte's growth. Without airport growth, the economy might falter, and jobs would be lost. This, at least, was the narrative of the pro-growth coalition.

The city of Charlotte was not asked to choose between noise pollution and jobs. Jobs, of course, are of great concern to mayors, city council members, and community leaders. At its peak, the ecology movement placed old-style local politicians in positions to which they were unaccustomed; issues of environmental protection were new to them. Many of these elected officials are now being outmaneuvered in the media by ecologists who present themselves as experts on the long-range effects of noise pollution. Politicians are also being circumvented in the media by federal government officials advocating stronger measures such as the institution of sanctions against companies failing to comply with federal environmental standards.

In 1985, the Airport Advisory Committee established the Neighborhood Task Force to determine the priorities for buying homes most affected by airport noise. The home-buying program was federally funded. By 1991 the *Charlotte Observer* reported that the plan to buy four hundred homes around the airport had not been completed. These were residences in the Morse Park, Whippoorwill Hills, and Withrow Road areas. In December, the city of Charlotte had made 127 offers and closed on 103 houses.[34] The city was turned down seven times, and the AAC was asked to monitor the process.

As a result of this rise in public consciousness, city council members were forced to deal with issues concerning the local environment. In turn, the council had to make hard choices. One official in Charlotte was quoted as saying, "Trying to measure noise is a little like trying to bottle fog—it's an elusive, constantly changing property perceived differently by each person."[35] The issues of noise raised some interesting questions for the pro-growth coalition. Is it better to raise the tolerance standards for measuring noise pollution, even though this discourages airlines from locating at Charlotte, thereby threatening the volume of jobs available? Is airplane noise a "product of success"? Was Birmingham right when he suggested that the "total effect is in the ear of the beholder?" If noise pollution is a matter of subjectivity, how can the relevant laws be enforced? What are the alternatives?

Charlotte found itself on the horns of a dilemma. Leaders and residents supported a bigger airport that would accommodate more takeoffs and landings and generate more noise. How would this affect the quality of life in the city? Above all, cities are living systems: they need clean air and less noise. Even the most ardent city boosters of economic growth will not gainsay airplanes' contribution to urban noise pollution. City governments had come a long way in turning down the volume of noise, but such pollution was still noticeable. And health statistics supported the need for change. (In fact, the relatively clean environment is one of the reasons why the southern Sunbelt has attracted new industries.)

If the airlines reduce their flights, Charlotte will find itself with many unemployed residents and fewer business transactions. On the other hand, the health of the people who live near the airport is at risk if the present rate of noise pollution is increased. When Charlotte Douglas Airport was built, approximately six miles of relatively empty space separated it from uptown Charlotte. Houses and retail shops subsequently filled in the gap. As city neighborhoods grew westward toward the airport, the facility needed more space. The dilemma was what to do with these homes and businesses. While home buyouts became the city's primary strategy for gaining more space for the airport, some homeowners refused to sell, and others took their case to the courts. Charlotte Douglas discovered that it would encounter legal problems anytime an individual decided to take on an airport. The noise pollution controversy illustrates why individual protest is futile. There was never a successful NIMBY (not in my backyard) movement in the communities surrounding the airport. Historian Janet R. Daly

Bednarek correctly states, "All airport noise is local."[36] Different cities handle the situation differently.

Considering a study of citizens' failed attempts to restrict the expansion of Chicago O'Hare Airport, Juline Cidell concludes that citizens as individuals are at a disadvantage when they confront airports. As Cidell states, it is a matter of scale.

> First, in multi-scalar conflicts such as airport expansion, individuals as scales are not politically powerful. In bringing up costs at the scale of the body or household in contrast to municipal or regional benefits, they can be dismissed as selfish or NIMBYS. An alternate political strategy might be to show that it is individuals who benefit from the proposed project (perhaps via construction contracts or airline profits) more than the "regional economy" or "international travelers," in order to make the scales equivalent.[37]

In other words, the courts have ruled in favor of the airport, not homeowners. Mounting an individual campaign against the pro-growth coalition and its "projects" is sometimes futile. When homeowners are able to get the media to support their cause, protests receive more publicity. To be successful, such groups will need allies on the city council.

One of the problems of environmental activists and homeowner associations is that cities are relatively new to the environmental protection business. Environmental management was not recognized as a local issue until the 1970s. In the beginning, municipal responsibilities were not clear. Remember that the EPA had not been created in 1970, and airport noise was considered the price one paid for having an airport. In 1972, Congress enacted the Noise Control Act. The Carter administration also supported the Quiet Community Act of 1978. This was the same year that airports and airlines were trying to address deregulation.

Despite the new laws, the city of Charlotte remains full of loud sounds. Cars, power tools, emergency vehicles, airplanes, and construction work all tend to pound the eardrum continually. Studies have shown that noise not only destroys hearing ability but also affects one's psychological disposition (e.g., level of irritability and stress). People who live near the airport experience different types of noises than others in the community. The sounds these residents are exposed to can have a cumulative physical and psychological effect, yet airline noise continues. Most complaints center on the blast of jet engines.

The regulatory power of municipalities has been seriously limited since the passage of the Noise Control Act of 1972. In general, the public has tolerated or adjusted to certain types of noise. Yet new or strange sounds are less likely to be accepted, and this issue was more salient for those living around the airport. In many cases, the state and federal governments set guidelines for noise pollution control. They do so despite the fact that some cities do not have expertise, manpower, or resources to effectively fight the problem. In deciding to accept national standards rather than creating citywide ones, elected officials are able to attack polluting companies who imperil the community's health.

THE POLITICS OF REVENUE BONDS REFERENDUM

As was suggested in the history chapter, bond issues have been won and lost regardless of the full support of the pro-growth coalition. Putting revenue bonds on a ballot without properly priming the electorate can be problematic. Although campaign literature for these elections claims that no taxes will be raised, some citizens routinely vote against the bonds. Why? Some voters take out their anti-tax resentments in the voting booth. Accordingly, a campaign for airport expansion had to be cast as a job creator, a matter of overall civic pride, and an opportunity for social betterment. Runway projects were presented as badly needed and cost efficient. Such campaigning usually had the backing of leading members of the various community groups in the city. Nevertheless, selling a terminal or a runway can be more difficult than selling a new stadium or park.

The media plays a central role in bond approval campaigning and mobilization. Newspapers were once the primary source of political news, and getting the support of the local paper was critical. A 1978 *Charlotte Observer* editorial admonished city residents for not being interested in or embarrassed about the quality of the airport infrastructure. The article described an apologetic airport sign posted between 1949 and 1954 that stated, "We solicited your patient consideration of these facilities." It pointed out that the "city only spent $14 million in bond money on what is now a $100 million asset." The editorial concluded, "Though the city's ambitions for the airport have been great, they have been frustrated by citizen reluctance to invest in airport facilities. Of seven airport issues put before the voters, three have been defeated. The reluctance is difficult to understand, for the airport has returned big benefits at small cost."[38]

Airport management had known since 1971 that the facility needed a new terminal. In 1973, the city brought in Arnold Thompson Associates Incorporated to evaluate the situation and make recommendations. The firm concluded, "Forecasts indicate the total annual passenger increase from the 1972 level of 2,095,000 to approximately 4,500,000 by 1980. . . . In order to process this number of passengers, approximately 385,000 square feet of terminal area, twenty-two aircraft parking positions and 3,600 public automobile parking spaces will be required."³⁹ The Airport Advisory Committee, consisting of former mayors Ben Douglas and Stanford Brookshire, supported the idea of a new terminal. The task that remained was convincing the public a new terminal was needed.

In 1975, the pro-growth coalition decided to use an appeal to civic pride to get support for the bond issue. This approach required citywide mobilization and efforts to educate voters. Don Davidson, head of the Charlotte Chamber of Commerce, led the 1975 campaign, which won backing from airport management, business leaders, elected officials, and consultants. An unexpected source of opposition came from the black community. The Black Political Caucus's (BPC's) Committee on the Issues, Campaign and Candidates had voted unanimously against the referendum.

On March 24, *Charlotte Observer* reporter Milton Jordan declared that the BPC had formed a coalition with the Steele Creek Community Association to oppose the referendum. The Steele Creek Community Association represented the areas adjacent to the airport. Ms. Sandra Reed, the association's chair, stated, "We think this whole bond proposal is a waste of taxpayers' money. Making Charlotte another Atlanta is going to hurt more people than it helps."⁴⁰

Two days later, the *Charlotte Observer* addressed the protests from the black community. The authors of an editorial entitled "Blacks and Bonds: Doubts Need Attention" stated, "This [protest] again underscores the price Charlotte is paying for not having more blacks in the political decision-making process. An underlying reason for the caucus's action is the distrust of City Hall and a desire to 'send a message' that blacks must be in on the formative stages of bond issues and other municipal projects if they are to lend support."⁴¹ The editorial also noted the BPC's displeasure with the city council's decision to appoint Harvey Gantt to a vacant seat on the council instead of drawing from five names offered by BPC. In addition, the editorial called the caucus's apprehension about airport expansion a "fairly vague concern."⁴² Writers urged the city council to take the initiative and invite BPC members to a hearing. They also warned readers that the caucus was promoting a negative view of city hall that could result in the referendum's defeat. The editorial concluded that the "caucus had made no cogent case against these projects."⁴³

On April 4, 1975, the *Charlotte Observer* published an editorial supporting the revenue bond for the airport. It stated that the $55 million would authorize the city to use tax revenues to retire airport bonds. Editorialists also wrote that "tax revenues would not be required except in the most extreme and unlikely of circumstances, such as the collapse of airlines and airline travel in the country."⁴⁴ They assured readers that airport revenues would fully pay for the bonds; indeed, these earnings could retire the bond without "absorbing tax money."⁴⁵ Two days later, the *Charlotte Observer* published another editorial supporting all items on the ballot.⁴⁶

On April 2, the local PBS television station, WTVI, channel 42, broadcasted an open forum on the referendum. City manager David Burkhalter represented Charlotte, Josh Birmingham represented the airport, and community activist Willie Strafford represented the Black Political Caucus. The black community had a variety of grievances against city hall. Aside from criticizing the airport's discriminatory hiring policies, BPC chair Robert Davis asserted, "It's more protest than opposition because of the way bond money has been spent in the past. We just feel the city fathers need to give an account for what's been done before asking us to write a blank check."⁴⁷ The bond issue also included funds for sidewalks and bikeways. Journalists from the *Charlotte Observer* could only identify two small groups of black citizens in favor of the referendum.⁴⁸ Several rumors emerged concerning bank money being put into black precincts to produce a favorable vote. Moreover, some people raised questions about the beneficiaries of airport expansion, as any airport construction put grand patronage at stake. Bond campaign chairman Don Davidson and others had to publicly deny they would profit from the expansion.⁴⁹

On April 8, the city's $55 million bond proposal to build a terminal was defeated by a vote of 16,888 to 14,575. Twenty-six percent of eligible voters turned out. In the five predominately black precincts, the combined vote against the airport bond was 695 to 412, and not one of those precincts voted for the bond. Furthermore, the measure barely won in Precincts Sixty-Five and Sixty-Nine, where affluent whites dominated.⁵⁰ These voters had always supported bond issues. It was a tough defeat for the pro-growth coalition and consultant Arnold Thompson, who reportedly sat glumly while results trickled in.⁵¹ Former director Jerry Orr remembered the defeat as "a low water mark" and said that a "sense of urgency" surrounded the airport.⁵²

Scholar Alex Coffin offers an explanation for the referendum failure: "The 1975 defeat was a casualty of a battle for control of the black community. The Black Political Caucus had been formed to break the lock that Fred Alexander, a former city councilman and later state senator, had on black voters. Bob Davis, president of the caucus, said after the referendum votes were counted that he was 'tired and elated' and that it showed 'people are more important than things.'"⁵³

Don Davidson, the bond campaign chairman, floated an alternative explanation for the failure of the referendum. In addition to the fact that the economy was suffering from stagflation, Americans were reacting to the fallout from the Watergate scandal and the 1975 New York City fiscal crisis. The New York crisis was caused in part by aggressive spending.[54] However, it is understandable that black leaders would claim credit for the referendum's defeat. The pro-growth coalition had not done a good job of including black residents in airport planning, and it learned from the 1975 failure. Black representatives were added to the Airport Advisory Committee, and a better campaign was launched three years later.

Voters approved the airport bond initiative on June 20, 1978, by a two-to-one margin.[55] They also wanted to expand the membership of the Charlotte City Council. Former mayor Gantt recalled the sequence of events:

> In 1975 the airport needed a new terminal. After the failure of the bond issue, neighborhood groups got together and stated that they [blacks and poor whites—residents of Charlotte's east side] wanted better representation. They felt unrepresented. They rose up against the airport. This was the first major loss for the airport. The black community, in general, had acquiesced to the business community's leadership traditionally over many years. There was a great deal of trust in the business community. Gradually that trust had dissipated, and the airport bond issue was a cause that they elected to oppose.[56]

The black community wanted a district form of city council representation. However, the city council voted against the idea. In 1976, citizens started an initiative petition, gathered the required signatures, and got on the ballot. In 1977, the proposal to change the council's structure passed by an eighty-vote margin. The Charlotte City Council had been an at-large system, and it then became a mixed one with seven single-member district seats (i.e., elected by designated districts) and four at-large seats (i.e., elected citywide). In 1978, a new revenue bond was constructed with funding for a terminal, capital improvements, and Mint Museum expansion. After the change, Gantt stated, "The airport was now a feasible situation."[57] He added, "It passed largely because of solid support by the new representatives."[58] Charlotte City Club historian Jack Claiborne concludes "that reform [adoption of mixed system] greatly diluted the business community's control of city affairs—and proportionally diminished the political influence of the City Club members."[59] As we shall see, the demise of the pro-growth coalition was greatly exaggerated. But it nevertheless marked a major transition in the politics of the "transformative city."

THE POLITICS OF RACE EQUALIZING

It is clear from this review of councilmanic politics in Charlotte that elected politicians supported the agenda of the pro-growth coalition and the aspirations of a transformative city. The pro-growth coalition reciprocated by helping political leaders address lingering social problems and make the city more inclusive. Social/racial deregulation—that is, promoting racial integration—was discussed in chapter 3. The council's attention to these issues may become more difficult to maintain as the gap in equality becomes more pronounced.

Members of the pro-growth coalition also recognized that they needed to improve Charlotte's workforce and upgrade its Uptown area. To make that happen, leading businessmen had to get personally involved in social and education endeavors. Ed Crutchfield, head of First Union Bank, started the Excellence in Education and Reading First Literacy Program. He also allowed his employees to volunteer in the city public schools. Hugh McColl, president of North Carolina National Bank, sponsored the NCNB Community Development Corporation that built condominium projects in Uptown. In addition, McColl served on the City Manager Areas Plan Task Force that created a master plan for Uptown. He explained,

> The business community has been deeply involved in the Central City. We need more affordable housing, more workforces housing and housing for working couples. Gentrification is explosive. People make so much money, that they push out the firemen and other workers, etc.
>
> The city and county government became interested in doing something about it [housing]. The bank is creating $50 million in equity, which should provide at least $500 million in housing. In the 4th Ward we built a whole neighborhood by providing the financing. We were lending the money at 6% in a 13% world. This was about half of the price of money at the time. In 3rd Ward there was a still standing black neighborhood. This was a middle-class community, they held middle level jobs, such as school principals, maître d's at clubs, etc. They [residents] ranged from the middle to upper class. They are integrated by choice. This was the first integration in the city. It was a matter of pleasure and hope.
>
> In 1st Ward Hope IV project. We built schools. Three of the four downtown wards changed, and the Bank did it.[60]

These programs obviously made an impact, but socioeconomic problems persist in the city's African American and Latino communities. These are complicated situations that intuitive solutions may not alleviate.

SUMMARY

Obviously, the churning of Charlotte politics has helped the city's transformational process. The new economy has helped some residents but not others because glaring fallouts always result from any fundamental economic change. Throughout history, elected leaders were careful not to kill too many golden geese. As the local economy changed, the city government structure followed it. The weak council-manager government has endured, and the 1978 switch to the district system of electing council members further opened up the government to disadvantaged individuals' complaints. This allows some councilpersons to cultivate a narrow constituency at the expense of the overall interest of the city, a situation Paul Peterson warns against in his work *City Limits*. The new partisanship also further compromised the city's history of consensus. Former acting city manager Pamela Syfert observed,

> During my whole career (thirty-five years in city government as budget director and eleven years as city manager) there was a sense of working together for the good of the community. There was a great consensus between the community, political leadership and the Chamber. There was a great focus on working toward a consensus. The business community would work on housing in the neighborhoods. It was not an either or [economic development or neighborhoods]. But in 2006–2007 I saw more signs that people were taking more partisan positions and were less inclined to work with the members from the opposite party. They would say that sounds like a bunch of Democrat talk or that sounds like it came out of Republican side. Since then there been less ability to come together.[61]

On the other hand, as Richard Schragger's *City Power* suggests, allowing such venting of dissatisfaction and partisanship could instill more agency in city government. Can this happen with the two-year term for elected officials and weak home rule?

More importantly for this study, would a change in local government structure advance Charlotte Douglas's development? Steven Erie cites Michael Denning's argument that infrastructure policies are not driven by government arrangements but rather technology and market forces.[62] In that case, Charlotte's council-manager form of city government was not at a disadvantage in balancing technology, economics, and community interest. Would the airport have evolved quicker if Charlotte had a strong mayor form of government? We may never know the answer to this question. We do know from Erie and Kogan's study of San Diego's government that the switch to a strong mayor form of government did not impede the plundering of the city.[63]

As we shall see in the next chapter, mayors, councilpersons, state representatives, Airport Advisory Committee members, and director Jerry Orr played critical roles in the North Carolina General Assembly's plot to take control of the airport from the city of Charlotte.

CHAPTER 8

The Plot That Failed

AS SUGGESTED IN THE EARLIER chapters, the building and expansion of Charlotte's airport required the cooperation of a pro-growth coalition of business leaders, mayors, airport managers, and federally mandated grants. Without this cooperation the airport and the "transformative city" would not have been possible. From the outside, Charlotte seemed to be progressing toward its goal of being the second regional city of the southeastern United States. The previous chapters outlined the volatility of the airline industry and the unending competition among cities, observing their impact on Charlotte city politics. Over the years Charlotte had developed a reputation for having a forward-looking city government and an aggressive business community. Obviously, the city demographics changed, as did the personalities of elected officials in the pro-growth coalition. Yet few people knew of possible internal conflicts, disparate interests, and plain partisanship and disagreements about the economic future of the city and its airport. Like a volcano, the pressure in Charlotte kept building until there was an eruption. The fissure in the pro-growth coalition manifested itself in the North Carolina state legislature's attempt to terminate the city's sole ownership of Charlotte Douglas International Airport.

Republican members of the Mecklenburg County delegation led the attempted takeover. But the story is more complicated than a simple partisan disagreement. The open conflict between Charlotte and the state legislature exposed a growing schism in a working coalition that had once been a consolidated front. The plot involved a variety of actors working covertly and overtly with state legislators to reorganize the airport's governance structure.

This chapter reviews the run-up to the state takeover attempt. It also details the reactions of city of Charlotte officials and airport managers to the North Carolina legislature's passage of a takeover law. This measure would have transferred the management and ownership of the Charlotte Douglas International Airport from the city to a regional authority. The law initially threw city officials off-balance, but they reacted quickly to stop the airport's appropriation. The general public considered the state's attempt an unwarranted and unwelcome seizure of city property. Several questions emerged from the takeover attempt: Was the powerful pro-growth coalition divided about the future of the airport?

What were the motives of Mecklenburg County Republican legislators? Was the takeover attempt purely partisan, or did it prompt a fight between the counties and the city? Was there a hidden subtext in the plan to seize the airport? How could Charlotte protect its most important economic assets? The attempted takeover became a pivotal moment for the transformative city. One of Charlotte's major economic assets was under threat, and the city's political power would be regionally dispersed. Efforts to acquire or displace the city-owned airport are not new.

During World War II, state legislation established the Charlotte Airport Commission to represent the city's interests when the military operated the airport. As chapter 2 showed, the Charlotte Chamber of Commerce Airport Committee established the Rogan Committee (1960) to study whether an authority should operate the airport. We also saw that two mayors had publicly suggested changes in the airport governing structure. In 1968, Mayor Brookshire suggested that Mecklenburg County take over the airport because it had a higher debt limit than the city of Charlotte. Richard Vinroot, the first Republican mayor, also suggested making the Airport Advisory Committee a regional one. In both cases the mayors argued that the airport served the metro region and even two states (North and South Carolina). Ergo, its governance should be more representative. Neither idea took root and the city of Charlotte continued to own and develop the airport.

In 2013, the city-state relationship changed. Charlotte Douglas International Airport received an unexpected jolt when the North Carolina state legislature proposed to reconfigure the facility from one owned and managed by the city to one controlled by multiple counties and states (i.e., an airport authority). To understand why the reorganization law was passed, one needs to understand the political context in which Charlotte Douglas operated and the type of the narratives espoused to justify the takeover attempt.

BACKGROUND OF THE TAKEOVER

Since the turn of the century, the political relationship between cities and state governments has undergone several important changes. We have seen a shift from a tutelage system in which state governments oversee cities to a system of quasi equality between local political leaders and state officials. We now live in a period of history when city administrators (i.e., a managerial class) are deemed rivals to state government officials, a situation very much akin to the classic adage of the tail wagging the dog. Strong home rule charters are seen as cities' bulwark against administrative encroachment. Cities are also somewhat protected by the fact that most of a state's voters live in metropolitan areas. Hence, statewide elected officials are not usually inclined to alienate this large bloc of voters.

Although cities have no political status in the U.S. Constitution, many large cities have achieved quasi autonomy from their host states. Cities like Charlotte enjoy a limited amount of independence from state legislative control. Charlotte lacks a home rule charter and cannot pass ordinances and tax levies as it sees fit. The state of North Carolina has the final say in these matters. Encroachment on a city's political turf happens when a city council decision is at variance with state policy. Charlotte's population advantage, which is important in statewide elections, protects it somewhat.

Supposedly, Charlotte's representatives in the state assembly also protect the city. State politicians from Charlotte and Mecklenburg County have gained equality with their rural counterparts. They chair committees, employ full-time staff, and lobby city workers and residents. Furthermore, they never let their colleagues forget that the largest percentage of the state's population lives in the city. Jim Morrill of the *Charlotte Observer* asserted, "For years Charlotte's legislative battles were often defined by geography. Urban vs. rural. 'The Great State of Mecklenburg' vs. the rest of North Carolina. Now it's a civil war, with city officials clashing with some of the county's own state lawmakers."[1]

City of Charlotte officials have consistently fought state encroachment into municipal governments' internal affairs. The fight over Charlotte Douglas International Airport publicly brought out these turf battles, exposing a situation replete with affronts. The underlying state and city conflicts have been smoldering for years for the reason discussed above. Reporter Jim Morrill quoted Bill McCoy, retired director of the Urban Institute at the University of North Carolina at Charlotte, as follows: "I can't ever recall anything like this. It seems like there's no common ground where people can talk about it. It's very personal."[2]

When city residents support local officials, they may be able to successfully resist or modify state probes into city affairs. Mayors and city council members can easily find sympathizers if they suggest that state legislators in Raleigh are meddling in local politics. This was clearly the case when the state wanted to change how the city operated and governed Charlotte Douglas Airport. As we shall we see, meddling is not without its perils.

Before the attempted state takeover, Charlotte Douglas International Airport was considered a well-managed, low-cost facility. Under the organizational structure the city council created after World War II, the airport experienced no problems attracting bondholders or getting good bond ratings. History shows that no surrounding counties demanded inclusion in the governing structures.

Former mayor Vinroot suggested that Airport Advisory Committee membership become regional. Mecklenburg County, the airport's host county, had not fought to assume control of the facility. Though some municipal debt limits existed, that was not a problem. Why, then, did the state legislature attempt a takeover? What were the background stories?

THE RUN-UP TO TAKEOVER OF THE AIRPORT

Several explanatory narratives were floated before the state takeover attempt. Increasing airport security problems formed the subtext of one narrative. This concern reflected the fact that many airports reported security breaches (fence jumping and theft). Since 2004, Charlotte Douglas has had six such incidents. The most notable one occurred in 2010, when teenager Delvonte Tisdale somehow penetrated the airport's security, lodged himself in an airplane's wheel well, and died while the plane was en route to Boston. This incident raised questions about the role of the airport police. Although Charlotte Douglas's police were trained by the Charlotte-Mecklenburg Police Department, they reported to the airport director. The conflict between the CMPD and the independent airport police department was long-standing. In 2012, the CMPD consolidated the two groups and officially took over security at the airport. While police are more visible at the airport, security remains an issue.

The second narrative was that airport management, under the auspices of the city government, was not aggressive and entrepreneurial enough. According to the *Charlotte Business Journal*, this narrative began circulating as soon as 2011, spread mainly by Johnny Harris, cofounder of Lincoln Harris, a major property developer in Charlotte.[3] Harris had earned a reputation and a record for developing Ballantyne, one of the city's most prestigious living areas. Harris had two thousand acres of land rezoned for this upscale, master-planned community. He also developed projects such Morrocroft, Piedmont Town Center, and over 545,000 square feet of commercial real estate. Known in the golf world as the president of Quail Hollow Club, home of the Wells Fargo Championship, Harris has been pro-growth throughout his career. Once a longtime U.S. Airways board member, he has also advocated the addition of light-rail at the Charlotte Douglas International Airport. When Harris speaks, the business community listens. According to this narrative, developers such as Harris coveted the western property surrounding the airport. Charlotte Douglas sits on six thousand acres of city-owned land. The freight yard and the Dixie-Berryhill area between the airport and the Catawba River were said to be "an intriguing area.... Jack Christine, deputy aviation director, declared, 'All of that acreage is in play.'"[4]

City politicians were characterized as falling behind the growth momentum. This narrative seems to have been an underhanded criticism of wayward airport management staffers and of elected officials preoccupied with other issues. An independent authority would keep employees focused on the airport alone. Consultant Stan Campbell—a former Republican member of the Charlotte City Council (1987–1995) and the founder of the Alliance for Better Charlotte—became a major player in the drive for an airport authority. Aside from desiring to force Jerry Orr to retire, Campbell also raised questions about the rumors of an ongoing FBI investigation of city officials. He told *Charlotte Business Journal* that he and others were concerned about mismanagement of the airport. Campbell took the idea of an airport authority to Republican state senator Bob Rucho of Mecklenburg County.[5] In addition, Wells Fargo economist Mark Vitner advanced this type of narrative in a speech to a real estate group:

> I don't know what to make of the idea of an airport authority. Whatever comes of it, we do have a very strong city manager in Charlotte, so it would make it harder to run into the problems that some other airports, like Atlanta and Philadelphia, have run into. The greatest threat that's out there is that city leaders will one day look at the airport as a piggy bank, and if some future mayor's son-in-law couldn't get a job, he'd wind up monitoring the TSA at the airport or making sure the automatic water sprinklers go on. Not that any of that has happened, but that's the worry about the airport, that instead of costing $3 to land a passenger it would cost $7, and the airline would go somewhere else. That's the threat that's out there. I don't think it's that immediate, but anything that guards the independence of the airport would be good. Whether that's staying as it is or an independent authority, it is an issue that deserves some attention.[6]

The third but related narrative focused on the fallout from former Charlotte mayor Patrick Cannon's influence peddling and corruption scandal. Apparently, he engaged in influence peddling of a personal type—putting money directly in his own hands. Cannon resigned, but the city received a lot of bad publicity as a result. Ensuing speculation concerned the level of influence peddling among city politicians. In some people's minds, this type of corruption could potentially spill over into the management of the Charlotte Douglas Airport. If the city got into fiscal trouble, would city politicians dip into the airport's funds?

Indeed, the *Charlotte Observer* gratuitously connected the mayoral scandal and the airport administration, stating, "Commission supporters expect last week's arrest of former Mayor Patrick Cannon will help buttress their case that the city should not be in charge of the airport, a vital economic engine for the region."[7] Senator Rucho asserted, "We were trying to find a way to ... insulate the airport from any type of cronyism. It was a collection of everything. The priority for keeping that airport economically viable is absolutely critical to this city and the region."[8] Orr used the occasion to again assert, "That's why you want an airport authority. That's why you want your governing board to be focused on the business, running the airport."[9] As we learned in chapter 4, federal law prohibits the use of airport revenues for nonairport purposes. Charlotte Douglas Airport cannot divert airport revenues into municipal coffers. No one in government has suggested this, but the claim can be used in partisan argument.

The fourth narrative, perhaps the principal one, argued that the airport was too important to the region's and state's economic future to be left in the hands of a single municipal government. Charlotte is the home of the second-largest banking center in the nation. Yet the metro region aspires to become a major player in the growing Sunbelt-oriented global economy. Continued growth of the airport is a critical part of the mantra of the pro-growth coalition of the state. Senator Rucho of Mecklenburg County, the leading advocate for the regional authority, contended that the airport was an "economic engine for the region and state."[10] The senator's comments were also linked to the transition surrounding Jerry Orr's retirement.

Suggestions of such radical change had to have a source. Rucho stated that the idea came from local business leaders whom he refused to name. Rucho had never played a role in airport politics and emerged as an unlikely leader in the battle for an airport authority. Johnny Harris, one of the leading critics of the airport, claimed he did not contact legislators regarding the takeover.[11] Former mayor Vinroot stated, "Bob Rucho did not go to Raleigh with an airport in mind. Somebody got his attention."[12] Who or what started this attempt to seize Charlotte Douglas? Rumors of a possible attempt to create an airport authority emerged as early as the beginning of the year. And the issue accelerated the churn of the city's day-to-day politics.

In May 2013, the *Charlotte Observer* polled 601 registered voters. By a three-to-one, or 65 percent, margin, the respondents wanted to keep the airport under the control of the city of Charlotte. Nineteen percent favored a proposal to create an independent authority. Another 16 percent were not sure. The *Observer* quoted U.S. Airways flight attendant Velvet Key as saying, "It's about a power grab by the state, I think there's money involved. There's something to be gained. . . . I don't see them clamoring to take over Concord's airport."[13] Obviously, the controversy upset some residents and was at variance with the norm of nurturing an inattentive citizenry.

Airport director Jerry Orr, who gained fame as an effective manager, decided not to remain neutral in the debate about the airport's governance structure. In doing so he disagreed with his supervisor, interim city manager Julie Birch, who reportedly asked him not to lobby for the authority. City manager Ron Carlee, Birch's successor, had stated publicly that the proposed bill would be disruptive. He also raised questions about city revenue bonds. Orr asserted to reporter Ely Portillo, "Should the bill pass, it will be a smooth transition. It has to be."[14] Orr insisted that the Airport Advisory Committee would continue until an authority board was appointed.

A related rumor was that U.S. Airways had wanted a new structure and had become concerned about developments at city hall. Consistent with the second narrative concerning the airport takeover, the airline, it acted. Former mayor Vinroot recalled events as follows:

> Someone said that U.S. Airways became concerned about what was happening at City Hall. The Mayor and City Council were looking to build a trolley from the Airport to the city with money from the airport.
>
> U.S. Airways sent a draft of a bill to Bob Rucho. He picked up on the idea for taking the airport from the city officials and putting it in a neutral body. Their [U.S. Airways'] motivation was concern about the cost increase.
>
> The City Council asked the state legislature to hold off on the bill. The council hired a consultant for $150,000 to study the idea for several months and they recommended a regional authority.[15]

In July 2013, the Republican-dominated North Carolina General Assembly voted thirty-three to sixteen along partisan lines to approve a bill transferring the ownership and management of Charlotte Douglas International Airport from the city to a thirteen-member regional authority. Led by Republican state senator Robert Rucho, state representative Bill Brawley, and Ruth Samuelson of Mecklenburg County, the legislature considered the airport bill as a local bill, thus facilitating its progress.

Samuelson and a group that included Rucho, Bill Brawley, Jacqueline Schaffer, Charles Jeter, Rob Bryan, and Jeff Tarte wrote an editorial in the *Charlotte Observer* stating that the airport's future should include "a truly regional perspective and a business mindset—free as much as possible from the influences of ward politics."[16] Ms. Samuelson said the legislature had tried to work with city council members who "were not willing to collaborate."[17] She further stated that business leaders believed a change was indicated. Rather than resembling a regular city department, Samuelson declared, "It [the airport] really is a business."[18] Her implication was that city government and elected officials were ill fitted to oversee a business.

Remember that Pat McCrory, former governor of North Carolina, had served as mayor of Charlotte for seven terms. He had initially claimed that the airport structure was a dispute between factions within Charlotte. He said that he did not want to get involved, but he thought the Charlotte politicians were interfering in the airport operations. Under the North Carolina Constitution a local bill does not require the governor's signature. McCrory later explained his bystander position: "It was a local bill. When I was mayor of Charlotte we kept the politics out of the airport. Our major client, U.S. Airways, and others were very concerned about politics interfering with our airport. We need to get politics out of Charlotte's airport. And that includes state politicians, and that includes city politicians, too. And we're working to do just that."[19]

No one could have predicted the political firestorm resulting from the idea of losing the airport Charlotte had nurtured for seventy-eight years. Why now and for what reason? Who would benefit? These were just a few of the questions citizens and the media were asking. Then came another surprise—in the middle of this ongoing political storm, longtime airport director Jerry Orr announced his resignation.

THE RESIGNATION OF MR. ORR

Director Jerry Orr, then seventy-one years old, proffered his resignation as airport director on July 18, 2013. He did so after officially accepting the directorship of the new Charlotte Douglas International Airport Authority. Until the time that he and the city council received Orr's resignation letter, city manager Ron Carlee discerned a pattern in the airport director's behavior.

> He [Orr] had been engaged in what most people would consider a highly insubordinate behavior working against his own employer which was the city of Charlotte at the time, engaging with the General Assembly in promoting legislation that was in conflict with the position of his employer, in order to separate himself and create basically his own independent agency. And it was hard to predict what the legislature is going to do and when they were going do it. We were in discussion with them on a variety of compromises. At the end of the day, the General Assembly woke up one day and said we are going to do it. . . . They pushed it through fairly quickly. It was written in a way that it took effect immediately. Mr. Orr thought he was being freed from the city and would be able to do what he wants to do in the new authority. What he did not anticipate that we would get an injunction in court. The authority would not be enacted. He was little bit too smart for his own good in that power play. He resigned, and I accepted his resignation and appointed a new director.[20]

While these transactions were taking place, Carlee had repeatedly spoken to Orr, who was his subordinate. As Orr's supervisor, Carlee wanted him to step down because he had gone against the wishes of his employer, the city of Charlotte. Even so, Carlee wanted Orr recognized as an outstanding public servant. Orr responded, "I don't consider myself as a public servant."[21] Though he resigned the airport directorship to assume directorship of the new airport authority and its successor the Airport Commission, the latter job did not exist.

The city council accepted Orr's resignation, and Carlee appointed Brent Cable the interim airport director. The Airport Advisory Committee was suspended during the takeover attempt. Meanwhile, the future of the airport remained uncertain, and city council members' modicum of support for Orr's continued service as a consultant quickly died. In a clever maneuver, the state legislature was attempting to force Charlotte's cooperation with the new airport authority by mandating that the city appoint members to it. The takeover fight was on.

THE STRUCTURE OF THE PROPOSED AIRPORT AUTHORITY

The N.C. General Assembly passed Session Law 2013–272 that established a nine-member regional airport authority. The authority's board would include one appointed member from the Charlotte City Council, and county commissioners from Mecklenburg, Cabarrus, Gaston, and Union Counties would also have a seat each. Interestingly, the governor, the state house speaker, the state senate president, and the Charlotte mayor would also have one appointment to the proposed airport authority.

The airport authority board would also include citizens selected by the nine board members to be at-large members. The only qualifications for citizen representatives were residence in the Carolinas and some experience in aviation. In effect, this new structure represents a fundamental attempt to eliminate the city of Charlotte's operating control of the airport and reduce its representation on the new authority to two seats on the board.

The Charlotte Douglas Airport restructuring and governance proposal would be unique in the state since it would include representatives from three counties. The Raleigh-Durham International Airport Authority (RDU) board has eight representatives, two of whom are from Wake and Durham Counties. The cities of Raleigh and Durham also have two representatives each. No state legislative appointees serve on the board, and neither does a representative from South Carolina.

The proposed authority for Charlotte Douglas International Airport and the composition of its governing board represented a major crisis for the city manager's authority over city departments and for the scope of the mayor's and the city council's appointment powers. Under the proposed authority, the mayor would have only one appointee. Other elected officials included a representative from both houses of the state legislature. Mecklenburg and surrounding counties would also have representatives, and the airport director and staff would work directly for the authority board. In effect, the new airport authority would eliminate the need for the city manager and the Airport Advisory Committee. The change elicited pushback because it could potentially introduce more state and county politics into the governance of the facility. It also created the potential for the takeover of city property. More importantly, possible outside disruptions could unravel plans for expanding and developing the airport as a major airline hub. Interestingly, few commentators mention such authorities in other states.

History shows that airport authorities predate some municipal airports. Established in 1928, the Louisville Airport Authority has a city-dominated board. The mayor heads the authority and has the power to appoint seven members. Kentucky's governor has three appointees. Additionally, each member serves a four-year staggered term, and the board appoints the airport director. Historian Janet R. Daly Bednarek finds that downtown Saint Louis business leaders promoted the idea of an authority.[22] The suburbs, however, opposed the plan. For its part, the federal government promoted the idea of regional authorities in the 1960s. As we observed, some states have imposed authorities on cities. However, such state actions are at variance with modern-day regionalization practices.

The Charlotte Douglas International Airport Authority proposal differed considerably from the proposal for the old Saint Louis Airport Authority model. Currently, the federal government does not support airport authorities. In Charlotte's case, downtown leaders were divided as to whether change was indicated. The push for an authority did not come from the citizens of Mecklenburg County or any surrounding counties. Rather, the proposal came from Republican legislators. Partisan lawmakers who designed the bill structured the regional authority to recruit area politicians by simply granting appointment authority to a wide variety of elected officials. In effect, making the airport a state-operated entity would yield some political patronage in the surrounding counties.

The crafting legislators were initially so successful for another reason—they had the support of some high-profile members of Charlotte's pro-growth coalition. It remains unclear whether support for the airport authority was split between counties and cities. Apparently, some members of the pro-growth coalition linked their future progress to an expanded airport with a regional governance structure. They shared the airlines' aspirations to accommodate more passengers and provide more international and intercity direct flights. Nevertheless, city leaders' nearly immediate negative response to the regional authority proposal forced the legislative leadership to amend the law.

As the legislation was being formulated, the issue of a revenue bond was raised. At the time, Charlotte was financing debt from more than $800 million in airport revenue bonds. Would the new airport authority assume responsibility for bonds servicing? Would the bonds be recalled and reissued? Could the city transfer them without bondholder consent? State senator Fletcher Hartwell, a Concord Republican and an authority supporter, stated, "That's playing with fire, until more is known about bond covenants, we're violating the dad-gum constitution again."[23] Bond counsel Donald Ubell stated that the city of Charlotte would default if bondholder consent was not obtained. Negative reaction to the issue triggered a number of political negotiations between city and state officials. Yet no compromise was reached. Former mayor Vinroot recalled, "I got a call from Jerry Orr. He said, 'I know you and like you. I anticipate the city will challenge the new law. I want your law firm to represent the new Authority. Will you represent us?' I told him that I would talk to my partners and let him know. The City filed the suit that day. We decided to represent the new Authority."[24] Meanwhile, the city legal team was organizing its response.

THE CITY RESPONSE

In *City Power*, Richard Schragger argues that cities have agency. They can act "if we let them," and they can protect themselves despite state constitutions.[25] The airport takeover attempt elicited strong public opposition from Anthony Foxx, Charlotte's Democratic mayor.[26] Some people in city government felt blindsided by the attempt to create an authority that would eliminate city control of the facility. Some were unaware of a scheme afoot involving members of the business community, officials from surrounding counties, and state legislators. In one of the most dramatic moments in the history of Charlotte City Council meetings, Airport Advisory Committee chair Shawn Dorsch was brought before the council and asked about these machinations.

A pilot and the former president of the Carolina Aviation Museum, Dorsch, who had gained recognition for bringing the actual plane that landed on the Hudson River ("Miracle on the Hudson") to the museum, was questioned about rumors, personalities, and deals made about the airport. During questioning about Charlotte Douglas rumors, personalities, and deals, Dorsch declared his approval of the draft consultant report supporting replacement of city controls with the airport authority. He told the *Charlotte Observer* that the authority was the "best form of governance."[27] Dorsch also stated that the AAC had not discussed the issue, and that he had been told not discuss it because the city was going to study the proposal. The issue had not been discussed with the Airport Advisory Committee. Mayor Anthony Foxx asked Dorsch three times, "Have you known about it since January 2012?" He also asked, "Were you a part of conversation about changing the airport to an Authority as early as January 2012?"[28] While before the city council, Shawn Dorsch refused to say who was behind the takeover attempt. He stated, "I don't think it is my role to identify people in this community and what their individual views are on things. It is up to them to make the decision when they want to publicly identify themselves and express their opinions."[29]

The council members wanted to know the names of the boosters who supported an airport authority. Councilperson David Howard asserted, "We are rolling down the road and the turd is getting bigger and bigger."[30] Several members of the council, including Foxx, thought that Dorsch should be removed from chairmanship of the AAC. When his testimony was characterized as "stonewalling," Dorsch stated, "I want to help you. I want to help the city. I will absolutely help you in any way I can. But I think it is improper for me to speak for other people. . . . Sir, it is not my job to out people. It is not my job to call out names publicly. Each citizen is entitled to their privacy."[31]

Near the end of questioning, Councilman David Howard asked if anyone had asked Dorsch to resign from the committee. He then asked those committee members to stand up. Five of the eleven members of the Airport Advisory Committee, including Vice Chair Andrew Riolo, an aviation lawyer and pilot, rose from their seats.

Mayor Foxx briefly delayed removing Dorsch as AAC chair and gave the committee an opportunity to handle the matter internally. In the end, Foxx removed Dorsch from the chairmanship and the committee's membership. The *Charlotte Observer* reported that Dorsch had encouraged the chairman of the board of commissioners in at least two neighboring counties to pass resolutions in support of the authority bill.[32] He claimed he had done so as a private citizen. Apparently, though, county commissioners considered his invitation or offer official.

Though the airport takeover attempt created several months of high drama, the Charlotte City Council responded quickly and comprehensively. Council members voiced unanimous support for retaining the airport. Even Republican councilman Andy Dulin wanted the airport to remain city owned.

As with anything related to the airport, the city sought to strengthen its management case with the help of a consultant firm. The council also appointed an oversight committee to assist the consultants. Its members included Shawn Dorsch of the Airport Advisory Committee, Frank Emory of the Charlotte Chamber of Commerce, LaWana Mayfield of the Charlotte City Council, Tom Murray of the Charlotte Regional Visitors Authority, and Mike Minerva of U.S. Airways.

The *Charlotte Observer* claimed that the city council asked Jerry Orr and U.S. Airways executives Chuck Allen and Mike Minerva about hiring a consultant. The spokesman for U.S. Airways told the *Charlotte Observer* that requests for consultants' names were "entirely normal." The airline recommended hiring Bob Hazel to conduct an airport governance study. Hazel worked for global consulting firm Oliver Wyman, and he claimed to have interviewed forty people including airport employees, local politicians, and state legislators. His sixty-two-page report cost the city $150,000 and recommended that an authority run Charlotte Douglas.[33] Hazel stated therein, "Our conclusion is nevertheless that the best form of governance for most public sector U.S. airports, including the Charlotte Airport, is a properly structured airport authority."[34] However, Hazel also recommended more representation for Charlotte-Mecklenburg by expanding the airport authority board's membership. Hazel did not recommend that Charlotte-Mecklenburg have a majority on the board.

The council members were reported as being "flummoxed" by the Hazel report.[35] It stated that the "airport was one of the best-run and low-cost airports in the nation and it should be run by an authority." In effect, the consultant supported the views of Jerry Orr, not the city council. Councilman David Howard said to Hazel, "It almost sounds like you think airports should be run by authorities, period. In your opinion, should any of them be run by cities?"[36] Interim city manager Julie Burch apologized for hiring Hazel and denied knowledge of his fixed opinion: "I did not know that was his predisposition."[37] She had hired Hazel before it was disclosed that U.S. Airways had met with authority supporters the previous year and had forwarded them draft legislation to create an authority via mail.

On June 13, 2013, the council followed the consultant's recommendation and passed a resolution that stated it would "vigorously resist any outside, unilateral effort" to transfer the airport to an independent authority. This resistance effort would be expensive.[38]

City attorney Bob Hagemann recalled the hectic days around the passage of the bill: "The vote was cast on Thursday, July 18, 2013. As soon as the vote was cast, (I had an audio from the state) I had a lawyer at the Courthouse and a judge standing by for Temporary Restraining Order (TRO) to maintain a status quo. The Judge (Summer) can decide to grant or not grant TRO."[39]

The Hagemann team made the following claims before the judge: The city had allegation or objection against the new law. The law was unconstitutionally taking property from Charlotte without compensation. The measure violated provisions of local acts in North Carolina. It also violated the Supremacy Clause of the United States Constitution. Finally, the law would cause the city to default on over $700,000 in revenue bonds. Hagemann said, "We [the City] had been put on verbal notice about the default as soon as the airport was gone. We knew that in order for it to become law, it needed ratification. Within five minutes the TRO was needed to get the Court order before the bill in Raleigh. Judge Robert Summers signed the TRO fifteen minutes before the bill was ratified, Thursday, 18 July 2013."[40]

After the law was passed, several attempts were made to reach a compromise. Compromise discussions allowed state politicians an opportunity to make deals and save face. To this end, Gov. Pat McCrory called a meeting at the Governor's Mansion, and Hagemann's team was in attendance. The city attorney's colleagues included Greensboro trial lawyer Jim Phillip and lawyer and former North Carolina judge Bob Orr. Former mayor Vinroot recalled the dynamics of the meeting.

> I talked them [authority proponents] out of the Authority ideas and to revert it into a Commission. The Regional Commission sounded like a good idea. A group met at the Governor's Mansion with the Governor to discuss the Authority. [Governor McCrory was in and out of the meeting.] Martin Brackett and I, representing the Authority, came from my firm. The Governor invited City Attorney Bob Hagemann and Jim Phillip, another Attorney. I proposed the idea of changing the authority to a Commission and have the majority of the members appointed by the city.[41]

Ten days later the airport authority's proponents asked the state legislature to pass a revision of the law. On July 19, 2013, the N.C. General Assembly passed Session Law 2013, also called the Douglas International Airport Commission Act. The same day the state bill passed, the city of Charlotte proposed a bill to the state legislature that would create an eleven-member Airport Commission under the city's control. The state law went into effect July 26, 2013. The N.C. legislature also passed the Clarification Act outlining the duties of the new commission. It stated,

Should the FAA or a court of competent jurisdiction determine that the Commission lacks any necessary FAA authorizations, the Commission shall not execute any rights, powers, or duties that require authorization from the FAA until the Commission either obtains such authorization to secures an appropriate determination from the FAA or a court of competent jurisdiction.[42]

This new Airport Commission was unlike the state-appointed Charlotte Airport Commission of the 1940s. The first commission was a holding mechanism. The state represented itself with the army but had no administrative authority over Morris Field. Under the new commission—the state version—Charlotte's mayor would have three appointees and the city council would have eight. One mayoral appointee would be a resident of Charlotte's west side, as would one city council appointee. Three members—one mayoral appointee and two from the city council—would not be Charlotte or Mecklenburg County residents. All appointees were required to have some experience in aviation and fields related to airport management. The mayor or council determines whether an appointee meets the qualifications. In addition, the new law appointed a five-member oversight committee to monitor the Airport Commission. Muriel Helms Shenbrook and Charlotte real estate developer Johnny Harris were the first two appointments to the oversight committee. Ultimately, the new Airport Commission would assume administrative control over the airport.

The new law revealed that state legislators had shifted their strategy, dumping the authority ownership provisions and allowing the city to retain ownership of the airport. Apparently, the increasing legal issues and potential for court intervention made the total takeover strategy untenable. The new proposal was called the Charlotte Douglas International Commission Clarification Act, House Bill 133. It established a city commission that would operate the airport on Charlotte's behalf. The new act also pushed back the Airport Commission's operating date until 2016.

City attorney Bob Hagemann noted that the new law "did away with the bond default issue."[43] The law gave Mecklenburg, Gaston, Cabarrus, Iredell, Lincoln, and Union Counties five appointees. The city of Charlotte was allotted seven appointees, four by the council and three by the mayor. The new act also mandated that city appointments be made before October 1, 2013. In effect, this measure forced the city to participate in the appointment process, apparently in an effort to legitimate the new commission.

On August 13, 2013, the city sought and got an injunction to prevent the Charlotte Douglas International Airport Commission from carrying out its duties. The commission had applied for an FAA operating certificate but never received it. Powerless without that certificate, the commission still mandated immediate appointments to its ranks from the city and the counties. On September 23, 2013, the city council appointed four members and Acting Mayor Patsy Kinsey appointed three members. Additional commission members included representatives from Gaston, Cabarrus, and Lincoln Counties. Charlotte's appointment of commission members did not mean the city accepted the state's imposition of this new airport governance structure. City attorney Bob Hagemann said as much before the city council.

Hagemann led the city government's legal strategy against the Airport Commission. He recalled that a suit was filed in the North Carolina Superior Court. When a judge subsequently provided the city with a temporary restraining order, there was no ruling on whether the commission was a separate entity. The city had ten days to make a full argument. Former Charlotte mayor Richard Vinroot represented the state and made the case for the new reorganization.

In September 2013, the Federal Aviation Administration (FAA) decided to leave the airport under the city's control. In effect, the FAA would not permit the Airport Commission to operate Charlotte Douglas unless the city of Charlotte's government requested it. In October 2013, Mecklenburg Superior Court judge Robert Ervin granted the city a restraining order against the commission takeover.

After the ruling the entire situation was at an impasse. On November 26, Governor McCrory told WFAE that the city should retain control of the airport. He also said that Orr should not get his old job back, asserting, "He's been great for the airport, but it's time to move on. I think Jerry could still add some value, but it's time to move on. This is not about an individual."[44] McCrory's comment elicited swift reaction. State representative Bob Rucho said, "This was never about Mr. Orr. It's always been about the airport."[45] City officials wished the governor had offered support earlier, helping them avoid the problems created by the takeover fight.

While the ownership crisis was in play, President Obama appointed forty-two-year-old Charlotte mayor Anthony Foxx secretary of the U.S. Department of Transportation (the home of the Federal Aviation Administration). After being sworn in, Foxx said, "There is no such thing as a Democratic or a Republican road, bridge, port, airfield or rail station. We must work together, across party lines, to enhance this nation's infrastructure."[46] As secretary, he retained his interest in Charlotte's infrastructure, including the airport.

After Foxx's appointment, Councilwoman Patsy Kinsey was named acting mayor. She was a strong supporter of city ownership of the airport, and she had to make the case against new takeover attempts. Yet an acting mayor's power has its limits. The city of Charlotte endured a period of political uncertainty while it waited for the voters to elect a new mayor. Charlotte Douglas's future remained an issue in the primary and general elections.

During the Democratic primary, candidate James Mitchell issued a campaign ad accusing his leading opponent Patrick Cannon of supporting state senator Bob Rucho's bill to take over the airport. Cannon, a city councilman, denied this charge, stating, "The senator is for an authority and I'm not. Nor does any periodical or broadcast suggest that. It's a total misrepresentation."[47] Cannon then won the Democratic primary.

In November 2013, Patrick Cannon, who rose from Fairview Home and Pine Valley Public Housing to run a successful parking management company, defeated Republican Edwin Peacock in the mayoral election. The *Charlotte Observer* characterized the new mayor "as less combative in his public statements about fighting with the state legislature over the airport."[48] Mayor Cannon apparently wanted to make a deal. In the primary he was accused of believing that Charlotte should consider other options. As mayor, he remained noncommittal about the new Airport Commission and its legitimacy, as well as about legal fees and the airport's future. "I don't want to micromanage the commission that has been put in place," Cannon stated.[49]

Cannon supported the Charlotte Chamber of Commerce's pro-growth agenda. He lauded the chamber for its Business First initiative, a joint venture with the city to help existing local businesses. In January, Cannon went to Washington to lobby the FAA for a new airport tower. The current thirty-year-old tower was obsolete, and flights to and from the airport had doubled. It was reported that Cannon and Governor McCrory tried to find a compromise for three months after the takeover battle began, but Charlotte Airport Commission chair Robert Stolz stated that these efforts had failed. Nevertheless, Cannon refused to give up. He said, "I do not believe that we have exhausted all options and remain hopeful that city and state leaders can find common ground."[50]

Then the unexpected happened. In March 2014, Patrick Cannon was arrested by undercover FBI agents, subsequently convicted of taking bribes, and sentenced to prison. In April 2014, the city council elected Daniel Clodfelter mayor of Charlotte. Clodfelter had served fifteen terms as a representative in the state assembly.

The law required the city to appoint members to the Airport Commission. As the year went on, it became clear that certain members of the business leadership and the new commission did not have the authority or budget to operate Charlotte Douglas. Charlotte had gotten the courts to stop the commission from taking control of the airport. Charlotte Airport Commission chair Robert

Stolz stated, "We are still stuck in the mud and maybe worse, we are stuck in a battlefield I would consider to be a no man's land." His fellow commission member Joe Carpenter agreed, declaring, "Hate to be in limbo, we've been in for a year, and I don't want to keep meeting and doing nothing."[51] The city of Charlotte continued to run the airport's day-to-day operations.

In October 2014, Judge Ervin ruled that the airport was permanently under city control unless the FAA decided otherwise. The Airport Commission was now barred from managing Charlotte Douglas without an FAA operating certificate. The ruling stated, "The Commission is permanently enjoined from operation of the Charlotte Douglas International Airport until the necessary operating certificate from the Federal Aviation Administration or a declaration from the Federal Aviation Administration that the Commission is permitted to operate the airport in reliance on the City's operating certificate."[52] On November 14, 2014, a letter was sent to the chief counsel of the FAA with copies of the judge's ruling. City attorney Bob Hagemann also sent a letter from Scott Lewis, a Boston lawyer with an FAA practice, supporting the city's position. This correspondence was at the FAA for a year. Accordingly, the commission had no authority to operate the airport. The city retained ownership and management of Charlotte Douglas International Airport, and the courts did not support the state's desire to assume a shared ownership. Nor does the research on such arrangements support shared ownership.

THE RUNDOWN FROM THE TAKEOVER

Four issues stand out in this review of North Carolina's relationship to Charlotte Douglas Airport. First is the matter of state control of local units or subgovernments. Under the Dillon Rule, states have the legal authority to dismantle, consolidate, and co-opt local entities, local governments, and special service districts. The state legislature controls most of the public policy in the county and in the city. According to Hunter Bacot and Jack Christine's 2006 survey research, airport authorities differ administratively and fiscally from special purpose governments such as regional sewer and health districts.[53] Airports do not have the same fiscal and debt problems that plague other special districts. Accordingly, a case cannot be made that a takeover will create financial difficulties for the state. The reference to a special district was eliminated from the revision of the state-mandated airport authority law. If the city had accepted the Airport Commission, it would have been a win-win proposition for the state. North Carolina would have gained more control of a municipal asset without having spent more funds. The state would have been able to redistribute the control of a major city asset to several counties and create a new set of stakeholders, all without making a major financial investment.

Second, the commission proposal contained a nascent partisan issue. Documented management issues were simply lacking. Why was the narrative initiated? Its source was partisanship. The Republican-dominated state legislature seemed to have wanted to limit the discretion of the largely Democratic Charlotte City Council. A subsequent airport takeover was attempted under the guise of establishing a city commission. This action follows a general trend of states tightening their grip on local governments. As large municipal airports become cash cows, state governments have taken more interest in the operations of such facilities. However, imposing layer upon layer of governance structure on airport administration is not without its perils.

Third, the reorganization produced no fiscal or management advantages. More representation does not always yield greater efficiency or reduced costs. The intent is to make airport governance more representative for the counties surrounding the facility. Granted, Charlotte Douglas served those counties and part of northern South Carolina, but there were no elaborate narratives about making representatives of these areas part of the airport's management. The question was whether the new entity would make the airport more efficient. No evidence was produced that it would.

Some considered the takeover a prologue to potential corruption. The situation at Charlotte Douglas paralleled the Atlanta Airport scandal of 1998. Atlanta's mayor at the time, Bill Campbell, fired independent airport manager Angela Gittens for not taking direction from city hall. Before the Gittens regime, the airport had been embroiled in a major scandal that resulted in several council members' conviction for bribery.[54] This scenario is unlikely in Charlotte because city council members are not that involved in airport business. In Atlanta the mayor can take direct action in cases of insubordination and scandals. The mayor of Charlotte does not hire and fire the airport director. Indeed, airport directors are structurally insulated from mayoral and council politics. They report directly to the city manager.

Fourth, the introduction of a small appointed membership (the airport commission) in the governance of the airport may have produced a different set of problems. Political scientist Sidney Verba defines small groups as "groups in which face-to-face communication is possible among all members."[55] There are several possible compositional dynamics associated with face-to-face decision-making citizen groups. Among them are county appointees versus city appointees and mayoral appointees versus city council appointees. Each group has incentives to justify its appointment and to change the way governance is done.

In addition, what would be the city manager's role in the reconfigured management of the airport? The old system involved a management hierarchy that was clear and simple and that allowed airport directors to achieve considerable administrative discretion.

By 2013, the story of the takeover was two years old. Hence, November 2014 was the month of resignations. Gov. Pat McCrory stated publicly that the city should keep the airport. Real estate developer Johnny Harris announced, "I really don't care anymore who runs Charlotte Airport, just keep costs down."[56] Interestingly, in his same 2014 speech expressing indifference to Charlotte Douglas governance structure, Harris resigned from his seat on the Airport Commission's oversight committee.

Similarly, U.S. Airways spokeswoman Katie Cody asserted, "We don't really care who governs the airport as long as it's done cost effectively and efficiently as it's been done in the past."[57] Robert Rucho and Ruth Samuelson had previously announced that they would not run for reelection.

Former Charlotte mayor and current U.S. secretary of transportation Anthony Foxx was also a player in the takeover efforts. (The U.S. Department of Transportation was the home of the FAA.) Journalists reported on some interesting statements and on characters such as Mecklenburg Republican Robert Rucho and former airport director Jerry Orr. While at a conference in 2012, Orr explained the pending construction booms at the airport. He tried to tell his audience that the new construction on the access roads would not leave the taxpayers debt if U.S. Airways merged with American Airlines and decided that it did not need Charlotte as a hub. According to Jerry Orr, Charlotte would share Pittsburgh's and Saint Louis's fate if the airline abandoned the city as a hub. Orr also asserted, "We spend a lot of money, we're moving forward at a rapid pace, but there is no risk for the taxpayers."[58] Displaying his dry sense of humor, he added, "There is no risk in charging ahead and spending money like a drunken sailor." If U.S. Airways decided to stop flying to Charlotte, Orr observed, "We wouldn't have to lay off any of our employees, and we could meet all of our debt."[59] This statement was meant to reassure businesses and citizen taxpayers that he had everything under control. A year later Orr would lose all managerial power. But as of this writing, the prediction that U.S. Airways' merger with American Airlines would not close Charlotte as a hub still holds. Indeed, the airport underwent the massive process of building a parking lot.

The city had every intention of keeping the airport, an economic asset. All drama around Charlotte Douglas and the proposed airport authority and commission seemed only indirectly related to the central question: Does shared ownership of airports work?

IS SHARED OWNERSHIP A SOLUTION?

Shared ownership of municipal facilities has a long tradition in American politics. If a city requests state support or assistance, then the basis for joint ownership can be established. Problems occur when two or more governmental entities claim exclusive ownership in overlapping activities without acknowledging one another's claims. These claims go beyond mere jurisdictional conflicts. Accordingly, the state's attempt to assume joint ownership of Charlotte Douglas encountered vigorous opposition. Any form of shared ownership jeopardized or was perceived to jeopardize organizational integrity and survival. Public administrators realize the danger associated with mixed or shared ownership. Consider the conclusions of economists Tae H. Oum, Jia Yun, and Chunyan Yu:

> Our key empirical findings are: (a) airports owned and/or controlled by majority private firms, autonomous public corporations or independent authorities are more efficient than those owned and/or controlled by government branch (city/state), multiple level governments, or U.S. ports authorities; (b) there is an almost 100% probability that airports controlled/operated by independent airport authorities are more efficient than those controlled/operated by U.S. port authorities, and there is 93% probability that U.S. city/state run airports are more efficient than those operated by U.S. port authorities; (c) there is about 80% probability that airports owned/operated by a majority private firm achieve higher efficiency than those owned/operated by the mixed enterprise with government majority ownership; and (d) airports owned/operated by Government controlled agencies (U.S. ports authorities, shared government ownership, U.S. city or state government, mixed enterprises with government majority ownership) have significantly lower efficiency in multiple airport markets than in single airport markets.[60]

City of Charlotte leaders concluded that mixed ownership was conducive to neither the airport's efficient operation nor its long-term interests. Pertinent research advises against creating a joint state ownership structure such as the Port Authority of New Jersey and New York. Oum, Yun, and Yu's research suggests that management efficiency of independent authorities was not more statistically significant than that of city-owned airports. City politicians may not have been aware of such research, but they knew efficiency was not one of the goals of the state takeover. As Charlotte's city manager Ron Carlee stated, "Authorities can be problematic. They can be used for political patronage."[61]

SUMMARY

A truly in-depth analysis of the state of North Carolina's attempt to take over Charlotte Douglas International Airport is impossible because some key actors refuse to be interviewed. Therefore, some conversations and proposed deals will never be made public. What exactly was the role of American Airlines? Who said what to whom and when may be lost to history. A surprising aspect of the takeover's politics was the open schism among the business members of the pro-growth coalition. Ordinarily supportive of pro-growth projects, the Charlotte City Council remained foursquare in support of keeping the airport under city control. Again, it was difficult to know what members of the pro-growth coalition were doing behind closed doors; their public statements are the only available record. Yet during the whole takeover process, the airport continued to function.

In mid-2013, Acting Mayor Patsy Kinsey was struggling. She wrote the U.S. Justice Department in support of the controversial merger between U.S. Airways and American Airlines. At first glance it may seem incongruous for the mayor to support this merger—after all, heads of airlines occupied the forefront of the push for an airport authority. A closer look suggests that local leaders were unaware of airline management's role. City politicians reportedly had problems with former city manager Curt Walton's choice of a director to replace Jerry Orr. The hearing on the airport takeover made it clear that the city council had no knowledge of either these reservations or Bob Hazel's connection to U.S. Airways. The *Charlotte Observer* reported that Hazel had been the airline's vice president of properties and facilities.[62] The hearing showed that the ball had been dropped concerning the city county's control and oversight of the consultant selection process.

Shawn Dorsch's testimony also provided evidence of the council's disagreements with Airport Advisory Committee members. The airlines and the airport director had outmaneuvered the city council. Council members found themselves on the defensive, claiming they were under the pressure of budget making and did not have time to fully vet Mr. Hazel. Apparently, it was not until the hearing that anyone picked up on the conflict of interest in Hazel's hiring.

When Charlotte won the battle over ownership of the airport, some state politicians shifted their positions while others remained quiet. Brent Cagle replaced Jerry Orr. Then in 2015, Charlotte Douglas made its first full annual report to the city council. Governor McCrory said publicly that the city owned the airport and should retain management. U.S. Airways, now American Airlines, stated that it was "agnostic" about whether the regional commission was an alternative to city control.

Finally, the politics of the airport reorganization produced a type of internecine behavior among state and local politicians. This can be counterproductive and distracting for Charlotte's long-term image and economic progress. The run-up to the passage of the airport authority law and its successor, the Airport Commission, had an eerily theatrical quality. Airport director Jerry Orr was found plotting against his employer, the city of Charlotte. Former Charlotte mayors were lining up against one another and against sitting elected officials. Governor Pat McCrory, once known as a relatively moderate Republican mayor, initially and bafflingly remained neutral. In August 2014, the governor appointed the eighteen-member Aviation Development Task Force to submit recommendations to the state secretary of transportation (Tony Tata).

The takeover was a story of trust in which an airport director was allowed absolute discretion. But the takeover was also a story of betrayal. The director conspired with the largest hub airlines, business leaders, state legislators, and the leader of the Airport Advisory Committee to change Charlotte Douglas's governance structure. Orr's personality and actions had been a tagline for the media. *Charlotte Business Journal* concluded, "During his tenure, Orr enjoyed a casual, at times flippant, relationship with city government. McCrory, during his gubernatorial campaign, told a local Rotary audience that he knew enough to stay out of the way when it came to Orr and the airport. Council routinely approved what Orr sought with minimal examination."[63]

Reporters Gesell and Sobotta predict the demise of directors like Orr, and they claim that the job of director has changed dramatically: "Airport managers, who in the 1940s and 1950s once thrived in the industry due to technical skill in aviation, have since been replaced by managers with disciplined education in business management, public administration and aviation specific management or business academic preparation."[64] The latter sort of manager describes Brent Cagle and his master's degree in public administration. His background and training are very different from his predecessors'; Birmingham and Orr were engineers. But as discussed in chapters concerning the airport's history and directors, outsiders are limited in what they can do for the pro-growth coalition. Outsiders can also be fired easily.

The airport takeover failed in part because it read as a partisan affair. Conflicts pitting Republicans against Democrats and the center city narrative against forces opposing Charlotte and Mecklenburg County overwhelmed the plan. The first state takeover law was hastily written despite the fact that legislators had an airport authority model proffered by an airline. This half-finished product allowed city lawyers to quickly point out legal problems, and it also allowed the courts and the Federal Aviation Administration to suspend the takeover process.

Finally, even within a weak council-manager government, Charlotte's leaders were able to exercise the city's agency to stop the state takeover of the airport. City officials had citizens' support and used their political capital in the courts and with the FAA. State officials may also have been aware that the city politicians' defiance could spill over to other issues. Charlotte was becoming a minority-majority city. Although the media coverage played down these dynamics, they loomed as factors in the state legislature's relations to the city. Interestingly, the so-called black political caucus did not take a public stand during the struggle for airport control.

In any case, it was clear that some officials' sole concern was whether American Airlines would continue to exist and use Charlotte as a hub landing. No elected official was willing to jeopardize that critical relationship. Yes, city agency can be mobilized in certain situations, but it is only episodically available.

CONCLUSIONS

ONE OF THE UNSPOKEN MYTHS of American cities is that they develop organically. Purportedly, cities start up as small settlements, attract retail businesses and people that help them create central business districts, and then grow indefinitely. If the matter were that simple, all cities located in similar environments would be approximately the same size, perform relatively the same functions, and have similar local politics. Accordingly, Jackson, Mississippi, would have grown like Charlotte, North Carolina. Obviously, few southern cities have the same economic development stories. In general, southern cities matured while encumbered by racial segregation and rural conservatism. Some did not heed the dress-up imperative, dawdled on social/racial deregulation, and lost the competition for people, businesses, and resources. Their competitors had prophetic leaders with resources to periodically rethink and remake their cities. Indeed, Charlotte had a prophetic civic leadership and an enabling infrastructure (i.e., the airport) to support growth. With growth comes changes in what residents want from their city.

WHAT CHARLOTTEANS WANT

Historian Thomas Hanchett states in *Sorting out the New South*, "Throughout the century from the mid-1870s to the mid-1970s, Charlotteans continually redefined their notions of 'a good place to live.'"[1] Hanchett regards Charlotte as a social organism responding to social desires. He thinks that what constitutes an acceptable urban form is "the product of particular historical forces, which shift kaleidoscopically with passing years."[2] In addition, Hanchett is concerned primarily with neighborhood development after Charlotte's economic functions changed and its race relations improved. Indeed, Charlotte is home to several communities. The "new Charlotteans" are out-of-state people and immigrants from a variety of cultures and places. They make up the growing high-tech and banking workforce, and they do not have the sentimental attachments to old cultural traditions and neighborhoods. New Charlotteans want a different lifestyle and will make more modern residential choices. Johnny Harris, the city's premier real estate developer, understood the need for upscale living when he and his brother-in-law Howard "Smoky" Bissell developed the Ballantyne areas and other properties.

A Charlotte Chamber of Commerce report titled "Best of Both Worlds" and published by the *Charlotte Observer* claimed that the city provides the convenience and livability of a midsize city, as well as the diversified business services found only in much larger metropolitan areas.[3] Charlotte is "an ideal headquarter city."[4] This is why the metro area features companies like Bank of America, Lowe's, Duke Energy, Sealed Air, Nocur, and Sonic.

Transforming a city's economy, resocializing its residents, and developing a competitive spirit are difficult enterprises. This transformation was a reaction to national economic shifts, expected generational change, and, again, providence. Charlotte had to formulate a new raison d'être (i.e., reason for being) to fully transform itself. In other words, Charlotte had to reinvent itself in order to grow. Leaders of the old city could not have anticipated that the new center of economic activity would be banking, or that computers and airplanes would put the city in the arena with world-class urban centers.

Charlotte is now a financial and service center. Becoming a transformative city required certain social and economic preconditions. As has been suggested, the first step in transforming a city is creating a reliable and dedicated progrowth coalition of local politicians and business leaders. Keeping economic leaders on the same page requires strong leadership in the chamber of commerce and other business advocacy groups. The current structure of the city of Charlotte's government works because it allows politicians to join the pro-growth coalition. Obviously, the government plays a critical role in legitimating the coalition's decisions. Problems arise when mayors and council members find themselves at variance with the pro-growth interests.

The long-standing symbiosis of elected officials and other members of the pro-growth coalition is why this book spends so much time reviewing Charlotte's political history. As we have seen, disagreements, but not fundamental ones, arose concerning the airport and economic development. The gist of this book's argument is that an infrastructure like a dynamic airport that can withstand the "ripple effects of technology" can create jobs. Jobs then create growth. Without jobs, Charlotte would not have attracted residents.

The second step in the transformation of the city's growth was welcoming foreign and domestic immigrants. A new economy requiring new skills needs a different talent set. Therefore, the pro-growth coalition had to be an aggregator of exceptional and trending talent. Leaders knew, perhaps earlier than the average resident, that to make this economic transition they had to recruit a workforce to match the new economy. In the future, cities' competition for talent will be a mad scramble.

Accordingly, this study goes further than Paul Peterson's *City Limits*, which highlights a city's calculated land use and tax policies as a way to attract businesses. The review of Charlotte's economic development strategy asserts that infrastructure development and willingness to recruit relevant talent are additional tools for economic development. Service economies like banking needed bean counters (accountants), number crunchers (data analysts), and economic planners. The postindustrial economy and financial capitalism demanded a highly trained workforce. Richard Florida claims that a creative class is needed for these jobs. Members of this group find their common identities "based on their economic function. Their social cultural preferences, consumption and buying habits, and their social identities all flow from this."[5] The creative class generally abhors social discrimination such as racism, sexism, and homophobia. In the past Charlotte had a history of southern racism, blue laws, and evangelicalism. Aware of that reputation, the pro-growth coalition fought to present a more progressive image.

It is impractical to recruit a first-class twenty-first-century workforce without off-loading a culture of social discrimination. Because modern banking is by nature international, banks need workers from around the world. The Immigrant and Nationality Act of 1965 that lifted the quota on workers from Asia and elsewhere who were entering the country helped facilitate this global recruitment effort. International flights at Charlotte Douglas made the city accessible for such individuals. They did not have to take a boat across the ocean and then take a train to Charlotte. Instead, these recruited employees could make the trip in several hours and with only two changes in airports. Charlotte's new openness also induced Latinos to locate in the Queen City. In order to grow, Charlotte's population needed to evolve so that the city was no longer 99 percent native-born as it had been in the 1930s and 1940s.

The third step in making Charlotte a transformative city was the decision to nurture an inattentive citizenry or a trusting citizenry. With the assistance of elected city officials, Charlotte's business leaders promoted a sense of local identity with residents. However, the narrative did not concern the city's loss of industries. Rather, it focused on Charlotteans' struggle with other cities (e.g., Atlanta and Nashville) for due recognition. It was a matter of other cities' perceived disrespect for Charlotte. The narrative addressed the city's residents in this manner: Charlotte is your city, and you should want the best for your city.

You deserve a bigger and growing city. Support for this corporate vision of a pro-growth Charlotte was supposed to redound to all residents. The city would grow and gain importance because of residents' faith in it.

This faith was implicit in the city's attempt to comply with the federal mandate to integrate public schools. Indeed, the 1976 special issue of *U.S. News and World Report* credited Charlotte's growth to these efforts. It stated that the city "managed to resolve the busing-for-integration issues before the city was torn apart."[6] Real estate moguls created new living spaces for high-income workers, new hotels appeared in the city, and Uptown was quasi-Manhattanized. Charlotte also acquired auxiliary amenities such as professional sports teams (the Carolina Panthers and Charlotte Hornets) and nonstop flights to distant cities. These new assets were confirming and reassuring to the citizenry.

In addition, the city of Charlotte and the state of North Carolina in general have a long history of anti-union politics and pro-business mantras. Organized labor leaders were deemed a complaining and questioning class. The state's right-to-work laws ensured the dominance of the business-class narrative. Accordingly, cultivating a nurturing and inattentive citizenry was relatively easy. Local politicians, the media, and community leaders worked to communicate a message that said, in part, "Let business leaders do it." Consequently, there were few voices of dissent. What minor opposition arose could never engage the general public. The glaring exception resulted when the state attempted to seize the city airport.

The confluence of these three factors—a desire to change the economy, a relatively open immigration policy, and a trusting citizenry—helped stabilize Charlotte's pro-growth coalition. Led by the chamber of commerce, real estate developers, and the city council, the pro-growth coalition began setting the new economic agenda after World War II. Charlotte's successful banking industry reconstructed or transformed the city.

THE ECONOMIC USES OF AIRPORT LANDINGS

Charlotte is a relative newcomer to the New South's high-flying growth rivalries. Selling the transformative city to outsiders is a massive marketing enterprise, and an attractive airport with multiple links to the rest of the world is part of that sale. Even connecting fliers who can get a dazzling view of the city's growing skyline are part of image building. Charlotte Airport's history as a feeder airport or landing strip was short, as it quickly became a secondary hub for the nascent Eastern Air Lines. Other airlines like Piedmont then followed Eastern.

Hub landings were located in cities like Charlotte because, in part, the city's leaders were enablers. Without consistent opposition from citizens, the pro-growth coalition openly promoted airport expansion and growth.

Hubs are built to collect regional passengers for commuter airlines and distribute them to major carriers. Some hub cities like Charlotte need to aspire toward obligatory landing status. Cities like Atlanta, Chicago, Los Angeles, New York, and Washington, D.C., have attained this standing. In these large cities, the political leadership works to maintain headquarters and to entice the creative class to become residents. Airlines must land in these locations to be considered among the leading carriers. When cities achieve obligatory landing status, their airports will be in a strong position to negotiate with airlines. This explains why discount airlines like Southwest and JetBlue keep pursuing gates in these cities. Southwest Airlines bought Air Tran Airlines partly to get gates in Atlanta and even Charlotte. However, the airlines continue to face the uncertainties of corporate investment, technological change, and globalization.

With the merger of U.S. Airways and American Airlines, the Charlotte Douglas International Airport is closing in on achieving obligatory landing status. Obviously, the city needs more residents, businesses, and members of the creative class to make this happen. In other words, it must have a truly diverse economy that attracts job-creating entities. Part of the reason for Charlotte's success thus far owes to solid support from the business community. The city also needs the airline industry and other business interests to help it fulfill transformational goals.

For Charlotte Douglas International Airport itself, becoming a truly international airport (obligatory landing status) or even one with a high number of nonstop flights required a major upgrade of facilities and willingness of the new American Airlines to invest heavily in the gates. Parking problems and the lack of public transportation to the airport have long been identified as impediments to accommodating more passengers and expanding the airport facilities. Currently, the airport lacks sufficient parking lots and a light-rail system running to and from the facility. Granted, the new construction is a major response to these demands, but more space may be indicated. If a passenger wants to make a same-day flight, he will have to park his car in an hourly parking lot with higher fees or take a cab. This adds to the cost of day trips.

The city of Charlotte's government has managed the airport and its development for over seventy years. Currently, American Airlines is the largest tenant at the airport. Although the carrier is headquartered in Dallas, its location in Charlotte allows it to compete with Delta Airlines, its rival. Compared to facilities in a city of equal size, the Charlotte Douglas Airport has a good record of maintenance, security, and enplanement. Before 2013, the city never asked the state government for assistance in sorting out Charlotte Douglas's management problems. The airport is not a financial burden for the state of North Carolina or the city of Charlotte.

Furthermore, the airport is one of the largest employers for Charlotte. It is also what economists call a multiplier; when the airport expands, it causes other related business activities to grow. Vendors, concessionaires, and the taxi industry saw an increase in business. Larger airports can also justify international landings. By supporting an international airport, Charlotte raised its international profile, thereby allowing itself to compete in a postindustrial world. Simply put, the airport makes Charlotte a global economic player.

Aside from not reaching obligatory landing status, Charlotte Douglas International Airport is still a long way from becoming what economist John Kasarda calls an "aerotropolis." As a hub, does Charlotte act as a "router" for "physical internet" that quickly connects high-value people and products? Kasarda defines an aerotropolis as "a metropolitan subregion whose infrastructure, land use and economy are centered around the airport. It consists of an airport's aeronautical, logistics and commercial elements, and it connects transportation infrastructure with clusters of aviation-oriented businesses and residential developments that continually feed off each other in their proximity to the airport." The Charlotte Douglas International Airport does offer what Kasarda characterizes as "business connectivity on a massive scale."[7] This may explain, in part, why the airport appointed Stuart Hair as the first economic affairs manager. His job is to attract companies other than airlines to locate facilities at the airport and in surrounding communities. As a hub with its variety of flights, the airport can play a critical role in meeting the special needs of a changing industry such as banking. A fascinating question is whether the city will allow the airport to gain aerotropolis status. Can an aerotropolis maintain itself as a separate entity?

Finance, insurance, and real estate (FIRE) industry employees can arrive in Charlotte, conduct their meetings at the airport, and never spend much time in the city proper. This possibility confirms studies that show a relationship between airline traffic and employment in U.S. metropolitan areas. Based on her empirical research on Chicago O'Hare, economist Jan Brueckner finds that a 10 percent increase in passengers leads to an approximately 1 percent increase in employment in service-related industries. She states, "Frequent service to a variety of destinations, reflected in high level of passenger enplanement, facilitates easy face-to-face contact with businesses in other cities, attracting new firms to the metro area and stimulating employment at established enterprises."[8] In the late 1990s, geographer William Graves researched the financial industry's impact on Charlotte's economy. He summarizes his findings as follows:

> Despite the city's importance as a command and control center for the banking industry, examinations of FIRE-industry employment and wages suggest that, as of 1997, Charlotte's economy was no more reliant on the financial industry than other metropolitan areas of similar size. However, while Charlotte has experienced a dramatic growth in FIRE-industry employment and wages, this growth did not appear to be at the expense of cities losing bank headquarters. These findings suggest that while bank acquisitions are highly visible events, they result in little change in the distribution of financial employment. This study also found evidence that the Charlotte banks generate fewer spillovers than other banks in similarly sized metropolitan areas. This lack of FIRE spillovers may indicate the trouble that the Charlotte banks have experienced entering more lucrative portions of the financial industry. . . . The high visibility of the banking industry in Charlotte overshadows the diversity of the area's economy.[9]

Charlotte can indeed be a center of service-related industries. Hugh McColl agrees with Graves's assessment, asserting, "Charlotte is not dependent on the banks today. There are now high-tech industries. The Duke Energy and Banks had a demand for technology. This helped drive the development. They attracted all kinds of businesses from insurance companies, money managers, high tech firms, headquarters like United Technology and Sealed Air [Corporation]. Charlotte is now an open city."[10]

Mr. McColl may refer to companies like Fintech Firm, AvidXchange, and Credit Karma. Together with other companies, these organizations hire over forty-five thousand workers. These jobs include computer system analysts, informational security analysts, and software, web, and app developers. If Charlotte ever hopes to enter the big league of high-tech workers, it needs to double or triple the number of these companies and workers. This situation involves a bit of a chicken-and-egg dilemma. Which comes first, recruiting such companies or creating a pool of these workers to entice them to come to Charlotte? Moreover, Charlotte has similar political problems to its sister New South cities but also some unique ones.

THE NEW POLITICAL REALITIES OF CHARLOTTE

For political leaders in Charlotte, the task is to separate myths from realities. The myth is that growth is a merit good that will lift all economic boats. The reality is that individuals may be at different ends of the same boat. According to conventional political wisdom, cities like Charlotte are subservient to the relentless economic realities of the global economy. Consequently, cities are rarely in the position to dictate future economic outcomes. Law professor Richard Schragger disagrees and cites examples of cities governing themselves for the sake of their residents.[11] Despite constitutional limitations and conservative state legislatures, these cities made things happen for the common good. In addition to expanding social services for the poor, they have passed ordinances that restrict what incoming industries and businesses can do, and they have enacted minimum wage laws. A brief summary of the realities of Charlotte's transformative journey and the airport that took the city to its new place in the nation's economy appears below.

1. The story of Charlotte's transformation is reminiscent of W. W. Rostow's stages of economic growth.[12] The city was once dominated by rural interests and textile industry leaders, and the precondition for Charlotte's takeoff was that industry had hit a wall. Yet federal funds seemed always available to airport development. Few knew at the time what the new economic step would be, but progress happened when banking and race relations were deregulated. Charlotte had the appropriate infrastructure (i.e., the airport) to facilitate its transition to the national mainstream economy. Accordingly, the parallel development of the airline industry and Charlotte's economy was a profitable concurrence.

2. The designation of Charlotte Douglas International Airport as an airline hub had both economic benefits and hidden costs for city residents. As the UNCC Urban Institute reports have demonstrated, the airport's economic benefits are measurable. The social cost is yet to be determined. Furthermore, overreliance on one industry is perilous. While Charlotte benefits from the active trucking and freight railroad industries, it could be argued that banking is the city's only high-paying and glamorous industry. Yet banking as we know it is not purely self-sustaining. As this study of Charlotte has indicated, economic growth is not self-generating, and the competition will intensify. In other words, if Charlotte does not diversity, it cannot adequately meet the new challenges of technology and work reimagination.

3. Airports like Charlotte Douglas International are constantly entangled with airline management uncertainties. Airline leadership changes regularly, and the individuals who hold these positions are invited to speak to local business leaders. Hub cities need a quasi-symbiotic relationship between local business leaders and airline executives. Airlines continue to merge, throwing

airport managers off-balance. In addition, pilots and flight attendants go on strike. Yet Charlotte Douglas International Airport plans to complete a new runway and new parking decks, roadways, and domestic gates, in addition to remodeling terminals. The construction cost will be over $1 billion, and the result will be what Daniel Boorstin called "parking temples."[13] Another cost will be an overall improvement of the city surface transportation system connecting to the airport. The airport's immediate future is unclear, but the long-term impact of financial commitments creates endless questions. Who will land where and at what hubs? Will this hub need more international nonstop flights? A transformative city needs to know these answers to make marketing decisions.

4. Although the Charlotte city manager supervises the airport director, the latter has great discretion in the day-to-day management of the facilities simply due to the nature of the job. Charlotte Douglas International Airport is an enterprise agency that operates on fees. Moreover, airport management often escapes the normal policy debates of the city council. There is a difference between tight oversight and loose oversight. Since Charlotte Douglas's inception, its managers did not make a separate annual report to the city. They did so for the first time in 2015. The question is whether this arrangement can continue as the city keeps changing.

5. Federal regulation of air travel and airlines imposes hidden costs on host cities. Airports cannot fully offset these costs because their financial stability is linked to concession and parking fees, as well as competition with other airports. Fortunately, airport development is considered distributive, rather than redistributive, public policy, so it usually enjoys bipartisan support. Yet global cities are expensive, and the increase in costs is unpredictable. A major miscalculation can cause a crash landing for the city and its airport.

6. To stay competitive with other hub cities and large airports like Atlanta's Hartsfield Jackson Airport, Charlotte Douglas has had to find new ways to make its enplanement cheaper for the airlines. Airports in so-called medium markets such as Charlotte have less leverage over airlines than larger markets where the airlines must have obligatory landing gates (e.g., Chicago, New York, Los Angeles). Accordingly, cities must grow so that their airports can attain obligatory landing status. However, I agree with historian Ray Clark, who concludes in his study of Dulles International Airport, "Simply building the most modern and efficient airport in the world does not guarantee its use or popularity."[14]

7. As Charlotte Douglas Airport grew as an economic generator, it impacted North Carolina's future economic ambitions. Accordingly, statewide business communities are stakeholders in the airport; they cannot afford to be bystanders while Charlotte develops as a global player. This regional anxiety manifested itself in the 2013 state takeover attempt. Hence, it is incumbent on city leaders to keep state leaders abreast of changes in the management of the airport.

8. The full impact of international travel and immigration on Charlotte is not clear. The next U.S. Census (2020) will be telling. Charlotte proper has grown exponentially, and new people bring new culture, ideas, and ambitions with them. The international political and postindustrial economy has created a labor market of highly skilled, ambitious nomadic workers. Do these members of the "creative class" have any political allegiance to their host city? To attract them, Charlotte has catered to their living preferences. In *The New Geography of Jobs*, geographer Enrico Moretti calls this phenomenon the great divergence.[15] For Moretti, residents' education level increasingly defines American cities' attractiveness. Charlotte banks attract a lot of bean counters and number crunchers, but it is not clear whether they are aspiring Charlotteans or itinerant workers in an increasingly variable worldwide labor market. Obviously, more survey research on these newcomers is needed.

    The creative class can make a city grow economically, but it also creates changes in the real estate arena, as evidenced by the city's luxury apartment buildings. The real estate industry responded to the market by building expensive condos on the Catawba River. Charlotte's streets filled with beautiful "ole trees" will disappear, and Uptown traffic will also change as the demographics change. In 1982 the Charlotte Uptown Development Corporation (CUDC) invited urban designer William H. Whyte to the city. Whyte advised city officials to congregate seats, trees, and retail shops in Uptown, stating, "People say they don't like to be crowded, but they do."[16]

9. Finally, the city of Charlotte must stay alert to changes in the national and international economy. Its government form and conservative politics have admirably served its transformative aspirations, but the city cannot afford to rest on its laurels. More changes are necessary to retain Charlotte's place in the national and global market. In 1998 the chamber of commerce hired a consultant to look at the future for the city and the metropolitan region. It urged Charlotte "to get out of the smokestack-chasing business and into the policy business."[17] The report also urged the city to invest in education,

training, transportation infrastructure, and university research in order to be "winners in a global economy."[18]

In 1987, *Atlanta Journal-Constitution* staff writer Bob Dean contended that it is difficult to quantify the relationship between airport development and economic growth. He further stated that "adequate air service is essential" to making cities like Charlotte more attractive to the high-tech and service industries.[19] Several years later, Chris Buritt, also of the *Atlanta Journal-Constitution*, asked rhetorically, "Will people eat herbed grits with halibut cheeks?" He then quoted the response of restaurant owner Sharon Talient: "It has taken awhile to grow people's palates. But they're coming to love us."[20] On the brink of an economic and demographic boom, Charlotte residents have to continue adjusting to relentless social change.[21]

The Charlotte Chamber of Commerce has been at the center of the marketing effort publishing attractive pamphlets hawking the advantages of doing business in the city. These materials stress access, talent, affordability, and the quality of life. As we learned earlier, Charlotte banks are investing and recruiting internationally. In the early 2000s, a case was made that New South cities like Charlotte were attractive locations to invest, live, and work. While Charlotte needed to upgrade its light-rail, create more amenities, and build more downtown (Uptown) living space, it was nevertheless a business-friendly city that had right-to-work laws and a hub-landing airport.

REMAKING CHARLOTTE'S IMAGE

Changing the identity of a southern city has not been easy. Historian David Goldfield's *Cotton Fields and Skyscrapers* traces the development of southern cities for three centuries, concluding that rural values such as biracialism, closed-mindedness, and other conservative predilections inhibited growth and development. Because the economy changed, the face of Sunbelt cities like Charlotte had to change as well. Goldfield asserts, "It is very different now. Over 10 million Americans have moved to the Southeast. There has been immigration from other parts of the world."[22] Indeed, Charlotte has come a long way since President Washington called it a "trifling place." Turn-of-the-twentieth-century textile buildings have been replaced by rectangular glass office buildings reaching thirty to forty stories high. Charlotte's legendary banker Hugh McColl once stated, "Our city will be only as healthy as its heart. We need to ensure an uptown that is alive and breathing."[23] Uptown is also the face of the city that the nation sees. Charlotte, a Sunbelt city, has to upgrade its infrastructure to be nationally and internationally competitive.

When the manufacturing cities of the Snowbelt reached their growth apex, they also became icons of economic nationalism and magnets for the best and the brightest. In the past, manufacturing cities like Chicago, with its "big shoulders," and New York City, "the Big Apple" with its five boroughs, accommodated immigrants from all over the world and elsewhere in the United States. Local airports played a critical role in these cities' ascendancies and dominations. In 1980 the chamber of commerce and its leaders were involved making a foreign-trade zone.[24]

To grow larger, Charlotte needs more nonstop international landings besides the United Kingdom and Germany. Achieving status as an airline hub and an elite New South city is not enough. Beyond this, the governing elites must wean themselves from their localism and embrace a more cosmopolitan and aggressive business posture. After reviewing Charlotte's prospects in 1991, Peter Applebome of the *New York Times* disagreed with this approach to the city's growth: "The flip side of the city's aggressiveness is a place that struts too much and crows too loudly, particularly when it is bragging about being 'international' and 'world class,' the mantras of every up-and-coming American city." He quoted skeptic Robert Raiford, a local radio commentator who billed himself as Charlotte's curmudgeon at large: "Charlotte is 90 percent foam and 10 percent beer. It's a city of Babbitts." Mr. Raiford also said that, despite its economic successes, Charlotte still took its cultural cues from the North. Raiford concluded, "It's made up of a bunch of local yokels who've seen 'Breakfast at Tiffany's' too many times, and they want to make Charlotte a city like that, a sterile sort of Manhattan. Let's face it, the performing arts here is stock car racing."[25]

It is obvious that if Charlotte embraces globalization, it has to link its existing central organizing story, or metanarrative, to this new narrative. This central story often takes years to refine, and it has to be deeper than civic jingoism, pride, or boosterism. Metanarratives are defined as "widely shared cultural stories by which a society, or social group, sometimes expresses the most fundamental ideals, or 'truths,' of their culture."[26] This story defines what the New South governing elite seeks to project as it embraces the global world. It is a matter of economic and trade connectivity. Consultant Michael Gallis observed, "We now live in factory earth where parts and pieces are made everywhere and assembled through supply chains wrapping the planet."[27]

An inevitable correlate of this new image projection is the need for a tranquil political environment. Richard Schragger's assertions about cities' proactive agency have their limits for a city like Charlotte. Charlotte is so constrained by not having absolute home rule, and it has not settled into being a race-neutral or immigrant-welcoming community. Indeed, widespread economic disparities among race and ethnic groups persist. Income inequality will grow as more people come to Charlotte to find jobs. Although the city has elected three black mayors, social grievances and tensions between blacks and whites remain. Crime will continue to be a problem, and affordable housing will still be scarce. Minority and progressive white city politicians have consistently argued for a more unified and economically equitable community. The media covers these aspirational proclamations, and the pro-growth coalition has supported them, but the resources needed to make these changes are beyond Charlotte's fiscal capacity. Then couple this circumstance with the fact that Charlotte is a blue city (i.e., one dominated by the Democratic Party) embroiled in a struggle with a recalcitrant red state legislature (i.e., one dominated by the Republican Party). The result has been a minimalist approach to the city's growing inequality problem. These issues may become exacerbated as Charlotte, like other cities, recruits a more cosmopolitan managerial class to run city departments.

If the recruitment is done nationally, some of these new managers will not be native born or educated in the Carolinas. Conventional wisdom holds that mobile managers are itinerants who have less psychological commitment to their employing city. Thus, their presence will mean more turnover and less of what former city manager Pam Syfert called "continuity." Syfert served eleven years and her predecessor Wendell White served fifteen years. Her staff selections included a deputy from the city budget office, and this continuity "trickled down" to the police and transit departments.[28]

It follows that this managerial class may not be fully cognizant of this continuity ethos. Its members may therefore be less civic minded because they are being judged on institutional performance rather than otherwise uplifting contributions to the city. Hence, there is still a need for a larger perspective than operational city leadership. The question becomes, Who is going to be the next John Belk, Stanford Brookshire, Ed Crutchfield, Hugh McColl, Harvey Gantt, and Johnny Harris? Can Charlotte depend on a new managerial class of outsiders such as the city managers, airport directors, and school superintendents to guide it to the next leap forward? Can the city continue to prosper and grow under a council-manager form of government? Will these elected officials and professional managers stay true to the pro-growth script? Will there be future hiring of what organizational theorists call ambidextrous leaders—that is, individuals who can at once do the job for which they were hired and suggest, promote, and implement new goals for the city?[29] The pro-growth coalition should ponder the above questions.

If Charlotte plans to remain a city that attracts the creative class and a productive bean-counting class, it needs to recruit world-class talent and cater to their needs. Urban theorist Richard Florida argues that the these professionals' locational choice is slanted toward "lifestyle" values.[30] As we saw earlier, this group of workers is not inclined to move to an area with a reputation for any type of social discrimination. This preference has forced some businesses to move to where the workers choose to live. Ballantyne, Myers Park, Dilworth, and South Park are interesting places to reside, but they are actually inside the city of Charlotte. Locational preferences of this group may also mean city leaders should develop additional swank living spaces outside Charlotte. Since the late 1990s, people have dreamed about creating a subcommunity between the Catawba River and the airport. After the discussion of the airport takeover diminished, the discussion of development of the Catawba River and the airport was revived.

The next development boom, an "edge city," would convert acreage near the airport into offices, warehouses, factories, and homes. Jack Christine was appointed a deputy aviation director in charge of economic development in the Dixie-Berryhill area. Charlotte Douglas Airport owns hundreds of acres and plans to buy more land to its west between Interstate 485 and the Catawba River. Christine asserted in a 2014 *Charlotte Observer* article, "There's about 5,000 acres between 485 and the river. There are another 1,500 acres south of the airport. All of that acreage is in play."[31] Such a development will require the city to provide waterlines, sewers, and roads, the most important thing of all. In fact, the city has allocated $45 million for widening Dixie River Road and Garrison Road.

The aforementioned improvements are part of the city's $816 million capital improvement plan, paid for with a 7.25 percent property tax increase.[32] Christine admitted that this is a long-term deal: "We've had preliminary conversations with a lot of developers. I don't think there's been a whole lot of commitment yet from the developer side, everyone's looking."[33] The *Charlotte Observer* also reported that Johnny Harris, one of the city's major real estate developers, had called Wayne Cooper, who owned eighty acres west of I-485. The largest landowner in the area is Crescent Communities, another developer. In 2015, the proposed development was called the River District. Developers envisioned four thousand residences and five hundred thousand square feet of shops, restaurants, and other retail venues. There would also be eight million square feet of office space, as well as more traffic and access roads.[34] Such a development would afford the residents and office workers close access to the airport. This could be a favorite waterfront property.

CHARLOTTE AND THE STATE OF NORTH CAROLINA

What happens in Raleigh does not always stay in Raleigh. North Carolina's state assembly dominates state politics. Accordingly, conflicts occasionally arise between the Republican-dominated assembly and the heavily Democratic Charlotte. This writer was told a joke about the North Carolina Republicans in Raleigh. In 1960, U.S. senator Howell Helfin of Alabama, a Democrat, called establishment Republicans the "Grey Poupon element of the Republican Party"—in his opinion, they were the "Gucci-clothed, Mercedes-driving, Jacuzzi-soaking, Perrier-drinking, Aspen-skiing Republicans."[35] In turn, highly partisan Democrats called North Carolina Republicans "a grit eating, NASCAR watching, time-share owning, high price bourbon drinking and Bible thumping bunch, but not in that order."[36] In the 1940s John Gunther recorded Charlotte's slogan, "The Greatest Church-Going Town in the World, Except Edinburgh."[37]

Since the turn of the century, Charlotte's national reputation has changed. It was a city on the rise. But for some Charlotteans economic and racial progress was not as important as church attendance and southern traditions. These views had to change. Banker Hugh McColl explained the circumstance plainly:

> Charlotte is a business community whose business is business. We are not a political city. It is hard to be a government center and business city. Politics in Charlotte is secondary. Our business community has always been elastic enough to have peace. "We had social peace." Charlotte is a Democrat [Democratic Party] city. The Black community and the business community were in lockstep. Ergo, they got along. Later the business community went Republican. This put the black community and business community on different sides. Sometimes there are issues.[38]

The black community has played an important role in the city's economic development. Many deem Charlotte progressive, yet some state Republicans supposedly do not consider it North Carolina's flagship city. Instead, they regard Charlotte as a blue city in a red state. The failed airport takeover attempt is cited as evidence of this bias.

In many ways, the debate about Charlotte as a flagship city is relatively settled. Skyline towers including the Bank of America building, the Duke Energy Center, and Hearst Tower hover over the city, but Charlotte lacks the status of a travel destination, and it is not a convention magnet like Atlanta and Miami. Not all North Carolina residents consider Charlotte the state's premier city. The capital is Raleigh, located near the Research Triangle. Some believe that Raleigh, Durham, or Winston-Salem could offer North Carolina the most promise for growth and development. Wisely, the state government has invested in all three cities. Obviously, the local Charlotte Chamber of Commerce would take exception to intrastate comparisons. City leaders see Charlotte as the lead city in the mid-South. Yet they recognize that Charlotte is not yet competitive with cities like Atlanta, Dallas, Houston, and Miami.

Money lies at the heart of relations between the state of North Carolina and the city of Charlotte. Charlotte needs state funding for bonded megaprojects (airport support with access roads) and unbonded projects (education and social welfare). City leaders need the entire North Carolina congressional delegation to help procure federal money for building plans. Traditionally, the state government has been amenable to requests for infrastructure. For example, during the fight over the airport, the state of North Carolina provided most of the funding for the $1 billion extensions of Charlotte's light-rail line. In addition, the state has funded access roads throughout the history of the airport.

Yet cities like Charlotte always claim that they send more money to the state than they receive in return. Indeed, the state of North Carolina must become more flexible when it comes to allowing Charlotte to find new tax revenues to build infrastructure and attract a talented workforce. The fight over Charlotte Douglas International Airport was in part a struggle over who controls the future of the city and the region. Despite the setback in the attempt to take the airport, planning for the development of land between the facility and the Catawba River continued. This is because the business community has kept its eyes on the prize. The pro-growth coalition apparently foresees yet another phase of Charlotte's "transformative" evolution, and a new story will therefore unfold for Charlotteans.

NOTES

PREFACE

1. Steve Harrison "DNC Economic Impact: $164 Million—the Convention Brought $91 Million in New Spending, Study Finds; Hotel Industry Was the Biggest Winner," *Charlotte Observer*, January 29, 2013, 1A.

INTRODUCTION

1. Daniel K. Bubb, *Landing in Las Vegas: Commercial Aviation and the Making of a Tourist City* (Reno: University of Nevada Press, 2012), 123.
2. Alan Altshuler and David Luberoff, *Mega-projects: The Changing Politics of Urban Public Investment* (Washington, D.C.: Brookings Institution Press, 2003), 236–237.
3. The idea of a city as a local growth machine is attributed to John Logan and Harvey L. Molotch, *Urban Fortunes* (Berkeley: University of California Press, 1987).
4. Historians are exceptions. Janet R. Daly Bednarek, *America's Airports: Airfield Development, 1918–1947* (College Station: Texas A&M University Press, 2001). Also see *Airports, Cities, and the Jet Age: US Airports Since 1945* (New York: Palgrave Macmillan, 2016).
5. Paul Stephen Dempsey, Andrew R. Goetz, and Joseph S. Szyliowicz, *Denver International Airport: Lessons Learned* (New York: McGraw-Hill. 1997), 520–522.
6. Nicholas Dagen Bloom, *The Metropolitan Airport* (Philadelphia: University of Pennsylvania Press, 2015), 197.
7. See Simon Mosbah and Megan S. Ryerson, "Can Metropolitan Areas Use Large Commercial Airports as Tools to Bolster Regional Economic Growth?," *Journal of Planning Literature* 31, no. 3 (2016): 317–333.
8. Interview with Hugh McColl, October 31, 2017.
9. Paul Barrett, "Cities and Their Airports: Policy Formation, 1926–1952," *Journal of Urban History* 14, no. 1 (November 1987): 116.
10. See Daniel Bell, *The Coming of the Post-Industrial Society* (New York: Basic Books, 1973).
11. Peter Mantius, "Economic Profiles of the Southeast: Charlotte, N.C.: Charlotte, N.C.: Bustling City Banks on Business-Financial Institutions' Help to Pave the Way," *Atlanta Journal-Constitution*, November 29, 1987, 1.
12. Benson J. Lossing, ed., *The Diary of George Washington, from 1789 to 1791; Embracing the Opening of the First Congress, and His Tours through New England, Long Island, and the Southern States* (Richmond: Press of Historical Society, 1861), 197.

13. Samuel Lubell, "Charlotte, NC," *Saturday Evening Post*, June 23, 1951, 33.

14. Ibid.

15. Timothy Mead, "Governing Charlotte-Mecklenburg," *State and Local Review* 32, no. 3 (Fall 2000): 194.

16. "On the Way Up: Four Cities Show How It Can Be Done," *U.S. News and World Report*, April 5, 1976, 62.

17. Ibid., 62–63.

18. Russell M. Smith, "An Examination of Municipal Annexation in North Carolina, 1990–2009," *Southeastern Geographer* 52, no. 2 (Summer 2012): 172–173. Also see R. L. Clark and P. B. Gubbins, "Real Spheres of Influence? North Mecklenburg Towns Have More Say in Outside Zoning," *Charlotte Observer*, November 19, 1986, 1.

19. Peter Applebome, "The Nation: Challenging Atlanta, The South Has Its Second Cities, and They Thrive," *New York Times*, April 23, 1989, 5E.

20. Charlotte Chamber of Commerce, *Metrolina: The Million Plus Market* (Charlotte: Chamber of Commerce, 1985), 5.

21. William Graves and Heather A. Smith, eds., *Charlotte, N.C.: The Global Evolution of a New South City* (Athens: University of Georgia Press, 2010), 2–3.

22. Kim Q. Hill, *Democracy in the Fifty States* (Lincoln: University of Nebraska Press, 1994), 67.

23. David Esler, "Why Your Community Needs Its Airport," *Business and Commercial Aviation*, August 2006, 46–55, http://www.calairports.com/Why%20Your%20Community%20Needs%20Your%20Airport.pdf.

24. Ibid., 52.

25. Wilbur C. Rich, *The Politics of Urban Personnel Policy: Reformers, Politicians, and Bureaucrats* (Port Washington, N.Y.: Kennikat, 1982), 33–34.

26. Interview with Ron Carlee, March 31, 2016.

27. See Clarence Stone, "Urban Regimes and the Capacity to Govern: A Political Economy Approach," *Journal of Urban Affairs* 15 (1993): 1–28.

28. Richard Maschal, "Correspondent's File," *Architectural Record* 190, no. 5, (May 2002): 78.

29. M. Boyle, "Civic Boosterism in the Politics of Local Economic Development," *Environment and Planning* 29 (November 1997): 1975–1997.

30. See Clarence N. Stone *Regime Politics: Governing Atlanta* (Lawrence: University Press of Kansas, 1989).

31. Website of the Charlotte Chamber of Commerce, Charlottechamber.com (2016).

32. Interview with Prof. Bill McCoy, October 4, 2017.

33. LeGette Blythe, "Clarence Kuester—He Was 'Mr. Charlotte,'" *Charlotte Observer*, February 28, 1950, 1J. Also see Harold L. Cooler, *Booster Kuester and Beyond* (Charlotte, N.C.: Okatie, 2009).

34. Cited in Harry J. Freeman, "Establishment of Municipal Airports as Public Purpose," *National Municipal Review* 18, no. 4 (April 1929): 263–264. Also in Bednarek, *America's Airports*, 64.

35. Chris Mead, *The Magicians of Main Street: America and Its Chambers of Commerce, 1768–1945* (Oakton, Va.: John Cruger Press, 2014), 3.

36. Ibid.

37. Jack Claiborne, *Crown of the Queen City: The Charlotte Chamber from 1870 to 1999* (Charlotte, N.C.: KPC Custom Publishing, 1999), 3.

38. Jane Hinkle, Bradley Wyatt, and Whitney Shaw, "The Chamber: Involved in Too Much?," *Charlotte Observer*, January 19, 1980, 7A.

39. Claiborne, *Crown of the Queen City*, 9.

40. Ibid., 10.

41. David Dawley, Robert Stephens, and David Stephen, "Dimensionality of Organizational Commitment in Volunteer Workers: Chamber of Commerce Board Members and Role Fulfillment," *Journal of Vocational Behavior* 67, no. 3 (December 2005): 514.

42. See Janet R. Daly Bednarek, *America's Airports: Airfield Development, 1918–1947* (College Station: Texas A&M University Press, 2001).

CHAPTER 1. TEXTILE CHARLOTTE LEARNS TO FLY

1. See Jay W. Forrester, *Urban Dynamics* (Cambridge, Mass.: MIT Press, 1969).

2. David Goldfield, "A Place to Come To," in *Charlotte, N.C.: The Global Evolution of a New South City*, ed. William Graves and Heather A. Smith (Athens: University of Georgia Press, 2010), 12–13.

3. "Advent of Flying Machine, Claims of the Wright Brothers," *Charlotte Observer*, January 7, 1904, 1.

4. "Wright Brothers Try Again," *Charlotte Observer*, May 28, 1904, 1.

5. "Promise Better Airship," *Charlotte Observer*, April 12, 1908, 1.

6. "Disaster to Aeronauts Aeroplane Wrecked," *Charlotte Observer*, May 16, 1908, 1.

7. "Mail Trains In and Out of City," *Charlotte Daily Observer*, January 15, 1914, 6.

8. Mildred G. Andrew, *The Men and the Mills* (Macon, Ga.: Mercer University Press, 1987), 76.

9. Ibid.

10. "Charlotte Is Southern Textile Center," *Charlotte Observer*, March 2, 1928, 17.

11. Gerry Bunn, "We Put the Question of Airport Expansion to the Vote," *Engineering and Technology* 6, no. 3 (2011): 26.

12. "Many Stunts Slated for Air Show Sunday," *Charlotte News*, July 11, 1947, 14A.

13. Frederick M. Kerby, "Airplane Mail Very Efficient," *Charlotte Observer*, November 27, 1918, 5.

14. Ibid.

15. "Coming of the Airplane," *Charlotte Observer*, November 25, 1918, 6.

16. "Want Air Mail Line Stop Here," *Charlotte Observer*, November 26, 1918, 3.

17. "Aero Club Is Formed Here," *Charlotte Observer*, July 15, 1929, 10.

18. Randy Johnson, "Blind Flying On the Beam: Aeronautical Communication, Navigation and Surveillance: Its Origins and the Politics of Technology," *Journal of Air Transportation* 8, no. 2 (2003): 64.

19. E. P. Goodrich, "Airports as a Factor in City Planning," supplement to *National Municipal Review* 17 (March 1928): 181.

20. Cited in Dr. Thomas W. Hanchett, "The Growth of Charlotte: A History,"

http://landmarkscommission.org/wp-content/uploads/2016/11/THE-GROWTH-OF-CHARLOTTE.pdf.

21. LeGette Blythe, "Charlotte Has Her Own Shopping and Financial Centers," *Charlotte Observer*, April 1, 1928, 7.

22. "Charlotte Aviator Johnny Crowell Dies," *Charlotte Observer*, October 17, 1983, 1C.

23. "Lund to Show Stunts Today," *Charlotte Observer*, June 21, 1931, 10.

24. "Thousands See First Mail," *Charlotte Observer*, April 2, 1930, 1.

25. Mary Kratt, *Charlotte, Spirit of the New South* (Winston-Salem, N.C.: J. F. Blair), 198.

26. H.G. Trotter, "Air Service for Charlotte Has Had Phenomenal Rise," *Charlotte Observer*, February 28, 1950, 5G.

27. "He Knew What He Was Doing," *Saturday Evening Post*, March 28, 1942, 26.

28. Ibid.

29. For an account of the flight, see Dan Hampton's *The Flight: Charles Lindbergh's Daring and Immortal 1927 Transatlantic Crossing* (New York: William Morrow, 2017).

30. Howard Stussman, "Bigger Planes Drive Airport from Pasture to Pavement," *Engineering News Record*, July 26, 1999, 45.

31. "Says Aid of City Needed for Airport," *Charlotte Observer*, July 19, 1927, 1.

32. "City's Need for Airport Vital, Expert States," *Charlotte Sunday Observer*, October 23, 1927, 1.

33. Ibid.

34. "Aid for Airport Expected Soon After Operations Start," *Charlotte Observer*, March 30, 1928, 1.

35. "Fight for Air Mail Route in Capital Today," *Charlotte Observer*, May 23, 1931, 1.

36. Cited in an article titled "New Floodlighting for Small Airports," *Aero Digest* 17, no. 6 (December 1930): 90.

37. Ibid.

38. "Effort to Sell Airport Bonds," *Charlotte Observer*, April 15, 1929, 1.

39. "Most Cities Own Their Airport," *Charlotte Observer*, October 27, 1931, 1.

40. "Bond Election Seen as Only Recourse Now: Chamber of Commerce at 'Rope's End' in Effort to Save Airport," *Charlotte Observer*, May 18, 1932, 1.

41. Ibid.

42. Stanley High, „They Build Men Into Jobs," *Saturday Evening Post*, April 27, 1940, 24–25, 82, 84, 87.

43. Janet R. Daly Bednarek, *America's Airports: Airfield Development, 1918–1947* (College Station: Texas A&M University Press, 2001), 61.

44. LeGette Blythe, "A. H. Wearn Is Defeated by Total of 670 Ballots," *Charlotte Observer*, May 8, 1935, 1A, 13.

45. Kratt, *Charlotte*, 198.

46. Ibid., 199.

47. "Will Ask the Council to Act on Airport," *Charlotte Observer*, August 21, 1935, 14.

48. "Airport Should Be City's No. 1 Project Grice Says," *Charlotte Observer*, August 11, 1935, 1.

49. "Club Vote to Help Election," *Charlotte Observer*, October 19, 1935, 15.

50. "Air Commerce Man to Be Placed Here," *Charlotte Observer*, October 20, 1935, 1.

51. "City Must Buy Airport to Get Aid," *Charlotte Observer*, August 16, 1935, sec. 2, p. 1.

52. "Air Commerce Man to Be Placed Here," 13.

53. See Douglas Carl Adams, *Conservative Constraints: North Carolina and the New Deal* (Jackson: University Press of Mississippi, 1992).

54. "Airport Should Be City's No. 1 Project," 1.

55. SteelerGrrl, "Charlotte's Blue Roots: The WPA, the Airport, and Professional Lacrosse," *Daily KOS*, August 18, 2013, http://www.dailykos.com/stories/2013/8/18/1231029/-Charlotte-s-blue-roots-the-WPA-the-airport-and-professional-lacrosse.

56. J. B. Marshall, *Annual Report of the City Manager for the Fiscal Year July 1, 1936, to June 30, 1937*, 2.

57. Kratt, *Charlotte*, 198.

58. H. G. Trotter, "Air Service for Charlotte Has Had Phenomenal Rise," *Charlotte Observer*, February 28, 1950, 6G.

59. "Frank Thies Made Fifth Planning Board Member," *Charlotte Observer*, June 13, 1945, 1B.

60. Trotter, "Air Service for Charlotte," 6G.

61. Bednarek, *America's Airports*, 98.

62. Johnson, "Blind Flying On the Beam," 73.

63. Cecil Brownlow, "Jet Age, Growth Strain Airports, Airways," *Aviation Week* 66 (February 1957): 149–150.

64. "Airport Bond Issue Beaten," *Charlotte News*, April 4, 1941, 1.

65. "Mayor Sets Assurance," *Charlotte News*, May 20, 1940, 21.

66. Mary James Cottrell, "Phone Strike Snags Morris Field Housing Transfer," *Charlotte Observer*, January 14, 1946, 1C.

67. Ibid.

68. "Clear Morris Field for Final Transfer," *Charlotte Observer*, January 25, 1946, 1.

69. Herbert Baxter to Roy Palmer, January 24, 1946, Herbert Baxter Papers, University of North Carolina at Charlotte Special Collections and Archives.

70. Lynn L. Bollinger, "Private versus Public Management of Airports," *Harvard Business Review* 24, no. 4 (July 1946): 520.

71. Edwin S. Mills, *Urban Economics* (New York: Scott, Foreman, 1972).

72. Douglas Karsner, "Aviation and Airports: The Impact on the Economic and Geographic Structure of American Cities, 1940s–1980s," *Journal of Urban History* 23, no. 4 (May 1, 1997): 430.

73. Rick Rothacker, *Banktown: The Rise and Struggles of Charlotte* (Winston-Salem, N.C.: John F. Blair, 2010).

74. Ibid., 10.

75. See Robert Dahl, *Who Governs? Democracy and Power in an American City* (New Haven, Conn.: Yale University Press, 1961).

76. See Deborah Gwen Douglas, "The Invention of Airports: A Political, Economic, and Technological History of Airports in the University: 1919–1939" (PhD diss., University of Pennsylvania, 1996).

CHAPTER 2. POSTWAR YEARS AND THE NEW AIRPORT

1. Mildred G. Andrew, *The Men and the Mills* (Macon, Ga.: Mercer University Press, 1987), 253.
2. Don Oberdorfer, "Transition Shakes Carolina Textiles," *Charlotte Observer*, August 11, 1957, 1D.
3. "Administrative Structure Would Cost $105,000; Extension or Runways Termed Necessary for Long-Range Program," *Charlotte Observer*, December 18, 1945, 1.
4. "Big or Little Airport?," *Time*, January 20, 1947, 90.
5. J. A. Daly, "City Makes Strong Plea for Air Lines," *Charlotte News*, July 25, 1946, 1B.
6. Ibid., 8.
7. Thomas E. Mullaney, "Growth of Commercial Flying: A Billion Dollar Business Comes of Age within Three Decades," *New York Times*, October 11, 1953, 28.
8. See *Charlotte, the Industrial Center of the Carolinas* (Charlotte, N.C.: Charlotte Chamber of Commerce, 1947).
9. "Kuester: Charlotte Booster," *Charlotte News*, May 10, 1948, 12C.
10. Samuel Hair, *A Survey and Analysis of Air Transportation at Charlotte North Carolina* (Washington, D.C.: Gotch and Crawford, January 27, 1954), 3.
11. Samuel Lubell, "Charlotte, N.C.," *Saturday Evening Post*, June 23, 1951, 46.
12. Rolf Neill, "Traffic, Hospital Beds, Airport in Chamber of Commerce Plans," *Charlotte Observer*, February 11, 1960, 8B.
13. Victor K. McElheny, "Charlotte Protests Air Route Proposal," *Charlotte Observer*, April 5, 1961.
14. Ed Martin, "Piedmont, Charlotte Flew in Tandem," *Charlotte Observer*, July 31, 1989, 1D.
15. See Walter R. Turner, "Building the Piedmont Airlines Hub in Charlotte North Carolina, 1978–1989," *North Carolina Historical Review* 83, no. 3 (July 2006): 366.
16. Ibid., 367–368.
17. Martin, "Piedmont, Charlotte Flew in Tandem," 1D.
18. Wingate Main, "59 Local Flights, 1000 Workers Hit," *Charlotte Observer*, July 8, 1966, 1A.
19. J. A. C. Dunn, "Advice to Air Travelers: Next Time Take Stagecoach," *Charlotte Observer*, July 9, 1966, 1.
20. Jack Claiborne, *Crown of the Queen City: The Charlotte Chamber from 1870 to 1999* (Charlotte, N.C.: KPC Custom Publishing, 1999), 88.
21. David Merritt, "CAB Opens Charlotte to Delta, United," *Charlotte Observer*, April 16, 1970, 1A.
22. See Mark Gottdiener, *Life in the Air: Surviving the New Culture of Air Travel* (Latham, Md.: Rowman and Littlefield, 2001).
23. Susan Jettson, "Airport Is Fastest Growing in the U.S." *Charlotte Observer*, June 3, 1974, 1C.
24. Ibid.
25. Kenneth Harris to Marvin S. Cohen, chair of Civil Aeronautics Board, February

15, 1979, Kenneth Harris Papers, University of North Carolina at Charlotte Special Collections and Archives.

26. Marion A. Ellis, "Major Carolinas Airports Surge with Explosion of Growth," *Charlotte Observer*, November 18, 1985, 1D.

27. Ibid.

28. Bill Bancroft, "New Air Terminal—Now or Next Decade," *Charlotte Observer*, May 7, 1978, 12A.

29. Robin Clark, "Airport's Namesake Watches His Effort Enter New Phase," *Charlotte Observer*, June 3, 1980, 4A.

30. Louise Hickman Lione, "Terminal Project a Production with Many Players," *Charlotte Observer*, April 25, 1982, 4H.

31. Ibid.

32. Ibid.

33. Bill Arthur, "Airport Terminal Ready to Takeoff," *Charlotte Observer*, April 25, 1982, 1H.

34. Cassandra Lawton, "50,00 Visitors Take a Look at Glossy New Airport Terminal," *Charlotte News*, April 26, 1982, 1.

35. See "Up & Away: Dedication Ceremony," Charlotte Municipal Airport, Department of Aviation, Charlotte, North Carolina, April 29, 1982, 1–4.

36. David Mildenberg, "Hollings Supports Piedmont," *Charlotte Observer*, December 10, 1996, 10E.

37. Jack Claiborne, *Crown of the Queen City*, 122.

38. "Airport Financing Set by Charlotte," *New York Times*, November 26, 1985, 21D.

39. Turner, "Building the Piedmont Airlines Hub," 366.

40. Bob Deans, "Airline Hubs Shaping Economic Destiny of Region as Rivers Did," *Atlanta Journal-Constitution*, February 8, 1987, 25S.

41. Kevin O'Brien, "Charlotte's Next 5 Years: Plums and Pitfalls," *Charlotte Observer*, June 15, 1988, 1C.

42. John Cleghorn, "Damage to Airport Put at $3 million," *Charlotte Observer*, September 27, 1989, 7C.

43. E. S. Savas, "It's Time to Privatize," *Fordham Urban Law Journal* 19, no. 3 (1992): 401–414, reprinted in *Government Union Review* 14, no. 1 (Winter 1993): 37–52. And E. S. Savas, "A Taxonomy of Privatization Strategies," *Policy Studies Journal* 18, no. 2 (Winter 1989–1990): 343–355.

44. Robert Poole, *Privatizing Airports*, Policy Study No. 199 (Santa Monica, Calif.: Reason Foundation, 1990), 20.

45. T. J. Orr memorandum to Julie Burch, assistant city manager, "Sale of Charlotte/Douglas International Airport," February 26, 1990, 1–2, Sue Myrick Papers, University of North Carolina at Charlotte Special Collections and Archives.

46. Ibid., 2.

47. Marion A. Ellis, "Eastern Airlines Curtails Charlotte Service, Citing 'Dropping 41 Flights, Trimming Payroll,'" *Charlotte Observer*, August 1, 1986, 1A.

48. Ibid.

49. Doug Smith, "USAir May Zing Charlotte's Retail Economy," *Charlotte Observer*, October 15, 1991, 1D.

50. Ibid.

51. John Day, "Charlotte/Douglas Air Traffic Soars," *Charlotte Observer*, December 25, 1991, 1D.

52. Joe Drape, "Charlotte's Queen City–Size Task: Managing Its Good Fortune," *Atlanta Journal-Constitution*, March 18, 1990, 7S.

53. Stella M. Eisele, "USAir Chief Sees More International Flights from Charlotte-Overtime," *Charlotte Observer*, November 17, 1992, 1D.

54. See Rick Rothacker, *Banktown: The Rise and Struggles of Charlotte's Big Banks* (Winston-Salem, N.C.: John F. Blair, 2010).

55. Amber Veverka, "For Banks, Big Event Turns Into 'Big Yawn,'" *Charlotte Observer*, January 1, 2000, 10A.

56. Ted Reed, "Passengers Discover No Glitches in Air Travel," *Charlotte Observer*, January 1, 2000, 10A.

57. John Gallagher, "Is U.S. Airways Too Big to Fail? Some Say Yes," *Charlotte Observer*, June 29, 2000, 1D.

58. Ibid.

59. Rothacker, *Banktown*, 46.

60. "Cities and Airport Security with Mayor Patrick McCrory," *Washington Journal*, on C-SPAN, October 25, 2001.

61. Rick Newman, "Ready to Takeoff," *U.S. News & World Report*, July 31, 2006, 47–48.

62. Jefferson George, "U.S. Airways Boss: Airlines Will Adapt—during Charlotte Visit, CEO Parker Says the Industry Will Figure Out a Way to Be Profitable in Future Despite Current Financial Crisis and Soaring Fuel Costs," *Charlotte Observer*, August 1, 2008, 1D.

63. H. McKinley Conway, *The Airport City: Development Concepts for the 21st Century* (Atlanta: Conway Publications, 1980), 28.

64. Martin, "Piedmont, Charlotte Flew in Tandem," 1D.

65. Interview with Ron Carlee, March 31, 2016.

CHAPTER 3. CHARLOTTE IN AN ERA OF DEREGULATION

1. Tom Fiedler, "A Fear of (Deregulated) Flying," *Charlotte Observer*, April 24, 1974, 1A.

2. Janet R. Daly Bednarek, *Airports, Cities, and the Jet Age: US Airports Since 1945* (New York: Palgrave Macmillan, 2016), 19.

3. Associated Press, "Carter Urges Congress to Ease Controls on Airlines," *Charlotte Observer*, March 5, 1977, 2.

4. See Martha Derthick and Paul Quirk, *The Politics of Deregulation* (Washington, DC: Brooking Institution, 1985).

5. See John M. Pfiffner and Robert Presthus, *Public Administration* (New York: Ronald Press, 1967), 457.

6. William E. Schmidt, "Deregulation Challenges Atlanta Airline Hub," *New York Times*, November 12, 1985, 1A.

7. *Nader v. Allegheny*, 426 U.S. 290 (1976).
8. Gary McDonnell, "What Caused Airline Deregulation: Economists or Economics?," *Independent Review* 19, no. 3 (Winter 2015): 391.
9. Airline Deregulation Act of 1978, Pub L. No. 95–504, 92 Stat 1706.
10. William J. Eaton, "Reform Plan for Airlines near Takeoff," *Charlotte Observer*, March 5, 1977, 2.
11. Laurence T. Phillips, "Structural Changes in the Airline Industry: Carrier Concentration at Large Airports and Its Implications for Competitive Behavior," *Transportation Journal* 25, no. 2 (Winter 1985): 18–28.
12. Jack Claiborne, *Crown of the Queen City: The Charlotte Chamber from 1870 to 1999* (Charlotte, N.C.: KPC Custom Publishing, 1999), 106.
13. Sen. Edward Kennedy, "Airline Deregulation, More Competition, Lower Fares," *Charlotte Observer*, July 17, 1979, 15A.
14. Edwin I. Colodny, "A Few Large Airlines Will Take Over," *Charlotte Observer*, July 17, 1979, 15A.
15. Richard A. Klein to R. C. Birmingham, December 4, 1978, Kenneth Harris Papers, University of North Carolina at Charlotte Special Collections and Archives.
16. Richard A. Klein to R. C. Birmingham, December 26, 1978, Kenneth Harris Papers, University of North Carolina at Charlotte Special Collections and Archives.
17. Bernard Wasow, "Airlines Are In a Tailspin," For the Record, *Charlotte Observer*, December 30, 1991, 6A.
18. Mark Potts, "Piedmont Rides Deregulation to High-Flying Business," *Washington Post*, May 23, 1983, 7.
19. Questionnaire sent by United States Conference of Mayors, August 8, 1979, 2, Kenneth Harris Papers, University of North Carolina at Charlotte Special Collections and Archives.
20. Henry Scott, "Reduction in Plane Services Keeping Travelers Up in Air," *Charlotte Observer*, March 5, 1979, 1A.
21. Ibid.
22. David A. NewMyer, "The Impact of Deregulation on Airports: An International Perspective," *Journal of Aviation/Aerospace Education and Research* 1, no. 1 (Spring 1990):62–63.
23. Ibid.
24. Laurence E. Gesell and Robin R. Sobotta, *The Administration of Public Airports*, 5th ed. (Chandler, Ariz.: Coast Aire Publications, 2007), 16.
25. Bill Arthur, "Airport Terminal Ready to Take Off," *Charlotte Observer*, April 25, 1982, 1H.
26. Jay McIntosh, "After Deregulation, Easter Faced Tough Competition," *Charlotte Observer*, August 1, 1986, 8A.
27. John H. Cushman, "Support for Airline Deregulation," *New York Times*, February 14, 1990, D1.
28. Stephen E. Creager, "Airline Deregulation and Airport Regulation," *Yale Law Journal* 93, no. 2 (December 1983): 338.

29. Tim Whitemire, "Forget Hornets, U.S. Airways' Woes Have Charlotte On the Edge," *Herald Sun*, May 2002, 4B.

30. Ibid.

31. Robert Crandall, "Charge More, Merge Less, Fly Better," *New York Times*, April 21, 2008, A21.

32. Cliford Winston and Steven A. Morrison, "With Deregulation, Everyone Gains," *New York Times*, April 8, 1990, 13.

33. Joe Nocera, "Merger Is What Airlines Do," *New York Times*, August 17, 2013, A19.

34. Frederick J. Stephenson and Frederick J. Beier, "The Effects of Airline Deregulation on Air Service to Small Communities," *Transportation Journal* 18, no. 4 (Summer 1981): 54–62.

35. David Mildenberg, "CCAIR Flying High Since Making Link to Piedmont System," *Charlotte Observer*, October 20, 1986, 3.

36. "5 Senators Zero in On Airline Industry," *Charlotte Observer*, March 5, 1992, 1D.

37. Wasow, "Airlines Are In a Tailspin," 6.

38. Peter C. Carstensen, "Evaluating 'Deregulation' of Commercial Air Travel: False Dichotomization, Untenable Theories, and Unimplemented Premises," *Washington & Lee Law Review* 46, no. 109 (1989): 124.

39. U.S. Department of Transportation, "Airports, Air Traffic Control, and Related Concerns. Office of the Secretary of Transportation, Secretary's Task Force on Competition in the U.S. Domestic Airline Industry, Washington, D.C. (1990)." The term "pocket of problems" was used by John H. Cushman in "Support for Airline Deregulation," *New York Times*, February 14, 1990, 1B.

40. Steven Morrison and Clifford Winsk, *The Economic Effects of Airline Deregulation* (Washington, D.C.: Brookings Institution, 1986).

41. Timothy M. Vowles, "The 'Southwest Effect' in Multi-Airport Regions," *Journal of Air Transport Management* 7 (2001): 251–258.

42. Interview with Hugh McColl, October 31, 2017.

43. Rick Rothacker, *Banktown: The Rise and Struggles of Charlotte* (Winston Salem, N.C.: John F. Blair, 2010), 23.

44. For a discussion of Hugh McColl's relationship to Clinton, see Ross Yockey, *McColl: The Man with America's Money* (Atlanta: Longstreet, 1999), 471–474.

45. Gail Russell Chaddock, "What It Took to Enact Banking Reform: Contributions, Compromise, and Having Powerful Friends in High Places," *Christian Science Monitor*, October 21, 1994.

46. For an understanding of how the 2008 recession affected banking, see Andrew Ross Sorkin, *Too Big to Fail: The Inside Story of How Wall Street and Washington Fought to Save the Financial System* (New York: Penguin Books, 2010).

47. For a discussion of how Charlotte lost its number two position in banking, see Deon Roberts and Rick Rothacker, "Charlotte No Longer the No. 2 U.S. Banking Center," *Charlotte Observer*, May 24, 2017, 1A.

48. "Airport Café Racial Policy Is Challenged," *Charlotte Observer*, July 1, 1954, 1B.

49. "Negroes to Fight Airport Decision," *Charlotte Observer*, July 15, 1954, 1B.

50. Bill Arthur, "Downtown Building Took a Great Leap Upward," *Charlotte Observer*, December 30, 1979, 4B.

51. Tom Eblen, "Major U.S. Airports Pressed for Elbowroom—after Deregulation, Air Passenger Traffic Increased Greatly. But Huge Costs, Plus the Opposition of Citizens' Groups, Often Means That—Expansion Plans Have Only a Wing and a Prayer of Being Realized," *Atlanta Journal-Constitution*, December 4, 1988, 1E.

52. Ibid.

53. Cushman, "Support for Airline Deregulation," 1D.

CHAPTER 4. ORGANIZING THE CITY'S GREATEST ASSET

1. John D. Kasarda, "Welcome to Aerotropolis, the City of the Future," *New Perspective Quarterly* 32, issue E (July 2015): 43–45.

2. John D. Kasarda and Greg Lindsay, *Aerotropolis: The Way We'll Live Next* (New York: Farrar, Straus and Giroux, 2011), 174.

3. Ely Portillo, "Airport Growth May Hinge on Merger—U.S. Airways, American Combination Could Have Increased Traffic," *Charlotte Observer*, August 15, 2013, 1A.

4. Ibid.

5. See Thomas Petzinger, *Hard Landing: The Epic Contest for Power and Profits That Plunged the Airlines Into Chaos* (New York: Random House, 1995).

6. Richard de Neufville and Amedeo Odoni, *Airport Systems: Planning, Design, and Management* (New York: McGraw-Hill, 2013), 30.

7. Ibid., 601.

8. R. C. Birmingham and J. B. Fennell, *Five Airport Expansion and Financial Proposal: Douglas Municipal Airport Development Program*, November 1979.

9. Portillo, "Airport Growth May Hinge On Merger," 1A.

10. Yap Yin Choo, "Factors Affecting Aeronautical Charges at Major US Airports," *Transportation Research Part A* 62 (April 2014), 61.

11. Ibid., 56.

12. Harriet Baskas, "Gloves Are Off as Airports Go After Their Rivals in Ads," *USA Today*, March 17, 2010, 2B.

13. 49 U.S.C. 1513 (1976).

14. 48 U.S.C. 40116.

15. Stephen E. Creager, "Airline Deregulation and Airport Regulation," *Yale Law Journal* 93, no. 2 (December 1983): 323–324.

16. Bernie Kohn, "Airport Expects Flak over $3 Tax," *Charlotte Observer*, April 7, 1993, 1D.

17. "Airport Study Might Cost Only $12,000," *Charlotte Observer*, September 27, 1967, 4C.

18. William Safire, "The Airport World," *New York Times*, November 20, 1978, 31.

19. Wyatt Brummitt, "The Airport Snaps Out of It," *Aero Digest* 17, no. 6 (December 1930): 88.

20. Marion A. Ellis, "Charlotte/Douglas Passenger Boarding Topples Projections," *Charlotte Observer*, September 11, 1985, 1.

21. Julie Fenster, "The Front Porch Comes to the Airport," *American Heritage* 57, no. 6 (November/December 2006): 17–18.

22. "City Will Settle Airport Cab Issue," *Charlotte Observer*, July 24, 1956, 1B.

23. Fenster, "Front Porch Comes to the Airport." 17

24. Ibid., 18.

25. Ted Reed, "Airport Ranks 6th in National Survey," *Charlotte Observer*, November 14, 2000, 1D.

26. Charisse Jones, "Airport Satisfaction Soars in New J. D. Power Study," *USA Today*, December 16, 2016, 1.

27. See Janet R. Bednarek, *Airports, Cities, and the Jet Age: US Airports Since 1945* (New York: Palgrave Macmillan, 2016), 138.

28. Walter R. Turner, "Building the Piedmont Airlines Hub in Charlotte, North Carolina, 1978–1989," *North Carolina Historical Review* 83, no. 3 (July 2006): 371.

29. Adams D. Steven, Yan Dong, and Martin Dresner, "Linkages Between Customer Service, Customer Satisfaction and Performance in the Airline Industry: Investigation of Non-linearities and Moderating Effects," *Transportation Research*, part E, vol. 48 (2012): 752.

30. James K. C. Chen, Amirita Batchuluun, and Javkhuu Batnasan, "Service Innovation Impact to Customer Satisfaction and Customer Value Enhancement in Airports," *Technology in Society* 43 (November 2015): 219–230.

31. Ibid., 228.

32. Yap Yin Choo, "Factors Affecting Aeronautical Charges," 54–55.

33. Valerie Reitman, "Piedmont Plans Charlotte Expansion," *Charlotte Observer*, November 10, 1986, 1A.

34. Ibid.

35. Ibid.

36. Kays Gary, "Airport Name Game," *Charlotte Observer*, May 15, 1982, 1B.

37. Ed Martin, "Delays Will Cost More at Airport [:] Report Discusses Charlotte's Future," *Charlotte Observer*, June 12, 1991, 1D.

38. Ibid.

CHAPTER 5. THE PRO-GROWTH COALITION AND THE HIRED HELP

1. Richard de Neufville and Amedeo Odoni, *Airport Systems: Planning, Design, and Management* (New York: McGraw-Hill, 2013), 82.

2. Ibid.

3. Bruce W. Fraser, "Consultants to the Rescue," *Nation's Business* 84, no. 7 (July 1996): 32.

4. Douglas Connah, "Airport Advisor Favor Pease Firm," *Charlotte Observer*, September, 1, 1961, 9A.

5. For a discussion of the Buckley firm, see Lucas C. Ross, "Charlotte's Airport Enters

the Jet Age: Charlotte Douglas, 1954–1983" (master's thesis, University of North Carolina at Charlotte, 2016).

6. Victor K. McElheny, "Al Quinn's Successor on Hot Seat," *Charlotte Observer*, January 31, 1962, 1B.

7. Susan Jetton, "Terminal Design Goes to Odell," *Charlotte Observer*, November 20, 1973, 1B.

8. Mark Ethridge and George Flum, "New Runway Isn't Needed," *Charlotte Observer*, December 14, 1975, 18A.

9. Ibid.

10. Interview with T. J. "Jerry" Orr, October 6, 2015.

11. Ibid.

12. Ibid.

13. Charlotte Chamber of Commerce, "The Need for Affirmative Action on the Expansion of Douglas Municipal Airport," June 16, 1976, 4.

14. See John Belk Papers, University of North Carolina at Charlotte Special Collection and Archives.

15. Bill Bancroft, "New Air Terminal—Now or Next Decade," *Charlotte Observer*, May 7, 1978, 12A.

16. Ibid.

17. Ibid.

18. Interview with T. J. "Jerry" Orr.

19. Bill Arthur, "Airport Terminal Ready to Take Off," *Charlotte Observer*, April 25, 1982, 8H.

20. Ibid.

21. Marion A. Ellis, "More Runways, Concourses, Even Terminals Will Be Needed," *Charlotte Observer*, November 18, 1985, 20B.

22. William Gamson, David Croteau, William Hoynes, and Theodore Sasson, "Media Images and the Social Construction of Reality," *Annual Review of Sociology* 18 (1992): 385.

23. "Delay Naming Airport Head," *Charlotte Observer*, June 29, 1946, 4B.

24. "Flack Names Rea Airport Manager," *Charlotte Observer*, August 13, 1946, 15.

25. "Records Cited in Sale of Air Base Building," *Charlotte Observer*, August 18, 1946, 1B.

26. Ibid., 3B.

27. Don Oberdorfer, "Has This Jet Age Gone to the Dogs?," *Charlotte Observer*, January 9, 1956, 12B.

28. Kays Gary, "Texan Is Named Airport Manager," *Charlotte Observer*, February 25, 1956, 1B.

29. McElheny, "Al Quinn's Successor on Hot Seat." 1B.

30. Hoke May, "New Airport Manager 'Must Find Greenback,'" *Charlotte Observer*, March 25, 1956, 4B.

31. "Charlotte on List for New Airport," *Charlotte Observer*, April 25, 1961, 1.

32. *Jewell Ridge Coal Corp. v. City of Charlotte, N.C.*, 204 F. Supp. 256 (1962).

33. Alex Coffin, *Brookshire and Belk: Business in City Hall* (Chapel Hill: University of North Carolina Press, 1994), 98.

34. Ibid.

35. Dwayne Walls, "Manager Quinn Quit at Airport," *Charlotte Observer*, January 31, 1961, 1.

36. McElheny, "Al Quinn's Successor on Hot Seat," 1B.

37. Joe Doster, "Council Still Up in Air Over Airport Contracts," *Charlotte Observer*, November 17, 1962, 1B.

38. Harriet Doar, "Mural at Airport Will Depict County History," *Charlotte Observer*, January 12, 1964, 2C.

39. Ibid.

40. Marion Ellis, "Knight a Jet Age Airport Manager," *Charlotte Observer*, June 12, 1967, 1.

41. Stan Brenan, "Airport Manager Ross Dies," *Charlotte Observer*, June 6, 1970, 1B.

42. See Porter Munn, "Meter Go in Airport's Face-Lifting," *Charlotte Observer*, September 27, 1967, 1C.

43. Marion Ellis, "Airport to Seek Key to Traffic," *Charlotte Observer*, August 3, 1967, 1C.

44. James K. Batten, "Airport's New Head Sees Clear Skies," *Charlotte Observer*, May 18, 1965, 8B.

45. Bill Arthur, "2 City Officials Considered for New Airport Manager," *Charlotte Observer*, April 12, 1971, 1C.

46. Ed Martin, "Airport Administrator Satisfied Working Behind the Scenes," *Charlotte News*, April 27, 1982, 6D.

47. Louise Hickman Lione, "Terminal Project a Production with Many Players," *Charlotte Observer*, April 25, 1982, 4H.

48. Susan Jetton, "Douglas Airport Nation's Fastest-Growing, Can't Stop," *Charlotte Observer*, June 3, 1974, 1C.

49. Ken Clark, "Charlotte: City of Many Means," *Charlotte Observer*, June 15, 1975, 1B.

50. Cited in Matthew Lassiter, "Searching for Respect: From New South to World Class at the Crossroads of the Carolinas," in *Charlotte, N.C.: The Global Evolution of a New South City*, ed. William Graves and Heather A. Smith (Athens: University of Georgia Press, 2010), 34.

51. Jetton, "Terminal Design Goes to Odell," 1B.

52. Josh Birmingham to H. Edward Knox, February 14, 1980, 2, H. Edward Knox Papers, University of North Carolina at Charlotte Special Collections and Archives.

53. Interview with Prof. Bill McCoy, October 4, 2017.

54. Interview with Ron Carlee, March 31, 2016.

55. Interview with Prof. Bill McCoy.

56. Interview with Michael Gallis, October 19, 2017.

57. Adele C. Schwartz, "Building on Faith," *Air Transport World* 38, no. 11 (November 2001): 83.

58. Walter R. Turner, "Building the Piedmont Airlines Hub in Charlotte, North Carolina, 1978–1989," *North Carolina Historical Review* 83, no. 3 (July 2006): 379.

59. Ed Martin, "General Aviation Flights Increased at Charlotte/Douglas," *Charlotte Observer*, October 4, 1991, 2D.

60. Ned Curran and Ed McMahan, "For the Record—Jerry Orr Has Made Charlotte Airport One of the World's Best," *Charlotte Observer*, February 25, 2011, 10A.

61. Ibid.

62. Ely Portillo, "Orr's Legacy in Limbo as Airport Drama Unfolds," *Charlotte Observer*, July 21, 2013, 1A.

63. Steve Harrison and Jim Morill, "City: Airport Change Needs Study, GOP's Rucho, Brawley Reject Call to Slow Airport Takeover," *Charlotte Observer*, February 20, 2013, 1A.

64. Interview with Brent Cagle, June 1, 2016.

65. David Gillen, "The Evolution of Airport Ownership and Governance," *Journal of Air Transport Management*, 17 (2011): 6.

66. Olga Johansson, "Inter-urban Competition and Air Transport in the Deregulated Era: The Nashville Case," *Journal of Transportation Geography* 15, no. 5 (September 2007): 378.

67. Alan Altshuler and David Luberoff, *Mega-projects: The Changing Politics of Urban Public Investment* (Washington, D.C.: Brookings Institution Press, 2003).

68. Karl A. Bosworth, "The Manager Is a Politician," *Public Administration Review* 18, no. 3 (Summer 1958): 216–222.

69. Interview with Hugh McColl, October 31, 2017.

CHAPTER 6. MESHING CITY POLITICS AND THE NEW ECONOMY

1. Peter Mantius, "Economic Profiles of the Southeast: Charlotte, N.C.: Charlotte: Bustling City Banks on Business-Financial Institutions Help to Pave the Way," *Atlanta Journal-Constitution*, November 29, 1987, 1.

2. Jerelyn Eddings and Jill Jordan Sieder, "Republicans Whistle Dixie," *U.S. News & World Report*, October 17, 1994, 32.

3. "Nonstop to Hell," *Charlotte Observer*, January 26, 1974, 12A.

4. Richard Maschal, "Correspondent's File," *Architectural Record* 190, no. 5 (May 2002): 77.

5. See "Charlotte: Economy," City-Data.com, http://www.city-data.com/us-cities/The-South/Charlotte-Economy.html#ixzz58E6zcA3y.

6. Richard Maschal, "Correspondent's File," 77.

7. Ted Mellnik, "Study's Task: The Selling of Charlotte," *Charlotte Observer*, June 21, 1990, 1C.

8. Larry Copeland, "Who's the Biggest Fish in the South?—Atlanta Has Long Been the Southeast's Star City. Charlotte, Nashville and Others Are Ready to Take a Bite Out of the Competition," *USA Today*, June 16, 2006, 3A.

9. Interview with Bob Morgan, May 31, 2016.

10. For a discussion of this effort, see Harry I. Chemotsky, "The Growth Impact of Globalization upon City Policies," *Policy Studies Review* 18, no. 3 (Autumn 2001): 29–48.

11. Darel E. Paul, "The Local Politics of 'Going Global': Making and Unmaking of Minneapolis–St. Paul as a World City," *Urban Studies* 42, no. 12 (November 2005): 2017.

12. Jack Claiborne, *Of Pleasure and Power: The Story of the Charlotte City Club* (Charlotte, N.C.: Deacon, 2007), 19.

13. Ibid.

14. Ibid.

15. LeGette Blythe and Charles R. Brockman, *Hornets' Nest: The Story of Charlotte and Mecklenburg County* (Charlotte, N.C.: McNally of Charlotte, 1961). See chapter 2.

16. Carl Abbott, *The New Urban America* (Chapel Hill: University of North Carolina Press, 1981), 140.

17. James Weinstein, "Organized Business and City Commission and Manager Movement," *Journal of Southern History* 28, no. 2 (May 1962): 178.

18. See Jeffrey L. Pressman, "Preconditions of Mayoral Leadership," *American Political Science Review* 66, no. 2 (June 1972): 511–524.

19. Jack Claiborne, "Airport Memorializes Former Mayor Ben Douglas," *Charlotte Observer*, April 25, 1982, 12H.

20. Chris Mead, *The Magicians of Main Street: America and Its Chambers of Commerce, 1768–1945* (Oakton, Va.: John Cruger Press, 2014), 193.

21. See Stephen Skowronek, *Presidential Leadership in Political Time* (Lawrence: University Press of Kansas, 2011).

22. Mead, *Magicians of Main Street*, 20.

23. See William H. Hansell Jr., "Council-Manager Government: Alive and Leading Today's Best Managed Communities," *National Civic Review* 90, no. 1 (Spring 2001): 41–44.

24. Ibid., 43.

25. James Svara, "Mayoral Leadership in Council-Manager Cities: Preconditions versus Preconceptions," *Journal of Politics* 49, no. 1 (February 1987): 214.

26. Edward Banfield and James Q. Wilson, *City Politics* (Cambridge, Mass.: Harvard University Press, 1963).

27. See David Truman, *The Government Process* (New York: Alfred A. Knopf, 1963).

28. Gary Mattson, „The Civic Boosterism, Corporate City Planning and Economic Development Policy of Smaller Great Plains Towns: Is Professionalism a Factor?," *Social Science Journal* 42 (2005): 42.

29. See Clarence Stone, "Urban Regimes and the Capacity to Govern: A Political Economy Approach," *Journal of Urban Affairs* 15 (1993): 1–28.

30. Thomas W. Hanchett, *Sorting Out the New South City: Race, Class, and Urban Development in Charlotte, 1875–1975* (Chapel Hill: University of North Carolina Press, 1998), 226.

31. Svara, "Mayoral Leadership," 218.

32. J. A. Daly, "Army in a Hurry to Set Up Base Here," *Charlotte News*, October 25, 1940, 6.

33. Jack Claiborne, *Crown of the Queen City: The Charlotte Chamber from 1870 to 1999* (Charlotte, N.C.: KPC Custom Publishing, 1999), 63.

34. Cited in Stephen Herman Dew, "The Queen City at War: Charlotte, North Carolina, during World War II, 1939–1945" (PhD diss., University of Arkansas, 1997).

35. "Douglas and Small Swap Verbal Blows on Airport Question," *Charlotte Observer*, March 16, 1941, 17.

36. Roy Covington, "Douglas Airport Had Its Opponent," *Charlotte Observer*, October, 2, 1967, 1B.

37. "Airport Aid Has Strings," *Charlotte Observer*, May 1, 1956, 2A.

38. "Hotels, Motels End Segregation," *Charlotte News*, April 24, 1963, 1B. Also see the Charlotte Mayor's Committee on Race Relations records at the Robinson-Spangler Carolina Room at the Charlotte Mecklenburg Public Library.

39. Pat Watters, *Charlotte* (Atlanta: Southern Regional Council, 1964), 4.

40. "Hotels, Motels End Segregation," 14B.

41. Watters, *Charlotte*, 2.

42. Hammer and Company Associates, *Metropolitan Charlotte: An Economic Study of Its Commercial Development Potential* (Atlanta, 1964), 121.

43. *Carolina International*, "N.C. Ports Are a Vital Link to Worldwide Business Connections," in *Charlotte Observer*, November 16, 1980, 4Y.

44. Emery Wister, "Andy Williams Is First Through West Concourse," *Charlotte News*, March 31, 1967, 1B.

45. Pat Stith, "Let County Take Control of Airport, Mayor Urges," *Charlotte News*, November 6, 1968, 1B.

46. Richard de Neufville and Amedeo Odoni, *Airport Systems: Planning, Design and Management* (New York: McGraw-Hill, 2013), 128.

47. Joe Flanders, "Baugh Proposes Regional Airport," *Charlotte News*, March 12, 1969, 1.

48. Ibid.

49. Ibid.

50. Paul Clancy, "New Airport Terminal Won't Raise Tax Rate," *Charlotte Observer*, January 21, 1969, 1.

51. Howard Covington, "Don't Expand, Abandon 'Lousy' Airport-Baugh," *Charlotte Observer*, March 5, 1969, 1B.

52. See Benjamin S. Horack Papers, 1968–1971, https://findingaids.uncc.edu/repositories/4/resources/352.

53. Katherine Peralta, "4 Ways the Belks Shaped Charlotte," *Charlotte Observer*, September 2, 2015, http://www.charlotteobserver.com/news/business/article33546450.html#storylink=cpy.

54. Mike Dembeck, "Mayors Want City to Annex Airport," *Charlotte News*, July 31, 1973, 1B.

55. Marion A. Ellis, "No One Suggests Revising Chamber's Old Power," *Charlotte Observer*, August 19, 1973, 16A.

56. Ibid.

57. Ibid.

58. Kenneth Harris to David C. Garrett, August 25, 1978, Kenneth Harris Papers, University of North Carolina at Charlotte Special Collections and Archives.

59. Alex Coffin, *Brookshire and Belk: Business in City Hall* (Chapel Hill: University of North Carolina Press, 1994), 216.

60. Ibid.

61. Ibid.

62. Bill Arthur, "Downtown Building Took a Great Leap Upward," *Charlotte Observer*, December 30, 1979, 4B.

63. Don Bedwell, "Boom Time for Charlotte," *Charlotte Observer*, August 10, 1979, 1A.

64. See Charles Shepard and M. S. Van Hecke, "Downtown Zoning Plans Unraveling Under Fire," *Charlotte Observer*, October 8, 1981, 1A, 8A.

65. See Don Bedwell, "Modest Heights Gets Some of Credit for McColl's Stature in Community," *Charlotte Observer*, January 25, 1981, 14A.

66. Interview with H. Edward Knox, July 24, 2016.

67. Kathleen Curry, "It's Charlotte; It's Douglas; and It's International," *Charlotte News*, May 11, 1982, 1A.

68. Jesse Helms to H. Edward Knox, April 29, 1980, H. Edward Knox Papers, University of North Carolina at Charlotte Special Collections and Archives.

69. Bill Arthur, "Report: No Fraud in Airport Contracts," *Charlotte Observer*, January 12, 1982, 1B.

70. *City of Richmond v. J. A. Croson Co.*, 488 U.S.(1989).

71. John Minter, "Ruling May Not Affect Charlotte Program," *Charlotte Observer*, January 24, 1989, 5A.

72. Ted Reed, "Southeast Airlines Brings Low Fares to Charlotte," *Charlotte Observer*, October 27, 2000), 1D.

73. See Doug Smith and Merle D. Kellerhals Jr., "Stock Issue Under Study for Downtown Projects," *Charlotte News*, February 18, 1981, 14A.

74. Interview with Harvey Gantt, August 11, 2013.

75. Tim Funk, "Mayor Gantt Urges N.C. Panel to Call for Home Rule Law," *Charlotte Observer*, January 28, 1986, 8C.

76. Jim Morrill, "Chamber Backing New Taxes," *Charlotte Observer*, May 17, 1986, 1A.

77. See Charlotte Uptown Development Corporation, *Uptown Charlotte Mixed Use Development* (August 1986).

78. Jean Marie Brown, "Region Should Pay Its Way, Vinroot Says," *Charlotte Observer*, December 3, 1991, 1A.

79. Interview with Richard Vinroot, May 3, 2016.

80. Ibid.

81. Dan Chapman, "Airport Workers Targeted in Probe," *Charlotte Observer*, April 19, 1995, 1A.

82. See Doug Smith, "Revamped CUDC Focus on New Vision for Uptown," *Charlotte Observer*, October 20, 1996, 1C.

83. "Economic Impact of Charlotte Douglas Airport," The Urban Institute at University of North Carolina, Charlotte, N.C., 1997, 10.

84. Edd Hauser, *Economic Impact Assessment of Charlotte Douglas International Airport* (Charlotte, N.C.: The Center for Transportation Policy Studies, 2005).

85. Minutes of the Aviation Advisory Committee, November 5, 1996, 3, University of North Carolina at Charlotte Special Collections and Archives.

86. *Competitive Air Service Assessment* (Evergreen, Colo.: Boyd Group / ASRC, 1999), 3.

87. Jerry Orr, "To Hub or Not to Hub," *Connections*, Spring 1999, 2.

88. See Karen Jacob, "How Nashville's Airport Bounced Back after Losing a Major Hub," *Business Insider*, June 3, 2014, www.businessinsider.com/r-former-hub-airports-find-new.

89. Vance Cariaga, "Task Force Has No Plans to Contact Any Low Fare Airlines," *Business Journal*, March 12, 1999, and "Task Force Plans to Take Its Case First to U.S. Airways," *Business Journal*, March 12, 1999.

90. Steve Harrison, "Foxx: Put Off Council Vote on Airport Taxis—Mayor Wants Closer Scrutiny of Airport, Joins Others Who Say Taxi Plan Needs Review," *Charlotte Observer*, February 12, 2011, 1B.

91. "Jerry Orr Departs CLT, Compromise Sought in Dispute," *Charlotte Business Journal*, December 20, 2013, http://www.bizjournals.com/charlotte/blog/queen_city_agenda/2013/12/jerry-orr-departs-clt-compromise-sought-in-dispute.html.

92. Eric Frazier, "Clodfelter Feels Bullish about the City's Future—'Charlotte Never Really Was a One-Horse Banking Town,' Mayor Tells Group," *Charlotte Observer*, October 22, 2015, 8A.

93. Ibid.

94. Ibid.

CHAPTER 7. CITY COUNCIL OVERSIGHT STYLE

1. Heinz Eulau and Robert Eyestone, "Policy Maps of City Councils and Policy Outcomes: A Developmental Analysis," *American Political Science Review* 62, no. 1 (March 1968): 143.

2. Hunter Bacot, "Civic Culture as a Policy Premise: Appraising Charlotte's Civic Culture," *Journal of Urban Affairs* 30, no. 4 (October 2008): 412–413.

3. Kevin R. Cox and Andrew Mair, "Locality and Community in Politics of Economic Development," *Annals of the Association of American Geographers* 78, no. 2 (June 1988): 318.

4. Eulau and Eyestone, "Policy Maps," 126.

5. Steve P. Erie, *Globalizing L.A.: Trade, Infrastructure, and Regional Development* (Stanford, Calif.: Stanford University Press, 2004), 35–39.

6. Jack Claiborne, *Of Pleasure and Power: The Story of The Charlottte Club* (Charlotte, N.C.: Deacon, 2007), 41.

7. James H. Svara, "Mayoral Leadership in Council-Manager Cities: Preconditions versus Preconceptions," *Journal of Politics* 49, no. 1 (February 1987): 207–227.

8. Michael Reisman, "Charlotte, N.C. Go-Ahead to Airport Expansion Debt," *Bond Buyer* 329, no. 30712 (August 25, 1999): 3.

9. John Minter, "2 Businessmen Square Off Over Airport Concession," *Charlotte Observer*, March 15, 1986, 1A.

10. Kelly Alexander, "The Airport Bonds: Are Jobs and Growth Worth Noise and Risk?," *Charlotte News*, June 19, 1978, 4A.

11. Minter, "2 Businessmen Square Off," 1A.

12. Ibid.

13. *Charlotte Douglas International Airport Annual Report* (1992/1993), 13.

264 | Notes to Chapter Seven

14. "Douglas Renamed to Airport Board," *Charlotte News*, September 11, 1973, 15A.
15. *United States v. Causby*, 328 U.S. 256 (1946).
16. Joe Doster, "Airport Committee Is Revised," *Charlotte Observer*, July 12, 1960, 1B.
17. *Griggs v. Allegheny County*, 369 U.S. 84, 82 S. Ct. 531 (1962).
18. Liz Chandler and Ricki Morell discuss the lack of diversity among Charlotte's citizen boards in their "Boards Loaded with White Men Southeast Charlotte Wields Much City, County Power," *Charlotte Observer*, October 8, 1992, 1A.
19. Kathleen Curry, "5 Named to Airport Panel," *Charlotte Observer*, September 29, 1987, 2C.
20. Ibid.
21. Ibid.
22. Paul Clancy, "New Airport Terminal Won't Raise Tax Rate," *Charlotte Observer*, January 21, 1969, 1B.
23. Ted Mellnik, "$115 Million Bond Issue for Airport Projects Okd," *Charlotte Observer*, November 19, 1985, 2C.
24. David Midenberg, "Panel Recommends Airport Plan," *Charlotte Observer*, December 10, 1986, 10E.
25. Kathleen Curry, "Airport Boosters: Growth Fuels Local Economy," *Charlotte Observer*, February 4, 1987, 10.
26. Ibid.
27. Ibid.
28. Kathleen Curry, "5 Named to Airport Panel," 2C.
29. Stella Eisele, "Airport Panel Delay Acting on Fee Plan," *Charlotte Observer*, December 9, 1992, 1D.
30. Ibid.
31. Stella M. Eisele, "Shuttles, Parking Lots May Face Airport Fee," *Charlotte Observer*, November 9, 1992, 1D.
32. Kathleen Curry, "Shape of Airport Noise Charted," *Charlotte Observer*, November 24, 1985, 1.
33. Gail Smith, "Airport Neighbors Rev Up Against Proposed 4th Runway," *Charlotte Observer*, November 14, 1985, 3C.
34. Pat Borden Gubbins, "Airport Buyouts Near Cruising Speed Some Owners Balk at Selling at Price Offered by City," *Charlotte Observer*, December 11, 1991, 3.
35. Curry, "Shape of Airport Noise Charted," 1.
stopped here
36. Janet R. Bednarek, *Airports, Cities, and the Jet Age: US Airports Since 1945* (New York: Palgrave Macmillan, 2016), 198.
37. Julie Cidell, "The Place of Individuals in the Politics of Scale," *Area* 38, no. 2 (2006): 196–203.
38. "A Gift Horse," *Charlotte Observer*, June 17, 1978.
39. *Apron/Terminal Areas Concept Study, Charlotte Douglas Municipal Airport* (White Plains, N.Y.: Arnold Thompson Associates, 1973), 4.
40. Milton Jordan, "Fight Bond Issue," *Charlotte Observer*, March 24, 1975, 1B.

41. "Blacks and Bonds: Doubts Need Attention," *Charlotte Observer*, March 27, 1975, 1C.
42. Ibid.
43. Ibid.
44. "City Taxes, Would Bond Raise Them?," *Charlotte Observer*, April 4, 1975, 24.
45. Ibid.
46. "'Yes' On Bonds," *Charlotte Observer*, April 6, 1975, 26.
47. Susan Jetton, "Sharp Jabs at Bonds Call for Hard Look at Facts," *Charlotte Observer*, April 3, 1975, 1C.
48. Nancy Brachey, "2 Black Group Speaks in Favor of Bond Issues," *Charlotte Observer*, April 6, 1975, 1C.
49. Jetton, "Sharp Jabs at Bonds," 1C.
50. Susan Jetton, "Voters OK Bus Purchase, Turn Down Airport Bond," *Charlotte Observer*, April 9, 1975, 1A.
51. Ibid., 6A.
52. Interview with T. J. "Jerry" Orr, October 6, 2015.
53. Alex Coffin, *Brookshire and Belk: Business in City Hall* (Chapel Hill: University of North Carolina Press, 1994), 213.
54. See Wilbur Rich, *The Politics of Personnel Policy* (Port Washington, N.Y.: Kennikat, 1982).
55. Walter R. Turner, "Building the Piedmont Airlines Hub in Charlotte, North Carolina, 1978–1989," *North Carolina Historical Review* 83, no. 3 (July 2006): 355–380.
56. Interview with Harvey Gantt, August 11, 2013.
57. Ibid.
58. Ibid.
59. Claiborne, *Of Pleasure and Power*, 76.
60. Interview with Hugh McColl, October 31, 2017.
61. Email correspondence with Pamela Syfert, August 2, 2018.
62. Erie, *Globalizing L.A.*, 32.
63. See Steven P. Erie and Vladimir Kogan, *Paradise Plundered: Fiscal Crisis and Governance Failure in San Diego* (Stanford, Calif.: Stanford University Press, 2011).

CHAPTER 8. THE PLOT THAT FAILED

1. Jim Morrill, "Dogfight for the Airport: The Bitterly Fought Takeover Has Left Charlotte at War with Suburban Legislators," *Charlotte Observer*, July, 21, 2013, 1A.
2. Ibid.
3. Erik Spanberg, "Jerry Orr: FAA 'Irregular' in CLT Analysis," *Charlotte Business Journal*, September 18, 2013, http://www.bizjournals.com/charlotte/blog/queen_city_agenda/2013/09/jerry-orr-faa-irregular-in-clt.html.
4. Ely Portillo, "City Has Big Ideas for Land Near CLT—Planners Talking with Developers About Transforming Thousands of Acres Near Airport with Factories, Offices, Homes," *Charlotte Observer*, January 26, 2014, 1A.
5. Rick Rothacker and Andre Dunn, "Scandal Gives New Life to Airport Tug-

of-War—Supporters of Change Say They'd Heard Rumors of Criminal Investigation," *Charlotte Observer*, March 30, 2014, 1A.

6. Will Boye, "Wells Fargo Economist Mark Vitner Speaks on Charlotte Airport, Other Topics at CCIM Event," *Charlotte Business Journal*, March 13, 2013, http://www.bizjournals.com/charlotte/blog/real_estate/2013/03/vitner-speaks-on-airport-and-other.html.

7. Rothacker and Dunn, "Scandal Gives New Life," 1A.

8. Ibid.

9. Ibid.

10. Jim Morrill, "City Closer to Losing Control of Its Airport—N.C. Senate Moves to Put Facilities Under an Independent Authority," *Charlotte Observer*, March 13, 2013, 1A.

11. Johnny Harris, "A Voice of Airport Concern: But Apparently Not the Voice of Its Authority Drama," *Charlotte Business Journal*, March 1, 2013.

12. Interview with Richard Vinroot, May 3, 2016.

13. Eric Frazier, "Poll: Most Want City to Control Airport—Nearly Two Thirds Opposed Taxpayer Help for Stadium Renovations," *Charlotte Observer*, May 12, 2013, 1A.

14. Ely Portillo, "Orr: Shift Would Be Smooth—Aviation Director Disputes City Manager's Claim the Airport Transition Would Be 'Chaos,'" *Charlotte Observer*, June 7, 2013, 6A.

15. Interview with Richard Vinroot.

16. Ruth Samuelson, "Lawmakers to Charlotte: Give it Up," *Charlotte Post*, July 25, 2013, 1A.

17. Ibid.

18. Ibid.

19. Ely Portillo and Steve Harrison, "McCrory: City Should Retain Airport—Governor Also Says Jerry Orr Shouldn't Return as Aviation Director," *Charlotte Observer*, November 26, 2013, 1A.

20. Interview with Ron Carlee, March 31, 2016.

21. Ibid.

22. Janet R. Daly Bednarek, *America's Airports: Airfield Development, 1918–1947* (College Station: Texas A&M University Press, 2001), 30.

23. Jim Morrill, "Airport Bill Flies in N.C. Senator Floor—One Backer Says Bill Is 'Playing with Fire' Over Question About Bonds," *Charlotte Observer*, February 28, 2013, 1A.

24. Interview with Richard Vinroot.

25. See Richard Schragger, "Can Strong Mayors Empower Weak Cities? On the Power of Local Executives in a Federal System," *Yale Law Journal*, 115, no. 9 (January 1, 2006): 2542–2578.

26. See emails from citizen input published in *Charlotte Airport Governance Study*, email comments received April 15–22. In conjunction with Public Input Hearings, April 16, 2013, 1–17, University of North Carolina at Charlotte Special Collections and Archives.

27. Ely Portillo and Steve Harrison, "City-Funded Study Recommends Airport Authority," *Charlotte Observer*, April 26, 2013, 1A.

28. Julie Rose, "Foxx Boots Dorsch From Airport Advisory Committee," *WFAE, Charlotte NPR News Source*, April 24, 2013, wfae.org/term/shawn-dorsch.

29. Ibid.

30. Ibid.

31. Ely Portillo and David Perlmutt, "Airport Advisor Stonewalls Council—Mayor Might Fire Chairman for Not Saying Who's behind Regional Airport Authority," *Charlotte Observer*, April 23, 2013, 1A.

32. Ely Portillo and Steven Harrison, "City-Funded Study," *Charlotte Observer*, April 26, 2013, 1A.

33. See Oliver Wyman, *Airport Governance Study, Charlotte International Airport, Draft Final Report* (Reston, Va., April 25, 2013), 22–23.

34. Portillo and Harrison, "City-Funded Study," 1A.

35. Steve Harrison and Ely Portillo, "Airline Suggested Hazel to Do Study—Consultant Says He Looked at Authority Issue with Open Mind," *Charlotte Observer*, May 9, 2013, 1B.

36. Ibid.

37. Ibid.

38. See Ely Portillo and Rick Rothacker, "Legal Fees Soaring in Airport Dispute—Tab for Both Parties Approaches $1 Million," *Charlotte Observer*, December 13, 2013, 1A.

39. Interview with Bob Hagemann, May 5, 2016.

40. Ibid.

41. interview with Richard Vinroot, May 3, 2016.

42. *City of Charlotte v. The State of North Carolina and Charlotte Douglas International Airport Commission* (2014).

43. Interview with Bob Hagemann.

44. Ely Portillo and Steve Harrison, "McCrory: City Should Retain Airport—Governor Also Says Jerry Orr Shouldn't Return as Aviation Director," *Charlotte Observer*, November 26, 2013, 1A.

45. Ibid.

46. Peter Baker and Michael D. Shear, "Charlotte Mayor Is Chosen as Transportation Chief," *New York Times*, April 30, 2013, 12A.

47. Steven Harrison, "Mitchell, Cannon Spar Over Airport Fight—Contentious Issue Sparks Barbs from Candidates," *Charlotte Observer*, August 30, 2013, 1B.

48. Steve Harrison, "Orr Out, Airport Rift Remains—Despite Challenges, City Manager Says, There's Interest in Finding a Solution," *Charlotte Observer*, December 22, 2013, 1B.

49. Steve Harrison, "Cannon Outlines Vision for First Term as Mayor—Job Creation, Easier Permitting, Tax Incentives for Businesses Highlight Mayor-Elect's Speech," *Charlotte Observer*, November 8, 2013, 1B.

50. Ibid.

51. "Charlotte Airport Commission Members Divided Over Legal Battle," *Legal Monitor Worldwide*, September 25, 2014.

52. *City of Charlotte v. The State of North Carolina and Charlotte Douglas International Airport Commission*.

53. Hunter Bacot and Jack Christine, "What's So Special About Airport Authorities? Assessing the Administrative Structure of the U.S. Airports," *Public Administration Review* 66, no. 2 (March 2006): 241–251.

54. Rothacker and Dunn, "Scandal Gives New Life," 1A.

55. Sidney Verba, *Small Groups and Political Behavior: A Study of Leadership* (Princeton, N.J.: Princeton University Press, 1961), 12.

56. Eric Frazier, "Harris: Costs Most Critical than Control-Developer: 'I Really Don't Care' Who Runs CLT Airport if Costs Stay Low," *Charlotte Observer*, November 14, 2014, 1A.

57. Ibid.

58. Ely Portillo, "'Spending Money Like a Drunken Sailor'—Aviation Director Jerry Orr Sees No Peril in Charlotte Douglas's $1B Expansion," *Charlotte Observer*, April 14, 2012, 10A.

59. Ibid.

60. Tae H. Oum, Jia Yan, and Chunyan Yu, "Ownership Forms Matter for Airport Efficiency: A Stochastic Frontier Investigation of Worldwide Airports," *Journal of Urban Economics* 64, no. 2 (September 2008): 432.

61. Interview with Ron Carlee, March 31, 2016.

62. Harrison and Portillo, "Airline Suggested Hazel," 1B.

63. "Jerry Orr Departs CLT, Compromise Sought in Dispute," *Charlotte Business Journal*, December 20, 2013, http://www.bizjournals.com/charlotte/blog/queen_city_agenda/2013/12/jerry-orr-departs-clt-compromise-sought-in-dispute.html.

64. Laurence E. Gesell and Robin R. Sobotta, *The Administration of Public Airports*, 5th ed. (Chandler, Ariz.: Coast Aire Publications, 2007), 33.

CONCLUSIONS

1. Thomas W. Hanchett, *Sorting Out the New South City: Race, Class, and Urban Development in Charlotte, 1875–1975* (Chapel Hill: University of North Carolina Press, 1998), 4.

2. Ibid., 240.

3. Roy Covington, "Report Praises Charlotte," *Charlotte Observer*, October 14, 1976, 7B.

4. Ibid.

5. Richard L. Florida, *The Rise of the Creative Class* (New York: Basic Books, 2003), 68.

6. "Big Cities: On the Way Up: Four Cities Show How It Can be Done; Houston: Standing On the Verge of Greatness," *U.S. News and World Report*, April 5, 1976, 62.

7. John D. Kasarda, "Welcome to Aerotropolis, the City of the Future," *New Perspective Quarterly* 32, issue 3 (July 28, 2015): 44.

8. Jan Brueckner, "Air Traffic and Urban Economic Development," *Urban Studies* 40, no. 8 (July 1, 2003): 1467.

9. William Graves, "Charlotte's Role as a Financial Center: Looking Beyond Bank Assets," *Southeastern Geographer* 41, no. 2 (November 2001): 242.

10. Interview with Hugh McColl, October 31, 2017.

11. See Richard Schragger's *City Power* (New York: Oxford University Press, 2016).

12. See W. W. Rostow, *The Stages of Economic Growth: A Non-Communist Manifesto* (Cambridge: Cambridge University Press, 1960).

13. Douglas Karsner, "Aviation and Airports: The Impact on the Economic and Geographic Structure of American Cities, 1940s–1980s," *Journal of Urban History* 23, no. 4 (May 1, 1997): 429.

14. Ray Clark, "A Public Airport for the District of Columbia: The History of Washington Dulles International Airport" (PhD diss., George Mason University, 2017), 378.

15. Enrico Moretti, *The New Geography of Jobs* (Boston: Houghton Mifflin Harcourt, 2012).

16. See Ken Eudy, "Urban Designer Studies Downtown," *Charlotte Observer*, July 21, 1982, 2D.

17. Cited in Jack Claiborne, *Crown of the Queen City: The Charlotte Chamber from 1870 to 1999* (Charlotte, N.C.: KPC Custom Publishing, 1999), 9.

18. Ibid.

19. Bob Deans, "Airline Hubs Shaping Economic Destiny of Region as Rivers Did," *Atlanta Journal-Constitution*, February 8, 1987, 25S.

20. Chris Burritt, "Charlotte Gets Ahead by Dreaming Big—Carolina Powerhouse May Show the Way to 21st Century, Some Say," *Atlanta Journal-Constitution*, April 17, 1994, 5.

21. Dan Chapman, "Charlotte at Brink of a Boom," *Charlotte Observer*, August 11, 1996, 1A.

22. Interview with David R. Goldfield, October 3, 2017.

23. Don Bedwell, "Banking on Downtown NCNB's McColl Invests in Its Future," *Charlotte Observer*, January 25, 1981, 14A.

24. "N.C. Ports Are a Vital Link to Worldwide Business Connections," *Carolina International*, in *Charlotte Observer*, November 16, 1980, 4Y. Also see Claiborne, *Crown of the Queen City*, 108.

25. Peter Applebome, "Banking Lifts Charlotte, City on the Rise, to the Top," *New York Times*, August 24, 1991, 10.

26. Charles Lemert, *Postmodernism Is Not What You Think* (Malden: Blackwell, 1997), 66.

27. Interview with Michael Gallis, October 19, 2017.

28. Email correspondence with Pamela Syfert, August 2, 2018.

29. See Tobias Keller and Jurgen Weibler, "What It Takes and Costs to Be an Ambidextrous Manager: Linking Leadership to Cognitive Strain to Balancing Exploration and Exploitation," *Journal of Leadership & Organizational Studies* 22, no. 1 (2015): 54–71.

30. Florida, *Rise of the Creative Class*, 224.

31. Ely Portillo, "City Has Big Ideas for Land Near CLT—Planners Talking with Developers About Transforming Thousands of Acres Near the Airport with Factories, Offices, Homes," *Charlotte Observer*, January 26, 2014, 1A.

32. Ibid.

33. Ibid.

34. For an update on the project, see Ely Portillo, "River District Development Likely to Get Millions of Dollars in Public Money for Roads," July 13, 2017, http://www.charlotteobserver.com/news/business/biz-columns-blogs/development/article122463709.html.

35. Robin Toner, "Stakes High in Contest for Alabama Governor," *New York Times*, September 25, 1990, www.nytimes.com/1990/09/26/us/stakes-high-in-contest-for . . .

36. This is a version of an old anti-Republican put-down.

37. Cited in Dixie Living, "Atlanta Is to Southerners What New York Is to Everyone Else," *Atlanta Journal-Constitution*, February 23, 1992, 1M.

38. Interview with Hugh McColl, October 31, 2017.

INDEX

Abbott, Carl, 155
Advantage Carolina, 15
Aerial League of America, 24
Aero Club of America, 25
aeromobility, 3
Aeronautics Bureau of the Department of Commerce, 74, 75
aerotropolis, 132, 233
Affirmative Action Plan, 173
A. G. Odell Associates, 56, 125, 126, 142
Air Commerce Act of 1926, 26, 74
Airline Deregulation Act of 1978, 58, 88, 95, 109, 120
Airlines Transportation Association (ATA), 100
Airmail Act of 1925, 26
Airmail Act of 1934, 29, 41
Airmail Act of 1938, 30
Airport Advisory Committee (AAC): origin, 16, 49, 52; relations with City Council, 55, 114, 137, 142, 156, 171, 188–194, 200, 203; relations with director, 110, 132, 139, 162; role in takeover, 205, 210, 212, 213, 214, 215, 225
Airport Airway Safety and Capacity Expansion Act of 1982, 62
Airport and Airway Improvement Act of 1982, 62
Airport and Airways Development Act of 1970, 53, 100
Airport Commission, 49, 218
Airport Development Acceleration Act of 1973, 109
Alander, Robert, 139
Alexander, Kelly, 188
Altshuler, Alan, 1, 149
American Airlines: Charlotte service, 60, 119; instability and, 87; merger, 61, 70, 84, 99–100, 106, 117, 119, 120, 225, 232; September 11 and, 11, 67
Andrew, Mildred, 22
Andrew, Thornwell, 22
Applebome, Peter, 239
Arthur, Bill, 85, 93
Ash Commission, 77
Atlanta Journal-Constitution, 61, 65, 152, 238
Aulty, Ron, 186

Bacot, Hunter, 183, 221
Banfield, Edward, 162
Bank of America, 1, 4, 5, 13, 19, 65, 92, 179
Barrett, Paul, 4
Baugh, Jack P., 169
Baxter, Herbert H., 28, 43, 44, 48, 166
Bednarek, Janet R. Daly, 16–17, 34, 40, 76, 116, 213
Bedwell, Don, 172
Belk, John M., 15, 55–56, 60, 127, 147, 156, 169, 170–171, 181, 240
Bell, Daniel, 5
Bernstein, Marvel, 78
Bidwell, Don, 172
Birmingham, Robert "Josh": airport development and, 57, 59, 113, 119, 126–127, 128, 131; as airport director, 13, 141–143, 145, 148, 175, 188, 226; Charlotte service and, 83
Black Political Caucus, 199
Bloom, Nicholas Dagen, 2
Blythe, LeGette, 27
Bollinger, Lynn, 44
Boorstin, Daniel, 236
Borman, Frank, 60
Bosworth, Karl A., 150
Boyd, Mike, 99, 106

271

Boyle, Mark, 12
British Airlines, 65, 84
Broderick, Sean, 108
Brookshire, Stanford, 15, 94, 139, 167–169, 181, 205, 240
Brown, Gene, 28
Brown, Walter, 28, 29
Brownlow, Cecil, 42,
Brown v. Board of Education, 170
Brueckner, Jan, 233
Brummitt, Wyatt, 112
Bubb, Daniel, 1
Bunn, Gerry, 23
Buritt, Chris, 238
Burkhalter, David, 199
Burnside, J. Ed, 168

Cagle, Brent, 131, 148, 212, 226
Cameron. C. C., 171, 172
Campbell, H. B., 49
Campbell, Stan, 40, 193, 208
Camp Nathanael Greene, 14, 23, 33
Cannon, Joseph Franklin, 51
Cannon, Patrick, 161, 186, 208, 220
Cannon Airfield, 25, 27, 33, 45
Cariaga, Vance, 179
Carlee, Ron, 10, 70, 143, 148, 210, 212, 224
Carnes, Eric, 33
Carpenter, Joe, 221
Carson, Ken, 191
Carstensen, Peter C., 89
Carter, Jimmy, 78, 80, 81, 196
Charlotte Aero Club, 25, 35, 139
Charlotte Airport Commission, 39, 49, 189, 205
Charlotte Army Missile Plant, 5
Charlotte Business Journal, 207–209, 226
Charlotte Chamber of Commerce: city image making, 154–155, 229, 238; history, 14–16, 18, 31, 45, 50, 65, 81, 83, 99, 127, 141, 162, 165, 167, 190–191, 205; relationship with elected officials, 158, 171; role in airport development, 31, 33–35
Charlotte City Council: airport takeover, 208, 215, 225; relationship to airport director, 16, 18, 105, 113, 132, 148, 186, 188–190, 193; relationship with mayor, 18, 37–38; structural changes, 155, 200, 212, 222
Charlotte Douglas International Airport, 3, 5, 32, 70, 112, 129, 211; city economic development and, 61, 97, 102, 104, 108, 120–122, 124, 129, 186, 204–206, 232; as hub, 90; terminal development and, 102
Charlotte Municipal Airport, 20, 42, 49, 76, 111
Charlotte News, 16, 20, 59
Charlotte Observer: airport bonds, 36; airport operations and, 32, 48, 52, 99, 102, 120, 126–127, 133, 139, 165–166; city growth and, 27, 137, 206; editorials, 24–25, 82–83, 153, 197–199, 208, 210, 229, 241; polls and, 209, 216, 220; rail transportation and, 22, 28; reporting, 14–16, 19–20
Charlotte Post, 20
Charlotte 220 History Mural, 140
Charlotte Uptown Development Corporation, 4, 177
Chen, James, 117
"CH factor," 12
Choo, Yap Yin, 108, 117
Christine, Jack, 221, 241
Cidell, Juline, 196
Civil Aeronautic Administration (CAA), 38, 48, 75–76
Civil Aeronautic Administration Act of 1938, 49–50, 75
Civil Aeronautic Board (CAB), 40, 73–76, 78–79, 83, 103
Civil Air Patrol (CAP), 142, 166
Civil Rights Act of 1964, 94, 167
Claiborne, Jack, 15, 55, 154–155, 158, 165
Clarification Act of 2013, 217
Clark, Ray, 236
Clodfelter, Dan, 161, 180, 220
Coffin, Alex, 138, 167, 171, 199
Colodny, Edwin I., 82
Connections, 179
Conway, H. McKinley, 69
Cox, Kevin, 183
Crandall, Robert, 87

Index | 273

Creager, Stephen, 86, 109
Crowell, Johnny, 27, 37
Crutchfield, Edward, 66, 92, 152, 201, 240
Cunningham, John R., 167
Curran, Ned, 147
Currie, E. McA., 166
Curry, Kathleen, 192

Dahl, Robert, 46
Davidson, Don, 200
Davis, Thomas, 53
Dawley, David, 16
Day and Zimmermann, 59
Delta Airlines: Charlotte service, 51–52, 54, 60–61, 68, 85, 108, 120, 138, 171, 232; merger, 84, 88, 90, 119
Dempsey, Paul Stephen, 2
de Neufville, Richard, 103, 124
Dennis, Harold D., 32
Denver International Airport, 2
Derthick, Martha, 77
Disadvantaged Business Enterprises Contracts, 189
Dorsch, Shawn, 214, 215, 225
Douglas, Benjamin Elbert: airport development, 35–37, 39, 51, 165, 184; election, 155–156, 161, 165–166, 181; referendum and, 38
dress up imperative, 4, 228
Duke Energy, 4, 13, 177, 229, 234
Dunn, J. A. C., 55

Earhart, Amelia, 14, 101
Eastern Airlines: Charlotte service, 40, 51, 53–57, 60, 82, 118, 168; deregulation, 85, 104; equipment change, 49, 59; as hub, 70, 231; instability, 64, 143;
Eastern Air Transport, 28, 30, 33, 38, 39, 54, 55
Eaton, Paul, 35
Eblen, Tom, 95
Economic Policy Institute, 89
Edding, Jerelyn, 152
Elliot, H. A., 34
Elroy v. Burns, 10
Epley, Joe, 170

Erie, Steve, 202
Erwin, John C., 110, 192, 221, 137
Esler, David, 9
Eulau, Heinz, 182
Evansville-Vanderburg Airport Authority District v. Delta Airlines (1972), 108
Eyestone, Robert, 182

Federal Aviation Act of 1946, 48
Federal Aviation Act of 1958, 52, 78
Federal Aviation Administration (FAA), 58, 99, 103, 139, 219, 227
Fenster, Julie M., 113, 115
Financial Institutions Reform Recovery and Enforcement Act of 1989, 91
Flack, A. W., 39, 136–137, 189
Florida, Richard, 230
Forrester, Jay Wright, 19
Foxx, Anthony, 179–180, 219
Fraser, Bruce, 124
Friday, Sue, 190, 192, 193
Friel, Dan, 64
Futterman, Evan, 128

Gallis, Michael, 144, 239
Gamson, William, 133
Gantt, Harvey, 60, 119, 174–176, 190, 198–200, 240
Garn-St. German Depository Institutions Act of 1982, 91
General Aviation Revitalization Act of 1994, 65
Gesell, Laurence E., 226
Gillen, David, 148
Golden, Harry, 93
Goldfield, David, 19, 238
Goodrich, E. P., 26
Gottdiener, Mark, 56
Government Accounting Office (GAO), 145, 178
Grand Patronage, 10, 103, 149
Graves, William, 7, 234
Greater Charlotte Club, 155
Grice, John, 37, 38
Griffith, E. G., 31, 32
Griffs, Leonard, 121

Griggs v. Allegheny County, 190
Gunther, John, 242

Hagemann, Robert, 217–219
Hair, Samuel C., 51
Hanchett, Thomas, 26, 163, 228
Hansell, William H., 159, 160
Harris, Johnny, 61, 207, 209, 218, 223, 228, 240, 241
Harris, Kenneth, 57, 161, 171, 240
Hartevelt, Henry, 99
Hartsfield, Fletcher, 214
Hawkins, Reginald A., 167
Hazel, Bob, 216, 225
Height, E. M., 37, 38
Helfin, Howell, 242
Helm, Jessie, 173, 176
Hendrick, Jerry, 83
Hill, Kim Q., 8
Hoover, Herbert, 29, 41
Howard, Bill, 63, 120
Howard, David, 215
Huntington, Samuel, 78
Huntley, Ben, 23
Hurricane Hugo, 62

inattentive citizenry, 183, 230

Jettson, Susan, 57
Johansson, Olga, 149
Johnson, Randy, 26, 44
Johnson, Roy, 59

Kahn, Alfred, 80
Karsner, Douglas, 45
Kasarda, John, 98, 177, 233
Kays, Gary, 120
Kelly, Clyde, 26
Kennedy, Edward (Ted), 81, 82
King, Jan, 126
Kinsey, Patsy, 225
Klein, Richard A., 82
Knight, Ross, 110, 140, 141, 150, 169
Knox, E. Edward, 83, 142, 172, 173, 193
Knox, Kenneth R., 142, 172, 173
Kolfenbach, Tom, 174

Kolkhoz, Gabriela, 78
Kratt, Mary, 28, 38, 39
Kuester, Clarence O., 14, 28, 33, 50, 153

La Guardia, Fiorello, 42
Lambeth, Charles, 12, 14, 25, 27, 35, 39, 186
Lassiter, John, 39
Lassiter, Robert, 39
Lawton, Cassandra, 59
Lee, Bill, 171
Lindbergh, Charles, 30
Lowrence, Bomar, 36
Lubell, Samuel, 6, 52
Luberoff, David, 1, 149
Lufthansa Airlines, 84
Lund, Freddie, 27

Mair, Andrew, 183
Marquette v. First of Omaha, 91
Marshall, J. B., 38
Martinelli, Louis, 59, 173
Maschal, Richard, 11, 12, 153
Mattson, Gary, 163
McCain, John, 89
McCarran-Lea Bill, 40
McColl, Hugh, 4, 65–66, 70, 91–92, 142, 150, 181, 201, 234, 238, 240, 242
McCoy, Bill, 14, 143, 144, 206
McCrory, Patrick, 62, 67, 86, 161, 177–180, 211, 217, 225–226
McDonnell, Gary, 80
McDuffie, James, 170
McFadden Act of 1927, 90, 92
McMahan, Ed, 147
McNary-Watres Act of 1930, 28, 29
McNinch, Frank R., 24, 25, 181
Mead, Chris, 14, 15, 157
Mead, Timothy, 6
Mead Act of 1946, 44
Mercer, Gene, 58
Metrolina, 6, 7, 121
Millett, Bill, 191
Mills, Edwin, 45
Mills, Elizabeth, 174
Minority Business Enterprises, 172
Mintzberg, Henry, 131, 132

Moretti, Enrico, 237
Morgan, Bob, 99, 154
Morrill, Jim, 206
Morris Air Base, 43–44, 48, 137, 218
Morrison, Steven A, 87
Mullaney, Thomas E., 50
Myers Park Crowd, 170
Myrick, Sue, 62, 70, 161

Nader, Ralph, 80, 81
Nash, V. L., 39, 136
National Airport System Plan, 53
National Association of States Aviation Officials, 9
National Transportation Safety Board, 57
Newman, Rick, 68
NewMyer, David, 84
New York Times, 79, 87, 110, 239
Nocera, Joe, 88
Noise Control Act of 1972, 196
North Carolina National Bank (NCNB), 1, 4, 5

Oberdorfer, Don, 47
obligatory landing, 236
Odoni, Amedeo, 103
Ogrodzinski, Henry, 9, 17
Orr, Jerry: defending airport policies, 62, 63–64, 86, 131, 164, 178–180, 193, 223; management reputation, 106, 146–148, 150–151, 226; relations with airlines, 53–54; role as assistant director, 113, 126–127, 143–145; role in state takeover, 203, 208–212, 225–226
Oum, Tae, 4, 224

Parker, Douglas, 69, 100, 119
"Pattern for Charlotte, A," 158
Paul, Darel, 154
Peltzman, Sam, 67, 100
People Airline (Express), 58, 60–61, 90
Peterson, Paul, 10, 202, 230
Petzinger, Thomas, 100
Phillip, Laurence T., 81
Piedmont Airlines: Charlotte service, 51–55, 60–61, 84, 86, 89, 118–119, 128, 143, 145; as hub, 81–83, 118, 119, 231; merger, 120
Pietro, Edwin G., 140
pocket of problems, 89, 95
political time, 157
Poole, Robert W., 63
Portillo, Ely, 210
Pressman, Jeffrey, 156
privatization, 63
pro-growth coalition: economic development, 174, 204, 209, 243; purpose and goals, 2, 3, 4, 16, 154; relationship to airport director, 122, 129, 133, 147, 149; relationship to elected leaders, 151, 155–157, 160, 168, 169, 180–181, 183, 189, 193, 201, 213, 225, 229–232, 240

Quick, Paul, 77
Quiet Community Act of 1978, 196
Quinn, Albert, 124, 137–139, 191

Rafferty, Thomas, 125, 139–140, 150, 191
Raiford, Robert, 239
Rea, David M., 39, 137, 139, 140, 150
Reagan, Ronald, 113
Reason Foundation, 63, 64
Reed, Sandra, 198
Rickenbacker, Eddie, 39, 57, 91, 92, 100
Riegle-Neal Interstate Banking and Branding Efficiency Act of 1944, 92
ripple effect of technology, 17, 71, 102, 229
River District, 241
Robinette, George, 64
Rogan Committee, 52, 205
Roosevelt, Franklin, 29, 31, 37, 40
Roosevelt, Theodore, 22
Rothacker, Rick, 45, 65, 91,
Rucho, Robert, 208–210, 219, 220, 223

Safire, William, 110
Samuelson, Ruth, 210
Saturday Evening Post, 29, 34
Savas, E. S., 63
Schneiderman, Michael, 172
Schofield, Seth, 65
Schragger, Richard, 202, 214, 235, 239

September 11, 2001, 122
Shaw, Victor, 52
Sieden, Jill Jordan, 152
Small, John H., 165
Smith, Heather, 7
Smith, Russell, 6
Snyder, J. Luther, 33
Sobotta, Robin, 226
Southeast Airlines, 174
Southwest Airlines, 90, 232
Sparrow, Glen, 185
Spoils Conference, 29, 73
Stephen, Robert, 16
Steven, Adam, 116
Stolz, Robert, 220–221
Stone, Clarence, 10, 12, 18
Stussman, Howard, 30
Svara, James, 160, 164, 185
Swann v. Charlotte-Mecklenburg Board of Education, 93, 170
Sweitzer, Charles, 140
Syfert, Pamela, 202, 240

Taylor, Sam, 61
technification of airports, 103
Thompson, Arnold, 127, 197
Thompson, Daniel, 154, 158
Thrasher Bros Flying Circus, 23
Time Magazine, 48
Tompkins, Daniel A., 154, 158
Transportation Security Administration (TSA), 68, 113
Trotter, H. G., 51
Truman, David, 162
Truman, Harry, 48
Tucker, Wayne, 116
Turner, Walter, 54, 116, 145

Ubell, Donald, 214
Underhill, Henry, 174
United Airlines, 40, 56, 66
United States Conference of Mayors, 83
United States v. Causby, 189
USAir: Charlotte service, 69, 90, 95; as hub, 145; instability and, 64–66

U.S. Airways: Charlotte service, 104, 178, 211; as hub, 89, 145, 178; instability and, 67, 86, 109; merger, 61, 70, 90, 120–121, 232
USA Today, 108, 153
U.S. Commerce Department, 36, 74, 75, 103
U.S. Department of Transportation, 53, 60, 76, 86, 89, 219
U.S. News and World Report, 6, 231
U.S. Postal Service, 30

Veeder, William, 59, 139, 171, 185
Verba, Sidney, 222
Vinroot, Richard, 62, 147, 161, 176, 205, 207, 209–210, 214, 217
Vitner, Mark, 208
Voting Rights Act of 1965, 94, 168
Vowles, Timothy, 90

Wachovia Bank, 1, 12, 13, 20, 62, 67, 92, 178, 179
Wade, Jo Ellen, 127
Washington, George, 6, 238
Washington Post, 83
Wasow, Bernard, 89
Watters, Pat, 168
Waynick, Capus M., 36
Weinstein, James, 155
Wellon, Robert A., 27
Wells Fargo, 1, 13, 98, 208
White, Wendell, 177
Whitten, Frank, 41
Whyte, William H., 237
Wilson, James Q., 162
Winston, Clifford, 87
Work Progress Administration (WPA), 37, 38
Wright, Orville, 20
Wright, Wilbur, 20–21
Wynne, Jack, 36

Yancey, Henry, 137
Young, Clarence M., 32
Yu, Chunyan, 224
Yun, Jia, 224

www.ingramcontent.com/pod-product-compliance
Lightning Source LLC
Chambersburg PA
CBHW011755220426
43672CB00018B/2964